Formal Methods, Informally

Learn to program more effectively, faster, with better results... and enjoy both the learning experience and the benefits it ultimately brings.

While this undergraduate-level textbook is *motivated* by formal methods, so encouraging habits that lead to correct and concise computer programs, its informal presentation sidesteps any rigid reliance on formal logic which programmers are sometimes led to believe is required. Instead, a straightforward and intuitive use of simple "What's true here?" comments encourages precision of thought without prescription of notation.

Drawing on decades of the author's experience in teaching/industry, the text's careful presentation concentrates on key principles of structuring and reasoning about programs, applying them first to small, understandable algorithms. Then students can concentrate on turning those reliably into their corresponding – and correct – program source codes. The text includes over 200 exercises, for many of which full solutions are provided. A set of all solutions is available for instructors' use.

Carroll Morgan has been an innovator, educator and researcher in computer science for his whole career: first in industry, then as Lecturer and Fellow at the University of Oxford, and finally as Professor at the University of New South Wales. He is best known for his pioneering work in systematic- and correctness-oriented methods of writing computer programs and systems, and especially for his text *Programming from Specifications*. He is a member of IFIP Working Groups 1.3, 1.7, 2.1 and 2.3 and received (jointly) the "Best Cybersecurity Paper of the Year" award from the National Security Agency in 2015.

"This accessible and compellingly written book will deepen your understanding of how code works and why it works correctly. It is full of practical insights for both students and experienced programmers, as well as university educators looking for a new – and better – way to teach programming."

Graeme Smith, University of Queensland

"Carroll Morgan's *Formal Methods, Informally* is a timely guide to checking everyday code by asking the right questions. Building on distilled logic and math mechanisms, rigorous thinking is promoted as a most valuable tool for developing verifiable software. This book is an insightful must-read for students, educators and practitioners alike."

Luigia Petre, Åbo Akademi University

Formal Methods, Informally

How to Write Programs That Work

CARROLL MORGAN

University of New South Wales, Sydney

CAMBRIDGE
UNIVERSITY PRESS

Shaftesbury Road, Cambridge CB2 8EA, United Kingdom

One Liberty Plaza, 20th Floor, New York, NY 10006, USA

477 Williamstown Road, Port Melbourne, VIC 3207, Australia

314–321, 3rd Floor, Plot 3, Splendor Forum, Jasola District Centre,
New Delhi – 110025, India

103 Penang Road, #05–06/07, Visioncrest Commercial, Singapore 238467

Cambridge University Press is part of Cambridge University Press & Assessment,
a department of the University of Cambridge.

We share the University's mission to contribute to society through the pursuit of
education, learning and research at the highest international levels of excellence.

www.cambridge.org
Information on this title: www.cambridge.org/highereducation/isbn/9781009420990

DOI: 10.1017/9781009421003

First published 2026

Cover image: Michael Phillips / Moment Open / Getty Images

A catalogue record for this publication is available from the British Library

A Cataloging-in-Publication data record for this book is available from the Library of Congress

ISBN 978-1-009-42099-0 Hardback
ISBN 978-1-009-42102-7 Paperback

Additional resources for this publication at www.cambridge.org/Morgan.

Contents

Preface

What is this text about, and who is it for?

This text is about how to program more effectively, faster, with better results... and how to enjoy doing so.

And it's intended for two kinds of people: those who have some experience of programming, but are not yet experts; and those who *are* experts, but might like to see a possible explanation of *why* they are. Thus its purpose is to introduce (to the first group) and make explicit (to the second group) some design- and coding techniques that can be used to organise, check and maintain large programs, especially those whose correct functioning is crucial (i.e. they must have as few bugs as possible).

But –in spite of that emphasis on "large"– the examples used in this text will be very small ones, in many cases programs that readers will have written already. In fact the more experienced programmers might have written them dozens of times.

Our use of familiar, simple examples to introduce formal methods *informally* is a deliberate, although possibly unusual, choice; and it is quite different from what is usually done.

THE USUAL APPROACH to teaching programming is to introduce a general-purpose, widely used programming language as a first step, and then to apply it initially to very simple problems. The idea there is to instil familiarity with *some* programming language –it does really not matter so much which one– and then, by choosing more and more ambitious examples, to move the students to a level where they realise that what they are learning has two main components. One of them is "how to find algorithms".

An *algorithm* describes steps that if followed will fulfil a task. Computers are used to follow algorithms' steps so that they can be carried out automatically, quickly and reliably. An algorithm is the "essence" of a computer program.

The other component of this "usual" approach is expressing algorithms (the essence) in computer-program *code* (i.e. in a programming language), so that the computer can carry them out, can "execute" them on its own.

But when programs are large and complex, it is not easy to be sure they will work as desired, or even at all. First, the algorithm itself might be complex, and not well understood. It could even be wrong. And second, even if the algorithm is not complex (but especially if it is), translating it into code can be tricky too, and sometimes very error prone. It's a bit like "typos" in ordinary writing — but actually it's much worse. A typo (think "misspelling") in a computer program is usually picked up automatically: the rules for programs, their "spelling and grammar", are very exact. Computers detect "syntax errors" in programs very easily.

What computers *don't* detect is grammatically correct programs that –actually– don't do what their programmers expect them to. Maybe the algorithm is wrong in the first place; maybe it was coded up incorrectly; maybe both. But –again "usually"– people simply accept all that as just a "fact of life" when writing computer programs.

BUT ANOTHER APPROACH is often taken by people who *don't* accept "all that ... as a fact of life" : it's called "formal methods".

Formal methods uses rigorous logic, sometimes in a very sophisticated form, to *prove* mathematically that a program does what it should. Obviously, to prove that, it must be known in the first place what "should" means, that is, what the program is actually supposed to do — and that knowledge must be exact, at least if the proof is to have any rigour at all. So to use formal methods properly, the program's *specification* must be written in mathematical language too, not just the proof. And it must be possible to translate the program's code into a mathematical form as well; and then after that more mathematics must be deployed to connect the (mathematised) program to the (mathematical) specification. So it's "mathematics all the way down".

Formal methods is therefore a very specialised part of computer science, and how it works –and especially *why* it works– are fascinating topics in their own right. This "second, alternative" approach to teaching programming, which we are describing in these paragraphs, presents formal methods first, though perhaps not at its highest intensity, as a sort of "limbering-up exercise" before students are even allowed to attempt and submit answers to real programming exercises, to "touch the computer at all" so to speak. After that, they are allowed to use the just-learned formal methods on real programs, first small ones and then steadily larger. . . and they proceed further as in the first approach above.

THE PROBLEM WITH *BOTH* OF THOSE TWO APPROACHES. . . is that *neither* of them gets us where we want to go: not the programmers, and not the people who depend on the programs they write. And that's why we don't adopt either of them in this text.

The first approach leads to enormous amounts of time wasted, as running programs are tested, debugged, tested again, debugged further. . . Nights and weekends are lost doing that, and –even then– there are further losses when users suffer because the programs *still* don't work, and their unexpected failures prevent ordinary people from doing their own jobs — or worse.

And the second approach simply puts off many people right from the start. You don't *have* to be a mathematician to be a programmer: "everyone knows that" — and actually they are right. Many students therefore reject the formal-methods-first approach: they develop scepticism towards the whole idea, and we all end up worse off than we would have been if we just went straight into programming, that is, without any "method" at all.

WHAT'S LEFT is what you will find in this text: neither of those two approaches. Here, we use simple programs, programs that people can write already; and at the same time, we use *general* ideas "lifted" from formal methods and made accessible and understandable in an everyday way. This approach really does deserve our title:[1]

Formal Methods, Informally .

"Informal" formal methods shows you how to combine the *ideas* of formal methods, a way of thinking about programs, and the *ideas* built into designing algorithms you want to program, into an approach that

---

[1] The course this text accompanies is called *(In-)Formal Methods: The Lost Art*. The "Lost Art" is explained in the Afterword.

- Does not require you to learn mathematical logic first, and yet...

- Still reduces the number of mistakes you make when coding.

- Helps you to divide a large programming job into smaller pieces, share them with colleagues, and then put the results back together again.

- Leaves behind a description of the essential ideas that were used during the coding (the "documentation"), so that the program can be easily understood and modified by others, later on.

- Helps you to understand where an error occurred in the design process if, after all, a bug turns up in the running code, so that the programming *process* (e.g. in your organisation, or just your daily life), can be tuned and improved. If a program ends up wrong, you need to fix not only the program *but also the way it was made.* Sometimes that involves "tweaking" the *social* processes involved. Formal methods, even informally, helps you find out which processes need attention.[2]

- Helps you to produce modular components that can be reused in many programs — not just the ones they were originally written for.

- Suggests ways in which the program (components) can be tested, both during coding and after it is complete.

The simple programming examples used in this text –the ones you have probably done already in a more traditional way– can be found listed under PROGRAM EXAMPLES in the index. The programming language used for those examples is `Python`, but the approach can easily be adapted to other, similar languages. (See also App. G.2.) More than 200 drills and exercises are included, targeted not only on writing small programs but also on how to think about the *process* of doing so.

The general algorithmic topics covered include sorting, searching, order of growth (complexity), data structures and encapsulation, loop correctness and –as a more advanced topic– concurrency.

But none of those topics is covered exhaustively: it would be more accurate to say that in *this* text they are only "visited". Our purpose here is to introduce and then encourage further interest in more specialised programming topics and techniques –which readers will later discover to have their own authoritative texts– and *at the same time* to give some idea of how to think effectively about those topics and how to use them. We don't tell the whole story here; rather we help people to find and better understand the more comprehensive stories, told by others, that will deepen and complete their knowledge.

Because of the simple examples chosen, the programs we study here are connected to what people already know: they can concentrate on the new *process* we are following, without having to wonder how the example program actually works. Introducing a new topic *and* how to think about it *and* why it works *and* the really difficult problems that it solves, all at the same time... for a general audience is often a bad idea...

...because most people learn best in layers, each layer building on the one before, each one benefiting from the proper assimilation of earlier material.

---

[2] An example of the importance of process in general (i.e. not necessarily computer-based), is the *Kansas City walkway collapse* where in 1981 a suspended bridge fell onto some 2,000 guests attending a gala dance-party below. The engineering-design "bug" (by analogy with the computing term), which led to the failure, could have been spotted by a first-year engineering student ... if she had ever been given the chance to look. But the human, i.e. the "social" processes followed by the designers and builders did not expose the design to proper scrutiny by anyone.

So our aim in this text, in this approach, is that when people get a bit further into their programming careers, meet new topics, stretch their capabilities, solve challenging problems, they will say

> *Oh yes! I met that in "Formal Methods, Informally" . . .*
> *and I learned there how to think about problems like this.*

And then they will get off to a running start — in the right direction.

Organisation and use

The material is presented in four major parts, and the first is the most important: "Everyday programs". It could be used on its own for an introductory university course, or for a short "summer school" of students meeting programming for the first time.

The text's more than 200 drills and exercises are cross-referenced to the topics that gave rise to them, and to each other.

The downward-pointing arrows within certain drills and exercises indicate that an answer is given in Appendix H or I, respectively. Marginal indications ("rubrics", like " Ex. 1.1 " on p. 3) refer to exercises that are directly relevant to that point in the text: they do not *need* to be followed then and there, but they do offer the opportunity for a closer look at the material they annotate. That is, to follow or not is the reader's choice. In any case, the exercises in turn refer back to the rubric, so it is easy to return to the text after having a look. (A complete set of answers is available, but many of them are reserved as a teaching resource.)

The material is based substantially on an "informal" formal methods course that has been given at The University of New South Wales and at Macquarie University, both in Sydney; and there are mini-project-sized assignments associated with the course (but not given here) that each can take several weeks to complete, depending on how they are presented. It's not hard to fit three of them into, say, a nine-week term.

Acknowledgments

I'm grateful for the support of the School of Computer Science and Engineering at the University of New South Wales, allowing me the flexibility to try out this approach on undergraduate students, over almost ten years so far, and similarly the Trustworthy Systems Group –at the time, part of the CSIRO's Data61 but now fully at UNSW– which has allowed me time to teach the course and to write this text and which provided the right intellectual environment for an experiment of this kind. It provided many of the students who have attended and helped to improve the course.

Indeed *very* many improvements and corrections to the text have been suggested by those using early drafts: the students at UNSW in 2021–3, Annabelle McIver (who has used it for teaching at Macquarie University) and Thomas Kunc, Enzo Lee Solano and Paula Tennent (all three veterans of it, and later invaluable as teaching assistants).

Tom was essential in holding together the delivery and presentation of the course in 2022, especially as we made the post-COVID transition from a small class size to a much larger one: he structured an approach to our (partly) automated assessment of the students' homework. Paula and Enzo were indispensable in 2023 for suggesting further improvements to the course presentation and organisation, and for helping to carry them out.

Many more people have been kind enough to read through evolving versions of this material, offering comments –*and* corrections– concerning technical, historical and grammatical matters. Among them are Cliff Jones, Rustan Leino, Sebastian Sequoia-Grayson, Graeme Smith and Trudy Weibel. Miki Tanaka and Junming Zhao organised an "informal methods" study group at Trustworthy Systems — which was not only fun and rewarding (I hope for *everyone* involved), but also led to significant changes in the way some of the material was explained.

David Tranah, from Cambridge University Press, encouraged vast improvements with his meticulous, tireless reading of every chapter — and his precise and always pertinent observations and suggestions. Very thorough copyediting by Laura Emsden and Susan Parkinson improved the presentation significantly.

Dedication

This presentation of how to *reason* about programs, rather than just writing them down, is dedicated to all the academics and computer-science professionals whose insights into how to employ both simplicity and power, at the most fundamental level, will eventually be recognised by *everyone* as the true determinant of how computers should be designed, programmed and deployed. A small number of them are cited here directly, indicated by bold-faced entries in the index.

And it is dedicated to my family, all my boys and girls.

In memoriam GEOFFREY SEWARD SMITH *and* JEAN-RAYMOND ABRIAL, *mentors both.*

Part I

Everyday programs

1

Programs that work

1.1 Introduction

This first part of the text deals with "ordinary" programs, those comprising assignment statements, conditionals and loops, and simple data structures (mainly)... and how to check that they work. The language for the program examples is `Python`, but the techniques apply to other "conventional" languages (such as Java and C) that also have those features. Program text will be usually written in `monospaced font`.[1]

Part of the novelty (perhaps) of what we are doing will be that we use "conditions", which can be thought of as Boolean-valued expressions, to write down what we expect the programs to achieve. What we call "checking" a program is simply making sure that the program *does* achieve those conditions. The conditions' syntax will be in the `Python` style as well, written just as you would write a condition in an `if`-statement: for example we'll write `x==2` instead of $x=2$, and `x!=2` instead of $x \neq 2$.

Although our aim is to write programs that work, we will begin our study of "everyday programs" with a famous case of one that *didn't* work. It's not hard, of course, to find programs that don't work — we all write them every day, and the point of this text is to help us to do that less often. More unusual, though, is to find a "doesn't work" program that was in the pockets of millions of people. So that will be our first example.

Before we do that, however, see Ex. 1.1 at the end of the chapter for a preview of what "checking a program" might mean.[2]

$\boxed{\text{Ex. 1.1}}$

---

[1] Comments about `Python` specifically will be mainly in footnotes, from here on.

[2] Boxed notes such as "Ex.1.1" suggest exercises particularly relevant to that part of the text. Some have answers included in Appendix I; but other answers are reserved for class exercises.

1.2 Jack be nimble, Jack be quick...

The following program was part of the operating system for a portable music player, of which millions were sold around the world. The variable d (for "day") was kept up to date by the player's hardware, giving at all times the day-number of "today", where Day 1 begins the "epoch" of 1 January 1980 and counts from there. When the player was switched on, one of its first tasks was to convert that internal day-number d to a displayable date in the calendar style: "the Dth day of month M in year YYYY".

Below is the program it used to calculate the YYYY part of that:[3]

```
# --- If 1/1/1980 is Day 1,
# --- and today is Day d counting from there,
# --- determine the Year y of today.
y= 1980
while d>365:
  if leapYear(y):
    if d>366:                                              (1.1)
      d= d-366
      y= y+1
  else:
    d= d-365
    y= y+1
# Today is in Year y.
```

Today's date could then be displayed on the player's screen in conventional form (after subsequent code dealt with month-in-year and day-in-month).

Yet on New Year's Eve –31 December– in the first *leap year* after the music player was released, every single one of those players in the whole world froze when it was turned on. Looking above at (1.1), can you see why?

There are many posts about that error on the internet, and many blog comments attached to them where the program is "fixed" by one reader — only to have the next reader find a new mistake introduced by the previous repair. But the "why" of that error is not the actual mistake in the program: the real cause of it is that programmers are often not given the chance to learn how to avoid simple mistakes like that in the first place. It's the process that *led* to that program that needs to be debugged.

That program should never have been installed. And even if the programmer was new, or inexperienced (but we do not know), more experienced colleagues should have been able to ask simple questions –as part of a code review, a checking process– that would have revealed the problem in spite of possible opinions that it was too obviously correct to be worth the attention.

> The problem is the culture that allowed that program to be written, installed and deployed.
>
> *Jack should have been encouraged to be less nimble, not so quick, and should have been shown how to be more careful.*

Can we do better than Jack? Yes. This book shows how.

---

[3] The original program was written in *C*; aside from that, this transliteration into Python is believed to be the exact code, except for the added comments.

1.3 When does a program "work"?

Suppose we have a sequence `A[0:N]` of numbers, indexed from 0 inclusive to N exclusive, and we want to calculate their sum. Does this program work?

```
s= 0 # Start from zero.
for n in range(N):                                          (1.2)
  s= s+A[n] # Add the current element.
```

To answer that question, we must check various things.

Is the intended sum `s` correctly initialised? *Yes.* Are all the sequence elements `A[n]` of `A` considered, exactly once? *Yes.* And does the `n`-indexing remain within the bounds of the sequence? (We remind ourselves that the elements of `A[0:N]` are indexed from 0 up to `N-1`, and that `n in range(N)` iterates over `0,1,...,N-1`.) Again *Yes.* Is the correct operator + being used in the loop body? *Yes.*

So –overall– *Yes.* It does work. For a program of that (tiny) size, we can be sure we've checked everything.

Or does it work, really... *What does that mean?* It does run without crashing. But you can't say that something works (or doesn't) *unless* you know what it's supposed to do. And there's nothing "officially" associated with (1.2) that says what it's actually *for.* All we have is the text "...we have a sequence `A[0:N]` of numbers, and we want to calculate their sum." written in a paragraph nearby (in this case, just above the program code). What if there had been a page break in the source-text file, in between? When asking whether a program works we have to point not only to the program, but also to a description of what it's supposed to do. (See Sec. 18.2.3.)

So it's probably a good idea to include a (rough) description of the program's purpose as *part of the program itself*, say as a comment at its beginning. That would give us

```
# --- Sum the elements of sequence A[0:N].
s= 0                                                        (1.3)
for n in range(N): s= s+A[n]        .
```

(We have removed the two comments that were there, possibly pointless, not really doing anything useful; and so the `for`-loop can now be all on one line.)

And so we can *now* ask simply "Does (1.3) work?" and it *does* make sense, provided we know we are following the convention that the comment at the front (for now, its *only* comment) is supposed to give the program's purpose. That is, the first line is "officially" where the purpose is to be stated, the *requirements*; and we have here the convention that the " `# ---` " in the comment identifies it as such. (Any other similar convention would do: we are not quibbling about syntax.)

More than that, though, we'll also write a comment at the *end* of the program that states, perhaps in more precise and technical terms, what the final state of the program is supposed to have achieved. That gives us the program

```
# --- Sum the elements of sequence A[0:N].
s= 0
for n in range(N): s= s+A[n]                                (1.4)
# s == ∑A[0:N] # We call this a "postcondition".
```

in which $\sum$ means "the sum of". It's a more technical comment, at the end because it is telling us what we expect to be true once the program's execution has finished. It can be thought of as a more precise, more detailed version of the `# ---` comment at the beginning.

Later we will see many more reasons that putting what we call a "postcondition" there, at the end, is a good idea.

1.4 Requirements and specifications: pre- and postconditions

In careful programming, the comment at (1.4)

```
# --- Sum the elements of sequence A[0:N].
```
(1.5)

might be called the *requirements*, and the comment

```
# s == ∑A[0:N]
```
(1.6)

would probably be called a *postcondition*. The requirements say what the program is supposed to achieve, and the postcondition states something that is supposed to be true (a Boolean *condition*) once the program has finished (*post*). That is, the requirements (1.5) express what our customer (or boss) wants the program for: and "gathering" requirements is an important topic on its own. (See Sec. 19.2.1.) The postcondition (1.6) states what the program will have achieved (made true) when it has ended.

Obviously, requirements and postconditions are related; but they do not have exactly the same purpose. We will explain at the end of this section what the difference between those two things is.

For now, however, we look at a third feature — *preconditions*. They go at the front of the program, and interact with postconditions in the following way. Suppose we have the slightly different program shown here, for finding the largest element in a sequence:

```
# --- Find the largest element of sequence A[0:N].
m= A[0]
for n in range(1,N): m= m max A[n] # Note! A[N] is not included.
# m == MAX A[0:N]      ,
```
(1.7)

where in general we are writing $a \max b$ for the maximum of a and b and MAX A for the overall maximum of a sequence A of values.[4]

If we check that program, as we checked (1.2) at the beginning of Sec. 1.3, we would look at similar things; but here we have deliberately introduced a slight complication. The requirements comment `# ---`   doesn't make sense if the sequence is empty; that is, there can't be a *largest* element if there is no element at all. So –if we are to meet the requirements– we must somehow make sure that the program is never run when A is empty, that is when N is zero... at least not by anyone who expects it to work. *That's what the precondition is for.*

Just as a postcondition states what should be true at a program's end, a precondition states what should be true at its beginning. To make it clear which is which, we will (often, but not always) write PRE and POST within the comments:

```
# PRE: 0<N
m= A[0]
for n in range(1,N): m= m max A[n]
# POST: m == MAX A[0:N]     .
```
(1.8)

One could read the whole of (1.8) as

---

[4] In Python "max" is written as a function; thus in the program we would find `max(m,A[n])`.

"If `0<N` is true at the beginning (PRE) of the program

```
m= A[0]
for n in range(1,N): m= m max A[n]     ,
```

then '`m == `the largest element in `A[0:N]`' will be true at its end (POST)."

Reading it in that way, i.e. saying "if" this "then" that, makes it clear who has responsibility for making those conditions true: the person who is *using* the program must ensure that the precondition is met *if* she wants to be sure that the program will operate correctly — that is, after all, exactly what "if" means. And the person who wrote the program must make sure that *if* its precondition holds *then* its postcondition will hold once the program ends. In the case of (1.8), that means "If `0<N` then the program will set m to the largest element in `A[0:N]`."

But if (1.8) is run when its precondition does not hold, what then? In that case, the program (and its programmer) is absolved from any responsibility for what happens. That takes us back to the requirements: does the program meet them? They were there in (1.7), that is

```
# --- Find the largest element of sequence A[0:N].     ,
```

and it's now clear that they are too strong: the requirements should read instead

```
# --- Find the largest element of non-empty sequence A[0:N].   (1.9)
```

and our overall program becomes   Ex. 1.2

```
# --- Find the largest element of non-empty sequence A[0:N].
# PRE: 0<N
m= A[0]                                                        (1.10)
for n in range(1,N): m= m max A[n]
# POST: m == MAX A[0:N]     .
```

That leaves "specifications" as the last keyword in the heading of this section. We'll call the pre- and postcondition pair together the *specification*: you could think of it as

$$\textit{precondition} \implies (\text{program}) \implies \textit{postcondition} \quad ,$$

where if a program is sitting between the two conditions then it should "satisfy" the specification that the pre- and postcondition together express. The difference between the requirements and the specification *precondition* $\Rightarrow \cdots \Rightarrow$ *postcondition* is then that the requirements can be thought of as the purpose of the program, and the specification can be thought of as a contract — one that the programmer has checked the program is guaranteed to meet (as in Meyer's "Design by Contract" [39]).

It's crucial that the specification should imply that the requirements are met — but, of course, also that the requirements in turn capture accurately what the "customer" wants. (That's part of what is called "requirements analysis", sometimes "validation" — see Chapter 19.) And of course it's just as crucial that the program be guaranteed to satisfy its (validated) specification. (That's "program correctness", sometimes called "verification".) But those are two separate aspects. In the next section, we will take a closer look at the second of those: checking that the program meets, "satisfies", its specification.

That is the programmer's responsibility: *your* responsibility.

1.5 Satisfying a specification: assertions

We now return to the original (1.2), but suppose additionally that `N` is 3 (an arbitrary choice) so that we can "unroll" the program. Because `A[0:N]` is now `A[0:3]` –i.e. it is `[ A[0],A[1],A[2] ]`– we get

```
# PRE: True
s= 0
s= s+A[0]
s= s+A[1]
s= s+A[2]
# POST: s == ∑A[0:3]
```
                                                                              (1.11)

where we have put a precondition `True` to indicate unambiguously that the precondition hasn't simply been left off by accident.[5] Does that program (the middle four lines) satisfy its specification (the first- and last lines taken together)?

It's intuitively clear that it does (once we remember –again– that the last element of `A[0:3]` is `A[2]`). But there is now a sense in which we can check that (can "verify" it), even though for such a small program it seems hardly worth it. Yet we do it anyway, because we want to see exactly how it is done. Start by splitting it up into smaller pieces.

The small program (1.11) is actually four tiny programs one after the other, and we can give each one a specification of its own. Instead of writing them as conventional comments, here we write them between braces {···} to help separate them textually from the program code in between. Their meaning is the same:

$$\{\,\text{PRE: True}\,\}\qquad \texttt{s= 0}\qquad \{\,\text{POST: } \texttt{s} == \textstyle\sum\texttt{A[0:0]}\,\}$$
$$\{\,\text{PRE: } \texttt{s} == \textstyle\sum\texttt{A[0:0]}\,\}\quad \texttt{s= s+A[0]}\quad \{\,\text{POST: } \texttt{s} == \textstyle\sum\texttt{A[0:1]}\,\}$$
$$\{\,\text{PRE: } \texttt{s} == \textstyle\sum\texttt{A[0:1]}\,\}\quad \texttt{s= s+A[1]}\quad \{\,\text{POST: } \texttt{s} == \textstyle\sum\texttt{A[0:2]}\,\}$$
$$\{\,\text{PRE: } \texttt{s} == \textstyle\sum\texttt{A[0:2]}\,\}\quad \texttt{s= s+A[2]}\quad \{\,\text{POST: } \texttt{s} == \textstyle\sum\texttt{A[0:3]}\,\}$$

The precondition of the first program is `True`, meaning that we are assuming nothing (because `True` is true no matter what the variables' values are). After that, though, the *post*-condition of each smaller program is the *pre*-condition of the next one, until –at the end– the final postcondition, i.e. of the final statement, is the postcondition of the whole original program. It's like passing a "baton of correctness".

Let's now look at the small program `s= s+A[1]` all on its own. If we write it vertically, we can include our conditions as comments again:

```
# PRE:  s == ∑A[0:1]
s= s+A[1]
# POST: s == ∑A[0:2]
```
                                                                              (1.12)

Its *pre* condition `s == ∑A[0:1]` will be true just before it is executed, because it is exactly the *post* condition of the previous program `s= s+A[0]`. And if that fragment (1.12) is itself correct, it will establish *its* postcondition `s == ∑A[0:2]`, which is then ready "to be passed" to the `s= s+A[2]` that follows. So each fragment "does its bit", and the next fragment assumes that "the previous bit" has been done.

But *does* the small program (1.12) work? (Yes.) How do we check that?

---

[5] We write `True`, i.e. in "`Python` font" as here, when it is a condition within a `Python` program that is identically true. See also App. D.1.

To find out whether (1.12) works, we take the postcondition $s == \sum A[0:2]$ and simply make the textual substitution given by the assignment statement, that is replacing s by s+A[1]. It's as simple as that, just doing it with a text editor: *find* s, then *replace* s *with* s+A[1]. Literally: just find, then replace. The new text is then s+A[1] $==$ $\sum A[0:2]$. Once that's done, we check that the new, edited, text is implied by ($\Rightarrow$) the precondition;[6] that is, we check that

$$
\begin{array}{ccc}
& \textit{implies} & \\
\text{---antecedent---} & & \text{---consequent---} \\
s == \sum A[0:1] & \Rightarrow & s+A[1] == \sum A[0:2]
\end{array} \quad , \tag{1.13}
$$

which is to say that "Whenever the *antecedent* (to the left of the $\Rightarrow$ arrow symbol) is true, then so is the *consequent* (to the right of the $\Rightarrow$ arrow symbol)." After some simplification, that boils down to just

$$
(\sum A[0:1]) + A[1] \quad == \quad \sum A[0:2] \quad ,
$$

and of course checking the other three small programs (i.e. including the initialisation s= 0) is just as simple, as you can see in App. B.1.1.

But now here is the magic: although we checked those program fragments separately,[7] we can be sure they will work when put all together — *without checking anything further* except that each postcondition implies the precondition immediately following it.

All of that is an example of decomposing one *fairly* simple problem into four *extremely* simple ones. Later however we will use the same technique to decompose not-so-simple problems into a number of simple-but-not-trivial problems. And later still, we will decompose complex problems into a number of less complicated ones, and those into less complicated ones still... until eventually we reach (at last) the extremely trivial again.

Overall, therefore, we are decomposing a large single complicated problem into a (large) number of very simple ones: it's like a tree with a large trunk (a complicated problem) whose branches split, and split again — getting smaller and smaller until we reach the leaves (many simple problems).

Because we have become used to preconditions and postconditions, and to writing them either as comments # $\cdots$ or between braces {$\cdots$}, just as we like, and to suppressing the PRE and POST annotations — we'll now write just

```
{ True }
s= 0
{ s == ∑A[0:0] }
s= s+A[0]
```

line 5
```
{ s == ∑A[0:1] }
```
line 6
```
s= s+A[1]
```
line 7
```
{ s == ∑A[0:2] }
```
$\left.\begin{array}{c} \\ \\ \\ \end{array}\right\}$ $\to$ Recall program (1.12) above. (1.14)

```
s= s+A[2]
{ s == ∑A[0:3] }
```

for the example above. The items {$\cdots$} are called *assertions*, and each one is at the same time the postcondition {POST: $\cdots$} of the program statement before it

---

[6] The implication "$\Rightarrow$" is discussed more thoroughly in App. D.10.1. For now, read it as "if... then".
[7] They could even have been checked by different people, at different times and in different places.

and the precondition {PRE: $\cdots$} of the one after: an example is lines 5–7 of the above, which together give our earlier (1.12) once we re-insert the PRE and the POST annotations and use the vertical format. If we wrote the whole thing out in that style, it would become

```
# PRE: True
s= 0
# POST:  s == ∑A[0:0]

# PRE:  s == ∑A[0:0]
s= s+A[0]
# POST:  s == ∑A[0:1]

# PRE:  s == ∑A[0:1]
s= s+A[1]
# POST:  s == ∑A[0:2]

# PRE:  s == ∑A[0:2]
s= s+A[2]
# POST:  s == ∑A[0:3]
```

line 5
line 6
line 7

$\left.\right\} \rightarrow$ *These are the same.* (1.15)

and that is why the whole, single program is correct provided each of its four smaller components is correct.

1.6 Turn the handle, and watch the program flow

An easy way to visualise (1.14) is to imagine its execution flowing from one statement to the next: we just follow the program's progress, the *program counter's* position, as it moves from the program's beginning to its end.[8]

When the program counter "flows through a *statement*", the statement is executed; and when it flows through an *assertion*, that assertion must be true. The second of those –that the assertion must be true– is the key to rigorous reasoning about programs of this kind.[9]

If each statement does its job, then the truth of its precondition guarantees the truth of its postcondition, which becomes in turn the precondition of the next statement... and so on. Taken all together, the truth initially of the very first precondition, i.e. of the first statement in the program and thus the precondition of the *whole* program, leads inevitably via this "baton passing" of what's-true-here assertions to the truth finally of the postcondition of the very last statement — which is the postcondition of the whole program.

It's like lining up dominoes, checking the adjacent pairs separately to be sure that as each one falls it is certain to strike the next. If *all* adjacent pairs have been checked, even if by different people at different times then pushing the very first "precondition domino" –no matter how many dominoes there are– will eventually cause the postcondition domino to fall.

---

[8] The *program counter* points to the program statement about to be executed.
[9] That second, complementary point of view was proposed by Robert W. Floyd — and it changed *everything*.

1.7 Assertions for loops: invariants

Our original (1.2) from Sec. 1.3 was a loop, and to discuss its correctness we added pre- and postconditions (1.15) and then "unrolled" the loop. We now repeat that, but this time we include the variable n that is initialised and then incremented "behind the scenes" by the iteration `for n in range(N)`. The initial (multiple) assignment `s,n= 0,0` sets both s and n to 0 and establishes the postcondition (of the initialisation), i.e. that $s == \sum A[0:n]$ which, because n==0 at that point, is the same as our earlier $s == \sum A[0:0]$. And all the subsequent assertions $s == \sum A[0:1]$ and $s == \sum A[0:2]$ and $s == \sum A[0:3]$ are also replaced by the same $s == \sum A[0:n]$, and for the same reason:

$$
\begin{aligned}
&\{\,\textsc{Pre: True}\,\} \\
&\texttt{s,n= 0,0} \qquad\qquad \downarrow \; \textit{Now these are all the same.} \\
&\{\,\textsc{Post: } \texttt{n==0 and } s == \textstyle\sum A[0:n]\,\}\ ^{10} \\[4pt]
&\{\,\textsc{Pre: } s == \textstyle\sum A[0:n]\,\} \\
&\texttt{s,n= s+A[0],n+1} \\
&\{\,\textsc{Post: } \texttt{n==1 and } s == \textstyle\sum A[0:n]\,\} \\[4pt]
&\{\,\textsc{Pre: } s == \textstyle\sum A[0:n]\,\} \\
&\texttt{s,n= s+A[1],n+1} \\
&\{\,\textsc{Post: } \texttt{n==2 and } s == \textstyle\sum A[0:n]\,\} \\[4pt]
&\{\,\textsc{Pre: } s == \textstyle\sum A[0:n]\,\} \\
&\texttt{s,n= s+A[2],n+1} \\
&\{\,\textsc{Post: } \texttt{n==3 and } s == \textstyle\sum A[0:n]\,\} \qquad .
\end{aligned}
\tag{1.16}
$$

But we can go even further: we can replace the A[0] and A[1] etc. in the assignments by A[n] in all cases, and we can remove the n==0 and n==1 etc. from the assertions. That gives

$$
\begin{aligned}
&\{\,\textsc{Pre: True}\,\} \\
&\texttt{s,n= 0,0} \qquad\qquad\qquad\quad \rightarrow \; \textit{This is the initialisation, but\ldots} \\
&\{\,\textsc{Post: } s == \textstyle\sum A[0:n]\,\} \\[4pt]
&\{\,\textsc{Pre: } s == \textstyle\sum A[0:n]\,\} \\
&\texttt{s,n= s+A[n],n+1} \qquad\quad \rightarrow \; \textit{\ldots this statement, and} \\
&\{\,\textsc{Post: } s == \textstyle\sum A[0:n]\,\} \\[4pt]
&\{\,\textsc{Pre: } s == \textstyle\sum A[0:n]\,\} \\
&\texttt{s,n= s+A[n],n+1} \qquad\quad \rightarrow \; \textit{\ldots this statement and} \\
&\{\,\textsc{Post: } s == \textstyle\sum A[0:n]\,\} \\[4pt]
&\{\,\textsc{Pre: } s == \textstyle\sum A[0:n]\,\} \\
&\texttt{s,n= s+A[n],n+1} \qquad\quad \rightarrow \; \textit{\ldots this statement are all the same.} \\
&\{\,\textsc{Post: } s == \textstyle\sum A[0:n]\,\}
\end{aligned}
$$

```
# But how do we know that n==3 here?
```

And so we find that all the component programs –and their assertions– are now the same (except the initialisation). If we could somehow add the postcondition { n==3 } at the very end, we would be able to assert { $s == \sum A[0:3]$ } there as well.

---

[10] For example, in `Python` "and" is used rather than "&&" for *conjunction* (App. E.2.1): it makes a single condition that holds just when both of its components (conjuncts) do.

As a final step, to recover our final assertion {n==3}, we'll "roll (1.16) up" again, but use a while-loop rather than a for-loop: the advantage of the while-loop is that it makes the incrementing and testing of the loop index n explicit. With coloured program statements, making them stand out from the assertions, that gives us

Ex. 1.3
Ex. 1.4
Ex. 1.5

{PRE: 0<=N}
s,n= 0,0
{POST: 0<=n<=N and s == $\sum$A[0:n]}

{PRE: 0<=n<=N and s == $\sum$A[0:n]}   ← so-called *loop invariant*
while n!=N:
    {n!=N and 0<=n<=N and s == $\sum$A[0:n]}

(1.17)

    {PRE: 0<=n<N and s == $\sum$A[0:n]}
    s,n= s+A[n],n+1
    {POST: 0<=n<=N and s == $\sum$A[0:n]}   ← POST *of loop body, invariant again*

{POST: n==N and 0<=n<=N and s == $\sum$A[0:n]}   ← POST *of whole loop*
Assertion just above ↑ must imply (⇒) the one just below ↓.[11]
{POST: s == $\sum$A[0:N]}   ← POST *of whole program*

Ex. 1.6
The assertion {0<=n<=N and s == $\sum$A[0:n]} just before the while-loop and at the end of its body (but still within the loop) is the *loop invariant*. Just after the while-loop however, at the beginning of the body, the invariant is joined (with an **and**) to the *loop guard* n!=N, the condition which determines whether the loop is entered; and after the *whole* loop it is joined with the *negation* of the loop guard n==N. (The first POST reminds us that the assertion there is at the end of the loop body; the second POST reminds us that the assertion is at the end of the whole loop; and the third POST is at the end of the whole program. It's POST in all cases, but of different program fragments.)

The while statement –on its own, without its body– appears to have *two* postconditions, because it can send the program execution in either of two directions: in one of them it enters the loop, where the loop guard n!=N is added; and in the other it exits the loop, where the negation of the guard, i.e. n==N, is added.

Again, the program has been split up into simpler pieces; but this time the number of pieces does not depend on N, as it did before (where for example there were N+1, i.e. four pieces when N was 3). Instead of having to write out an instance of the loop body for every time it's executed, we can write it just once — because the pre- and postconditions are the same every time:

– Initialisation

{PRE: 0<=N} s,n= 0,0 {POST: 0<=n<=N and s == $\sum$A[0:n]}

If we treat the assignment statement just as we did at (1.13), and make the substitution, we need only check that

0<=N ⇒ 0<=0 and 0<=N and 0 == $\sum$A[0:0]   ,

which is indeed easy.

– Test for loop entry

{PRE: ···} while n!=N {n!=N and ··· n<=N ···} (loop body)

---

[11] When assertions are vertical, each must imply (⇒) the one below.

Figure 1.1 Flowchart for program (1.17)

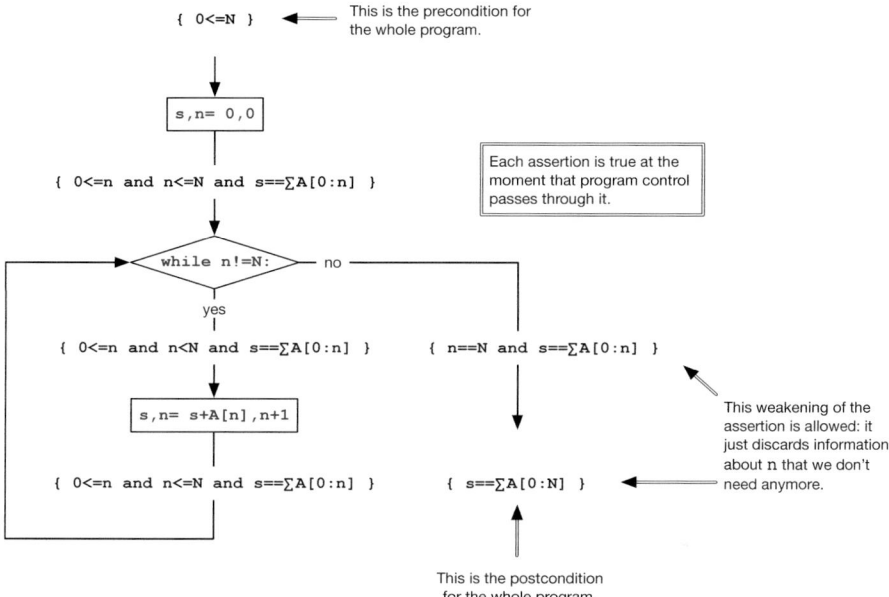

The overall precondition of the program is `0<=N`, at its top; and its overall postcondition is $s == \sum A[0:N]$, at its bottom.

If you imagine starting the program in a state where its precondition `0<=N` is true, and then travelling with the program counter through the program as it executes, you'll notice two things:

(a) Every time you reach an assertion, the program variables' values at that moment make the assertion evaluate to `True` (as a Boolean).

(b) Every time you travel through a statement, it will make its postcondition true (the assertion after it) provided its precondition was true (the assertion before it). Either it changes the variables' values (an assignment statement) or it chooses the correct exit path (using `if` or `while`).

As a result, when the program is finished and you have therefore reached the *overall* post-condition, that is of the whole program, that assertion will be true too.

The effect of entering the loop is to add the loop-entry condition, its guard
n!=N , to the loop body's precondition (to be found at ↘).

– Loop body

$$\{ \text{PRE:} \ \cdots \ \text{n<N} \ \cdots \} \ \text{s,n= s+A[n],n+1} \ \{ \text{POST:} \ \cdots \}$$

Here the precondition is not *textually* the same as the postcondition given earlier,
but it is nevertheless equivalent in meaning: if n<=N and n!=N then n<N (and
vice versa).

We must check that

$$\text{0<=n<N and s} == \sum \text{A[0:n]}$$
$$\Rightarrow \ \text{0<=(n+1) and (n+1)<=N and s+A[n]} == \sum \text{A[0:n+1]} \quad .$$

– Loop exit

$$\{ \text{PRE:} \ \cdots \} \ \text{while n!=N (exit loop)} \ \{ \text{POST:} \ \text{n==N and} \ \cdots \}$$

Here the effect of *not* entering the loop is to add the negation of the loop-entry
guard to the loop's postcondition, in this case n==N , to get the postcondition
for the whole loop.

– End of program

$$\{ \text{POST:} \ \text{s} == \sum \text{A[0:N]} \ \}$$

This *second* postcondition is the postcondition for the whole program, and it is
strictly weaker than the postcondition that was "baton-passed" to it from the
while-loop: we are no longer interested in n .

It is always allowed to have several assertions in a row vertically, as long as each
one is implied by ($\Rightarrow$) the one before.

Each of the five parts in the above list corresponds to taking one step in the execution
of the program, as shown in the flowchart of Fig. 1.1.

Even the "weakening of the final postcondition" (the final item above) corresponds
to a step in the flowchart, though it is not a step in the program (because there is no
program statement there). But it makes sense, because if the first assertion implies
the second, and the first is true, then you will find that the second is true as well.

Ex. 1.7

1.8 Avoiding infinite loops: variants

Our original summing program (1.3) cannot loop forever, because it's a "for-loop"
— a loop where the number of iterations, and the values of the index variable, are
fixed in advance. (That is an advantage of for-loops.) As long as the code in the
loop body does not assign to the index (and it should not), the loop will eventually
end. Here is (1.3) again, with assertions added and an invariant introduced with its
keyword INV :[12]

```
# --- Sum the elements of sequence A[0:N].
s= 0
for n in range(N): # INV: s== ∑A[0:n]      ← the invariant      (1.18)
    s= s+A[n]
# s== ∑A[0:N]      .
```

---

[12] The notations PRE, POST and INV do not affect the meaning of the assertions at all: they are just
there as reminders of what those assertions are telling us. We write the INV *on* the for-line, rather
than before it as for while, because the variable n is initialised by the   for   itself.

We have split the `for`-loop into two lines so that there is a convenient place to write the invariant, that is the assertion $s == \sum A[0\!:\!n]$. It's called the *invariant* of the loop because (as we saw above, with the `while`-loop) it's true every time that the `for` (or `while`) is reached — and that is precisely what allowed us to "roll up" the separate program fragments (the values of n being $0, 1, 2$ etc.) into a single piece of code.

For "`while`-loops", by contrast, it *is* possible that the loop will never end: and usually, at least in simple programs such as (1.1), that constitutes a mistake. But luckily –again, for simple programs– there is an easy way to check that a loop cannot iterate forever: we look for an integer expression that can never become negative, and we show that each execution of the loop body must execute assignment statements that strictly decrease that expression. It's called a *variant*. In the `while`-loop version of the summing program, which was

```
# --- Sum the elements of sequence A[0:N].
# 0<=N
s,n= 0,0
# Inv: 0<=n<=N and s == ∑A[0:n]      ← the invariant               (1.19)
while n!=N:
  s,n= s+A[n],n+1
# s == ∑A[0:N]      ,
```

a suitable variant would be the expression `N-n`. From the invariant's `n<=N` we see that `N-n` can never be negative; and from the loop body's `n= n+1` we see that it must decrease every time the loop body is executed (since N does not change). With some practice, one simply says that `n` on its own is an "increasing" variant (which therefore must be bounded *above*).

And now, if we go all the way back to (1.1) from Sec. 1.2, that is (repeated here for convenience)

```
# --- Calculate the year number of Day d,
# Pre: where 1/1/1980 was Day 1.
y= 1980
while d>365:
  if leapYear(y):
    if d>366:
      d= d-366
      y= y+1
  else:
    d= d-365
    y= y+1
# Post: The current year is y.      ,
```

we can see that there is *no possible variant* for its termination: there can't be one, because in some circumstances it does not terminate.[13] When y is a leap year and `d==366`, the first `if`-test evaluates to `True` and the second one to `False`; and in that case the loop body makes no assignments at all — it can't decrease anything, variant or otherwise.

If the social process for creating that program had included "What's the variant?", the program would never have passed inspection.

---

[13] What is the relevance of propositional rule (E.30) to this?

1.9 Summary

We've now concluded our introduction to checking programs, to making sure that they work: the *ideas* are extremely simple, though often overlooked (and –surprisingly– not taught). They become complicated only when they are applied to complicated programs. But –as we will see in subsequent chapters– keeping invariants and variants in mind when writing complicated programs can actually help to *construct* the program, and indeed often that can result in programs that are simpler than they might otherwise have been.

Following is a summary of what we have covered so far — and you can do a lot with just this alone.

(a) **What are requirements?** Requirements state informally, "in English" what the program is for, what it is supposed to achieve. They should not be too technical, nor swamped in detail.

(b) **What are specifications?** Specifications are precondition/postcondition pairs: as a pair, together they should satisfy the requirements. And they should be detailed enough to check that the program code actually works.

(c) **What are preconditions?** Preconditions are assertions written before a program fragment. They state with reasonable rigour the conditions that the fragment relies on in its initial state.

(d) **What are postconditions?** Postconditions are assertions written after a program fragment. They state with similar rigour the conditions that the fragment must establish when it reaches its final state, provided the precondition(s) were met in its initial state.

(e) **What are assertions? When are they supposed to be true?**
Assertions are Boolean expressions that should be true whenever the program is executing at that point. Preconditions, postconditions and invariants are all assertions: the label of an assertion (if it has one) is just to remind us of what we are using it for.

(f) **What is an invariant?** An invariant is an assertion used to check that a loop works, that it does what it is supposed to do: it is written before the loop, at the end of the loop body, and it appears as well at the beginning of the loop body (**and** the loop guard) and after the whole loop (**and** the negated loop guard).

Ex. 1.8   Introduced in Sec. 1.7 above, they are the principal topic of Chapter 3.

(g) **What is a variant?** A variant is an integer-valued expression used to check that a loop cannot be "infinite", i.e. that it cannot iterate forever (Sec. 1.8).

Ex. 1.9   They are the principal topic of Chapter 4.

(h) **What are comments good for?** Comments help people understand the program: they can state what the program is supposed to do; they can explain why certain code is the way it is; and they can give conditions (assertions, pre- and postconditions, invariants) that help to check that the program works.

They are especially useful when they state what should be true "here", i.e. at that point in the program.

(i) **What does it mean for a program to satisfy its specification?** A program satisfies a specification if it treats the pre- and postconditions as described at

(c) and (d) above, and if checking the program code is successful. The rules for checking programs are summarised in Appendix B, but are gradually introduced in the main text between here and there.

(j) **When can you say a program "works"?** A program works just when it satisfies its specification.

(k) **How do you show that an assignment statement satisfies a specification?** Treat the assignment statement as a textual substitution, replacing in the specification's postcondition all occurrences of the variables on the assignment's left-hand side by the corresponding expressions on the right-hand side. Then check that the specification's precondition implies the result of that substitution.

(l) **How do we decompose big complicated programs into smaller, more simple ones?** We split the program between its statements, inserting assertions there: they become the postcondition of the first statement and, simultaneously, the precondition of the second. Each precondition/statement/postcondition is treated as a small program on its own, and checked with respect to its own "local" precondition and postcondition. As with the "tree" analogy mentioned earlier, those smaller programs can themselves be split again.

(m) **What's the connection between specifications and requirements?** Requirements are the interface between the programmer and the client, and can be informal — but they should be clear. Specifications state in more rigorous terms what a program should do, and they should imply the requirements; but that can only be checked informally.

The rigour of specifications is what makes them useful for checking reliably that the program works. Check carefully that the program satisfies its specification, by splitting the program up into smaller pieces connected by assertions; but check also that the specification meets the requirements.

(n) Here is a final example of all the above:

requirements — Find the (integer) quotient $num//den$ and remainder $num\%den$ of non-negative numerator num and strictly positive denominator den.

specification — $\{\,\textsc{Pre}: num>=0 \text{ and } den>0\,\}$
        $\cdots$
        $\{\,\textsc{Post}: q==num//den \text{ and } r==num\%den\,\}$

program (which works) $\boxed{\text{Ex. 1.10}}$

```
# --- Find the quotient and remainder
# --- of non-negative num and den.
# PRE: num>=0 and den>0
q,r= 0,num
# INV: q*den+r ==num and 0<=r
while r>=den:
  q,r= q+1,r-den
{q*den+r ==num and 0<=r<den }
# POST: q==num//den and r==num%den
```
                                                                          (1.20)

We wrote "Inv" to remind us that the assertion we have placed there is the loop invariant.

1.10 Exercises

Exercises for which an answer is given in Appendix I are indicated by a small vertical arrow before the start of the exercise.

Exercise 1.1 (p. 3) This program sets m to a maximum value among a, b and c:

```
if a>=b:
  if a>=c: m= a
  else:    m= c
else:
  if b<=c: m= c
  else:    m= b    .
```
(1.21)

A conventional approach to checking it would be to examine all four paths it might follow when run. Write out the four paths, and the checks you would have to do.

If you extended that program in the same style, to include a fourth variable d, how many paths would you have to check then?

Exercise 1.2 (p. 7) ⇓ Program (1.10) finds the largest element of a sequence, and it was introduced as an example to motivate *pre* conditions, because it works only on non-empty sequences: there cannot be a largest element of a sequence if the sequence has no elements at all. If we rephrase its requirements slightly, however, we can make the program more general — provided we assume for now that the programming language includes the value that will be the answer to Ex. 1.18 below. It becomes

```
# --- Find the maximum of the elements in A[0:N],
# --- even if there are none.
# PRE: 0<=N
m= ???
for n in range(N): # INV: m == MAX A[0:n]
  { What assertion goes here? }
  m= m max A[n]
  { What assertion goes here? }
# POST: m == MAX A[0:N]    .
```

Note that we are alternating freely between writing assertions as $\{\cdots\}$ between braces and assertions as comments # $\cdots$. They are the same thing: but we are following a convention that the $\{\cdots\}$ form is used for checking that a program works –as we write it– and the # $\cdots$ form is used for conditions that we would like to retain in the program afterwards, as comments, for its documentation. Thus, in the above, the loop-invariant comment # INV: m == MAX A[0:n] should remain as part of the program's documentation — but of course it's also an assertion that we actually use when reasoning about whether the program works. On the other hand, we can probably remove the two "{ *What goes here?* }" assertions above once we are happy they have done their job.

Can you fill in the two "{ *What goes here?* }" assertions above? Use them to check that the program works.

Exercise 1.3 (p. 12) ⇓ In (1.17) there was the program fragment

Ex. 1.11
Ex. 1.12
Ex. 1.13

```
{ PRE:  0<=n<N and s == ∑A[0:n] }
s,n= s+A[n],n+1
{ POST: 0<=n<=N and s == ∑A[0:n] }      ,
```

where we included PRE and the POST annotations as {···}-assertions just to remind us what we are using those assertions for at that point. If you perform the substitution of s+A[n] for s and n+1 for n in the postcondition, as the assignment statement suggests, what exact condition do you get? *Just do the substitution*: do not simplify it (yet).

Exercise 1.4 (p. 12) The following program is like (1.17) except that it goes in the opposite direction, from high n==N to low n==0. The presentation is simplified by removing some of the assertions, and most of the PRE's and POST's; and some question marks, "?", have been introduced for you to fill in:

```
{ PRE:  0<=N }

s,n= 0,N
{ 0<=n<=N and s == ∑A[?:?] }                    # Start here.
while n!=0:
  { 0<n<=N and s == ∑A[?:?] }
  n= n-1                                                        (1.22)
  { ??? } # And finally calculate this from the one below.
  s= s+A[n]
  { 0<=n<=N and s == ∑A[?:?] }         # Then copy it here.
{ n==0 and s == ∑A[?:?] }

{ POST:  s == ∑A[0:N] }       .
```

Fill in the missing pieces, indicated by ?'s, in the order suggested: first the top, then the bottom and finally the middle one.

Hint: It's easier to calculate assertions *backwards*, working from postconditions to preconditions, that is from later assertions towards earlier ones. For example, the assertion marked "Start here." is the loop "invariant": figure it out first, and check that it is established by the initial assignment (given the program's overall precondition 0<=N). Then –because it's invariant– the assertion marked "Then copy it here.", at the end, should be exactly the same.

Only after all that, use substitution to calculate the intermediate assertion in the middle. Make sure it justifies the indexing A[n].

Exercise 1.5 (p. 12) ⇓ The three remaining comments in this version of (1.17) should be enough for checking that it works:

```
# --- Calculate the sum of sequence A[0:N].
# 0<=N
s,n= 0,0
while n!=N: # s == ∑A[0:n]                                      (1.23)
  s,n= s+A[n],n+1
# s == ∑A[0:N]       .
```

Why are those three comments enough? The reason is that the requirements comment can be checked against the other two "assertion" comments to see that the program is doing what the customer wants. Then the assertion comments can be turned into *actual* assertions, with the obvious "housekeeping" inequalities on n added. Finally, the intermediate assertions can be generated by substitution, and the implications checked by arithmetic and sequence-based reasoning. The PRE and POST labels are not necessary — we use them just to explain how the reasoning works. Any assertion is simply considered to be a *pre* condition of the statement after it, and a *post* condition of the one before it.

In the end, the only significant, i.e. "non-routine" fact turns out to be that

$$0<=n<N \qquad \Rightarrow \qquad \sum A[0:(n+1)] \ == \ \sum A[0:n] + A[n] \qquad ,$$

Ex. 1.14 which is actually a law of sequences (not of programs): it is that for any two sequences A and B we have

$$\sum (A+B) \qquad == \qquad \sum A \ + \ \sum B \qquad , \tag{1.24}$$

where the (+) on the left sticks two sequences together, "concatenates" them. (On the right it's just normal addition of numbers.)

Starting from (1.23), go through the process of (re-)generating all the assertions that were needed while (1.17) was being constructed. (Do not go back and copy them! Regenerate them here.)

You should do a painstaking, nit-picking exercise like that at least once in your life. Later, you will develop your own style: you will learn which assertions you should include and which ones you can safely leave out, which implications you should check carefully and which ones you can just "eyeball".

And indeed there are program-checking tools that can generate many assertions for you automatically, at least the simple ones. (See Sec. 18.2 for more about that.) But *before* you use those tools, you must know how to do it yourself! Otherwise you will never understand what the tools are doing for you and –worse– you might not spot that they are not doing what you think they do.

Exercise 1.6 (p. 12) In (1.17), where have we checked that sequence A is always being accessed within its bounds, that is without an indexing error?

Exercise 1.7 (p. 14) ⇓ A simple example of a *continued fraction* is $1 + \frac{1}{2}$, which has the value $\frac{3}{2}$. If we go two more steps we might have

$$1 + \cfrac{1}{2 + \frac{1}{3}} \qquad \text{and} \qquad 1 + \cfrac{1}{2 + \cfrac{1}{3 + \frac{1}{4}}} \qquad ,$$

which have values $\frac{10}{7}$ and $\frac{43}{30}$ respectively.

Suppose we represent a continued fraction in general as a (finite) non-empty sequence of integers A[0:N], where A[0] is the leading term and elements A[1:N] give the subsequent denominators. (They do not have to follow a rule like 1, 2, 3 as in the continued fraction above: that was just an example.) Thus [a] would be a and [a,b] would be $a + \frac{1}{b}$ and [a,b,c] would be $a + \frac{1}{b + \frac{1}{c}}$ and so on.

Write a program in the style of this chapter that, given a sequence of positive integers, calculates the value of the continued fraction it represents.

"In the style of this chapter" means

(a) Include an initial *requirements* comment.

(b) Write the *precondition* of the whole program as a comment at its beginning.

(c) Write the *postcondition* of the whole program as a comment at its end.

(d) Give an *invariant* for your loop; write it as an # INV: -comment immediately after the colon on the for-loop or before the while-loop header.

Note that the *way* you write these assertions/comments does not have to be super-rigorous: it's the ideas they express that are important.

After all, the summation sign $\sum$ was introduced into an assertion at (1.4) in the running example for this chapter, wholly without rigour — we never defined it, except informally in words. But we did use a property of it, which turned to be all we needed: it is the "law" (1.24) (stated without proof) in Ex. 1.5 above.

The whole idea of checking programs this way is to reduce the job systematically to a number of much smaller and, crucially, *separate and independent* checks where "eyeballing" suffices for each one on its own. A good example of that technique was given at (1.17) and its flowchart in Fig. 1.1.

Exercise 1.8 (p. 16) ⇓ Use the invariant "Today is Day d, where 1/1/y was Day 1." to rewrite (1.1) so that it actually works; assume that you have a function DiY(y) giving the number of days in Year y.

Do not use **break** to escape the loop; instead call DiY() twice if necessary.

> Ex. 1.15

Exercise 1.9 (p. 16) What is the variant of the program you wrote for Ex. 1.8, which you need in order to show that its loop terminates? How do you know that your variant strictly decreases on each iteration?

Note that (integer) variants do not have to be non-negative: it's enough to show that they are bounded below. "Non-negative" is just the special case where the below-bound is zero.

Exercise 1.10 (p. 17) ⇓ What is the variant that ensures that the loop in (1.20) does not iterate forever?

Exercise 1.11 (p. 19) Use arithmetic and facts about sequences (and $\sum$) to simplify your answer to Ex. 1.3 as much as you can.

Exercise 1.12 (p. 19) Suppose the program of Ex. 1.3 is split into two assignments, one after the other:

```
{ PRE: 0<=n<N and s == ∑A[0:n] }
s= s+A[n]
{ What assertion goes here? }
n= n+1
{ POST: 0<=n<=N and s == ∑A[0:n] }     .
```

Use the postcondition and the substitution implied by the second assignment n= n+1 to *tell you* what assertion should go "in the middle", between the statements: that way, you do not have to guess.

Simplify your middle assertion, and then substitute into it as suggested by the first statement s= s+A[n] . Simplify *that* and, finally, check that the simplification is implied by the overall precondition.

Exercise 1.13 (p. 19) Split the program of Ex. 1.3 into two assignments, one after the other as in Ex. 1.12, but this time the other way around:

> { PRE: 0<=n<N and s == $\sum$A[0:n] }
> n= n+1
> { *What assertion goes here?* }
> s= s+A[n]
> { POST: 0<=n<=N and s == $\sum$A[0:n] }   .

Use substitution (as in Ex. 1.12, i.e. from the postcondition back through the assignment just before it) to tell you which assertion should go between the two statements. Then perform the substitution into that assertion that is induced by the first assignment. Is the resulting precondition of that first assignment implied by the precondition of the whole program?

Ex. 1.16   Does the program check?

Exercise 1.14 (p. 20)

In Ex. 1.5 we mentioned a "law" (1.24) that related addition of numbers and con-
Ex. 1.19 catenation of sequences. How would you use that law to argue that the sum of the
empty sequence must be zero, i.e. that $\sum$[] == 0 ?
Ex. 1.18
What is the product $\prod$[] of the empty sequence?

Ex. 1.17 **Exercise 1.15** (p. 21) In your answer to Ex. 1.8 you might have called function DiY(y) in two places. Figure out how to use assertions to check loops that use **break**, and then write a version of (1.1) that uses **break**, and so needs only one call of DiY(). Introduce an extra variable **n** if you need it.

How would you use assertions to reason about **continue**?

Exercise 1.16 (p. 22) ⇓ If the program in Ex. 1.13 does not check, i.e. the intermediate assertion you found by substitution is *not* implied by the precondition, can you by some other means find an intermediate assertion that *does* show that the program works? If not, what does that tell you about the intermediate assertion found for you by that substitution?

Exercise 1.17 (p. 22) ⇓ Make a flowchart for your answer to Ex. 1.15 in the style of Fig. 1.1. Check that all assertions are true as program control passes through them.

Exercise 1.18 (p. 22) By analogy with + and $\sum$, and similarly ∗ and $\prod$, define max to be the maximum of two numbers, and MAX to be the maximum of a whole sequence. Thus 1 max 2 == 2 and MAX[1,3,2] == 3.

What is the maximum MAX[] of the empty sequence?

Exercise 1.19 (p. 22) ⇓ Any square matrix (of numbers) has a *determinant*. For the three matrices

$$(a) \quad \text{and} \quad \begin{pmatrix} a & b \\ c & d \end{pmatrix} \quad \text{and} \quad \begin{pmatrix} a & b & c \\ d & e & f \\ g & h & i \end{pmatrix}$$

the determinants are a and $ad - bc$ and

$$a\begin{vmatrix} e & f \\ h & i \end{vmatrix} + b\begin{vmatrix} f & d \\ i & g \end{vmatrix} + c\begin{vmatrix} d & e \\ g & h \end{vmatrix}$$

respectively.

What is the determinant of the empty matrix?

Exercise 1.20 Suppose that today is 1 January 2021, so that "one day ago" would be 31 December 2020, and "366 days ago" would be 1 January 2020 (because 2020 was a leap year). Assume (as above) that you have a function DiY such that DiY(y) is the number of days in Year y.

Given a natural number G (for aGo), design a program that calculates the day number d and year number y for "G days ago from today".

Hint: Invent the notation d/-/y for Day d counting from 1/1/y as Day 1 (i.e. as for conventional notation, but missing the month), where however d may be any integer at all, positive negative or zero. Then the purpose of the program is to establish that (1-G)/-/2021 is the same day as d/-/y (a good choice for the invariant?) while ensuring that d is within the proper range for year y, that is 1<=d<=DiY(y) .

Let G>=0 and "Today is 1 January 2021." be the precondition. Could d<=DiY(y) be part of the invariant as well? What loop guard will eventually establish 1<=d ?

Exercise 1.21 Look carefully at the precondition (on G) in Ex. 1.20, and consider whether perhaps you could let it be weaker. In particular, are there situations in which G is negative but the answer to Ex. 1.20 is still guaranteed to establish its postcondition?

Now, more generally than in Ex. 1.20, suppose that today is Day D in Year Y (rather than 1 January 2021). Otherwise, the purpose of the program is the same: to find d and y such that "G days ago" (from D//Y) is Day d in Year y. How would you approach writing that program? And what is its precondition?

2

Using invariants to design loops

2.1 Introduction

In this chapter, we will go through a program-design process in three different ways, but all three for the *same* problem. The first two ways will use a conventional approach (although we do mention invariants, after the fact, to help check them); but the third uses an invariant *before* the fact, to help design the program in the first place.[1]

2.2 The longest *Good* subsegment problem

Assume we have a property $Bad(a, b, c)$ of three integers, for some (not yet made precise) property of "badness". Here are some examples of what $Bad(a, b, c)$ might be:

- All equal: $a = b = c$ is bad.

- In a run, up or down: either $a+1 = b$ and $b+1 = c$, or $a-1 = b$ and $b-1 = c$.

- Able to make a triangle: thus $a+b+c \geq 2\,(a \max b \max c)$.

- The negation (i.e. opposite) of any of the above.

Suppose further we are working (as usual) with a sequence `A[0:N]` and that we have implemented a Boolean function `Bad(n)` that determines $Bad(\texttt{A[n]}, \texttt{A[n+1]}, \texttt{A[n+2]})$ for us. (Note that the function `Bad` has just one argument `n` but examines `A` in three places.) It is a programming error –index out of range– if `n<0` or `n+3>N`.

Recall that a *subsegment* of `A[0:N]` is any consecutive run `A[i:j]` of elements with `0<=i<=j<=N`.[2] We will say that such a subsegment of `A` is *Good* just when it has no *Bad* subsegments inside it: and therefore a *Good* subsegment of `A` can potentially be of any length up to the length `N` of `A` itself. Any subsegment of length 2 or less is necessarily *Good*, since it is too short to contain a *Bad* subsegment. Remember that *Bad* subsegments have length exactly 3 and, since they can overlap, it's clear that `A` can contain anywhere from 0 up to `N-2` of them.

---

[1] This problem was taken from a first-year university course "Introduction to Programming in *C*".
[2] A sub*sequence* can have "holes", so that `ac` is a subsequence of `abc` but not a subsegment.

The requirements for this program might be written as follows:

```
# --- Determine the length of the longest Good subsegment
# --- of sequence A[0:N], where a Good subsegment has no
# --- subsegment of three (consecutive) elements inside it
# --- that is Bad.
# --- Assume that the Boolean function Bad(n) determines
# --- whether A[n:n+3] is Bad, for 0<=n<=N-3.
```
(2.1)

The program's specification, making the requirements more precise, might be

```
# PRE: Bad(n) is well defined for 0<=n and n+3<=N.

... # Program text goes here.

# POST: good == "a largest value such that
#        there is a low with 0<=low and low+good<=N and
#        for no n with low<=n and n+3<=low+good
#        does Bad(n) hold."
```
(2.2)

Notice that the requirements state that Bad() must actually calculate *Bad*, but the specification does not: it makes no demands on Bad(n) except that it be well defined for 0<=n and n+3<=N. This is deliberate: given the many possible definitions of *Bad*, it might be a distraction if the programming task were to depend on what Bad() actually calculates.

We now design the first of our three programs for the above specification.

2.3 First attempt: operational intuition and diagrams

A straightforward approach to solving the above problem might be along these lines.

First go through all of sequence A and store its "bad-subsegment positions" in an extra array B. Then find the differences between adjacent elements of B. Finally –after some careful thought– set good to the largest of those differences.[3]

Notice in the previous paragraph the operational phrasing "go through" and the slightly fuzzy "after some careful thought... " (One more than the difference? One less than? Exactly?) A typical approach to the programming process might be to write code at this point, using the guess above, and see whether the program's answers look right. If not — well, then the bugs can be discovered by further testing, and then "tweaked" until the program seems to be correct. Probably the tweaks here will be one-off errors related to the differences calculated from B.

With the above intuitions, the program is easy to code: it's shown in Fig. 2.1. There are in that program, however, a number of careful calculations necessary to figure out the length of *Good* subsegments as they are discovered, plus the special

---

[3] The "careful thought" here –which is actually fun– is to figure out what the longest *Good* subsegment can be that includes neither *Bad* subsegment A[b0:b0+3] nor *Bad* subsegment A[b1:b1+3], where b0<b1 and they are the two adjacent bad positions with diff == b1-b0. It must start at-or-after b0+1, in order to leave out A[b0:b0+3], and it must end at-or-before b1+2-1 to leave out A[b1:b1+3]. So its greatest possible length is "where it starts" minus "where it ends" plus 1, that is (b1+2-1)-(b0+1)+1 which simplifies to b1-b0+1. Since the largest such b1-b0 is diff itself, the correct value for good is diff+1 — and not diff+2 as we initially guessed above.

This "guessing" and then "tweaking until correct" is a common approach — especially because it *is* fun. But is it reliable?

Figure 2.1 First program — 9 lines of code, and extra sequence B (Sec. 2.3)

```
# Sequence B must have length at least N-2.

bads= 0 # Number of Bad subsegments found.
for b in range(N-2): # Find starting points of Bad subsegments.
  if Bad(b): B[bads],bads= b,bads+1
# Now we know where the Bad subsegments are.

if bads==0: good= N # Special case.                              (2.3)
else:
    good= B[0]+2 # First Bad subsegment gives first Good subsegment.
    for n in range(1,bads): # More Bad subsegments... except last.
      good= good max (B[n]-B[n-1]+1) # ...give subsequent Good's.
    good= good max (N-B[bads-1]-1) # Very last Bad subsegment.
```

The first part of the program records the starting indices of all *Bad* triples in A. Its invariant is that B[0:bads], which we abbreviate B[:bads], records all such indices found so far, in A[:n].

For the second part of the program there are three cases. If there are no *Bad* subsegments at all, then the whole of A is *Good*, and it has length N.

If not, then the first *Good* subsegment begins at A[0] and ends at A[B[0]+1] (inclusive), and so has length B[0]+2.

And the last *Good* subsegment (which –remember– might be the same subsegment as the first one!) begins at A[B[bads-1]+1] and ends at A[N-1] (again inclusive), and so has length N-B[bads-1]-1. The general case has length B[n]-B[n-1]+1.

See Fig. 2.2 for helpful sketches. In between, the invariant is that **good** is correct for all *Bad* subsegments recorded in B[:b] — that is, again "so far".

---

cases of "no *Bad* subsegments" and "exactly one *Bad* subsegment" (when the first and the last *Bad* subsegments are the same), and finally the *Good* subsegments that run right from the start of A, or right up to the end of A.

Although it's "easy to code" this program... perhaps it's not so easy to *check* it. Part of the checking process might involve small "off line" sketches like those given in Fig. 2.2. Do the sketches become part of the program's documentation?

2.4 Second attempt: operational intuition and a caterpillar

A second program can be derived from the first. Suppose we realise that having the extra array B is useful for separating the problem into sub-problems, but logically speaking it is a waste of space: a more efficient program uses only a "conceptual" extra array B — that is, one for which only the two currently interesting elements are maintained as you go along: they're called a0 and a1.

That's a nice idea, and it improves (2.3) so that it becomes (2.4) in Fig. 2.3 — so it's probably worth the effort. The result, given in Fig. 2.3, might even be considered a clearer coding than the first program: the caterpillar analogy described in Fig. 2.3 really helps to see what's going on — see below. For example, the sketches of Fig. 2.2

Figure 2.2 Sketches to check index calculations in (2.3) above

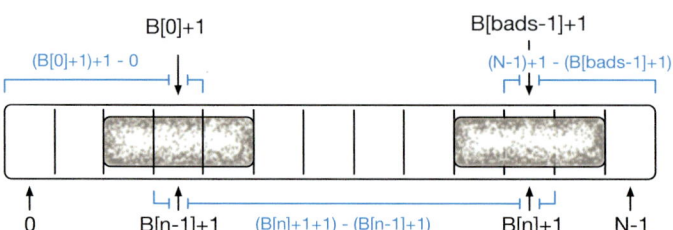

The length of subsegment `A[low:high]` is `high-low` in all cases.

---

aren't necessary any more.

Ex. 2.3 The program is slightly marred, though, by the mysterious "-1" assignments in its initialisation: see (2.4).

Its invariant is (1) that as a0 and a1 hop through the indices of A, the caterpillar's tail `A[a0]` and head `A[a1]` rest on the start of two adjacent *Bad* subsegments, so that `A[a0+1:a1+2]` is a non-extendable *Good* subsegment; and (2) that the value of good is always up-to-date with respect to the prefix `A[:a1]` of A examined so far.

2.5 Third attempt: use an invariant to design the program

We saw in Chapter 1 that assertions –a special kind of "What's true here?" comment– can help to check that a program works. (That's why we gave invariants to help in checking the two earlier version of this program.) Special cases were *preconditions*, which state what a program(mer) can assume about the initial state, *postconditions*, which state what the final state must satisfy and *invariants*, which state what should be true every time a loop guard is evaluated (to decide whether to (re-)enter the loop or not).

The first two are external, because they are directly related to the requirements: from the programmer's point of view they are "given". The invariants, on the other hand (one per loop) help to see *why* the loop is doing the right thing: they are internal, up to the programmer to find.

But invariants can do more — they can also be used to *design* the loop, and then the loop works because the invariant was used to *make* it, not (just) to check it. We are about to see how the example considered in this chapter illustrates that nicely.

Let's write for brevity `lgs(n)` for the length of the largest *Good* subsegment in the prefix `A[:n]` of A, so that the program's specification becomes simply

```
# PRE: Bad(n) is well defined for 0<=n and n+3<=N.
...
# POST: good == lgs(N)   ← Using N here means "the whole of A".
```

For many simple programs (like that one) we can find a candidate invariant immediately by "splitting the postcondition" into two pieces: the first piece is n==N, and the second is good == lgs(n), referring now to a new variable n that will be the index for the loop we are about to create. (It is the technique "iterate up" from Sec. 3.3.1

Figure 2.3 Second program — 8 lines of code, no extra sequence (Sec. 2.4)

```
a0,a1,good= -1,-1,0 # Pretend there is a Bad subsegment at -1.
while True:
  a1= a1+1 # Look for the next Bad subsegment.
  if a1+3>N: # There isn't one.
    good= good max (N-a0-1) # Take last a0 into account.                (2.4)
    break
  if Bad(a1): # Found one: update good from a0,a1 and carry on.
    good,a0= good max (a1-a0+1), a1
```

This second program improves the first in two major ways: it doesn't need an extra sequence B, and there are fewer special cases.

Think of a0 and a1 as being the tail and head respectively of a caterpillar. The tail always rests on the start of a *Bad* subsegment; and on each iteration the head advances to the start of the very next *Bad* subsegment further along. Then good is updated by max'ing it with the current length of the caterpillar; and finally the caterpillar brings its tail a0 up to its head a1 (as caterpillars do). The process then repeats.

At the beginning, the caterpillar is bunched up at -1, in effect pretending there's a *Bad* subsegment there. At the end, the caterpillar pretends there's a *Bad* subsegment at N.

---

below.) The Boolean n==N is the negation of the loop guard (if we use a while-loop) or the actual termination condition (if we use a for-loop). That small step alone allows us to begin writing the program — but we write it *from the outside in* rather than from front to rear, or in one part and then another.

Our first step is

```
# PRE: Bad(n) is well defined for 0<=n and n+3<=N.
n,good= 0,0
{ good == lgs(n) }
# INV: good == lgs(n) and 0<=n<=N   ←invariant
while n!=N:
    { PRE: good == lgs(n) and n<N }
    ···       # Loop body will go here.
    { POST: good == lgs(n+1) and n<N }       ← This specifies the loop body.
    n= n+1
    { POST: good == lgs(n)   and n<=N }
{ n==N and good == lgs(n) }
# POST: good == lgs(N)     ,
```

where the assertions $\{\cdots\}$ can be thought of as "What's true here?" comments: they are not to be executed — but they do remind the programmer of the structure as the program develops, grown from the outside in.

In some places we leave out parts of 0<=n<=N in the invariant, to reduce clutter; but we do put them in where they're important.

The programming is now reduced to finding the loop body, the "inside": the rest of the program, the "outside", is already there. And the specification of the loop body (at "} ←" above) tells us exactly what it must do. If good == lgs(n) at this point, as the precondition says, and we are considering A[n], which we know is well defined because of n<N, how do we "update" good so that it now takes A[n] into account as well?

"Updating good" means increasing it if a longer *Good* subsegment is found than the ones already considered. All the subsegments of A[:n] were considered (says the invariant) and so if good must change, it must be because of a *Good* subsegment that ends exactly at the newly considered element A[n]. So we add a new variable low to keep track of that, and a second invariant

INV2: A[low:n] is the longest *Good* suffix of A[:n]   .

(See Sec. 3.5 below for a more general discussion of that, a "cascading" invariant.) We'll call the second invariant Inv2(n), and our earlier invariant we'll now rename to Inv1(n). Both of them apply. Our program becomes

```
# PRE: Bad(n) is well defined for 0<=n and n+3<=N.

n,good,low= 0,0,0
{ Inv1(0) and Inv2(0) }

# INV: Inv1(n) and Inv2(n)          ← invariants
while n!=N:
```

$\qquad$ {PRE: Inv1(n) and Inv2(n) and n!=N}
$\qquad$ ... $\Big\}$ ← *How* low *must be updated.*
$\qquad$ {POST: Inv1(n) and Inv2(n+1)}

These are the same:
$\qquad\qquad\qquad\qquad\qquad$ $\Updownarrow$

$\qquad$ {PRE: Inv1(n) and Inv2(n+1)}
$\qquad$ good= good max (n+1-low) $\Big\}$ ← *This is correct by inspection.*
$\qquad$ {POST: Inv1(n+1) and Inv2(n+1)}

$\qquad$ {PRE: Inv1(n+1) and Inv2(n+1)}
$\qquad$ n= n+1
$\qquad$ {POST: Inv1(n) and Inv2(n)}   ← *invariants re-established.*

$\quad$ {n==N and good == lgs(n)}   ← *loop exit:* not (n!=N) *and* Inv1(n) ,
$\quad$ # POST: good == lgs(N)   ←   *implies overall postcondition.*

Notice at the double-headed vertical arrow how the *post*condition of the low-update becomes the *pre*condition of the good-update, and has told us what that good-update must be here — *even though we do not yet know what the* low *update –just before it– will turn out to be.* And the to-be-completed "···" has shrunk, from the whole of the loop body to just this portion.

And only now do we go back and update low as its specification directs. If the last three elements of A[:n+1], that is A[n-2], A[n-1] and A[n], are *Bad* then low must become n-1. (Remember that A[n-1:n+1], of length only 2, cannot be *Bad*.) On the other hand, if they are not *Bad* then low need not be changed. Bearing in mind that the subsegment must be of length 3 –and that there must be room for it– the final jigsaw piece is

$\qquad\qquad$ if 2<=n and Bad(n-2): low= n-1   .

If we insert that into the above program, and then remove all the "scaffolding" –that is, the {···} assertions we used, along the way, to help us *design* the program– then the result is the very concise Fig. 2.4. Here's how it compares with the two earlier programs:

Ex. 2.1
Ex. 2.2

Figure 2.4 Third program: recommended method

```
# PRE: Bad(n) is well defined for 0<=n and n+3<=N.

# Inv1(n) is "good is the length
#              of a longest Good subsegment of A[:n]."
# Inv2(n) is "A[low:n] is the longest Good suffix of A[:n]."

n,good,low= 0,0,0

# INV: Inv1(n) and Inv2(n) and 0<=n<=N
while n!=N:
  if n>=2 and Bad(n-2): low= n-1
  good,n= good max (n+1-low), n+1

# POST: Inv1(N).
```
(2.5)

- No extra array "B" is used (2.3).
- No off-line sketches are required (Fig. 2.2 for (2.3)).
- There are no mysterious −1 initialisations (2.4).
- There is no special treatment needed for the beginning or the end of A (or both).
- max is used only once.
- It is the shortest (only half the size, at 4 lines — not 8 or 9).
- We do not need to check it afterwards (though we *must* test it: Sec. 19.3) since it was checked automatically by the construction process as we went along.[4]

2.6 Exercises

Exercise 2.1 (p. 30) ⇓ Explain how we know that (2.5) in Fig. 2.4 cannot index A out-of-range with its call of Bad. Then write the program as a for-loop.

Since a subsegment must have length at least 3 to be *Bad*, is it true that the program always sets good to at least 2?

Exercise 2.2 (p. 30) Modify the postcondition for (2.5) from Sec. 2.5 so that the subsegment A[start:end], that is A[start], A[start+1],...,A[end-1], is an actual *Good* subsegment of maximum length. Modify the invariant to take account of that. And write the program that results.

(There should not be too much to change.)

Exercise 2.3 (p. 28) ⇓ In Sec. 2.4 it's stated that the invariant of (2.3) is "...as a0 and a1 hop through the indices of A, the caterpillar's tail A[a0] and head A[a1] rest on the start of two adjacent *Bad* subsegments..." (That gives the length of the non-extendable *Good* subsegment found between them as (a1+2)-(a0+1).)

And yet, strictly speaking, that is *not* the invariant of the simple loop given there. Why not? Could it be the invariant of an outer loop? If so, what would the invariant of the inner loop be?

---

[4] All three programs in this chapter were run on thousands of sample A's, generated by Python's hypothesis tester: it confirmed that their answers were equal in every generated case.

3

Finding invariants

3.1 Introduction

Invariants were introduced in Sec. 1.7 as assertions, there used specifically for design-ing and checking loops; and indeed we devoted all of the previous chapter to a single extended example of how that is done. Using "conventional" design techniques gave programs that were twice as long as the one we found, finally, by choosing an invariant *first* — before beginning to code.

And so invariants turn out to be one of the major skills that lead to simple, efficient and evidently correct programs that are easy to check — even when the problems those programs address appear at first to be difficult, or at least "fiddly" and "tricky" (as in the first two sections of Chapter 2).

Here in this chapter we will be more general, looking at some of the techniques used to find invariants *before* you write the program, then using them to help design the program so that it is "automatically" easy to check — precisely because it was developed with checking in mind.

We begin with the most common invariant-finding technique: it's called "splitting a conjunct".

3.2 Split a conjunct

This first invariant-finding technique is the simplest, and is indeed the most common. We introduce it by returning to our very first topic — date finding (Sec. 1.2). But this time we will concentrate on months rather than years.

Suppose we have a function `DiM(m)` that gives for any month m from 1 to 12 inclusive the number of days in that month: thus `DiM(1)==31` and `DiM(6)==30` etc. We'll ignore leap years for now.

Our program will convert "today", given as a day-in-year d again starting at 1, to a month-number m and a day-in-month number d:

```
# --- Given the day-number in a year,
# --- find the month-number
# --- and the day-number in that month.
# --- Ignore leap years.
# PRE: 1<=d<=365 and "Today is Day d counting 1 January as Day 1."
# PRE: DiM() contains correct values.
...
# POST: Today's month is m and d is the day number in it.
```

We begin by rewriting the postcondition as

"Today is Day d of Month m." and 1<=d and d<=DiM(m)   ,

and we see that the postcondition is in three pieces, joined by and's: those are called "conjuncts". We will take the first two of them for the invariant, and use the third by making its opposite (i.e. its negation not...) the condition of a loop: that is, we "split" the three conjuncts between the second and the third. That gives

```
# PRE: 1<=d<=365 and "Today is Day d where 1 January was Day 1."
m= 1
# INV: 1<=d and "Today is Day d in Month m."
while d>DiM(m):
    ...
```

$\Rightarrow$
$\Rightarrow$

```
{d>DiM(m) must be False if the loop has finished.  And so... }
{ (not d>DiM(m)) and 1<=d and (still) "Today is d days from Day 1 of m."}
{ 1<=d<=DiM(m) and "Today is d days from Day 1 of m."}
# POST: Today is Day d in Month m of this year.
```

The "$\Rightarrow$" implication symbols to the left of the last two assertions are just to remind us here that when assertions are arranged vertically, each should be implied by the one above it. (Once we are used to that, we do not have to write the $\Rightarrow$'s any more.)

Now that we've found an invariant, our job is to code a loop body that maintains it. Notice that the "to be written "$\cdots$" has again –as in Sec. 2.5– moved inwards: this program too is being developed from the outside in.

The loop body $\cdots$ is d,m= d-DiM(m),m+1, giving the program

```
m= 1
# INV: 1<=d and "Today is Day d counting from Day 1 of Month m."
while d>DiM(m):
    { 1<=d and "Today is Day d counting from Day 1 of Month m." and d>DiM(m) }
    d,m= d-DiM(m),m+1 # Maintain the invariant.

{ 1<=d<=DiM(m) and "Today is Day d counting from Day 1 of Month m." }
# POST: Today is Day d in Month m.
```

(3.1)

Ex. 3.1   And that's our program done.

Recalling Jack's difficulties at the end of Sec. 1.2, however, we will as well check carefully that this program cannot loop forever. For that we use a "variant" (mentioned in Sec. 1.8, and also the topic of Chapter 4) — as we will see, it's an expression that cannot be forever decreased. The variant for this loop is d itself, which the invariant bounds below by 1. And the subtraction d= d-DiM(m) strictly decreases d, because from the overall precondition (that DiM() contains correct values), we know that DiM(m)>=1; and so that is sufficient for a strict decrease. This loop cannot iterate forever.

We must check also, of course, that the invariant really is respected by the loop body — that is, the loop must give the right answer when it *does* terminate. Applying the rule for checking assignments to the loop body, we are therefore checking the program fragment

```
# PRE: d>DiM(m) and 1<=d and "Today is d days from Day 1 of Month m."
d,m= d-DiM(m),m+1
# POST: 1<=d and "Today is d days from Day 1 of Month m."          ,
```

where we note the extra conjunct d>DiM(m) in the precondition: it is the while-condition. If it were not true, we could not *be* in the loop.

As at (1.13) earlier, to check an assignment we make the substitution and then check the implication. In this case the implication is

> d>DiM(m) and 1<=d and "Today is d days from Day 1 of Month m."
> $\Rightarrow$ 1<=d-DiM(m) and "Today is d-DiM(m) days from Day 1 of Month m+1."   .

Because d>DiM(m) $\Rightarrow$ 1<=d-DiM(m) , we can simplify that implication to

> Today is d days from Day 1 of Month m.
> $\Rightarrow$ Today is d-DiM(m) days from Day 1 of Month m+1.   ,

which (again) follows from the precondition that DiM() contains correct values.

3.3 Introduce a new variable

The second common invariant-finding technique is often used together with the first, and the result is a program with a loop that goes up or down in regular steps.

3.3.1 Iterating up, or down

Indeed most of the examples we have done so far use an invariant that could have been found by introducing a new variable. The find-sum and find-max programs in Chapter 1 were all of the form

```
# PRE: A is a sequence of length N.
...
# POST: r == FUN(A)     ,
```

in other words "Assign to result-variable r the value of some function FUN applied to the whole sequence A." Function FUN might be "the sum of" ($\sum$) or "the product of" ($\prod$) or "the maximum of" (MAX); and in each case the invariant-finding strategy is

(a) Replace (just) A in the postcondition by the more explicit A[0:N].

(b) Introduce a new variable n and rewrite the postcondition as

> r == FUN(A[:n]) and n==N   ,

which makes not n==N , that is n!=N, become the loop guard.

(c) Split the conjunct (Sec. 3.2 just above), and use the invariant

$$\texttt{0<=n<=N and r ==} \textsc{Fun}\texttt{(A[:n])} \quad .$$

The program becomes

```
# PRE: A is a sequence of length N.
n,r= 0, FUN([])
# INV: 0<=n<=N and r == FUN(A[:n])
while n!=N:
  { PRE: 0<=n<N and r == FUN(A[:n]) }
  ··· # Examine A[n]; update r.
  { POST: r == FUN(A[:n+1]) }

  n= n+1 # Invariant restored.
  { r == FUN(A[:n]) }
{ n==N and r == FUN(A[:n]) }
{ r == FUN(A[0:N]) }
# POST: r == FUN(A)          ,
```

$$(3.2)$$

which "iterates up" from 0 towards N.

Ex. 3.2

For the analogous "iterating down" technique, see Ex. 3.2.

For a not-completely-trivial example of iterating up, let FUN be "the largest absolute difference between any two adjacent elements" — call it lad. From the above, once we have followed the routine steps described there, we are left with the loop body

```
{ PRE: 0<=n<N and r == lad(A[:n]) }
···
{ POST: r == lad(A[:n+1]) }

n= n+1
```

in which the assignment ··· is clearly r= r max abs(A[n]-A[n-1]). Or is it?

The value max'ed with r has to be –writing very carefully– the absolute difference between two adjacent elements where the second one is A[n]. But unless 0<=n-1, there isn't such a pair. So we must write if n>=1: r= r max abs(A[n]-A[n-1]).

And we mustn't forget the initialisation, which should include r= lad([]). Since our program produces only non-negative results, we can take 0 –the least non-negative number– for lad([]), and the program becomes

```
# PRE: 0<=N
n,r= 0,0
# INV: 0<=n<=N and r == lad(A[:n])
while n!=N:
  if n>=1: r= r max abs(A[n]-A[n-1])
  n= n+1
# POST: r == lad(A)
```

$$(3.3)$$

But this is not the program that most people would expect: do we have to test n>=1 every time in the loop body, when it is obvious that only the first test matters? We deal with that next.

3.3.2 A note on efficiency, "tweaking" and loop-unrolling

It's true that (3.3) has the irritating feature of testing `n>=1` again and again, where we can easily see that only one test is required. To avoid that, we just "tweak" it, that is we rewrite it as

```
# PRE: 0<=N
n,r= 1,0 # Note!
# INV: 1<=n<=N and r==lad(A[:n])
while n<N: # INV: 1<=n<=N and r==lad(A[:n])          (3.4)
    r= r max abs(A[n]-A[n-1])
    n= n+1
# POST: r==lad(A)     .
```

But should we *really* be indulging ourselves with a quick fix at the last moment?

Surely there's no point in carefully developing a program, checking at each stage... and then risking its correctness –all that work– with a casual, off-the-cuff adjustment.[1] So we will instead do it in stages, and alter the invariant to take account of what we do. Quick fixes should be avoided... and we'll use this program as an example of how to proceed carefully.

The first stage is to "unroll" the loop in (3.3) just once, so that the program becomes

```
n,r= 0,0
if n!=N:                                # n==0 here,
    if n>=1: r= r max abs(A[n]-A[n-1])  # and here.
    n= n+1
    while n!=N:
        if n>=1: r= r max abs(A[n]-A[n-1])
        n= n+1
else: {n==N} pass  2
```

and –crucially– the code above does not have to be checked again: if the loop was correct before unrolling, it's still correct afterwards.

A further step is then to replace `n` with `0` in the places where the unrolling has made `n==0` true. (Just replace it: don't simplify yet. Small, careful steps are the key...) That gives

```
n,r= 0,0
if 0!=N:                                # n was 0 here,
    if 0>=1: r= r max abs(A[0]-A[0-1])  # and here,
    n= 0+1                              # and here.
    while n!=N:
        if n>=1: r= r max abs(A[n]-A[n-1])
        n= n+1
else: {0==N} pass    ,
```

where the illegal sequence-indexing `A[0-1]` is not a problem — because it's behind an " `if 0>=1:` ", that is an " `if False` ", it's dead code and will never be reached during execution.

Ex. 3.3

---

[1] ...perhaps just as you are leaving for lunch? And what you just did was not documented?
[2] In Python, the statement **pass** means "do nothing". In other languages it is **skip**, or **no-op**.

The third step is to simplify what we now have, trivially *and therefore reliably*, to

```
n,r= 1,0
if 0!=N:
  {0!=N} ← Allows loop guard n!=N to become n<N.
  # INV: 1<=n<=N and r == lad(A[:n])
  while n<N:
    r= r max abs(A[n]-A[n-1])
    n= n+1
  {POST: r == lad(A) }                         # ← These are
else: {0==N} pass {POST: r == lad(A) }         # ← the same.
```

where we can see that the statement if 0!=N can be removed: given the assertions, its two branches establish the same postcondition (just under different circumstances). And so if itself can be removed, leaving the program (3.4) from above that we guessed by tweaking.

Ex. 3.4   A final step might be to turn the while-loop into a for-loop.

The lesson here, just as for loops "with or without early exits" (mentioned elsewhere), is that it is a good strategy to write programs first in a way that makes them easy to check. Only after that do you make small changes, if necessary, to increase their efficiency. There's a good chance that the extra checking for those changes will be quite small, and the earlier checks "come along for the ride".

3.3.3 Iterating towards the middle: binary search

In this example we look at iterations that go both up *and* down: it is based on Ex. 3.5 below. Our program is given a sequence A[0:N] that is sorted into ascending order, and a value x, and it must find where x occurs in the sequence:

```
# --- Find the location of a given value in a sorted sequence.
# PRE: Sequence A[0:N] is sorted into ascending order.
# POST: A[:n]<x and x<=A[n:]        ,
```

where an omitted low index (as in A[:n]) means A[0:n], and an omitted high index (as in A[n:]) means A[n:len(A)].

In general we write A[l:h]<x to mean that *all* elements in that subsegment of A are strictly less than x, and similarly for other comparisons: for example A[l:h]==x

Ex. 3.5   means that all values in A[l:h] are equal to x (and hence also to each other).

In Ex. 3.5 you are asked to work out the conclusions that can be drawn from the result, that is from the postcondition A[:n]<x and x<=A[n:] of the above program. Here however we will concentrate on how to discover a good invariant that *leads* to that postcondition. We begin by introducing a new variable m ("just before n"), and replace the first n in the postcondition by that — and then we add a conjunct m==n so that the new postcondition implies the one we really want. The postcondition is now

```
A[:m]<x and x<=A[n:] and m==n        .
```

Then we apply "split a conjunct", from Sec. 3.2 above, to "and m==n" — allowing us to add more code to our growing program. As usual, we try to work from the outside in, and we get

```
# PRE: Sequence A[:N] is sorted into ascending order.
m,n= 0,N
# INV: 0<=m<=n<=N and A[:m]<x and x<=A[n:]
while m!=n:
  { 0<=m<n<=N and A[:m]<x and x<=A[n:] }
  ··· # Need to look at some A[p] in A[m:n].
{ A[:m]<x and x<=A[n:] and m==n }
# POST: A[:n]<x and x<=A[n:]        .
```

The "Need to look at..." comment is a temporary note to ourselves, a hint to our own intuition: since the invariant says, for example, that x is *not* in A[:m] –it is strictly greater than all of them– we must have "looked at those elements already".[3] Similar reasoning suggests that we have looked at A[n:] already, and therefore that the only place left to look is A[m:n], the "middle" segment.

Being precise at this stage is quite helpful, as we are about to see. It is indeed true that the elements we need still to look at are "the ones in the middle" — but since we *can* say exactly which ones those are, we should use that information. The earlier the accessible information is brought to light, the easier our later steps will be.

And indeed our first payoff is to know how to choose p. If A[p] is to lie within A[m:n], then we must have m<=p<n: that's direct and obvious, without any of the usual "Is it < or <= ?" guesswork involved. All that is taken care of for us. (Remember that subsegment indexing is inclusive/exclusive.) Our precise identification of the subsegment of possible "p targets" is what told us that the inequality must be <= ··· < — that is less-than-or-equal-to on the left, and strictly-less-than on the right. No head-scratching is required.

Now the one thing that everybody knows about binary search is that somewhere in the middle there is a statement something along the lines of p= (m+n)//2, where // is integer division (rounding down). And then A[p] is compared with x. But that "something along the lines of"... Should we maybe round up? Does it matter?

Let's see. The remainder of our program is now

Ex. 3.6

```
# PRE: 0<=m<n<=N and A[:m]<x and x<=A[n:]
p= (m+n)//2 # Now m<=p<n, used in (3.6) and (3.7) below.
if A[p]<x:  { A[:m]<x and A[p]<x  and x<=A[n:] } ···
else:       { A[:m]<x and x<=A[p] and x<=A[n:] } ···
# n-m has decreased.
# POST: 0<=m<n<=N and A[:m]<x and x<=A[n:]
```
                                                                        (3.5)

where, with the comment # n-m *has decreased*, we are stating that the variant is n-m and we are using it to check that the loop cannot continue forever. Notice that the precondition of this remaining portion (3.5) has m<n, which comes from the invariant's m<=n and the loop guard m!=n. We can't check "# n-m *has decreased*" yet, because we have not seen what the if-branches do; but by writing it now, we make sure we won't miss it.

As usual, we try to reason in small pieces: here, that means "one if-branch at a time." (See however App. B.6.3 for a more advanced technique that allows such reasoning to be deferred until later.)

---

[3] This is operational reasoning, talking about "what we did" rather than "what is true", and it does aid our intuition. But we do not *rely* on it.

The first branch (with inessential conjuncts removed) is now

```
# PRE:   A[:m]<x and m<=p and A[p]<x
m= p+1
# POST: A[:m]<x and n-m has decreased    ,
```
(3.6)

where the number `p+1` comes from our careful observation that we must set `m` in such a way that `p` is the final index included in `[:m]` — and that final index is `m-1` (not `m`). That is, to establish `m-1 == p` we must set `m= p+1`. That being so, we see that "`n-m` *has decreased*" is satisfied because `m` has increased and `n` has not changed.

When we move to the second if-branch, that is to the `else` part, we can forget about the `then` part: it's already done, and we already know it's right. So we just look at

```
# PRE:   x<=A[n:]  and p<n and x<=A[p]
n= p
# POST: x<=A[n:]  and n-m has decreased    ,
```
(3.7)

Ex. 3.7 all on its own, where `n= p` is justified because `A[n]` (not `A[n+1]` or `A[n-1]`) is the first element of `A[n:]`, and because `p<n` ensures (again) the decrease of `n-m`.

Once we put the whole thing together, we have

```
# --- Binary Search:
# --- Find the location of a given value in a sorted sequence.
# PRE: Sequence A[0:N] is sorted into ascending order.

m,n= 0,N
# INV: 0<=m<=n<=N and A[:m]<x and x<=A[n:]
while m!=n:
  p= (m+n)//2
  if A[p]<x: m= p+1
  else: n= p
  # VAR: n-m has decreased.

# POST: A[:n]<x  and  x<=A[n:]       .
```
(3.8)

As usual, in the final program most of the assertions we used along the way have been removed — that's because we can regenerate them, if we need to, from the ones we did *not* remove: the important ones that were left behind. The VAR comment identifies the variant, which we leave as part of the program's documentation because Ex. 3.8 of its importance, for this program, and the fact that it's not *completely* obvious.

3.4 "Tail" invariants

Until now, most of our programs have used an invariant of the form "this partial result is correct for the portion examined so far". And the termination condition of the loop is "the portion examined so far is actually the whole thing". So when "so far" has become "the whole thing", similarly "partial result" has become "total result" — and we are done.

A *tail* invariant, on the other hand, often mentions the desired result explicitly in the invariant itself: "The *overall* result is –and remains– what we have done so far combined with the partial result of what we have *yet* to do."

The program at (1.19) –a very simple one– can be used to contrast the two approaches: recall that its invariant was the conventional $s == \sum A[0:n]$. A tail invariant for the same problem could be $\sum A == s + \sum A[n:]$, where the desired overall result ($\sum A$) is on the left of ==, and on the right we have what we have done so far (s) combined with (+) the partial result of what we still have to do ($\sum A[n:]$). But in this case it leads to the same program, and so here a tail invariant is not worth the trouble: it's longer, and gives no extra program-development opportunities.

We now look at two examples where a tail invariant *is* worth the trouble, leading to better programs than the more straightforward approaches do. Neither program is reliably coded without finding that invariant first: working from the outside in is especially important here.

Our first example is a calculation of the exponential B**E in time *logarithmic* in the exponent E. The obvious algorithm takes time proportional to (is "linear in") E.

3.4.1 The logarithmic–time exponential calculation

A given base value B is to be raised to a non-negative integer exponent E: our starting point, the requirement and overall pre- and postcondition, is

```
# --- Raise a given base to a non-negative integer power.
# PRE: 0<=E
...
# POST: p == B**E     .
```

Introducing a new variable (as in Sec. 3.3, here replacing E by e), we take as invariant p == B**e and –with the corresponding postcondition-conjunct e==E that negates the guard– we are then led immediately to the program

```
# PRE: 0<=E
p,e= 1,0
# INV: 0<=e<=E and p == B**e
while e!=E:                                                      (3.9)
    p,e= p*B,e+1
{p == B**e and e==E}
# POST: p == B**E     .
```

But that program (in spite of this subsection's title) takes time *linear* in the exponent E: we say that the time "complexity" of the algorithm is $O(E)$, which means that the time it takes to execute is no worse than some constant multiple of E.[4]

Indeed we simply used the "iterate up" (Sec. 3.3.1) strategy to find the invariant. However simple it might be, having an invariant still helps: we are more likely to get the initialisation (p,e= 1,0) and the loop guard (e!=E) right first time... *if* we have an invariant to refer to.[5] And we do not need to know *anything* about the loop body (yet), as we do that: it's the invariant that will ensure it's the *right* loop body, when the time comes.

Ex. 3.9

Now we will design a faster program: one that takes time only $O(\log E)$. Our *tail* invariant is B**E == p*b**e, and –on the left– it contains the overall goal B**E. Here is what motivates us to do that.

In our original invariant, we had only two variables, p,e, to manipulate in the loop body, but in the proposed tail invariant we have three: they are p,e and now

---

[4] The value of that constant depends on the speed of the computer, the efficiency of the compiler-generated code etc. But whatever those are, the $O(E)$ means that if the value of E is say doubled, and it is reasonably large, then the runtime is no worse than doubled.

[5] Once you have got used to invariants, for simple programs like the above you will just use them automatically, unconsciously, without having to write them down.

b as well. That extra freedom allows us to exploit the key insight that when e is even, the calculation can be speeded up enormously by using `b,e= b*b,e//2` in the loop body instead of the assignment `p,e= p*B,e+1` we used in (3.9) above — the remaining exponent E-e is halved, rather than simply being decreased by 1, and the base b is squared, to compensate.

But when e is odd, we can't exploit that speed-up: and so there we proceed –more or less– as we did in (3.9) (which was the reason we looked at that one first, as a warm-up). The alternative (and *much* faster) program that we have now is

```
# PRE: 0<=E
p,b,e= 1,B,E
# INV: B**E == p*b**e
while e!=0:
    if e%2 == 0: b,e= b*b,e//2
    else: p,e= p*b,e-1
{ B**E == p*b**e and e==0 }
# POST: p == B**E     .
```
(3.10)

To see just how much faster it is, we note that (3.9) needs 1,000 iterations for 2^{1000}, but the more efficient (3.10) needs only 10. If `print(e)` is inserted at the beginning of the loop body for (3.10), and `print(p)` at the end of the whole program, we see

```
1000 500 250 125 124 62 31 30 15 14 7 6 3 2 1
```

```
10715086071862673209484250490600018105614048117055336074437503837...
03510511249361224931983788156958581275946729175531468251871452856 9...
23140435984577574698574803934567774824230985421074605062371141877 9...
54182153046474983581941267398767559165543946077062914571196477686 5...
42167660429831652624386837205668069376     ,
```

where the last five lines taken together give the answer 2^{1000}, written out as one huge 302-digit integer.

In a nutshell, the advantage the tail invariant gave us was to have *two* possible approaches for progress towards termination (in the loop body):[6] *either* halve e *or* decrease it by 1 — adjusting b appropriately in each case. In the conventional approach we had only the latter possibility.

3.4.2 The strict majority

Our second example in this section again has a tail-invariant quality, though it is not so explicit as in the first; yet it is possibly even more surprising. The obvious algorithm (we will see) is $O(\text{N}\log\text{N})$; but with the invariant we will design a "non-obvious" version, one that can be reduced to linear complexity, that is $O(\text{N})$. Here is the description of the program's purpose.

Say that a value x is a *strict majority* in sequence `A[0:N]` just when it occurs strictly more than half the time. Thus a is a strict majority in $[a,b,a]$, because $2 > \frac{3}{2}$ — but it is not a strict majority in $[a,b,a,b]$ (because $2 \not> \frac{4}{2}$). As special cases, the empty list `[]` has *no* strict majority, because every element occurs 0 times, which is not strictly more than half its length (also 0); and in the singleton list `[a]` the element a is a strict majority because it occurs once, which is strictly more than $\frac{1}{2}$ times.

The obvious approach, mentioned above, is to sort the list –which takes time $O(\text{N}\log\text{N})$– and then look for the longest run of equal elements. (The point of sorting

---

[6] That tail invariants have greater flexibility is argued more generally by E.W. Dijkstra [15].

in this case is not in fact to put the elements in order: it is just to make sure that
equal elements come together in subsegments, and so can easily be counted.)   Ex. 3.23

But –in spite of all the above– we will use quite a different method. Start by
writing $\underline{csm}$(x,S), for "conditional strict majority", meaning that the value x is a
strict majority in the sequence S *if there is such a majority*. (If there is no strict
majority in S, then $\underline{csm}$(x,S) allows x to be anything at all.)

Our first step in designing the program is then

```
# --- If there is a value occurring strictly
# --- more than half the time in A[0:N],
# --- then set x to that value.
# PRE:   0<=N
...
# POST:  csm(x,A[0:N])     .
```
(3.11)

The straightforward approach mentioned above would be to take a sorting program
"off the shelf" and then, using the invariant-finding techniques "split a conjunct" and
"introduce a new variable" (Secs. 3.2 and 3.3), develop the following program:

```
# PRE: 0<=N
# Put a "sort sequence A" program fragment here. 7
# POST: A is sorted.

# PRE: A is sorted.
c,e= 0,0 # n will be set to 0 initially by the for-loop.
# Inv1(n) is "x occurs c times, and is
#               a most frequent occurrence in A[0:n]."
# Inv2(n) is "e indexes the start of the longest
#               all-equal suffix of A[0:n]."
for n in range(N): # INV: Inv1(n) and Inv2(n)
  # See Ex. 3.21 for this.
# POST: x is a most frequently occurring value in A,
#       and occurs c times.
# POST: csm(x,A[0:N])     .
```
(3.12)

If c>N/2 then x is a strict majority; otherwise, there is no strict majority.

Program (3.12) takes time $O(N \log N)$, however, because its first part –the sorting–
takes that long to sort A. (The second part of the program is only $O(N)$, but that is
dominated by the $O(N \log N)$ of the first part.)

Now we develop code for (3.11) that takes only linear time. The crucial insight
that leads to it is that

> if some sequence S has a *strict* majority, and you remove two *unequal*
> elements from it, then what's still in S has that same strict majority.
(3.13)

And that is where the "tail-invariant" nature of this approach appears: the invariant
is that the overall answer remains the same (though it is not explicitly written) in
spite of the manipulations carried out by the loop body; and –as for (3.10)– there are
several (in fact three) possible manipulations available, not just one.

A counting argument suffices to understand (3.13). Since the two removed elements are unequal, at most one of them can be a *strict* majority — and its count

---

[7] Look ahead to Sec. 12.2 and Ex. 12.4 to see how to put a specification here.

decreases by 1 exactly. But the length of the overall sequence S decreases by 2 —
and so the same strict majority (if there is one) will remain in what's left, because
$c > N/2 \Rrightarrow (c-1) > (N-2)/2$. Our sequence S here will be A[0:N] initially, and our
program will simulate removing elements from it.

We aim for a tail-like invariant of the form

> If A has a strict majority, then
> > "Here is something with the same strict majority as A,
> > but one that is easier to determine."

Our loop's termination condition will be that the "simpler something", once the loop
is done, is *so* simple that its strict majority (if it has one) is obvious.

A structure that suffices for the simpler version comprises "the rest of A " in the
usual way, plus a "pile" of elements we have examined in A but did *not* remove,
because they were *not* unequal. Our invariant is therefore

$$\text{Inv(n):}\quad \begin{array}{l}\text{If A has a strict majority, then}\\ \text{[x]}*\text{r} + \text{A[n:] has the same strict majority}\end{array} \quad , \qquad (3.14)$$

where [x]*r is the sequence in which x is repeated exactly r times and (recall) + is
sequence concatenation. The whole expression   [x]*r+A[n:]   is our "simulation" of
the simplification of A. The "rest of A " is A[n:], and [x]*r is the "pile" (of equal
elements) that we did not remove.[8]

The invariant (3.14) is established by r,n= 0,0. And when finally we have n==N,
that invariant tells us that if A has a strict majority at all then [x]*r+A[N:N] –that
is [x]*r *by itself*– has that same strict majority. And that would have to be x.

The body of the loop will therefore be

```
# PRE: Inv(n)
if    r==0:   x,r= A[n],1              # Case r==0
elif: x!=A[n]: r= r-1       # Case r>0 and x!=A[n]
else:         r= r+1        # Case r>0 and x==A[n]
# Inv(n+1)

n= n+1
# POST: Inv(n)    ,
```

where we have considered the three cases separately, simply referring to the invariant
alone (and, in particular, referring neither to other cases nor to program text lying
outside). The if-statement maintains the invariant because each of its three branches
does:

— **Case** r==0   Here we have [x]*r+A[n:] == [A[n]]*1 + A[n+1:], because both
   are equal to A[n:] itself.

— **Case** r>0 and x!=A[n]   Remove the two unequal elements x and A[n].

— **Case** r>0 and x==A[n]   Move x to the pile.

Notice how much simpler it is to examine the cases each one on its own, rather than
trying to write the whole if-statement at once.

The overall program is given in Fig. 3.1. A shorter version –a slight surprise– is
given in Ex. 3.15.

Ex. 3.13
Ex. 3.14
Ex. 3.15

---

[8] More explicitly, our tail invariant is " <u>csm</u>(x',A) $\Rightarrow$ <u>csm</u>(x', [x]*r + A[n:]) for all x' ".

Figure 3.1 The conditional strict majority found in linear time

```
# --- If there is a value occurring strictly more
# --- than half the time in A[0:N]
# --- then set x to that value.

# PRE: 0<=N

r= 0
for n in range(N): # INV: Inv(n)                              (3.15)
    if    r==0:      x,r= A[n],1                    # Case r==0
    elif x!=A[n]:    r= r-1          # Case r>0 and x!=A[n]
    else:            r= r+1          # Case r>0 and x==A[n]
{ Inv(N) }

# POST: csm(x,A)
```

Note that x is not explicitly initialised!

3.5 Cascading invariants: one leads to another

A "cascade" of invariants occurs when –having found one invariant– we discover that, in order to maintain it, we need a second one. (In fact that occurred in the example of Sec. 2.5, earlier, where we first suggested Inv but found that we needed another invariant to maintain it: then Inv became Inv1, and Inv2 was introduced to help maintain it.)

The general situation is that when we have found one invariant, say Inv1(n), we might find that we need another invariant Inv2(n) to take the step from Inv1(n) to Inv1(n+1). The typical pattern in the loop body (with program statements indicated by $\cdots$) is

```
{ Inv1(n) and Inv2(n) }
...                          # Update Inv2 to hold for n+1,
...                          # given that Inv1,2 hold for n.
{ Inv1(n) and Inv2(n+1) }                                    (3.16)
...                          # Update Inv1 to hold for n+1,
...                          # given that Inv2 already does.
{ Inv1(n+1) and Inv2(n+1) }    ,
```

and indeed we saw that in (3.12) as well. Its invariant Inv1 was found using one of the techniques above, and then its Inv2 was derived from that.

Here is another example: the maximum segment-sum. It is to...

```
# --- Find the largest sum of any (contiguous) subsegment of A[0:N].
# PRE: 0<=N
...
# POST: m= mss A    ,
```

where mss –the maximum segment-sum– of a sequence A is the largest value of $\sum A[l:h]$ for any 0<=l<=h<=len(A).

Of course there is a straightforward "brute force" program for that, namely

```
m= 0                                    #  m for "max"
for l in range(N+1):                    #  l for "low"
  for h in range(l,N+1):                #  h for "high"        (3.17)
    s= 0                                #  s for "sum"
    for n in range(l,h): s= s+A[n]
    m= m max s
```

which simply sums *all* subsegments –one by one and including the empty ones– and then returns the largest sum found.[9] Unfortunately however it takes time $O(N^3)$ to do so. But we will have a closer look at (3.17) anyway, before finding a much more efficient approach.

Although (3.17) looks simple enough not to need invariants, it's still good practice (in both senses) to think about them: if the program really is simple, its invariants will be simple too; and even simple invariants help to prevent one-off indexing errors and such.

For that program, it's clear that it calculates the sums of the subsegments A[0:0], A[0:1],... A[0:N], then A[1:1],... and finally A[N-1:N], A[N:N] –in the order shown– and so for brevity we'll write $\underline{muh}(\ell,h)$ for

Ex. 3.16

the Maximum segment sum in the above order
Up to just before Here   ,   (3.18)

where "Here" is (ℓ,h), describing the segment we are *just about* to examine: i.e. the sum $\sum A[\ell:h]$ is itself not yet included. With its invariants, and one helpful extra assertion, (3.17) becomes

```
m= 0
for ℓ in range(N+1):              #  Inv1: m==muh(ℓ,ℓ)
  for h in range(ℓ,N+1):          #  Inv2: m==muh(ℓ,h)
    s= 0
    for n in range(ℓ,h):          #  Inv3: s==∑A[ℓ:n]
      s= s+A[n]
    { s==∑A[ℓ:h] }          ← Put this postcondition in Inv2 ?
    m= m max s      .
```

Now **Inv3** suggests that the program's efficiency can be improved to $O(N^2)$ by moving its associated assertion $s == \sum A[\ell:h]$ into **Inv2**, and that gives

```
m= 0
for ℓ in range(N+1): #  Inv: Inv1(n): m==muh(ℓ,ℓ)
  s= 0
  for h in range(ℓ,N+1): #  Inv: Inv2(n): m==muh(ℓ,h)        (3.19)
               #              and  s==∑A[ℓ:h]
    m= m max s
    s= s+A[h] ← Oops!      ,
```

which is shorter and faster, only $O(N^2)$ — except for the fact that the s= s+A[h] would index A[N] –which is out of range– on the last iteration of the inner loop, when

Ex. 3.17 h==N. That did not occur in (3.17); why has it occurred here?

Figure 3.2 Outer structure of the maximum segment-sum algorithm

```
# PRE: 0<=N
n,s= 0,0
# INV: Inv1(n): 0<=n<=N and s==mss(A[:n])
while n!=N:
   {0<=n<N and m==mss(A[:n])}
   ...                                  } ← Code needed here.
   {0<=n<N and m==mss(A[:n+1])}
   n= n+1
# POST: s= mss A
```

Ex. 3.18

Instead of pursuing that issue now we'll use a different invariant altogether, based on *iterating up* (Sec. 3.3.1). We aim for a linear, that is an $O(N)$ program, and begin with the program of Fig. 3.2, whose loop body taken alone is as follows, and where for brevity we now write just $mss(n)$ etc., that is leaving out the "A[0:]":

```
# PRE: 0<=n<N and m==mss(n)
...                              }  ←  This specifies the missing loop
# POST: 0<=n<N and m==mss(n+1)            body. (See App. B.6.3.)
```

In $mss(n)$, all the subsegments $A[\ell:h]$ with $0<=\ell<=h<=n$ have been considered; and for $mss(n+1)$ we must therefore take into account only the subsegments $A[\ell:n+1]$ with $0<=\ell<=n+1$, because they are exactly the subsegments of $A[:n+1]$ that are not subsegments of $A[:n]$ as well. And that gives us our second invariant.

Define $mes(n)$ –the maximum *end* sum– to be the maximum sum of all *suffixes* of $A[:n]$ and define Inv2(n) to be $e==mes(n)$. Our loop body becomes (with some assertions suppressed) an example of (3.16), that is,

```
{e==mes(n)}
...
{m==mss(n) and e==mes(n+1)}
m= m max e
{m==mss(n+1) and e==mes(n+1)}      .
```

Then to "fill in the dots" we realise that there are two possible values for $mes(n+1)$: either it is $e+A[n]$, since e is the earlier maximum (and + distributes into max), or it is 0 in the case that $e+A[n]$ turns out to be negative. The latter case corresponds to taking the empty suffix $A[n+1:n+1]$.

For example, when $A[:n+1]$ is [3,-4,2,1, 5] –thus with $A[n]==A[4]==5$– the $mes(n+1)$ will become $(2+1)+5$, that is 8 because 2+1 was the mes beforehand, i.e. in $A[:n]$. But if $A[:n+1]$ was instead [3,-4,2,1, -5], then we would take 0 for $mes(n+1)$ — since adding the final -5 to the greatest suffix sum (2+1) of $A[0:4]$ that

---

[9] We include the empty ones for two reasons. One is that if the whole sequence is empty, we still have one subsegment to consider: the sequence itself. The other reason is that this program *scheme* is more generally useful, and might for example be used for the maximum segment "something else", where the something-else of the empty subsegment is not necessarily the least. (See Ex. 3.18.)

Figure 3.3 The maximum segment-sum program

```
# PRE: 0<=N
n,m,e= 0,0,0
# INV: 0<=n<=N and m==mss(n) and e==mes(n)
while n!=N:
  e= e+A[n] max 0    # Establish e==mes(n+1) given e==mes(n).
  m= m max e    # Establish m==mes(n+1) given m==mes(n) and e==mes(n+1).
  n= n+1
# POST: m= mss A
```

With the above as a guide, we can write the program as below, a `for`-loop, slightly more concisely. Remember however that it is usually easier to *check* a program in its original `while` form:

```
# PRE: 0<=N
m,e= 0,0
for n in range(N): # INV: 0<=n<=N and m==mss(n) and e==mes(n)
  e= e+A[n] max 0
  m= m max e
# POST: m= mss A
```

This version of the maximum segment-sum program runs in linear time, and has no problems with indexing errors.

---

we had before would still be less than we can achieve by just summing the empty subsegment.

Thus the missing piece of the loop body is `e= e+A[n] max 0`. Putting it all together gives the program in Fig. 3.3.

Ex. 3.19
Ex. 3.20
Ex. 3.21

3.6 Invariants should be "inductive"

We have seen above that invariants, whether written as "What's true here." comments or as {···} assertions, must hold (evaluate to `True`) at the beginning of a loop, at the beginning of its every iteration, and at its end. But simply "holding", being true, is not enough.

Checking an invariant includes showing that if it holds at the beginning of a loop body, and the loop guard holds as well, then it will hold at the end of the loop body again, thus it is *maintained* and –in establishing that– *we look only at the loop body itself.* In particular, we do not take account of what might have happened earlier in the program, or even in previous iterations of the same loop: the invariant should be *inductive* all on its own, through a *single* iteration. Simply being true at the beginning of each iteration is not enough: the invariant must be shown to be *maintained* by each

Ex. 3.10   iteration of the loop body acting in isolation (but assuming the loop guard of course).

The reason for that is precisely that we want to make the checking as reliable as we possibly can — and part of doing that is making it *local* in the sense that to justify checking carried out here we do not have to look for "over there", possibly pages away.

An analogy is the mathematical "proof by induction" technique, where to prove that $F(n)$ holds for all non-negative n we show $F(0)$ (the "base case") and we show, that for all non-negative n, the truth of $F(n)$ is sufficient *on its own* to establish the truth of $F(n+1)$ (the "inductive step").

3.7 Exercises

Exercise 3.1 (p. 34)   Combine (3.1) with your answer to Ex. 1.8 to write *and check* this program:

```
# --- Given that today is d days from 1 January 1980,
# --- determine today's date in the form d/m/y.
# --- Assume correctly operating functions DiY(y) and DiM(m,y).
# PRE:  ???
  ...
# POST: ???
```

Fill in the precondition and postcondition yourself, making sure they agree with the requirements. Take leap years into account, supplying your own functions DiY(y) and DiM(m,y). Use break if you wish; but make sure it does not interfere with your program-checking.

One approach to "filling-in the dots" is to code first *without* using break, because the checking is easier with "pure" while-loops, and it is more reliable. Once that is done, modify your program to use break, if it helps to avoid repeated tests or function calls; but carry over your assertions as much as possible.

The DiMY function could easily be implemented based on a fixed sequence and using m-1 as index: [31,28,31,30,31,30,31,31,30,31,30,31] .

Exercise 3.2 (p. 36) ⇓ Replay the invariant-finding strategy of Sec. 3.3.1 for a program that "iterates down".

Exercise 3.3 (p. 37) Would anything be gained by unrolling (3.4) a *second* time?

Exercise 3.4 (p. 38) ⇓ Rewrite the "tweaked" code of (3.4) as a for-loop.

Exercise 3.5 (p. 38)   For 0<=n<=N let

```
# PRE: 0<=N and A[0:N] is sorted in ascending order.
  ...
# POST: 0<=n<=N and A[:n]<x and x<=A[n:]
```

be the specification of the binary-search program (Sec. 3.3.3), which finds value x within A[0:N] if it is there. As before, read A[:n]<x as "Every element of A[:n] is less than x." etc.

(a) Why is A[0:0]<x always true, no matter what the value of x is?

(b) If x is strictly less than every element of A, what will the final value of n be?

(c) If x is strictly greater than all of A, what will the final value of n be?

(d) Describe informally what the final value of n will be if neither of the above holds, but still x does not occur anywhere in A.

(e) Describe informally what the final value of n will be if x occurs in A exactly once.

(f) Describe informally what the final value of n will be if x occurs in A more than once.

(g) Write an if-statement that branches *after* the above program depending on whether x is in A or not: that is, complete

```
# PRE: 0<=n<=N and A[:n]<x and x<=A[n:]
if ???: # x is in A.
else:   # x is not in A.
```

Exercise 3.6 (p. 39) As we remarked in Sec. 3.3, the integer division p= (m+n)//2 rounds down, so that for example 3//2 == 1 — it is the *floor* of the actual quotient 1.5. How would you write an expression that rounds up instead? (Can you do it without using the "ceiling" function?)

Would our binary search have worked if we had rounded up instead of down? If so, say why; if not, explain how it might fail and –in particular– state where our process of program-checking would have discovered the error before it was too late.

Exercise 3.7 (p. 40) The binary search program (3.8) used the assignment statement p= (m+n)//2 to establish the assertion m<=p<n afterwards, given that m<n held before: that is, the program

```
# PRE: m<n
p= (m+n)//2
# POST: m<=p<n
```

checked. But doesn't the simpler

```
# PRE: m<n
p= m
# POST: m<=p<n
```

also check? If so, then the resulting program as a whole also checks, doesn't it: it searches for x in A, just as binary search did. But what kind of search is it *really*?

(See also (B.6) in App. B.6.3.)

Exercise 3.8 (p. 40) ⇓ Where in our development of binary search did we use that A is in ascending order?

Exercise 3.9 (p. 41) The program

```
p,B,E= 1,2,10
for e in range(E): # INV: p==B**e
  p= p*B
{p==B**e and e==E}      ← Incorrect!
print(p,e)
```

prints 1024 9 — which is the correct answer for 2^E but gives a misleading impression. And the assertion shown there is incorrect. Why? *Hint*: See App. G.3.

Exercise 3.10 (p. 48) *All roads lead to Rome.* Suppose every city in the Roman Empire had a sign in its centre indicating the shortest route to Rome from there. A citizen travelling from Paris to Rome, and familiar with our "What's true here?" approach to thinking about loops, might reason as follows:

> I will "execute" a (`while`) loop whose initialisation is `This city is Paris`, whose body is

```
Follow the " to Rome " sign from this city to the next ,
```

and whose loop guard is `This city is not Rome`.
My loop invariant (Sec. 3.6) is

```
I have taken the shortest route from Paris
to this city, i.e. where I am now .
```

> Correctness will follow (she reasons) from the invariant and the negated guard conjoined, that is

```
        I have taken the shortest route from Paris to this city ,
and     this city is now Rome .
```
hence (overall postcondition)

```
I have taken the shortest route from Paris to Rome.
```

Although her *conclusion* is correct –she will have taken the shortest route from Paris to Rome– her *reasoning* is not correct.
Why not?

Exercise 3.11 *All roads lead to Rome (continued).* Call a route from Paris all the way to Rome a *green* route just when it is of minimum length overall. (There might be several green routes, but all green routes have that same minimum length of course.)
Show that if Citizen z has followed a green(-route) prefix to the current city c, and she then follows the "to Rome" sign to the next city c', then z will have followed a green prefix to that c' as well.

What should z's inductive invariant have been? Is it a tail invariant (Sec. 3.4)?
Hint: Compare Prim's *minimum spanning tree* algorithm [11].

Exercise 3.12 ⇓ *All roads lead to Rome (concluded).* Show that if the citizen follows the "to Rome" signs at every stage (as in Ex. 3.10) then it will be true that

> In every city c along the way she has indeed travelled a shortest route from Paris to c.

Exercise 3.13 (p. 44) In program (3.15) of Fig. 3.1 the result variable x is not assigned-to at all if `N==0`. How can the program be considered to be "working" in that case?

Exercise 3.14 (p. 44) In (3.15) it is possible that the final value of r is 0, even when N is not zero: in that case, the program has established only that <u>csm</u>(x,[x]*0+[]), that is <u>csm</u>(x,[]), which is trivially true for all possible values of x.

In this case, the program therefore guarantees nothing at all about x finally, even though it has been busily assigning to x throughout the run.

How can the program be said to be "working" in that case?

Exercise 3.15 (p. 44) ⇓ Explain why program (3.15) is equivalent to this slightly smaller program — only four lines:

```
# --- Find a conditional strict majority in A[0:N] .
r= 0
for n in range(N): # Inv3(n): see (3.14).
  if r==0 or x==A[n]: x,r= A[n],r+1
  else: r= r-1
```

Exercise 3.16 (p. 46) Does the program

```
for l in range(N+1):
  for h in range(l,N+1):
    print(l,h)
```

print the expected inclusive/exclusive indices of all the subsegments in A[0:N], including all the empty ones, in the order suggested?

Exercise 3.17 (p. 47) In program (3.19) a bug was introduced *("Oops!")* by what seemed to be a perfectly reasonable manipulation of the program just before. What is the root cause of that problem?

Exercise 3.18 (p. 47) ⇓ The "Oops!" difficulty with (3.19) in particular arises partly from its examining *every* subsegment, including all the empty ones: that is, the empties A[n:n] for every n from 0 up to N inclusive. If we skipped those (which sum to zero anyway, all of them), we could use `range(1,N)` for the inner loop and avoid the index-out-of-range. But skipping the empties is perhaps a bad idea. Why?

Instead, rewrite the inner for-loop as a `while True:` ··· `break` ··· loop, and so avoid the index error while continuing to visit every segment, including all the empty ones. Include invariants and helpful assertions.

Ex. 3.22 **Exercise 3.19** (p. 48) ⇓ Use the strategy of Sec. 3.5 to write programs that consider sums of *non-empty* segments only: both the $O(N^2)$ and $O(N)$ versions. Use the value $-\infty$ if necessary; if you do use it, say why.

Exercise 3.20 (p. 48) Use the strategy of Sec. 3.5 to write an $O(N)$ program for the maximum segment *product* in A[0:N]. Include empty segments.

Hint: You will have to "cascade" twice.

Suggestion: Try figuring out what the invariants will be before writing *any* code.

Exercise 3.21 (p. 48) Write <u>lr</u>(n) for the length of a longest run (subsegment of equal Dr. A.25(A.4) values) in the sequence A[0:N]. Make and check a program to find the length of a longest run in all of A, that is, to establish the postcondition { Post: l==<u>lr</u>(N) }.

Hint: First use Sec. 3.3.1 to suggest an invariant Inv1; then use Sec. 3.5 to suggest a second invariant Inv2. *Only then* write the program code: it should practically check itself.

Exercise 3.22 (p. 52) ⇓ If you used -∞ in your answers to Ex. 3.19, write new versions without it in which you assume that A itself is non-empty, i.e. that 0<N.

Hint: Do it by modifying your answers to Ex. 3.19 in just one place, and explain why you do not have to check the whole program again.

What's the new invariant for m? It can no longer just be m==<u>mss</u>(n), because <u>mss</u>(0)!=A[0] and so it would not be true initially.

Exercise 3.23 (p. 43) Write <u>sr</u>(n) for the length of the *shortest* run of equal values in the prefix A[:n] of A that cannot be extended on either side. Write and check a program to find the length of the shortest such run in all of A, that is, to establish the postcondition { Post: l==<u>sr</u>(N) }.

Hint: First use Sec. 3.3.1 to suggest an invariant Inv1; but then use choose the same second invariant Inv2 that you used in Ex. 3.21. Then write the program code.

Use ∞ in your code (since you're min'ing) if it's convenient: don't try to program your way around it. Test your program however by defining INF to be something suitable. What?

4

Finding variants

4.1 Introduction: simple variants

We have by now seen that there are two aspects to checking programs: one is to make sure they have the right answer when they terminate: that is called *partial correctness*, and invariants (and other assertions) generally are the main tools for that.

The other aspect is to make sure they actually *do* terminate, and there we use a different tool: "variants". Finding a variant is *usually* quite easy, which (unfortunately) is precisely why it is sometimes not bothered with: it's "obvious" — even if it turns out that there isn't one. (Remember Jack in Sec. 1.2, who did not have a variant. Did he look for one?)

When a loop is checked for partial correctness *and* it is checked for termination, then we say that it has been checked for *total correctness*.

Unlike an *in*variant (which must be maintained by each loop iteration), a *variant* is an integer expression (not a Boolean) that every iteration of the loop is guaranteed to decrease strictly but at the same time is also guaranteed never to make negative. A variant with those two guarantees ensures that the loop cannot iterate forever.

A typical example of a variant is found in (1.22) from Ex. 1.4, partly reproduced here:

```
# PRE: 0<=N
s,n= 0,N
{ 0<=n<=N }                      # Start the loop at n==N.
while n!=0:  # VAR: n
  { 0<n==V }
  n= n-1
  s= s+A[n]
  { 0<=n<V }
{ n==0 }                         # Finish the loop when n==0.
# POST: s==∑A
```

$$(4.1)$$

This program obviously terminates: the variable n starts at N and goes down in steps of 1 until it reaches 0. And in fact the expression n all by itself is the variant in this case, indicated by the VAR: it is an integer; it is decreased strictly on each iteration;

and it cannot go below 0. The variable V is an "auxiliary" variable,[1] which we can think of as capturing the value of the variant n at the beginning of each iteration, allowing us to check at the end of the loop body that it has decreased but not gone below 0 — the invariant is `0<=n<V`. (We return to auxiliary variables in Sec. 8.5.1.)

The postcondition of the loop body depends on (the value of) V in its precondition.

Another example is found in (1.19), where however the iteration goes up instead of down, from `n==0` up to `n==N`; in that case the "actual" variant is `N-n`. In general, a variant can be any integer expression *expr* that either always increases strictly or always decreases strictly (but not a mixture of the two) and which is bounded by a constant in the direction that it is moving: if it's decreasing and bounded below by L (rather than by 0), the "actual" variant is *expr*-L. If it's increasing and bounded above by H, then the actual variant is H-*expr*.

But variants that turn out to be simple might *not* be so simple to find. For example, in Euclid's algorithm for calculating the greatest common divisor, the gcd of two positive integers A and B, the loop body decreases either a or b (but never both). Thus neither a nor b can be used as the variant on its own, since on any given iteration it might be the other one that decreases. The algorithm is

```
# --- Euclid's algorithm
# PRE: 0<A and 0<B
a,b= A,B
# INV: 0<a and 0<b and gcd(a,b)==gcd(A,B)
while a!=b:
  if a<b: b= b-a
  else: {b<a} a= a-b                    # Why not {b<=a} ?
# POST: a == b == gcd(A,B)
```

$$(4.2)$$

Ex. 4.1 The important invariant of this loop for partial correctness is gcd(A,B)==gcd(a,b), maintained because

$$\text{gcd}(A,B) \ == \ \text{gcd}(a-b,b) \ == \ \text{gcd}(a,b-a) \qquad ,$$

and the loop checks as a whole because gcd(A,B) == gcd(a,b) == a == b when the loop terminates with the loop guard negated — that is, when not(a!=b).[2]

But here we will concentrate on the variant. It is neither a nor b on its own, because –as we observed above– sometimes one is decreased and sometimes the other. The variant is in fact the sum a+b, which is decreased whichever branch of the if is taken. It is a *strict* decrease (i.e. of at least 1) because we know from the *in*variant that both a and b are strictly positive. And we know also from the invariant that the variant a+b can never become negative: in fact it is always at least 2.

---

[1] Auxiliary variables are also called "ghost variables".
[2] This is an example of a "tail invariant": recall Sec. 3.4.

4.2 Lexicographic variants: not so simple

Another kind of variant is called "lexicographic", because it resembles the order of words in a dictionary.

An example is the old-style British "imperial" currency, where 12 pence make one shilling (12d = 1s) and 20 shillings make one pound (20s = £1). The program below models an *ATM* that allows non-zero withdrawals until the account is empty, and then terminates. If an attempt is made to withdraw more than the account contains, an error exit is taken:[3]

```
# Allow withdrawals from a bank account until it is empty.
# PRE: L>=0 and S>=0 and D>=0

while L>0 or S>0 or D>0:          # Account is not empty.
  read(p,s,d) # Requested withdrawal.
    # Assume input validation ensures that
    # 0<=p and 0<=s<20 and 0<=d<12,
    # and (0<p or 0<s or 0<d).

  L,S,D= L-p,S-s,D-d
  S= S + D//12                    # // is integer division.
  D= D%12                            # % is remainder.
  L= L + S//20
  S= S%20
  if L>=0 write("Please take your cash.")
  else:
    write("Insufficient funds.")
    break # Possible fraud: Account suspended.
```
(4.3)

The program is (deliberately) a bit cryptic, because such complications do occur — and we want to be able to check them regardless. Here we are concentrating only on whether the bank account will eventually be empty (and not so much on whether the debits are being done correctly — but see (4.6) in Ex. 4.2).

Ex. 4.2

Ex. 4.3

Ex. 4.4

What is the variant for termination? It cannot be any of L or S or D on its own, because for each variable separately there are situations in which that variable does not decrease: withdrawing 1d from £1/0s/0d leaves 19s/11d, where the number of shillings and the number of pence have both increased. The same example shows that it cannot be L+S+D either, because their sum just above has increased from 1+0+0 = 1 to 19+11 = 30.

The variant (of course!) is the number of pence in the account altogether –that is (20*L+S)*12+D– which can be written out as 240*L+12*S+D. And, with some calculation, that sum can be shown to decrease strictly with each withdrawal.

Ex. 4.5

But that involves a lot of annoying (and perhaps error-prone?) arithmetic; an easier approach is to use a *lexicographic* variant directly, in which the three variables are ordered by importance, not alphabetically –first L then S then D in this case– and less important variables may *in*crease as long as there is a more important variable that *de*creases at the same time: in the example above both S and D increased, but that decreased the lexicographic variant (L,S,D) because the more important (in both cases) variable L decreased from 1 to 0.

---

[3] "L" is used here for pounds (written £ normally), because it comes from the Latin *libra*, scales for weighing, as in "equilibrium"; but for lower-case pounds we use "p" to avoid confusing "l" with the digit one, i.e. "1". The "D" for pence comes from the Latin *denarius*.

In more detail: if L does not decrease then S or D decreases and, if in turn S does not, then D must decrease. That alone is sufficient for termination — without any tedious arithmetic at all.

Ex. 4.6

Ex. 4.7

Some lexicographic variants are so obvious that we don't notice they are there: for example decreasing an integer considered as a string of three digits H,T,U for "hundreds, tens, units" uses as variant the actual integer the digits together represent. We don't notice it because, in this case, the multipliers are all the same (10) instead of the unusual 20, 12 from the pounds/shillings/pence example.

Ex. 4.8

Ex. 4.9

And concerning "dictionary order": as you move from "banana" to "apple" in the dictionary, the second letter has "increased" from "a" to "p"; but the (more important) first letter has decreased from "b" to "a". One word is "less than" another if the first letter where they differ is going in the right direction, that is towards "a".

Ex. 4.10

4.3 Structural variants

In programming languages where structured data-types can be declared directly, giving something like [4]

$$\text{DATA tree: Leaf int | Node tree tree} \qquad , \qquad\qquad (4.4)$$

a variant function can be defined on the new data-type directly (tree in this case): any value in the type is strictly greater than any of its components. For example Node (Leaf 9) (Node (Leaf 17) (Leaf 23)) is strictly greater than both Leaf 9 and Node (Leaf 17) (Leaf 23), since they are its two direct components; and the second of those is in turn greater than both Leaf 17 and Leaf 23. The values Leaf 9 and Leaf 27 and Leaf 23 are not greater than anything, and thus play the role of zero in the simple variant. They are however not minim*um* elements: rather they are (all three) minim*al* elements: the difference is that a minimum element is less than *all others*, whereas a minimal element has nothing less than *it*. For example, in a family tree the "age in seconds" order has a minimum element, the youngest person (barring coincidences); but the "is a descendant of" order usually has only minimal elements, those with no children.

Ex. 4.11

In languages without declarations like (4.4) directly, but where types like that can still be represented by other means (for example sequences represented as linked lists with pointers, or classes and their instances), structural variants can still be used *provided* you have as an invariant that the representation is correct.

As for lexicographic variants, it is often possible to reduce a structural variant to a simple one: in (4.4) for example the simple variant would be the number of Node's in the tree (or equivalently the number of Leaf's, with minimum 1). But using the structural variant directly avoids having to go that extra conceptual step.

Ex. 4.12

Ex. 4.13

---

[4] This kind of definition does not seem to be possible in Python without using classes at the same time.

4.4 Well–founded variants, and even "real valued"

In general, a variant's values can come from any set –with an order defined on it–
provided that order is "well-founded". The non-negative integers, that is those that
are bounded below by 0, with its $\leq$ order, provide just one example of a well-founded
set, a type of set on which we have focussed so far because it occurs so often.[5]

More generally, a "partially" ordered set S has a non-strict order $\sqsubseteq$ between its
elements (which is usually written in the ascending direction). It's called *partial* if
there can be different elements of S that are not ordered with respect to each other
in either direction. If on the other hand every pair *is* ordered one way or the other,
then we have a *total* order. Thus the order $\leq$ on *integers* is total; but the order $\subseteq$ on
sets of integers is only partial, because neither $\{1\} \subseteq \{2\}$ nor $\{2\} \subseteq \{1\}$ is true.

A total order is therefore a special case of a partial order.

Partial orders are reflexive ($s \sqsubseteq s$ for any s), antisymmetric (if both $s \sqsubseteq s'$ and $s' \sqsubseteq s$
then $s = s'$) and transitive (if $s \sqsubseteq s'$ and $s' \sqsubseteq s''$ then also $s \sqsubseteq s''$).

A partially ordered set S is *well-founded* if its partial order $\sqsubseteq$ does not allow an
infinite strictly descending chain of the set's elements $s \sqsupset s' \sqsupset s'' \sqsupset \cdots$, that is a chain
that "descends" forever. That's why the set $\mathbb{N}$ of natural numbers with its order $\leq$
is well-founded:[6] there cannot be $n > n' > n'' > \cdots$ going on forever, because that
descending chain must reach 0 eventually, and there is no natural number strictly
less than 0 that would allow it to go further. Similarly the integers $\mathbb{Z}$ (including its
negatives) but ordered in the other direction, and bounded *above* by say $2^{32}-1$, is
well-founded — but its chains $n < n' < n'' < \cdots$ go the other way. They must stop at
"maxint" (or before).

It's just when there are no infinite (descending) $\sqsupset$-chains in a partially ordered set
that it is (in addition) well-founded. A nice example is when S is the set of *finite*
sets of integers, and $\subseteq$ is its (partial) order. There are no infinite descending chains
$s \supset s' \supset s'' \supset \cdots$ in S because, no matter how big your initial set s from S might be,
it's still finite (even though S itself is infinite); and you cannot keep taking elements
from that finite s forever.

Ex. 4.14

Finally, it's worth noting that a termination argument that appears to require a
real-valued variant can sometimes be dealt with using only natural numbers, even
when there are no integers explicitly in the program. Here is an example:

Ex. 4.15

Ex. 4.16

```
# Pre: e>0
x= 1.0 # x is real-valued.
# Inv: 0<x<=1                                             (4.5)
while x>e: x= x/2
# Post: x<=e     .
```

Although it's clear just from the loop guard alone that the postcondition x<=e is
established on termination –since that is what a loop guard is for– nevertheless termination *itself* must be checked. The invariant 0<x<=1 does guarantee the strict
decrease of x bounded below by 0 –because the 0<x part implies x>x/2>0– but x is
not an *integer*, and so it cannot be used directly as the variant.

Ex. 4.17

The solution is to require that *real*-valued variants decrease by at least some fixed[7]
and strictly positive value, in this case e/2. (This can be reduced to our usual

---

[5] We have used integers n that are ascending as well, bounded above by some fixed N; there the
"actual" variant is $N - n$.

[6] By $s \sqsupset s'$ we mean $s' \sqsubseteq s$ and $s \neq s'$. The order $\leq$ on $\mathbb{N}$ is a *total* (well-founded) order.

[7] By "fixed" is meant "the same strictly positive value for the whole of the loop's execution".

variant rule by noting that the "actual" variant is the integer `floor(2x/e)`, where the precondition's `0<e` avoids dividing by 0.)

4.5 Exercises

Exercise 4.1 (p. 56) ⇓ On the `else` branch of the conditional in (4.2) there is the assertion `{b<a}`, a reminder of the fact that the `0<a` part of the invariant will be preserved by the subtraction `a= a-b`.

Why do we use `{b<a}` rather than the exact negation `{b<=a}` of the `if` condition? And why is that important?

Exercise 4.2 (p. 57) ⇓ Integer quotient (`//`) and remainder (`%`) are related by this equality: when `d!=0` we have

$$(q//d)*d + q\%d == q \quad . \tag{4.6}$$

Use that to check this program:

```
# PRE: ss == 20*L + S
L= L-p + (S-s)//20 # Write "p" rather than lower-case "l".
S= (S-s)%20
# POST: ss == 20*(L+p) + (S+s)     .
```

Hint: Use substitution (App. B.1.1) to check the assignments, and work from postcondition to precondition. Don't forget (4.6).

Exercise 4.3 (p. 57) Why is evaluating only `L>=0` (i.e. not also `S` and `D`) correct in (4.3)?

Exercise 4.4 (p. 57) ⇓ What happens in (4.3) if `D= D-d` makes `D` negative?

Exercise 4.5 (p. 57) Give some other examples of lexicographic variants in everyday life, and of how you could reduce them to a simple variant.

Exercise 4.6 (p. 58) ⇓ At (3.18) in Sec. 3.5 there was an "up to just before here" -order introduced, used to express invariants for a program

```
...
for l in range(N+1):
  for h in range(l,N+1):
    # Process A[l,h].
...
```

that examined every subsegment `A[0:0]`, `A[0:1]`, ... of a given sequence `A`. Can you relate that to the idea of a lexicographic order, one that might be used for a variant?

Exercise 4.7 (p. 58) ⇓ Suppose variables a:ℕ and b:ℕ are non-negative integers, and thus each could be used as a variant on its own — they're both bounded below by 0. But if our program needs to use (a,b) *together*, as a lexicographic variant, must we also have an *upper* bound B for b? For –without such a B– we can't convert (a,b) to a simple variant a+B*b.

Exercise 4.8 (p. 58) Explain the fact that "dictionary order" does not work as a lexicographic variant if the words can be arbitrarily long.

If however there is a maximum length (however large), give a simple argument that dictionary order does work as a (lexicographic) variant.

Exercise 4.9 (p. 58) We remarked in Sec. 4.2 that three-digit non-negative integers HTU (hundreds, tens, units) give a lexicographic order with each H "worth" 10 T and each T worth 10 U. Yet in Ex. 4.8 it's stated that lexicographic order does not work for variants if the "words" can be arbitrarily long.

But non-negative integer variants *do* work for checking termination, no matter how many digits they have. What's going on?

Exercise 4.10 (p. 58) Suppose in the example of "banana" and "apple" the lexicographic variant was over six-letter words, including trailing blanks but no other punctuation. Thus "apple" would be "apple␣" — and the symbol '␣' would be letter 0, then 'a' would be 1 and finally 'z' would be 26. If you converted "banana" and "apple␣" to simple non-negative integer variant values, what would they become? Would there be a strict decrease from "banana" to "apple␣"?

Hint: The absolute difference between the two is 6,330,151.

Exercise 4.11 (p. 58) ⇓ Give some examples of genealogical family trees which have minim*um* (rather than just minim*al*) elements in the "is a descendant" order.

Exercise 4.12 (p. 58) ⇓ A (finite, non-circular) list of characters could be defined as the structured type

        DATA list: Empty | Cons char list   ,

and for example Cons 'a' (Cons 'b' Empty) would be greater than both Empty and Cons 'b' Empty.[8]

How would you reduce this structural variant to a simple one? Is this equivalently a lexicographic variant?

Exercise 4.13 (p. 58) If you reduce a structural variant to an integer variant (as suggested in Ex. 4.12 or, earlier, by counting the number of Leaf's in a tree), it's possible that several of the original data-type values could reduce to the same integer. Does that matter?

---

[8] The Cons notation for "Stick an element onto the front of a list of such elements." comes from the functional programming language Lisp, but ultimately from the architecture of the IBM 704 computer of the 1950s, on which Lisp was first implemented.

Exercise 4.14 (p. 59) Why is any *finite* partially ordered set well-founded?

Exercise 4.15 (p. 59) Does the program below terminate? If so, can you find a simple variant in the style of Ex. 4.5?

```
# PRE: All variables read are non-negative integers.
read(a,b,c)              # a,b,c can be arbitrarily large.
while not (a==b==c==0):
  if c>0: c= c-1
  else:
    read(c)              # c can be arbitrarily large.
    if b>0: b= b-1
    else:
      read(b)            # b can be arbitrarily large.
    {a>0} a= a-1
# POST: a==b==c==0
```

Why does a>0 equal **True** where indicated?

Exercise 4.16 (p. 59) Is the set *of all sets* of integers well-founded under subset? What about the (infinite) set of all *finite* sets of integers?
   Hint: Is $\{0, 1, 2, \ldots\}$ a strict superset of $\{1, 2, 3, \ldots\}$?

Exercise 4.17 (p. 59) Check carefully that `floor(2x/e)` satisfies the conditions for being an integer-valued variant in (4.5), justifying the use of x as a real-valued variant there.
   Do not guess! Take small steps that seem to be inevitable — because that very inevitability makes them easier to understand.

Exercise 4.18 The inhabitants of Flatland are polygons of at least three sides; and the more sides they have, the greater their social status. Triangles are the least-respected Flatlanders of all.
   When a polygon dies, as they all eventually do, with its last gasp it "spawns" baby polygons, arbitrarily many but all of strictly lesser status than it had: a dying hexagon might spawn a million pentagons, a hundred squares and a billion triangles. But the lowly triangles do not spawn: since there are no polygons of degree 2,1 or 0, when a triangle dies it leaves no legacy at all.
   Suppose the polygon species began with a single *ur*-polygon, a circle with infinitely many sides (thus a polygon only on a technicality — but who was there to complain?) When it died, it left behind an enormous (but finite) number of polygons each of arbitrarily large (but finite) status.
   In spite of all the polygons the *ur*-polygon might have created when it died, will Flatland's polygon-species nevertheless eventually become extinct?

Exercise 4.19 ⇓ You are given a (rectangular) matrix of numbers, positive, negative or zero; and you can choose any row or any column and negate all the numbers in it. Show that by doing that repeatedly, each time with a row or column of your choice, you can eventually bring the matrix into a state where no row or column has a strictly negative sum.

The difficulty of course is that negating a row (or column) might disturb the numbers in the other columns (or rows) that it crosses, possibly changing *their* sum from positive to negative (just as fixing one face in a Rubik's Cube can disturb other faces).

That activity can be expressed as a program:

> while *"Some row or column has a negative sum."*:
>   *"Choose a row or a column."* # ← What's your strategy here?
>   *"Negate every number in it."*
> # Post: *"No row or column has a negative sum."*   .

Can you find a strategy that works, and a variant that checks it?

Exercise 4.20 There is a train yard with strings of coupled carriages in it: let that be represented by a sequence cs of positive integers with each integer being the length of a string of coupled carriages. Thus there are initially len(cs) strings of carriages in the yard, and $\sum$cs carriages in total. Your aim is to empty the yard.

But only single carriages can be removed from the train yard, one at a time; and the only other move allowed is to separate some string of carriages into two (smaller) strings.

As in Ex. 4.19, that activity can be expressed as a program:

> while cs!=[]:
>   *"Choose any single string c of carriages in cs."*
>   if c==1: *"Remove that c from cs (i.e. from the yard)."*
>   else: # It's not a single carriage.
>   *"Choose any positive c1,c2 so that c == c1+c2."*
>   *"Replace c in cs with [c1,c2]."* # Break c into two pieces.
> # Post: *"The train yard is empty: cs==[]."*   .

Show that no matter how the two *"any"* choices are made above, the above program is guaranteed to terminate. (Note: This is not "Find a strategy to empty the yard." Rather it to show that *any* strategy will empty the yard.)

Exercise 4.21 ⇓ For safety during a pandemic, people who queue are required to stand on painted circles along a line: each circle is 1.5 metres from the next. But sometimes –in spite of that– several people stand together on the same circle, and so they have to be asked to separate.

A single police officer enforces this separation repeatedly: if two or more people are on the same circle, one of them is asked to move one circle forward, and another one is asked to move one circle backward.[9] (If there is no circle there to accommodate a move, the officer paints a new one.)

The moves might of course create new multiple occupancies, with the original circle itself still multiply occupied: for example 6 consecutive circles and 11 people arranged [1,1,2+2,4,0,1] could become [1,1+1,2,1+4,0,1], where there are now three multiple occupancies 1+1, 2 and 1+4 instead of the two original 2+2 and 4; and –worse– one of the new multiple occupancies (1+4) is now more crowded than any that were there before.

Nevertheless... show that no matter in what order the officer visits the circles, and which people are moved, eventually there will be no multiple occupancies left.

---

[9] Strictly speaking, moving just one of the people would be enough to separate her from the others remaining on that circle; but then termination might not be assured. Why not?

Exercise 4.22 ⇓ This gives the answer to Ex. 4.21.
But be sure to try it yourself first!

Checking assignments and conditionals

5.1 Introduction

So far, our checking of assignments and conditionals has been partly (but not wholly) intuitive, because we have been concentrating on the bigger issue of how to design and check loops — which requires some inspiration and experience.

Here however we will look at those basic building blocks more closely, because in many cases checking them is a relatively mechanical process.[1]

5.2 Checking assignments

At (1.13) in Sec. 1.5 we checked an assignment statement s= s+A[1], repeated here:

$$
\begin{aligned}
&\text{\# PRE: } s == \sum A[0:1]\\
&s= s+A[1]\\
&\text{\# POST: } s == \sum A[0:2] \quad .
\end{aligned}
\tag{5.1}
$$

By substituting s+A[1] for s in the postcondition $s == \sum A[0:2]$, just as a text editor would, we got (s+A[1]) $== \sum A[0:2]$, and we had to show that the resulting assertion was implied by the precondition. (The parentheses have been inserted only to group the substituted text together; usually they can be removed.) Again we use that reasoning here: because $(\sum A[0:1]) + A[1] == \sum A[0:2]$ we have the implication

$$
s == \sum A[0:1] \quad \Rightarrow \quad s+A[1] == \sum A[0:2] \quad ,
\tag{5.2}
$$

and because of that (and we need no other reason), we know that (5.1) works. Notice the *two* steps we have done here, however: the first was substitution, where we did not need to know about sequences at all; and the second was about sequences and addition, where we did not need to know about programs at all. That's an important technique generally: don't try to think about two things at once, if thinking about them separately is sufficient. Reduce your risk of error.

Here are some further examples:

---

[1] A summary is given in Appendix B.

(a) x= 1 {Post: x==1} checks because True $\Rightarrow$ 1==1. (Remember that the default precondition is True.) Here the equality 1==1 comes from substitution, but its *truth* comes from arithmetic: again two steps. Since 1==1 is unconditionally True, this program would work no matter what its precondition was, because *pre* $\Rightarrow$ True holds for any *pre*.

(b) {Pre: x==1} x= x+1 {Post: x==2} works because x==1 $\Rightarrow$ (x+1)==2. Here, the precondition True would not check.

(c) {Pre: x==X} x= x-1 {Post: x<X} works because x==X $\Rightarrow$ (x-1)<X. The X in the precondition is also a variable, but one that is not in the program body x= x-1: that's how we write postconditions that depend on the precondition. Often the "capture the value before" variable X is auxiliary.

(d) {Pre: 0<n==V} n= n-1 {Post: 0<=n<V} works since 0<n==V $\Rightarrow$ 0<=(n-1)<V, and is the typical check you might do for the variant in a loop that is iterating down. We're using (auxiliary?) V for the initial value of n.

(e) {Pre: V==n<N} n= n+1 {Post: V<n<=N} works since V==n<N $\Rightarrow$ V<(n+1)<=N, and is the typical check you might do for a variant in a loop that is iterating up.

Ex. 5.1

(f) {Pre: x==X and y==Y} x,y= y,x {Post: x==Y and y==X} works because of the implication (actually equivalence — but implication is enough)

$$x==X \text{ and } y==Y \quad \Rightarrow \quad y==Y \text{ and } x==X \quad .$$

(g) {Pre: x==X and y==Y} x= y; y= x {Post: x==Y and y==X} does *not* work, however. With two statements one after the other, the substitutions are also done one after the other, and we pass the assertions along as usual, from back to front: the program is actually

```
{x==X and y==Y}
x= y
{???}                                            (5.3)
y= x
{Post: x==Y and y==X}     ,
```

and in fact there is *no* "intermediate" assertion ??? which, placed in the middle, would make both

$$\{Pre: x==X \text{ and } y==Y\} \ x= y \ \{Post: ???\}$$
and $$\{Pre: ???\} \ y= x \ \{Post: x==Y \text{ and } y==X\}$$

work. One of them *must* fail: so if you always check the intermediate assertion (in both directions), you will never write (5.3) by mistake.[2]

A good (perhaps desperate?) guess for ??? comes from the substitution we'd carry out for the second assignment: that would give us {x==Y and x==X}, which does look unlikely: we are not allowed to assume that X and Y are equal. But if we apply the first assignment's substitution to that anyway, we get {y==Y and y==X}, which is not implied by x==X and y==Y unless indeed x==y.

---

[2] In Sec. 18.2 you will see that sometimes those checks can be done automatically for you by Dafny.

So not only do we see that x= y; y= x does not swap x and y in general, we discover the precise conditions when actually it would: just when x and y are equal already.[3]

(h) As our final example, we show that the following well-known "swap x and y" program *does* work:

{PRE: x==X and y==Y} t= x; x= y; y= t {POST: x==Y and y==X}

As usual for chains of assignments, we figure out the assertions from the end towards the beginning, simply one substitution after another: we get

```
     # PRE: x==X and y==Y   # ...which is implied by this.
⇒ ↑  {y==Y and x==X}                # and then this ...
     t= x
   ↑ {y==Y and t==X}                # and then this,
     x= y
   ↑ {x==Y and t==X}                 # then do this,
     y= t
   ↑ # POST: x==Y and y==X           # Start here,
```

Reason from back to front.

... after which we show the implication x==X and y==Y ⇒ y==Y and x==X, which is what in general allows us to put one assertion after another: the first must imply (⇒) the second. In this case, however, they are actually equivalent (≡). Alternatively, we could imagine that there is a skip at the beginning, giving

```
     # PRE: x==X and y==Y
     skip
⇒  {y==Y and x==X}     ,
     ⋮
```

where the implication ⇒ comes from the explanation of how to check skip, given in Sec. 5.3 below. (See Sec. 18.2.3 for how these simple intermediate assertions can sometimes be found and checked automatically.)   Ex. 5.2

5.3 The "do nothing" statement skip

The program {PRE: *pre*} skip {POST: *post*} works just when *pre* ⇒ *post*, because skip does nothing at all.[4]

Like zero (as a number), it's not terribly useful on its own. (Who wants to have zero oranges?) But it is useful in checking programs, just as zero is useful in checking arithmetic. One use for it is explaining why, when two assertions are placed directly after another as we saw just above, the first must imply the second. Another use is in explaining how to check else-less if-statements. (See App. B.3.2.)

---

[3] In Python, the swap can be done with x,y= y,x, a multiple assignment. But we are pretending that multiple assignment is not available here, because not all languages have it. For example *C* does not have it in that form.

[4] In Python skip is called pass.

5.4 Checking conditionals

We have already extensively used conditionals, that is the construct `if` *condition*:
while writing and checking programs (for example in Secs. 2.2, 3.3.3, 3.4.1 and 3.4.2).
But occasionally it's an "`if`" itself that needs checking. We'll start with an example,
the following program which sorts a,b,c into ascending order:

```
if a>b: a,b= b,a
{a<=b}
if b>c: b,c= c,b          } → Concentrate on this step.
{a<=c and b<=c}

if a>b: a,b= b,a
# Post: a<=b<=c     .
```

We check the second statement more closely: pulled out of context, and presented for
independent checking, it becomes

```
# Pre: a<=b
if b>c: b,c= c,b
# Post: a<=c and b<=c     .
```

If the `if` condition `b>c` is false then `b<=c` holds, and so it can be in the postcondition
without action on our part. (You can see it there as the second conjunct.) But how
do we justify the first conjunct `a<=c`? And why don't we have the precondition's
`a<=b` any more? These questions are answered by looking more closely at how `if`'s
are checked in detail (when we need to do so).

The first conjunct comes from taking the precondition `a<=b` and the negation of
the if-condition `b>c` together: they give a<=b<=c, and the first conjunct `a<=c` in the
postcondition above is a consequence of that. (It's *transitivity* of `<=`.)

The reason we must discard the `a<=b` however –it is *not* in the postcondition– is
that it does not (necessarily) hold when the `if` condition is true, because b,c are then
swapped, potentially decreasing b's value — and so *invalidating* `a<=b`.

Let's leave that for a moment, though, while we look at the first branch of the
`if` statement in the case that `b>c` *does* hold. The overall precondition, and the
truth of the condition `b>c`, together –going forwards– give a first extra assertion
(1), and applying the assignment `b,c= c,b` as a substitution to the postcondition
`a<=c and b<=c` –going backwards– gives a second extra assertion (2):

```
        # Pre: a<=b
        if b>c: {a<=b and b>c}              # (1)
   ⇒       {a<=b and c<=b}                  # (2)
           b,c= c,b
        # Post: a<=c and b<=c     ,
```

Since the assertions (1) and (2) are next to each other vertically, we must check as
usual that the first implies the second, i.e. that `a<=b and b>c` ⇒ `a<=b and c<=b`;
and indeed it does.

And now we can see, by analogy, that what we should be checking, in the case that
the `if` condition is false, is the implication `a<=b and not b>c` ⇒ `a<=b and b<=c`;
and that holds too.

Ex. 5.3

The overall pattern of checking an `if` is easier to see if we include the `else` part of the conditional explicitly: to check the program fragment

```
# Pre:  pre
if cond: thenBranch
else:    elseBranch
# Post: post
```

we check each branch separately; thus we check both

```
# Pre:  pre and cond
thenBranch
# Post: post
```

and

```
# Pre:  pre and not cond
elseBranch
# Post: post        ,
```

which is precisely what we did in the example above — but because in that case the second branch was actually `skip`, we could check it with an implication, since checking `skip` is *always* done with an implication, as we saw in Sec. 5.3.

Most of the time, conditionals don't need such careful attention; but sometimes they do. (The small program containing (1) and (2) above is one of them; and what if we had a fourth variable `d` as well?) An example is the binary-search program | Ex. 5.5 | from Sec. 3.3.3, in particular checking that it does not go into an infinite loop. The variant for that program is `n-m`, and we need to check that it decreases strictly in each iteration. Here is the part of the binary-search program where that happens, with assertions concentrating on the variant:

```
# Pre: 0<=m<n<=N and V==n-m
p= (m+n)//2
{ m<=p<n }
if A[p]<x:  m= p+1
else:       n= p
# Post: 0<=n-m<V
```

Applying the checks explained above, but concentrating only on `m`, the two checks for the branches are

```
# Pre: 0<V==n-m and m<=p<n
m= p+1
# Post: 0<=n-m<V
```

and

```
# Pre: 0<V==n-m and m<=p<n
n= p
# Post: 0<=n-m<V      ,
```

and the implications that result from them (after carrying out the substitutions) are separately

$$0<V==n-m \text{ and } m<=p<n \quad \Rightarrow \quad 0<=n-(p+1)<V$$
$$\text{and} \quad 0<V==n-m \text{ and } m<=p<n \quad \Rightarrow \quad 0<=p-m<V \quad .$$

Both of those hold.

Notice how we have introduced the auxiliary variable V to capture the value of n-m before the loop body, so that we could check that afterwards that it had been decreased strictly.

5.5 Exercises

Exercise 5.1 (p. 66) ⇓ Example (e) in Sec. 5.2 can be (re-)written as a decreasing variant, bounded below by 0: it becomes

$$\{\,\text{PRE: } V==(N-n)>0\,\} \quad n= n+1 \quad \{\,\text{POST: } V>(N-n)>=0\,\}$$

— that is, the (decreasing) variant is N-n, not just n on its own. What implication must be checked for that?

Exercise 5.2 (p. 67) Show that this program works:

$$\{\,\text{PRE: } x==X \text{ and } y==Y\,\} \quad x= y-x; \; y= y-x; \; x= x+y \quad \{\,\text{POST: } x==Y \text{ and } y==X\,\} \quad .$$

Hint: Remember to figure out the assertions *from the end* of the program towards the beginning. Simplify the conditions, if you can, as you go along.

Exercise 5.3 (p. 68) Here is how assertions are placed inline when checking conditional statements:

```
# PRE: pre
if cond:
  { PRE: cond and pre }
  ...
  { POST: post }
else:
  { PRE: (not cond) and pre }
  ...
  { POST: post }
# POST: post    .
```

Set out a similar procedure for if on its own (no else).

Hint: Use the above, with skip for the else part. (See also App. B.3.3.)

Then show how to check if *and* elif and else.

Exercise 5.4 This program sets m to the largest value among a, b, c and d:

```
m= a
if b>m: m= b
if c>m: m= c
if d>m: m= d
```

Add assertions between the statements that will allow the program to be easily checked.

Hint: Write [a,b,c]<=d for a<=d and b<=d and c<=d etc.

How many paths need to be checked in this program? With an extra variable e, how much longer would the program have to be?

Exercise 5.5 (p. 69) Add assertions to check the "sort *four* variables" program

```
{ PRE: True }
if a>b: a,b= b,a
if b>c: b,c= c,b
if c>d: c,d= d,c
if a>b: a,b= b,a
if b>c: b,c= c,b
if a>b: a,b= b,a
{ POST: a<=b<=c<=d }      .
```

Hint: See the hint for Ex. 5.4, which suggests for example that the condition
`a<=c and b<=c` from there could be written more concisely as `[a,b]<=c`.   Ex. 5.6

Exercise 5.6 (p. 71) ⇓ The following (incomplete) Bubble Sort program uses the ideas
of Ex. 5.5 to sort a whole sequence `A[0:N]` of N values instead of just four named
variables `a,b,c,d`. Its invariants are suggested by the assertions you would have used
in your answer to Ex. 5.5.

```
{ PRE: ··· }
for i in range(?1?): # INV: Inv1
  for j in range (?2?): # INV: Inv2
    if ?3?: ?4?
  { ?5? }
# A[0:N] are in their final sorted positions.
# POST: The whole of A is sorted.       ,
```

where `Inv1` is "`A[i:]` are in their final sorted positions." and `Inv2` is
`A[:j]<=A[j]` and

(a) `range(?1?)` should establish `Inv1` initially, and should imply that `A[0:N]` are
in their final sorted positions when the outer `for`-loop has terminated. What
should `?1?` be?

Hint: Use `range(high,low,-1)` to "iterate down" in the outer `for`-loop.

(b) `range(?2?)` should establish `Inv2` initially, and imply `?5?` when the inner `for`-
loop has terminated. What are `?2?` and `?5?` and why?

(c) The code of the inner-loop body will be

$$
\begin{array}{ll}
\texttt{\{ PRE: A[:j]<=A[j] \}} & \\
\texttt{if ?3?: ?4?} & (5.4) \\
\texttt{\{ POST: A[:j+1]<=A[j+1] \}} &
\end{array}
$$

What do `?3?` and `?4?` have to be so that the code checks?

Hint: Do the `else` part first.

(d) Explain in words why your completed (5.4) checks. Note however that Bubble
Sort is quite inefficient.

Exercise 5.7 Another elementary (and similarly inefficient) sorting program is Insertion Sort:

```
{PRE: ···}
for i in range(?1?): # INV: A[i:]  are in order.
  for j in range(?2): # INV: Inv2 ?6?
    if ?3?: ?4?
  {?5?}
{A[0:N] are in order.}
{POST: ···}      .
```

Complete the missing assertions and code fragments. (Note the new one, ?6?.) Like Bubble Sort, Insertion Sort is quite inefficient.

Exercise 5.8 ⇓ This simple program sorts a sequence A[0:N] by continuing to swap until no more swaps can be done. What is its invariant ?I?? What is its variant ?V?? What should the assertion ??? be? Remember that an invariant is a Boolean condition, whereas a variant is a non-negative integer.

```
# --- Sort sequence A[0:N] into ascending order.
# PRE: 0<=N

while True: # Var: ?V?
  noSwaps= True
  for n in range(N-1): # Inv(n): ?I?
    if A[n]>A[n+1]:
      A[n],A[n+1]= A[n+1],A[n]
      noSwaps= False
  {Inv(N-1)}
  if noSwaps: {???} break

# POST: A[0:N] is sorted
```

Like Bubble Sort and Insertion sort, Exchange Sort is quite inefficient.

6

Summary of Part I

6.1 What's not obvious

Programming is both a skill and an engineering discipline.

As a skill, people learn to "code" (so-called to make it sound less forbidding?) — possibly at school, but perhaps also from their parents, siblings and friends as well. Coding is not very hard, and so by the time they start university, most of those whose interests lie there are already quite good at it; and a substantial subset of those have discovered that they have a natural aptitude for programming, and even computer science in general.

There is a difference though between a skill and a discipline *based* on that skill: it's the difference from being able to build a garden shed yourself and *organising* the construction of an office block or a bridge or an aeroplane (with help from perhaps hundreds of people you have not yet met). In the first case, with a skill you have an instinctive understanding of what to do, based on (years of) experience, and you have a built-in rapport with the people who are helping: maybe you eat breakfast with them every day. In the second case, instinct is only a start, and actually you might *never* meet some of the team who are working for you. It's the difference between being able to tune your motorcycle yourself ... and being able to design one from scratch, then organise its being manufactured and sold.

That difference, the small vs. the large, the instinct vs. the science, is why there are four-year university courses in engineering, indeed in various different *kinds* of engineering, and professional bodies that accredit engineers so that we can trust what they build and what they organise others to build. What is the analogue for programming?

Unlike engineering in general, the *technical* gap between skill and discipline in programming is actually

astonishingly small,

possibly because programming requires so little in the way of raw materials: once you have a computer and a compiler, you can (try to) write programs as large and as complicated as you like. The organisational and social gap however remains as wide as ever, as big as it is for any other branch of engineering. Yet that small technical gap is very easily bridged — if only you are given the chance. We need accreditation there too.

And so the techniques explained in Part I show that –for example– instead of figuring out how to write a loop by following the conventional thought processes. . .

- Imagining what a typical iteration must do. ("It must add another one of the array elements to the current running total.")

- Taking one step back from the first iteration, to guess what the initialisation must be. ("After the first addition, the running total must be the first element alone: so we start at zero. But what if the list is empty, so that there *is* no first element?")

- Figuring out what the last iteration must do in order to make the loop complete. ("We mustn't forget to add the very last element, so the index on the last iteration must be N-1. . . Or is it N? And maybe the last step is a special case?")

- Checking the edge cases. ("How do you know you've covered them all?")

(6.1)

. . . instead you might do better by remembering the program (1.18)[1], and then perhaps send those thought processes in a different, and startlingly more efficient direction. Once you get the hang of it, for (1.18) you'll think

- The *invariant* is that the running total is the sum of the sequence prefix so far. And to preserve that invariant you simply add the current element to the sum, and lengthen the prefix by one position.

- At the beginning, "the prefix so far" is empty, and the sum of an empty list is zero. So the initial running total must be zero as well: no "edge case" to worry about here.

(6.2)

- At the end, "the prefix so far" must be the whole sequence, which means that you have indeed *summed* the whole sequence: no "edge case" here either.

- Thus both edge cases are handled automatically.

You might not have heard of a loop invariant before — **but you have now**. Are invariants "unconventional"? Perhaps. But most of the time they make your programs easier to write, easier to check and sometimes even more efficient. And soon they will become the *conventional* process for you.

Remember that the difference between the approaches (6.1) and (6.2) above is not necessarily "an amount of work". Indeed, for small programs the amount of work is about the same. For larger programs, however, the approach of (6.2) is substantially *less* work in the end, when you factor in the reduction in testing,[2] debugging and other program maintenance that will still have to be done. Instead of "an amount of work", the difference is a *point of view* — plus the astounding advantage that the second approach brings, these four extra benefits:

1. Approach (6.2) scales up.

   However, checking a program in terms of "What steps does it carry out in this situation? And that situation? And the situation that my customer mentioned

---

[1] . . . or, worse, the tortuous examples of Sec. 2.3 and Sec. 2.4.
[2] . . . reduction in, but not elimination of testing.

only yesterday?", as in (6.1), becomes harder at a much faster rate than the
size of the problem itself. Recall Ex. 1.1 where, even in that small program,
every new variable *doubled* the amount of checking needed — if done in the
conventional style.

2. Approach (6.2) makes it easier for team members to collaborate.

   The idea of documenting "What's *true* at this point in the program?", as in (6.2),
   instead of "What does this do?", as in (6.1), is the glue that binds together large
   teams of programmers and allows big programs to be divided into small pieces
   that can be handled separately.

3. For very important programming projects, where failure is extremely expensive,
   even catastrophic, the approach (6.2) can to some extent be automated. (See
   Part IV.) For (6.1), that is much more difficult.

4. And when something *does* go wrong, in spite of all your careful reasoning, testing, walk-throughs –all of which remain necessary– the approach (6.2) leaves an
   "audit trail", the assertions, that helps you to find where in your *process* the
   mistake was made — and how to avoid similar mistakes in the future.

Because the difference in effort required –that is, to move from thinking in the (6.1)
style to thinking in the (6.2) style– is *so small* but makes *so much difference*, we have
started in Part I with programs that you already know and understand — and that
means you can concentrate on *how* you are thinking about them, rather than having
to worry at the same time about *what* those programs are actually doing.

Later, however, we will see the payoff that "What's true here?" thinking brings. As
just one example, the program you will encounter in Chapter 16 (Fig. 16.4) is just
four lines long (plus another four that are a symmetric copy of the first four): but
it took 15 years to discover that program, and the person who did is still celebrated
today.[3] *More than 50* program-execution paths would be followed were we to check
those four lines of code conventionally.

What is *not* obvious about the above insights, when you think about your programs
in that different way? The only non-obvious thing (before you found yourself reading
this text) was that those insights have been there for decades: you *can* learn them; it
is possible to apply them.

But you were not taught; and nobody showed you how. Until now?

6.2 What *is* obvious

Once you know this style of thinking about programming, and have had some practice,
it is indeed pretty obvious in most cases how to do it. Figure 1.1 showed a flowchart
for summing a sequence (program (1.18) again). And it's very clear what's going on:
the operations of the program occur within the boxes –rectangles for assignments,
diamonds for tests– and the lines (with arrows where necessary) show how the program
moves from one action to the next.

Inside each box is written what it does; and you can simulate the program's actions,
execute them "in your head", just by following the lines around.

---

[3] Peterson's mutual-exclusion algorithm: 40 years later, at the time of writing.

But there is much more to *our* flowcharts than that: on the lines *between* their boxes is written "what should be true when the program is travelling along this line." [4] The principal reason it is so much easier to use those for checking –to use what's *between* the boxes rather than what's *in* them– is that, if you use the boxes alone, then to check whether a particular box is doing the right thing you must look at the box before, to see what *it* did; and for that one, you must look at the one before it, and so on. The more boxes there are, the further back you must look.

On the other hand, if you use what's written on the lines *between* the boxes, you need only check whether the box successfully takes you from what was written on its *incoming* line to what is written on its *outgoing* line. If that checks then this box is working, and you do not need to check *other* boxes to see whether *this* box works. And even more significantly,

> if you check *every box* in that style ("Does it take you from its incoming line to its outgoing line?") even if you check each box *separately*, even at different times, even with different people... and they all work, then the whole program works too.

That is, those other boxes can be checked by other people, or yourself on other days; and what's written on the lines, our pre- and postconditions, are the "glue" that puts all the checks together, that reminds you tomorrow what you have to check then (even if by tomorrow you have forgotten the details of what you checked today). Or it tells your colleagues what they have to check, separately, in order for the whole thing to work properly when it's assembled.

The more you practise checking programs, using the techniques we've introduced so far, the more you will appreciate those techniques in all senses of that word: you will appreciate that you were told about them, you will appreciate how they work — and you will appreciate a sense of satisfaction from the way they inspire *your* confidence in what you are doing.

---

[4] They are not *our* invention, of course: that conceptual innovation was proposed by Robert W. Floyd in 1967 [19]. Still, if you look at flowcharts as they are used in general today, you are very unlikely to find assertions on the *lines*. Their absence is an example of the "Lost Art" (p. 215).

Part II

Data structures
and their encapsulation

Introduction to Part II

7.1 Data vs. data *structures*

The data values manipulated by a program are stored in its variables; in the simplest cases they are things like numbers (integers, floating point), characters, Booleans — and they are called "basic", or "primitive" data *types*. Using those basic types, that is "building" on them, gives us more interesting structures, such as sequences of integers, characters, Booleans, strings and more generally sets of *those* things, tuples of them and so on. There you get more than just the *basic* data-types: you get data *structures*.

As a first example, let's take people's names and ages, which are both basic types,[1] and make a data structure from them: we can build a small database using a sequence variable `dir` as a sequence of triples. It might be initialised with the assignment

```
dir= [("Alex", "Smith", 35), ("John", "Jones", 60)]    ,
```

so that it stores that information for just two people: Alex Smith is aged 35; and John Jones is aged 60. The data structure here, the *type* of `dir`, is a sequence of triples, with each tuple also a structure, in that case made from two basic types: two strings and an integer.

The family name of the first person in `dir` is `dir[0][1]`, where `dir[0]` is the triple for the first person (because we index lists from 0), and $\cdots$`[1]` is the second component of that triple — `"Smith"`.

You can do a lot with that structure. But if your directory `dir` grows to contain thousands of entries, or you want to store middle names as well, then two problems arise:

1. Having a simple sequence of entries might make it quite inefficient to search the whole directory: using linear search might take too long.

2. Expanding the directory to include middle names (with `""` for "none") would give things like

```
dir=  [("Alex", "", "Smith", 35),
       ("John", "Paul", "Jones", 60)]    ,
```

---

[1] Strictly speaking, the type "string" is not basic, because it is a sequence of characters. We'll ignore that, however: where you start is to some extent flexible. Isn't a character in turn a sequence of bits?

and the use of `dir[0][1]`, to access the family name "Smith" of Person 0, would have to be changed to `dir[0][2]` –everywhere, throughout your whole program– because all the family names are now in the third position.

The solution to both problems is to use procedures and functions to access and update the data structure; and then when you want to have a faster lookup you might alter the `search` function to use binary search instead of linear search (Sec. 3.3.3). But at the same time you would have to alter the `add` procedure to put new entries in the right place, so that the sequence of triples is always sorted (since binary search doesn't work, otherwise). All the various procedures to do with `dir` would have to be modified in a consistent way.

Also, the second problem above (a simpler one) is solved by using procedures and functions: in that case you would probably have to make only one change: the "`getFamilyName`" function would have its "$\cdots$`[1]`" altered to "$\cdots$`[2]`".

7.2 Data encapsulation

Data encapsulation is the practice –recommended just above– of gathering all the code for the declaration, initialisation, access and updating of a data-type, all of it, together in one place for each conceptual data structure. So for example the declaration and initialisation of `dir`, and its related functions, would all be grouped together. Data related to some other, possibly different, concept (say a directed graph) would also be grouped together — but in their own, separate encapsulation.

Doing all that is the topic of Part II, together with encapsulation's advantages and how it is organised, and how –in particular– changes like the two mentioned above (many entries, middle name), and others, can be carried out in a way that does not undo the checking that might *already* have been done in any surrounding program that used the data structure in its original form. Overall, it is likely to take less time to carry out the checks *with* encapsulation than it would have taken without it.

Very simple examples will be used to illustrate the process, pretending we have discovered the idea of encapsulation –and its advantages– for the very first time. See App. G.4, however, for a brief discussion of encapsulation's role in what has become known as object-oriented programming, and the further concepts that arise.

As in Part I, but now for encapsulation, the key tools are assertions and, in particular, invariants.

Coupling invariants

8.1 Introduction

Invariants –we recall– are assertions that are intended to describe things that are repeatedly true, like the condition that always holds every time your program begins a particular loop's body. Those are *loop* invariants, of course.

But invariants are used in many more places, and for many more purposes. Here we look at another application of them, the "coupling" invariants that state the relationship that always holds between two different representations of the same data. Often one of the representations is "abstract" and the other (more) "concrete"; and the process of relating one correctly to the other is called "data refinement".[1]

We'll begin with a data-type Set as a running example of coupling invariants.

8.2 Implementing sets as sequences

Our first illustration of coupling invariants concerns writing program code at a "low level" that expresses an algorithmic idea formulated at a "higher level". The low-level code here will involve sequences; the higher-level idea involves sets.[2]

Suppose we can write programs that use finite sets directly, with statements like ss= {} which assigns the empty set to set-typed variable ss,[3] or like ss= ss∪{s}, which adds element s to set ss, or like the conditional s∈ss, which determines whether s is in ss. That is the "higher level".

The reality at the "lower level" however might be that actually you *can't* use sets directly in your code, because your programming language doesn't support them: but you still have to write that program. In that case, you might decide to represent the set ss as a sequence qs, and write your code directly at that lower level, translating as you go: you'd write

- qs= []   to initialise the "set" to the empty set, and

---

[1] It is also called "data reification". They are synonyms.

[2] In fact Python supports sets directly; but here we are pretending it does not — and indeed the language *you* are actually using might not. Sets are not built-in to *C*, for example. The techniques we'll use here apply to more or less any language.

[3] In Python you must write set() for the empty set: the two-brace notation "{}" is reserved for empty "dictionary". Here however we will use {}.

- `qs= qs+[s]` or `qs.append(d)` to add an element `s` to the set, in the first case using sequence concatenation `+`, and

- the small program[4]

  ```
  b= False
  for q in qs:
      if q==s: b= True; break
  ```
  (8.1)

for setting Boolean `b` depending on whether some element `s` is in the "set" `qs`. (If (8.1) were a function, instead of inline as shown, we would add `return b` at its end.)

Here, instead of a single statement, we have had to use a small linear-search loop to search the "set" for the element.

In this case the low level is the actual code you are writing: the higher level is in your head.

Ex. 8.1

So now imagine that you wanted to add a new operation, to take some element `s` out of the set, that is to remove it. With sets directly, that is "in your head", you are *thinking* `ss= ss-{s}`. But that's not what you *write*: you are implementing the set directly, as a sequence `qs` and "translating from concept to code as you go". And so you must now decide whether to take "just one" `s` out of `qs`, or "all of them". But *how* do you decide?

In the implementation above, you would have to take them *all* out; and, to have discovered that, you would have had to examine the code of `add(s)` (perhaps pages away) to see whether it is possible for elements to be repeated in `qs`. Indeed our use of `append` above would show us that adding an element `s` "a second time" to our conceptual set `ss` will include it twice in the "actual" `qs`.

And –another variation– what if for efficiency of searching you decided to keep the sequence `qs` in ascending order? In that case, you could use binary search for membership checking, but then a loop, rather than a single statement, would be necessary for insertion (and deletion).

Our example here simply reminds us that if we are using a collection of procedures and low-level data to implement a higher-level concept, the collection must be consistent: the procedures in that collection must cooperate with each other. Here we will show why therefore it's a good idea to group them all together, and to introduce a "coupling invariant" that states clearly and explicitly what "cooperating with each other" actually means.

In fact programmers carry out "representation" exercises like the above in almost every program they write. Often it is trivial to do so, and easy to keep track of. But a clear advantage of putting all the information in one place, and having a coupling invariant, is that it makes the consistency checking so much easier. If say there were 5 procedures associated with the concrete representation of the data, then checking each against all the others would amount to 10 $(= 5 \times (5-1)/2)$ pairwise checks. With a coupling invariant, it would instead be only 5 checks: each procedure checked against the coupling invariant directly. If there were 10 procedures, it would be 45 checks vs. 10. The more procedures there are, the bigger the difference becomes.

---

[4] Python implements "`in`" for sequences directly; but many languages do not. We are pretending here that Python does not.

As remarked in the introduction to this chapter, we have seen assertions already as "What's true at this point in the program." comments; and we have seen a more specialised use of them as "What's true every time this loop evaluates its guard?" What we will now see is a third use: how assertions can describe the connection between the variables we would *like* to have –such as sets– and the variables we actually *do* have, in this case sequences. Those assertions are called *coupling invariants*, and the coupling invariant for our example above is

> The elements in the sequence qs, ignoring repeats, are the members
> of the set ss that we are actually thinking about as we write the   (8.2)
> program.

It's a condition on variables' values, just like the others we have written, in this case referring to the two variables ss and qs — that is, both the high level and the low level, the "abstract" and the "concrete". The coupling invariant (8.2) tells us, for example, that add(s) can append s to qs even if s is already there; but it tells us also that –as a consequence– remove(s) must examine the whole sequence, because it must delete *every* occurrence of s .

8.3 Sentinels as "high-level" data

Another use of coupling invariants is to implement "sentinels". Though sentinels are widely used, they are not so often presented in an "abstract vs. concrete" way.

A *sentinel* is an extra, "special" value added to data in order to simplify program code.[5] For example, we might want to find program code "···" below such that this program would check:

```
# --- Find the position of some value in a given sequence,
# --- if the value is there.
# --- If it's not there, report that.
# PRE: 0<=N
...
# POST: A[n]==x  if  x∈A  else  n==N
```
(8.3)

Notice that the requirements are (deliberately) a bit loose, but they do state the general purpose of the program. For example, they do not say *how* "not there" is reported: but the person looking for this search functionality does not care (yet): she just wants to know the functionality *is* there. (When she needs it, she'll find that detail in the program's postcondition.)

And indeed the postcondition is more precise: it says which sequence (A) is to be searched for x; which variable (n) is to receive its index, if it is there; and how "x is not there" is to be indicated.

We'll do it with linear search.

Linear search is not a hard program. But it would be slightly easier to code if we knew that x was in A somewhere, because the search for x would then be guaranteed to succeed — we would not have to worry about "falling off the end". `Ex. 8.2`

To use a sentinel for that, we imagine extending A with an extra element x at position N, "beyond the end" of A — that is, we would use a sequence B[0:N+1] that was equal to A+[x]. We'd therefore have B[n]==A[n] when 0<=n<N but B[N]==x in particular. Searching for the x that *might* be in A is then the same as searching for

---

[5] The NUL at the end of character strings in C is a sentinel.

the x that *must* be in B... somewhere. If x is not in A at all, then it won't be in B[0:N] either, in which case our program will set n to N — and that's exactly what the sentinel B[N]==x does so neatly.

Here is the program that uses our "imaginary", high-level B with its sentinel, and correspondingly an extra conjunct x∈B in the precondition:

```
# --- Find x in B[0:N+1].
# Pre: 0<=N and x∈B      ← Notice the extra precondition conjunct.
n= 0
# Inv: See Ex.8.3.                                                    (8.4)
while x!=B[n]:
  n= n+1
# Post: 0<=n<=N and x∉B[:n] and x==B[n]
```

The extra conjunct x∉B[:n] in the postcondition –that x is not in the portion examined so far– is important (and comes from the invariant): without it we could simply write the single line n= N on its own for the whole program! As usual, the postcondition is just the invariant **and** the negated loop guard.

Ex. 8.3

What we will now look at is how to translate the program (8.4) –with its "imaginary" B– back to a program about our "actual" low-level sequence A — from which variable B will have been removed. And that is done with a coupling invariant.

As we have said, a coupling invariant –like other invariants– states a condition that the program maintains: it links two or more variables together. In Sec. 8.2 the variables were ss and qs; here they are B and A.

In the earlier example of Sec. 8.2, we wanted to think in terms of sets, but we had to program in terms of sequences. The coupling invariant expressed that the "set we are thinking of" is the set "that the sequence represents". In addition, the coupling invariant might express extra constraints such as "the set has no more than N elements", or "the sequence is sorted" or "the sequence does not contain repeated elements". We won't pursue that now; but we will return to it in Sec. 10.2.

In *this* example we do something much simpler: we use a coupling invariant to link our original A to our fictitious B. Indeed we mentioned it above already: it's just

$$B \ == \ A+[x] \quad . \tag{8.5}$$

Since neither A nor B is being updated by our linear-search program, we do not have to figure out corresponding updates to keep the coupling invariant true. We do however need to use it for converting references to B into corresponding references to A. There are three places where B is referred to in (8.4):

- in the precondition, with x∈B;

- in the loop guard, with x!=B[n]; and

- in the postcondition, with x∉B[:n] and x==B[n] .

One of the principal advantages of invariants generally (i.e. loop invariants as well) is that they allow us to deal with things one at a time, knowing that if each thing separately respects the invariant then all of them together will respect it as well. In the case of a loop invariant, that translates into checking that the invariant is established by the loop initialisation (one thing), then checking that the loop body maintains it (another thing), and then being able to use the fact that the invariant holds when the loop terminates — in effect the "all of them together" payoff. In Sec. 8.2 it was the point about having to do only 10 checks instead of 45.

The same thing will happen with this small program:

- In the precondition x∈B becomes x∈(A+[x]), which is trivially true. So it can be deleted altogether from the precondition.

- The loop guard x!=B[n] becomes x!=(A+[x])[n], which we deal with in two cases: either n==N or n!=N. In the n==N case it's trivially false; but in the other case it is just x!=A[n]. The loop guard therefore translates to

        n==N and False   or   n!=N and x!=A[n]   ,

  and that in turn simplifies to just n!=N and x!=A[n].[6]   Ex. 8.4

- In the postcondition, the conjuncts x∉B[:n] and B[n]==x become

        x∉(A+[x])[:n] and (A+[x])[n] == x   ,

  and again we can separate that into the two cases. This time we get

            n==N and x∉A and True [7]
        or n!=N and x∉A[:n] and A[n]==x   .

  If we discard the "and True", and weaken the postcondition by discarding the x∉A[:n] as well, which we can do because the requirements didn't ask for the *first* occurrence of x, then we get

        # Post: A[n]==x if n!=N else x∉A   .

When we make those substitutions, replacing references to B by corresponding references to A as figured out just above, we get the linear search program

```
# --- Find x in A[0:N].
# Pre: 0<=N
n= 0                                                                    (8.6)
while n!=N and A[n]!=x: n= n+1
# Post: A[n]==x if n!=N else x∉A          ← Different from (8.3)!
```

Curiously however the postcondition of this (8.6) is not the same as the postcondition A[n]==x if x∈A else n==N of our earlier version (8.3) above. Why?   Ex. 8.5

We are not of course saying that (8.6) is complicated, or that it could not have   Ex. 8.6
been written in that form directly. What we *are* saying is that here we have used   Ex. 8.7
the (coupling) invariant to *construct* that program; and if (8.4), the "B version", is   Ex. 8.8
correct then (8.6) –its corresponding A version– must be as well. There's no need here
to check it again.

---

[6] Notice again how (as for assignments) we do the substitution first and *then* the reasoning separately (in this case, about sequences). In more complex cases, that reduces mistakes significantly.
[7] Remember that (A+[x])[:N] == A .

8.4 Writing abstract data-types

We now put the ideas of the two previous sections together: having simultaneously an "abstract" and a "concrete" view of our data (e.g. as sets and as sequences in Sec. 8.2, or with- and without a sentinel in Sec. 8.3); and using a coupling invariant to transform one view into the other.

We concentrate on the Set example, collecting a set-valued variable ss, and the functions that use it, all together in one place:[8]

```
class Set: # Pretend that sets cannot be implemented directly.
  local:⁹ ss= {}        # Initialise the set to "{}", yet

  def makeEmpty:
    ss= {}              # our abstract language has no "{}",

  def add(s):
    ss= ss∪{s}                              # no "∪",

  def isIn(s):
    return s∈ss                             # and no "∈".
```
$$(8.7)$$

The code above does not itself make a set: it is more like declaring a Set type. We write things like ss1= Set() to make a set-valued variable, in this case called ss1. With ss2= Set() we could make a second one.

Given however that (we are pretending) there are no "real" sets in our programming language, the code above is fantasy: it won't compile, and we can't run it.

So it's tempting to call (8.7) "pseudocode" — but in fact it is much more than that. Here's why: suppose we have a program that actually *uses* our (more than) "pseudocode", for example

```
# PRE: True
ss1= Set()
ss1.add(2*2)
has4= ss1.isIn(4)
# POST: has4    .
```
$$(8.8)$$

It initialises set ss1 to empty, adds the element 2*2 to the set, and then sets Boolean has4 to whether an element 4 is in the set. *Can we check this program, even though we can't compile it, can't run it?*

Yes. We can check this program with the methods we have already, as usual by inserting assertions in between the statements. We "inline" the procedure calls, that is, we replace the call to the procedure with the code that's *in* the procedure (making appropriate substitutions of any parameters) — and then we check *that*. As usual, we start from the bottom (the postcondition) and work towards the top (the

---

[8] We're using something like the Python syntax for declaring a "class", and will explain it as we go. Remember though that we are pretending that the statements ss= ss∪{s} and similar are *not* Python (even though actually they are), because sets might not be in whatever language we are actually using.

[9] The "local" is not a keyword of Python, where global- vs. local scope is determined implicitly: we use it here to make reasoning easier. It both indicates which variables are local (inaccessible from outside the class), and initialises them.

precondition), getting

```
# PRE: True                   # And confirm that it checks. ←
{ 4 ∈ {4} }                                      # Simplify.  ↑
{ 4 ∈ {}∪{4} }        # Inline the "local"; substitute.  ↑
ss1= Set()
{ 4 ∈ ss1.ss ∪ {4} }                            # Arithmetic.  ↑
{ 4 ∈ (ss1.ss ∪ {2*2}) }   # Inline add(2*2), substitute.  ↑   (8.9)
ss1.add(2*2)
{ 4 ∈ ss1.ss }                              # Inline isIn(4).  ↑
{ ss1.isIn(4) }                                 # Substitute.  ↑
has4= ss1.isIn(4)               # Work towards the front.  ↑
# POST: has4    ,              # Start checking here.  ↑
```

and we see that indeed it checks. But in doing that check, we have done something that ordinary pseudocode *cannot* do, and that is why this is *more* than pseudocode. *You cannot reason rigorously about pseudocode.* The best you can do is "execute it in your head."

> We have reasoned about code (the set operations) that is not only not really there, it can *never* be there in the language we imagine we are using. $\qquad$ (8.10)

> But –in spite of that– we can check our programs anyway.

That is what the abstract/concrete approach allows us to do. If we check the abstract, and then construct the concrete using the steps explained in this Part II, we will not need to (re-)check the concrete: the checking is in effect done automatically for us, by the construction process. It's the beneficial side-effect of the methods we are using.

The reason we call (8.7) an "abstract" data-type is that it *is* a data-type, and we can reason about it, but it *abstracts* from the details of the particular programming language we might be using.

8.5 Coding concrete data–types

At (8.10) we noted that we were able to check a real program (8.8) without actually having real, runnable code for the data it was using. We did it at (8.9) by using the abstract version of the data-type *as if* it had been real code. But in the end we do need real code, in a real programming language that we can compile and run on a real computer — if ever we are to *use* our program. And so we now use the ideas of Sec. 8.3 to do the complementary thing: we reason about the abstract data-type *itself* without having to worry about the programs that might be using it (however many and varied they might be).

That's worth emphasising: on the one hand, we can check programs that use the data *without* having the actual code that manipulates the data — we did that in Sec. 8.4 above. But we are now about to see that we can in turn implement the actual code that manipulates the data *without* having to see the programs that use the data: a complementary view, looking in exactly the opposite direction. That is, we won't have to look at "use cases" at all, things like (8.9), while we are figuring out how to implement the encapsulation in (8.7).

It's *coupling invariants* that make it possible to separate the two activities: writing the code without having an implementation of the data-type, then –complementarily–

implementing the data-type without knowing anything about the code that's using it.[10]

Here the coupling invariant was given in Sec. 8.2 at (8.2), and we will use it just as we did in Sec. 8.3 for sentinels, where B was abstract and A was concrete.

In general, translating an abstract data-type to a concrete data-type is done in three steps (Secs. 8.5.2–8.5.4 below), and we will use both Sec. 8.2 and Sec. 8.3 as examples. As mentioned above (Sec. 8.1), that process is called "data refinement".

First, however, in Sec. 8.5.1 we discuss "auxiliary variables", the tools used for that job.

8.5.1 Auxiliary (aka. ghost) variables

An *auxiliary* variable, sometimes called a "ghost" variable, is one that is never used in assignments except to itself; it is not used in any condition (e.g. if, elif, else, while etc.); and it is not used in a return value from, or a formal parameter to, a function (since both are effectively assignments in disguise). More generally, a *group* of variables is collectively auxiliary if no member of the group takes part in an assignment to any variable not in the group (and no member is used in any condition etc.) So far we have seen auxiliaries used to describe loop variants (Sec. 4.1); and later we will see them used to reason about concurrent programs (e.g. Sec. 15.2 in Part III). Here they will be used to reason about transforming abstract data-types into concrete ones.

In every case, the (only) point of introducing auxiliaries is to allow them to be used in "What's true here." comments, that is, in assertions; and variants give perhaps the simplest example. An assignment n= n-1 decreases the value of n, and it might be that the decrease is all we care about. To express that with assertions, we would naturally think of

$$\leftarrow \text{ What was } n\text{'s value here?}$$
$$\dots$$
$$n= n-1$$
$$\{ \text{ n } < \text{ "the value that } n \text{ had } before \text{ the } \dots \text{ above" } \} \quad ,$$

but we would not be able to write it in that way: we cannot access n's earlier value, in the assertion, because any n written there refers to its *current* value. An obvious work-around would be to introduce another variable V say, and write

$$V= n \qquad \# \leftarrow Capture \text{ n's "before" value here,}$$
$$\dots$$
$$n= n-1 \qquad\qquad\qquad\qquad\qquad\qquad\qquad (8.11)$$
$$\{ \text{ n} < \text{V } \} \quad \# \leftarrow and \text{ it can now be referred to from here.}$$

in which V –not used in the program's actual computation– still allows us to *reason* about the program, in this case to refer to n's previous value. But if (8.11) were compiled and run "as is", both variables n and V would be present in the compiled code, even though V itself makes no contribution at all to the result(s) the program produces (and outputs), indeed does not affect the program's behaviour in any way. (Variable n does contribute of course: it is not auxiliary.) So the point of making V auxiliary is that it can be left out of the *compiled* code, but can still be used for reasoning *about* the code.[11]

---

[10] One could say that the left hand does not need to know what the right hand is doing.

[11] A sophisticated compiler might even remove V from the compiled code automatically.

Erasing it from the program text altogether would affect only our ability to *reason* about the program.

We will now use auxiliary variables to help transform an abstract program into a concrete one.

8.5.2 First step: add concrete (auxiliary) variables

We start with the Set data-type, (8.7) with its ss, and convert it gradually into one that uses a sequence qs instead. Our first step is to add the concrete, variable(s) –in this case just qs, a single sequence– to the abstract data-type, and then add further statements that maintain the coupling invariant between the abstract and concrete variables we have just added. That is, we will temporarily have *both* ss (abstract) and qs (concrete); the qs however will be only an auxiliary variable, at first, one that (as explained in Sec. 8.5.1 just above) has no effect on the execution of the procedures (methods) of the data-type: we have (temporarily) a kind of abstract/concrete hybrid and, for now, the concrete variable "just goes along for the ride". This first step gives

```
class Set:
  local:
    ss= {} # Abstract.          }    Together: but
    qs= [] # Concrete, auxiliary. } →  qs is auxiliary.

    # Coupling invariant ss == set(qs) is established,
    # because {} == set([]).

  def makeEmpty:
    # PRE: Coupling invariant holds here, but is not needed.
    ss,qs= {},[]                                          (8.12)
    # POST: Coupling invariant holds here unconditionally.

  def add(s):
    # PRE: If coupling invariant holds here,
    ss,qs= ss∪{s},qs+[s]
    # POST: then it holds here too.

  def isIn(s):
    # PRE: Coupling invariant holds here;
    return s∈ss # but we don't use it yet.
```

Ex. 8.9

In the code above (8.12), the coupling invariant between ss and qs must hold after any initialisation (local), before any read-only function (isIn), and before –and after– any updating procedure (makeEmpty, add). But we are not using it yet.

That was the first step.

8.5.3 Second step: use the coupling invariant

The second step in the translation procedure is to use the coupling invariant to swap the roles of the abstract and the concrete variables. In (8.12) the abstract variable ss is "real" and the concrete qs is auxiliary. We want to swap that around, to make qs become real and ss become auxiliary; and so we must remove ss from the return of isIn while preserving the meaning of what is returned: when ss becomes auxiliary, it is no longer allowed to appear (in this case) in a return statement. For that we introduce the loop from (8.1). For the moment, provided it terminates (and it does), it has no effect on isIn() at all:

```
class Set:
  ⋮
  def isIn(s):
    # PRE: Coupling invariant holds here, before.
    b= False
    for q in qs:
      if q==s: b= True; break
    { b == s∈set(qs) }      ⟵ Established by the loop above.
    # Coupling invariant still holds here, which gives us...
    { b == s∈ss }    ⟸ this also (where ss has replaced set(qs)),
    return b         allowing "return s∈ss" to become "return b".
```
(8.13)

But it allows us to rewrite the **return** statement so that it no longer refers to **ss**. That is, because the loop establishes the postcondition ⟵ , the coupling invariant then tells us that ⟸ holds too, and it is what allows us to replace the **return s∈ss** by **return b**, which by eliminating the reference to **ss** has made it auxiliary in the class as a whole. (Its use elsewhere is only in assignments to itself.)

Ex. 8.10

8.5.4 Third step: remove abstract (now auxiliary) variables

After our changes in Sec. 8.5.3 just above, we find that it is now **ss** that is auxiliary, and **qs** has become "real" in its place — exactly the opposite of the situation in Sec. 8.5.2 earlier. And because it's **ss** that is now auxiliary, we can remove it altogether; that gives

```
class Set:  # This is the actual implementation.
  local: qs= []

  def makeEmpty: qs= []
  def add(s): qs= qs+[s]

  def isIn(s):
    b= False
    for q in qs:
      if q==s: b= True; break
    return b    .
```
(8.14)

Ex. 8.11 One might now ask "How do we re-check our reasoning at (8.9) about (8.8) –which reasoning used the *abstract* Set in (8.7)– now that we are supplying the *concrete* Set in (8.14) instead?"

The (surprising) answer –hinted above– is that *we don't have to (re-)check at all!* The check (8.9) using the abstract form remains valid. That is, we checked our program using the abstract data-type, but when we run it we supply the concrete data-type — *and we can be sure that it will still work...*

> ... provided the abstract and concrete data-types together respect the coupling invariant,

> *and we follow the rules illustrated here, and summarised in Chapter 10 below.*

The reason for splitting this process into two pieces –writing the surrounding program in terms of the abstract data-type, then implementing the abstract data-type using concrete types– is that the surrounding program is more easily checked with the abstract data-type, because we are reasoning at a higher level, as in (8.9). But for the actual code we need the concrete data-type, because the abstract code might not be supported by our programming language.

8.6 Exercises

Exercise 8.1 (p. 82) ⇓ Introduce requirements, pre- and postconditions for (8.1), and then add a loop invariant so you can check it.

Exercise 8.2 (p. 83) Find the code for (8.3) directly in terms of `A` (i.e. without using a sentinel), using the invariant

$$0<=n<=N \text{ and } x \notin A[:n] \qquad .$$

Exercise 8.3 (p. 84) What is the invariant for (8.4)? What is the variant? Check the program carefully with the invariant and variant you have chosen.

Be especially careful with the bound for the variant.

Exercise 8.4 (p. 85) ⇓ Explain why

$$n==N \text{ and False} \qquad \text{or} \qquad n!=N \text{ and } x!=A[n]$$

simplifies to just `n!=N and x!=A[n]` .

Exercise 8.5 (p. 85) Explain why

$$\text{not } (n!=N \text{ and } A[n]!=x) \qquad \text{is the same as} \qquad n==N \text{ or } A[n]==x \qquad .$$

Is it the same as `n!=N` $\Rightarrow$ `A[n]==x` ?
Is it the same as `n!=N` $\Rrightarrow$ `A[n]==x` ?

Exercise 8.6 (p. 85) ⇓ The postcondition of program (8.6) is not the same as the postcondition of program (8.3), which was our original goal. Indeed both of them are missing `0<=n<=N`, which really should be there. But even then they are *still* not the same.

Give an example that shows they are not the same, and explain "methodologically", that is in terms of moving from requirements to specifications (Sec. 19.2.2), how the difference might have arisen. Speculate about what the consequences might be.

Exercise 8.7 (p. 85) ⇓ Use the coupling invariant (8.5) to translate the assertion

$$x \notin B[:n] \text{ and } x==B[n]$$

to an assertion about `A` alone.

Hint: Consider the two cases in other examples of a similar translation.

Exercise 8.8 (p. 85) ⇓ Give the most concise formulation you can of the condition

x∉A if n==N else x==A[n] and x∉A[:n]   .

Use some natural language too, if it helps.

Exercise 8.9 (p. 89) Why is qs an auxiliary variable in (8.12)?

Exercise 8.10 (p. 90) ⇓ To check (8.13), in particular to check its { b == s∈ss }, we need an invariant for the linear-searching for-loop in isIn. What is it?

    What checking rule do we use (from App. B.2.2) to move from (⟵) to (⟸) in (8.13),? And why does it check?

Exercise 8.11 (p. 90) ⇓ Often the concrete data-type can be simplified, a sort of "tweaking" process, once the abstract variables are gone — and that is the case with isIn at (8.14). What is the simplified code for inIn? Why is it all right to change it now?

Case study
in coupling invariants:
Fibonacci numbers

9.1 Introduction: definition vs. implementation

The well-known *Fibonacci numbers* start with two 1's, then $2, 3, 5, 8 \ldots$ where each new number is the sum of the two just before.[1] Their usual definition is

$$\text{FIB}(n{+}2) \;=\; \text{FIB}(n{+}1) + \text{FIB}(n), \quad \text{with } \text{FIB}(1) = \text{FIB}(0) = 1 \quad , \quad (9.1)$$

and that leads directly to an easy (recursive) program to calculate them:

```
# --- Calculate the Nth Fibonacci number.
# PRE: N>=0
def fib(N):
    if N==0: return 1
    elif N==1: return 1
    else: return fib(N-1)+fib(N-2)
# POST: fib(N) returns FIB(N)    .
```
(9.2)

The above function is "recursive" because it can call itself, but the reason it is not a circular definition is that it does not *always* call itself. Eventually, it stops doing that and instead starts to construct the answer. The check that it *does* stop, eventually, is done with a variant; and the check that it returns the right answer, when it stops, is done with an invariant. And it's an easy check. Ex. 9.1

What makes (9.2) impractical, though, as an implementation of the requirements (9.1), is that for an N of any reasonable size it's simply too inefficient: to calculate $\text{FIB}(0)$ and $\text{FIB}(1)$ takes one call of `fib` (each), but to calculate $\text{FIB}(2)$ takes three; and $\text{FIB}(3)$ takes five. The number of calls is exponential in N . Ex. 9.2

---

[1] Some definitions start with $0, 1$, but that makes no essential difference here. Indeed Fibonacci himself started from $1, 2$.

The more efficient program that is typically used to calculate Fibonacci numbers is instead the one given in the next section, and we will explain it in detail –even though it's well known– because it illustrates two of our invariant-finding techniques from Chapter 3. And it takes time *linear* in n.

The aim of this chapter however (from Sec. 9.4 on) is to show how, using a coupling invariant, we can calculate FIB (n) in *logarithmic* time. The final (astonishing) program is given at (9.10) in Sec. 9.5.

9.2 Linear-time Fibonacci

The usual program for calculating Fibonacci numbers is this one:

```
# --- Calculate the N-th Fibonacci number FIB(N).
{ PRE: N>=0 }
f,g= 1,0 # Say that FIB(-1)==0.
for n in range(N): # INV: f==FIB(n) and g==FIB(n-1)
   f,g= f+g,f
{ POST: f==FIB(N) }     ,
```
(9.3)

where we note that in the multiple assignment `f,g= f+g,f` the before-the-assignment values of `f` and `g` are used on the right-hand side. To simplify the invariant, we introduce the convenient fiction that FIB(-1)==0.

Checking –indeed designing– that program is an example of the *iterate up* and *cascading invariants* strategies from Secs. 3.5 and 3.3.1 — the first step, iterate up, is to propose the (obvious) invariant `f==FIB(n)`. But then to code the loop body, which must calculate the next value FIB(n+1) of `f` from its current value FIB(n), we discover that we need FIB(n-1) as well, and that is the second step: the "cascaded invariant" is `g==FIB(n-1)`. And then it's done.

The next step, however, is to introduce a different representation of `f` and `g`.

Ex. 9.3
Ex. 9.4

9.3 Introducing matrices, but still linear time

If we look at the loop body of (9.3) just above, that is `f,g= f+g,f`, we see that it is equivalently the matrix multiplication

$$\begin{pmatrix} f \\ g \end{pmatrix} = \begin{pmatrix} 1 & 1 \\ 1 & 0 \end{pmatrix} \begin{pmatrix} f \\ g \end{pmatrix} \quad ;$$

and so we can rewrite (9.3) as shown in Fig. 9.1. Although the matrices make it *look* more complicated, it is in fact a simpler program because it no longer needs a cascaded invariant: it has become a simple exponential-calculating program, with the `n` and `n-1` cases combined together in the column vector for `f` and `g`. Nevertheless (9.4), like (9.3), takes linear time.

But it *is* an exponential-calculating program — and we recall that our earlier program (3.10) calculated B**E for scalars in the much more efficient *logarithmic* time, using a halving-and-squaring strategy. (It was the straightforward, but slower algorithm (3.9) that took time linear in E.) With the cleverer invariant B**E == p*b**e (though it was not an obvious one) the faster, logarithmic-time program was easy to write and check.

Using a coupling invariant, we can therefore transform (9.4) into a much faster program that calculates the Nth Fibonacci number in logarithmic time. It uses matrices rather than integers but is otherwise structurally the same as (3.10).

Figure 9.1 Fibonacci as matrix exponential

PRE: N>=0

$$\begin{pmatrix} f \\ g \end{pmatrix} = \begin{pmatrix} 1 \\ 0 \end{pmatrix}$$

for n in range(N): # INV: Inv as just below.   (9.4)

$$\begin{pmatrix} f \\ g \end{pmatrix} = \begin{pmatrix} 1 & 1 \\ 1 & 0 \end{pmatrix}\begin{pmatrix} f \\ g \end{pmatrix}$$

POST: f==FIB(N)   ,

where Inv is

$$\begin{pmatrix} f \\ g \end{pmatrix} == \begin{pmatrix} 1 & 1 \\ 1 & 0 \end{pmatrix}^{n}\begin{pmatrix} 1 \\ 0 \end{pmatrix} \quad .$$ (9.5)

This linear-time Fibonacci program, using matrices, is a simple example of *iterating up* from Sec. 3.5. It does not need a cascaded invariant as the original program (9.3) did.

9.4 Achieving logarithmic–time with matrices

Below is (3.10), the logarithmic-time exponential calculator from Sec. 3.4.1 for simple numbers, repeated here for convenience but with E,e changed to N,n:

```
# PRE: 0<=N
p,b,n= 1,B,N
# INV: B**N==p*b**n
while n!=0:
    if n%2==0: b,n= b*b,n//2
    else: p,n= p*b,n-1
{B**N==p*b**n and n==0}
# POST: p==B**N    .
```
                    (9.6)

The checking we did for that program, in Sec. 3.4.1, relied mainly on associativity of multiplication for ordinary numbers, that $a(bc) = (ab)c$. In general, an associative operator is one that can be used several times in a row without needing parentheses. Another example that does not need parentheses is $a+b+c$, because $(a+b)+c = a+(b+c)$. In particular, checking that the assignments in the above loop body maintained the loop invariant required things like

$$p * b**n \quad == \quad p * (b*b)**(n//2) \qquad \text{when n is even}$$
$$\text{and} \quad p * b**n \quad == \quad p * b * b**(n-1) \qquad \text{when n>0} .$$

Since *matrix* multiplication is associative, just as for scalars, we should be able to use the same checking strategy. (Matrix multiplication is not commutative, however.)

And so we will replace the "abstract" matrix-typed variables b and p by "concrete" integer variables, using one concrete variable for each of the four positions in a 2×2 matrix. The concrete variables are b00, b01, b10, b11 and p00, p01, p10 and p11, and the *coupling invariant* will be

$$b == \begin{pmatrix} b00 & b01 \\ b10 & b11 \end{pmatrix} \qquad p == \begin{pmatrix} p00 & p01 \\ p10 & p11 \end{pmatrix} \quad ,$$

so that the ordinary multiplications in (9.6) are replaced by matrix multiplications. The result is program (9.7) below, where the final assignment `f= p00` implements the multiplication of the final matrix by the initial (column) vector (1 0).

And indeed (9.7) calculates FIB(N) in *logarithmic* time. But now we will use invariants and auxiliary variables to simplify it significantly.

```
# Variable N is given.
b00,b01,b10,b11= 1,1,1,0                    # from (9.6) above
p00,p01,p10,p11= 1,0,0,1    # the matrix equivalent of 1
n= N

while n!=0:
  if n%2==0:
    b00,b01,b10,b11= b00*b00+b01*b10, \
                     b00*b01+b01*b11, \
                     b10*b00+b11*b10, \
                     b10*b01+b11*b11
    n= n//2
  else:
    p00,p01,p10,p11= p00*b00+p01*b10, \
                     p00*b01+p01*b11, \
                     p10*b00+p11*b10, \
                     p10*b01+p11*b11
    n= n-1
f= p00
```
(9.7)

9.5 Removing auxiliary variables

In the final assignment to `f` in (9.7) just above, only one of the four instances of `p` appears on the right-hand side. In fact, in the whole program the variables `p10` and `p11` appear only in assignments to themselves, which means they are (jointly) auxiliary. But `p01` is used in an assignment to `p00` — so it is not auxiliary, and must remain. If we remove the auxiliaries `p10` and `p11`, however, we get the new, smaller (but equivalent) program

```
b00,b01,b10,b11= 1,1,1,0
p00,p01= 1,0
n= N

while n!=0:
  if n%2 == 0:
    b00,b01,b10,b11= b00*b00+b01*b10, \
                     b00*b01+b01*b11, \
                     b10*b00+b11*b10, \
                     b10*b01+b11*b11
    n= n//2
  else:
    p00,p01= p00*b00+p01*b10, p00*b01+p01*b11
    n= n-1
f= p00      .
```
(9.8)

Yet there is more: in fact two further variables can be removed, once we notice that the program satisfies the loop invariant Ex. 9.5

$$b00 == b10+b11 \quad \text{and} \quad b01 == b10 \quad . \tag{9.9}$$

So far, that invariant has not been used — because we didn't even know it was there. But we will use it now: it means we can remove b00 and b01 (and assignments to them), replacing them on the right-hand sides as in (9.9). Doing that is another example of "tweaking" — we have already checked the program, but we are now making it slightly neater (and more efficient).

The substitutions (9.9) reduce (9.8) to the equivalent

```
b10,b11,p00,p01,n= 1,0,1,0,N
while n!=0:
  if n%2 == 0:
    b10,b11= b10*(b10+b11)+b11*b10, b10*b10+b11*b11
    n= n//2
  else:
    p00,p01= p00*(b10+b11)+p01*b10, p00*b10+p01*b11
    n= n-1
f= p00     ,
```

which (still) calculates FIB(N) in time logarithmic in N. We finish off by renaming the variables to reduce the clutter: say b10 becomes just b, and b11 becomes c, and similarly for each p. Then we get the following compact (and intriguing) program, one that is however *already checked*: it is

```
# --- Calculate FIB(N) in logarithmic time
# PRE: N>=0
b,c,f,g,n= 1,0,1,0,N
while n!=0:
  if n%2 == 0: b,c,n= b*(b+2*c),   b*b+c*c, n//2
  else:        f,g,n= f*(b+c)+g*b, f*b+g*c, n-1
# POST: f == FIB(N)    ,
```
(9.10)

where the renaming of p00 to f allowed us to delete the final assignment f= p00. (Note that if you transliterate program (9.10) into a language without multiple assignments, they will have to be replaced by single assignments done one after the other.)

9.6 Summary

What we have seen in this chapter is the transformation of a whole program from abstract to concrete form. The abstract form used matrices, and the concrete form used ordinary numbers, i.e. scalars. But the matrices occurred only *within* the program: the input and output of the program remained scalars. An added point of interest is that checking the abstract program, the matrices, had already been done when *it* was constructed in its scalar form, involving only ordinary exponentiation. Only because of that check –its explicit reliance on associativity of multiplication, for example– could we just "carry it over" to matrices, without having to start again from scratch. It's the assertions, and in particular the invariants, that made that possible.

Similarly, in Sec. 8.3 we transformed a whole (sequential search) program from an abstract form, using B, to its concrete form using A. In both cases, transformation of the program/procedure/function transformed everything except the inputs and outputs (i.e. the initial and final states). Only the "internal workings" were affected, and they were not visible from the outside — which is the main reason that such transformations work.

In Sec. 8.2, however, the various procedures of the Set class *do* input and output their internal state, in the sense that each one passes its final state on to the next procedure, where it becomes an initial state; and it's essential for their correct working that those internals are not exposed to the outside world, that is, to the surrounding program. That's achieved by "encapsulation", which is the subject of the next chapter. The internal state that is *shared* by all those functions and procedures (e.g. clear, add and isIn for the Set encapsulation) is *hidden*, accessible only by the procedures and functions supplied. It's as if the state is put in a box, on exit from one of the procedures, and the box is locked; only entering another procedure from the same encapsulation can unlock it. *Users* of the encapsulation, the surrounding program, cannot get inside the box.

9.7 Exercises

Exercise 9.1 (p. 93) ⇓ How would you adapt our invariant/variant techniques so that you could check *recursive* procedures and functions?

Exercise 9.2 (p. 93) Exactly how many calls of fib() in (9.2) does it take altogether (including recursive calls) to calculate FIB(10)? (It's nearly 200.)

Give a simple argument to show that the number FIB(n) itself is exponential in n, and then express the number of calls needed to calculate FIB(n) in terms of FIB itself... and conclude that the number of calls needed is also exponential.

Hint: "Exponential" is this context means "is at least c^n for *some* $c > 1$." You don't have to give the actual c.

Exercise 9.3 (p. 94) Fill in the detailed assertions for checking (9.3), but do it without using multiple assignment f,g=⋯ (for example because you are programming in C, whose multiple assignments behave differently). Instead introduce a "temporary" variable t to carry out the update as (three) separate assignments in the loop body.

Exercise 9.4 (p. 94) ⇓ Repeat Ex. 9.3 but this time do not introduce an extra variable t. Instead, do something "tricky" with f, g to get the effect of the multiple assignment but using only (two) single assignments. (This is how you would have to do it in *C*.) Fill in the detailed assertions that you need.

Hint: This is an excellent small problem for practising how to check assignments. Do it! You might also need App. B.2.2.

Exercise 9.5 (p. 97) Show that (9.9) is an invariant of the loop in (9.8).

Hint: Do it using substitutions for the assignments, as explained in App. B.1.1. Although it's tempting to write down equations based on what you think the loop body is doing, that's a bad idea: it would then be very easy to become confused between those variables that are "before the assignment" and those that are "after the assignment". Thinking operationally here is very prone to error.

Much better is to use the substitution approach, which avoids all that, and uses the same (elementary) algebra anyway. Actually, it organises your work so that in the end you are doing the *right* elementary algebra.

Exercise 9.6 The variables of (9.10) are b, c, p, q and of course n and N. Use a coupling invariant

$$\texttt{b' == b\%1000000 and } \cdots \texttt{ and q' == q\%1000000}$$

to transform (9.10) into one that calculates only the last six digits of FIB(N).

Since keeping only the last six digits prevents the numbers from growing arbitrarily large, you can run this program for huge values of N.

What are the last six digits of FIB(1000000)? What are the last six digits of FIB(1000000000)?[2] Can you see something surprising in those two answers?

Is it a coincidence?

---

[2] On a platform that supports unlimited-precision integer arithmetic (e.g. `Python` and `Dafny`) you can run `fastFib` without the mod and print the *whole* answer. *Roughly how many decimal digits does the N th Fibonacci number have?*

10

Encapsulated data–types: how exactly is it done?

10.1 Introduction

In Chapter 8 we introduced "coupling invariants" as a way of tying the abstract and the concrete versions of a data-type together. Like loop invariants (Chapters 2 and 3), the key idea was (again) something that is "always true", in fact "inductively true" (Sec. 3.6).

Here we will look a bit behind the scenes and see that coupling invariants are a special case of something more generally useful: the "data-type" invariant, which can describe an "always truth" for *any* data-type representation... in particular, not only those made by fusing abstract and concrete variables together (as in Sec. 8.5.2, which we will see is a special case).

10.2 Data–type invariants

Data-type invariants in general ensure that a data-type is used *consistently* in a way that preserves some important property of it. Thus coupling invariants are indeed a special case, where the important (inductive) property is that the abstract and concrete variables are coupled and remain so. It's the *consistency* that matters.

For example you might decide to represent a set as a *sorted* sequence –unlike the representation in Sec. 8.5, where sequence qs was unsorted– because you want membership tests to be efficient (say by using binary search). You would make sure that, whenever you add an element to the set, the new element is put in its proper place in the (sorted) sequence representing that set.

How can we be sure that the property of being sorted, used for (log time) efficiency in isIn(s), propagates to an entirely different function add(s) and becomes a requirement there for maintaining the "is sorted" property?

Or –a different example– if it's add(s) that has to be fast then new elements can simply be appended to the sequence that represents the set; in that case, however, when an element is removed from the set, *all* of its occurrences must be removed, not just the first one found. (Recall Sec. 8.2.) How does that propagate from "possibly add a duplicate (now)" to "remove all occurrences (later)"?

Those are two examples of "propagation" that should be highlighted, forced upon us automatically by the program-development process we follow: and coupling invariants are how it is done.

Further, using a sorted-sequence/no-duplicates example above could easily be a *second* stage of abstract-to-concrete translation: the first stage, a "quick and dirty" implementation of ss in terms of a sequence qs with possibly repeated elements (Sec. 8.5 again), might be only a prototype. Then the second stage, implemented when time allows (or the need arises), is a more sophisticated sequence version with a sorted, no-duplicates sqs, where all the procedures are altered systematically to be consistent with the fact that the sequence is now sorted. As we will see, the second translation does not have to refer to the original abstract ss version: its work –representing the set as a sequence– has been done already by our having introduced qs. The second translation works directly from qs itself, imposing only the *additional* constraint that the sequence be kept in order and without duplicates: it's still a sequence, and the original set ss is not referred to. Thus coupling invariants can compose, one after the other, as many as you like: first change a set to a sequence; then change "any" sequence to a sorted sequence. Again, a larger job can be done in smaller pieces.

All of that is, admittedly, familiar to experienced programmers (and soon will become so, for others): but writing code that works is as much an exercise in care, and good organisation, as it is in brilliant insight. As we've already remarked, it's for that reason that when a data-type representation contributes in many places to a program, it's helpful to gather all its definitions in one place textually, defined within a class, say: for then it becomes an encapsulation. The advantage is clear: it makes it easy to see whether the data-type is being used consistently, because all references to it are in one place textually. You do not have to search through the program's whole source file to find them. And if your compiler enforces the encapsulation properly, that is if the encapsulation's introduction of local scope around its internal variables is respected, you *know* that the data has been gathered in that one place — because you would get a compile-time error otherwise.

Not so familiar perhaps, but still very important, is that when the data is gathered, i.e. encapsulated that way, it is possible to check that an abstract data-type has been correctly implemented by a concrete version of it (as sets were by sequences in Sec. 8.2), again *without* searching through the rest of the program: it's all done in one place, inside the encapsulation. And if, later, you want to change the representation (which abstractly is still sets, but perhaps is now implemented concretely as binary search trees), that too is done in one place — the *same* place, inside the encapsulation.

With all that in mind, we now look at data-type invariants specifically, continuing with the Set example from Sec. 8.5.

In program (8.14) we gave an implementation for Set: earlier it had been specified abstractly in (8.7), where we showed with (8.9) how even in that earlier form it could have been used to help write a program that *used* a set for its own purposes. (It was the discussion about "more than pseudocode".) The concrete implementation we provided, in terms of sequences, was then *guaranteed* not to invalidate any of the checks that might have been performed on a surrounding program that referred only to the abstract version. "For its own purposes" means that we don't know how the set was used, and –because we followed the abstract-to-concrete transformation that a coupling invariant enables– in fact *we don't care*.

But now we might want to go even further: the implementation we have chosen uses sequences, which are possibly expensive to implement (because they might be copied around): for efficiency, we might use arrays instead. Arrays are like sequences, but are allocated just once and do not move around afterwards; but their disadvantage is that –once allocated– they are not easily extended. Can we implement our Set data-type of (8.7) with a fixed-size array, instead of the sequences we used in (8.14)? How do we find out?

What we find out is that actually we cannot implement (8.7) that way if we follow the rules we have explained, at least not as it currently stands: it will not check. Again, our systematic approach prevents us from making a mistake. Whatever the allocated size of the array we used, say some N no matter how big, if a surrounding program makes N+1 calls to its procedure add(s) with a different, that is a new s each time, an N-length array inside the encapsulation would have to store N+1 distinct values — which would be impossible for our concrete version. Since it *is* possible for the abstract version, the postulated array-based concrete version cannot be a correct representation of it.

Ex. 10.1

Thus we will have to change the abstract Set specification slightly, and we introduce some new features as we do it. Below is the altered version of the abstract data-type, a slightly different specification, written out all together in one place. We indicate the data-type invariant for the class with "DTI" (instead of the "INV" we use for loops) at its beginning, to reflect its special purpose:

```
class Set(N):  # New abstract version, capacity limited.
  # DTI: |ss|<=N                    # Data-type invariant.

  local:
    # PRE: N>=0                     # Data-type precondition.
    ss= {}

  def makeEmpty:                                                    (10.1)
    ss= {}

  def add(s):
    PRE: |ss|!=N        # Must hold when add() is called.
    ss= ss∪{s}

  def isIn(s):
    return s∈ss   .
```

It has four new features (of which the fourth, the "data-type invariant", is the most important conceptually) as follows.

The FIRST new feature is the parameter N for the whole Set class — it is the size of the set the class must be able to represent.

The SECOND new feature is the precondition PRE following the local keyword.[1] Here its condition N>=0 applies to the initialisation of the whole class, effectively a precondition for creating a Set (in this case): if that condition is false, then checking any program that creates an instance of the class *will fail.*[2] (Obviously it is pointless asking the set to be able to store at least a negative number of elements.)

The THIRD new feature is the precondition |ss|!=N placed at the beginning of add(s), which indicates *to the caller* that unless that condition holds when add(s) is

---

[1] The "local" is not a keyword in Python, where the treatment of variable scope and class initialisation is different. In Python style, however, we use a colon and indentation when several statements are needed.

[2] The precondition of the class can refer to other, global variables as well: it must hold whenever a new instance is created. See also Sec. 10.5(d) below.

Ex. 10.2
Ex. 10.3
Ex. 10.4
called, the result of the call could be arbitrary. That is, if the program calling `add(s)` does not establish the precondition, then the call will not check.

Preconditions, like the above, can be implemented at runtime by `assert` statements, common in programming languages,[3] and are intended principally as an aid to debugging. When executed, they check the condition given and, if that condition evaluates to `False`, the program is halted at that point — usually with a helpful error message that the programmer attached to the `assert` statement (and, at the very least, an indication of which `assert` it was, e.g. a line number and a trace-back). Assert statements are especially useful for catching bugs that are caused by coding errors in one place but –without the `assert`– might not actually crash the program until it had reached some other place, possibly far away.[4]

But we can (and should) check `assert` statements ourselves, while we are *writing* the program and, therefore, before the program is ever run. When you *check* an assert statement, you are making sure that its condition can never *be* false at runtime; it's the same as checking a precondition, which is why we write it that way and how we use them here. (We discuss `assert` statements further in Sec. 12.2(d) and give the rule for checking them in App. B.6.1.)

Indeed if we placed `assert |ss|!=N` at the beginning of `add(s)` (instead of the precondition), we would equivalently be forcing anyone who is checking a program that *uses* this class to make sure that `add(s)` is never called when `|ss| ==N`, because otherwise that *calling* program would fail. (This is a good way to encourage colleagues to respect the precondition *you* wrote even if they themselves have not yet learned thoroughly what Pre means.)

And now it's this new, slightly weaker specification of `Set(N)` that *can* after all be implemented with arrays, provided that the check for duplicates is done: if the encapsulation stores each element in the array only once then the Set-*user's* checks (whether encouraged by Pre or `assert`) will make sure that `add(s)` is never called in a situation where it would cause the array to overfill. That is, the assertion is imposing an obligation on the Set-user, not on the Set-implementer.

The FOURTH new feature, and our main focus, is the *data-type invariant*: it states a property that

(a) Must be established by the class initialisation, given the class precondition. (It is so established here, given the class precondition `N>=0` just after `local`.)

(b) Must be true on successful termination of any externally accessible procedure. It is, here, provided it...

Ex. 10.5
(c) ...can be assumed to hold at the *beginning* of any externally accessible procedure. It is, here, provided that only procedures in the class can assign to its variables. That is justified because whichever procedure of the class was last called before the current one, and successfully terminated, must by (b) have left the coupling invariant true.

In (10.1) within Fig. 10.2 the data-type invariant is `|ss|<=N`, written after the "# DTI" at the very beginning of the class.

A data-type invariant is therefore considered to be a checking obligation on the whole class: it is an implicit (conjunct of) the pre- and postcondition of every procedure — with the one exception that it is not a precondition of the class initialisation.

---

[3] `Python` has them.
[4] See for comparison Sec. 18.2.1 below, where it is described how an `assert` can be checked at *compile* time.

The initialisation must *establish* the data-type invariant using only the precondition for the data-type initialisation itself.

Thus in our example all three procedures `makeEmpty()`, `add(s)` and `isIn(s)` must be checked to see that they *maintain* the data-type invariant (to ensure that it is inductively true):

- The check for the initialisation is { PRE: N>=0 } ss= {} { POST: |ss|<=N }. Its precondition is supplied by the class precondition PRE (in the `local`) just before, an obligation on the calling program creating the `Set`.

- The check for `makeEmpty` is { PRE: |ss|<=N } ss= {} { POST: |ss|<=N }. Its precondition is the data-type invariant, ensuring that N>=0; that ensures the truth of the postcondition, since |{}| == 0.

- The check for `isIn(s)` is { PRE: |ss|<=N } return s∈ss { POST: |ss|<=N }. Here the check is trivial, because the procedure does not change ss.

- The check for `add(s)` is

$$\{\text{PRE:}\ |ss|<=N\ \textbf{and}\ |ss|!=N\}$$
$$ss=\ ss\cup\{s\} \tag{10.2}$$
$$\{\text{POST:}\ |ss|<=N\}\quad,$$

  where the |ss|!=N has just been supplied by the procedure's precondition, again an obligation on the caller who is warned –by the very presence of that extra conjunct– that only N distinct elements may be added to this set.[5] The precondition's two conjuncts can be simplified to merely { PRE: |ss|<N }, but here it is written out to show where its two components come from: the first is the data-type invariant, and the second is the initial assertion in `add(s)` itself.

Figure 10.1 is a possible concrete implementation of the size-limited `Set`, now using arrays and taking advantage of the assertions we have just been discussing.[6]

Ex. 10.6
Ex. 10.7

Most of that implementation is straightforward — except perhaps for the behaviour of `add(s)` when "too many" elements are added. What does `add(s)` actually do in that case? Should there be an `assert` statement there? Or a PRE: ?

(Remember that the "local" procedure `find` cannot be accessed from outside the encapsulation, and so has no data-type-invariant restrictions.)

If `ar` is full (i.e. if n==N) and a new element is added –one that isn't in the set ss already (in the abstract view)– then the array update `ar[n]= x` will actually be the assignment `ar[N]= x`, a runtime error (in the concrete view): *index out-of-range*.

But that *is acceptable* (!) in this situation (though inconvenient) because of the precondition |ss|!=N that was in the *abstract* specification of `add(s)` –at its beginning– warning that, if "too many" elements are added, then the user cannot place any reliance on the outcome. And it's the abstract encapsulation that is (or should be) the first thing the user looks at. If the surrounding program has been checked (i.e. the program for which *the user* has responsibility), the assertion will have made sure that the "too many elements" error can never occur. That is why it's *the user's* responsibility.

---

[5] Actually, what it literally says is that no element may be passed to `add` when the size of the set is already N. As we will see in Fig. 10.2, that condition can be slightly weakened.

[6] We continue to write in the `Python` style; but we will use the sequence `ar` only in "array like" ways.

Figure 10.1 An array-based implementation of Set

```
class Set(N):
  # DTI: Array "ar" contains no repeated values.

  local:
    # PRE: 0<=n<=N              # "ar" has constant size N>=0;
    ar,n= [0]*N,0              # but only ar[:n] is in use.

    local def find(s):                       # local procedure
      for i in range(n):
        if ar[i]==s: return i
      return n                                               (10.3)

  def makeEmpty: n= 0

  def add(s):
    i= find(s)
    if i==n:                  # If i!=n, then s is already there.
      ar[n],n= s,n+1
  def isIn(s):
    return find(s)!=n
```

In practice, however, as an instance of "defensive programming", we would still probably rewrite the concrete procedure add(s) as follows:

```
    ⋮
  def add(s):
    i= find(s)
    if i==n:                                                 (10.4)
      assert n!=N,"Set is already full."
      ar[n],n= s,n+1
    ⋮
```

The "assert condition,message" statement, executed at runtime, evaluates the condition and, if it is False, halts the program at that point and prints message.[7] — which is so much more informative than "Index out of range."

Here, assert is being used in both ways: at checking time, it should ensure that a user, one who is looking at this concrete version, writes code that calls add(s) properly. But if the user does not check this code, or the abstract version, and add(s) is –after all– called improperly, then at runtime the assert statement will catch the error at that point, and prevent it from propagating further. (And it will place the blame for the error where it belongs: with the *caller*.)

Ex. 10.8   *Better late than never.*

---

[7] That is Python's version of assert.

10.3 Rules for encapsulation: the basics summarised

Now that we have dealt with data-type invariants, we can bring all the earlier material of Part II together: the principal idea of encapsulation is that data –at least, non-trivial data– should be grouped textually together with the code that accesses and changes it. As already pointed out, aside from the fairly obvious general advantage of having things all in one place, there is the technical advantage that the representation of the data, or the trade-offs between speed of access and complexity of coding, can be done without affecting other parts of the program. It could be something as simple as deciding not to keep duplicates in a sequence that's representing a set (mentioned in Sec. 8.2, speeding-up deletions but slowing-down insertions) or something as complex as storing the set as a balanced binary tree (which would slow down insertions and deletions, but speed up searches).

As long as the rules below are followed, changes like that can be made behind the scenes, even when the software is already delivered and running in the field. But what are the rules, and what precisely do they guarantee?

The basic rules are given here; more advanced possibilities (including encapsulated *global* variables) are discussed in Sec. 10.5.

Rules for encapsulated data-types:

(a) The data should be gathered and declared in one place, and enclosed by an explicit indication of where the data-type definition (the class) begins and ends.[8]

This is the "encapsulation". The compiler should check automatically (with scope rules etc.) that it is enforced, in other words that statements outside the class cannot refer to variables declared locally within the class.

(b) Within the encapsulation there are a number of declarations:

(i) A declaration of all the local variables used to represent the data-type. These will not be accessible directly (i.e. will not be in scope) from outside the encapsulation, that is not directly from the surrounding program (again a compile-time error). The only way local variables can be read or written will be via procedures and functions declared *within* the encapsulation.

If the class as a whole has a precondition, it goes here.

(ii) A declaration of procedures and functions that the surrounding program can use to access the local variables. The simplest form of those is sometimes called "get-and-set methods"; but in general they may access/update the local variables in any way.

Generally such procedures/functions are called "methods".

(iii) A declaration of local procedures and functions that can be used by the procedures and functions of (ii) but may not themselves be called directly from the surrounding program. (Again, a program that does that should generate a compile-time error.) An example is `find(s)` in Fig. 10.1.

(iv) A declaration of formal parameters (if desired) of the encapsulation as a whole, which will be determined by the surrounding program when the data-type is initialised. There might be

---

[8] We have been using `Python`'s `class` declaration for that.

Figure 10.2 Part of the abstract definition of a more robust class `Set`

```
class Set(N):
    ⋮
    def add(s):
        assert  s∉ss ⇒ |ss|!=N
        ss= ss∪{s}
    ⋮
```

(10.5)

This abstract definition of the data-type `Set` is as for (10.1), but has a more tolerant `Add(s)` procedure.

---

            preconditions imposed on the formal parameters by the local-variable declarations in (b)(i). (See also (e) below.)

(c) The encapsulation may have a data-type invariant (which we have labelled DTI). If several are given, they all apply. Each (non-`local`) procedure or function may assume that the invariant holds when it is called, and must re-establish it (if necessary) if it returns to the surrounding program; but the procedure or function does not have to maintain that DTI-invariant "in between" call and return (though often it will, especially if the procedure is read-only) — *except* that it must not call one of its own non-local procedures (either directly or indirectly) if the invariant is not true at that point of call. (Why not? See App. G.4.)

    The data-type invariant usually refers only to the local variables of the encapsulation and possibly the formal parameters of the whole encapsulation. (See however Sec. 10.5.)

(d) The procedures and functions may have extra assertions, either pre-conditions or written with `assert`, and it is the *caller's* obligation to satisfy them. (An example is the assertion |ss|!=N in the `add(s)` of (10.1) for the data-type `Set`.) Each such assertion, or its corresponding `assert`, can be written at any point within the procedure or function, except that all PRE instances should be put at its beginning.

    To repeat: it is the *user* of the encapsulation that must make sure those assertions –the extra ones, not part of the data-type invariant– don't fail.

(e) The local variables may have an initialisation, and there can be a precondition that refers to the formal parameters of the class. Again, it is the class-user's responsibility to ensure that the precondition is true when the data-type is initialised.

    Given the precondition, the initialisation must establish the data-type invariant, if there is one.

  Our `Set` data-type gives us two examples of encapsulation as described above, which we now look at more closely. One we have called "abstract"; the other is "concrete". Figure 10.2 gives a slightly more robust version of (10.1).

The first, abstract example is (10.1) (and as modified in Fig. 10.2), where the local variable is (simply) the set `ss`, within the explicit indication of the data-type scope, beginning immediately after the `class Set:` declaration and ending when the outer indentation level is resumed. The surrounding program cannot refer to `ss` directly. That is (a).

Its declaration is given immediately after the `local`. That is (i). Often[9] the type of the local variable would be given here.

The procedures and functions that can access the local variable `ss` are `makeEmpty`, `add(s)` and `isIn(s)`. That is (ii). There are no local procedures or functions, as stated in (iii).

The formal parameter of the size-limited `Set` class is `N`, the maximum size of the set. That is (iv).

The data-type invariant of this class is `|ss|<=N`, that is, the size of the set `ss` may not exceed `N`. That is (c). All the externally accessible functions `makeEmpty`, `add(s)` and `isIn(s)` may assume that the invariant holds when they are called.

The procedure `add(s)` in Fig. 10.2 has an assertion $s \notin ss \Rightarrow |ss| \neq N$ which it is the obligation of the surrounding program to make true when it calls `add(s)`. It's slightly weaker than the assertion we gave earlier, in (10.1). If it is not true, the *surrounding* program could not have been checked successfully. If for some reason `add(s)` was called anyway, then it might crash — and it is allowed to do so. But recall defensive programming as in (10.4). That is (d).

The initialisation `ss= {}` has an assertion `N>=0`: it is the surrounding program's responsibility to make sure the assertion is true when the class is initialised. That is (e).

The second example is the concrete version of the `Set` class, the fixed-size array implementation (10.3) in Fig. 10.1 that we saw before:

The concrete version (10.6) from Fig. 10.3 has two encapsulation features that the abstract version did not need. It has a local procedure `find`, which is not accessible from the surrounding program; and the procedure `add(s)` has only an "implicit" precondition, which (as we will see) turns out to be the same as the *explicit* precondition in the abstract version. In concrete terms, though, if it were made explicit it would be `n==N` $\Rightarrow$ `s∈ar`, because on the concrete level there is no "ss" — instead `|ss|` is `n` and `s∈ss` is `s∈ar[:n]`.

---

[9] In `Python`, this typing is sometimes implicit.

Figure 10.3 A concrete version of Set, without `assert`

```
class Set(N):
  # DTI: 0<=n<=N
  # DTI: Array ar[:n] contains no repeated values.

  local:
    # PRE: N>=0
    ar= [0]*N
    n= 0                                    # Initially empty.

    local def find(s):                      # local procedure
    for i in range(n):                                              (10.6)
      if ar[i]==s: return i
    return n

  def makeEmpty: n= 0

  def add(s):                          # No explicit precondition.
    i= find(s)
    if i==n: ar[n],n= s,n+1

  def isIn(s):
    return find(s)!=n
```

10.4 Encapsulation rules justified

In the previous section, the rules for encapsulation were simply stated: to motivate them, we now look at Fig. 10.4. If a program –*any* program– is successfully checked using the left-hand class in Fig. 10.4 then replacing the left-hand class by the right-hand class must not invalidate that check. And it's precisely the rules for encapsulation that make that possible: by following them, we make sure that no user of the right-hand class can ever be sure that "There's not a real set ss in there."

And –as we said earlier– the process can be repeated: we could at a later stage replace the Set class a second time, for example putting in a bit more programming effort to keep the array sorted in order to speed up membership tests. And *still* no surrounding program would be affected.[10]

Indeed this second step was the motivating example we used in Sec. 8.2 and returned to in Sec. 8.4. To replace sequence qs by a *sorted* sequence sqs with no repeating variables, we would use the following coupling invariant:

> The sequences qs and sqs contain the same elements
> (ignoring repeats in qs), but sqs is sorted into
> ascending order and does not contain repeats.

The resulting new (and more efficient?) concrete encapsulation Set of sets would be as in Fig. 10.5, but functionally speaking it would *still* be indistinguishable from the original qs or ss version.

Ex. 10.9

Ex. 10.10

The relation between the left- and the right-hand programs in Fig. 10.4 is called "refinement". Saying that one piece of code, whether standing alone or an encapsulated data-type, is a *refinement* of another means that any check that succeeds on the first (less refined) one will succeed on the second (more refined) one too. If the

---

[10] We are concentrating only on the values returned by the procedures, not how fast the procedures run or how much space they take — and that is called "functional correctness". The other issues are important too but are not covered by our encapsulation rules here.

Figure 10.4 Two versions of class Set: abstract and concrete

```
class Set(N): # Abstract              class Set(N): # Concrete
  # DTI: |ss|<=N                        # DTI: Array ar[:n] contains no repeated values.
  local:                               # DTI: 0<=n<=N
    # PRE: N>=0                         local:
    ss= {}                               # PRE: N>=0
  def makeEmpty():  ss= {}              ar,n= [0]*N,0
                                       def makeEmpty: n= 0
  def add(s):
    assert |ss|!=N                     def add(s):
    ss= ss∪{s}                           i= find(s)
                                         if i==n: ar[n],n= s,n+1
  def isIn(s):
    return s∈ss                        def isIn(s):
                                         return find(s)!=n

                                       local def find(s):
                                         for i in range(n):
                                           if ar[i]==s: return i
                                         return n
```

Replacing the left-hand implementation of a fixed-size set by the right-hand one cannot invalidate the checking of any surrounding program.

We are using the original, less tolerant, `assert` on the left and have not included the "defensive" `assert` in `add(s)` on the right. (See also App. C.4.)

Figure 10.5 Implementation with sorted non-repeating sequences

```
class Set:  # Concrete, sorted, no repeats.
  # DTI: Sequence sqs is sorted, without repeats.

  local: sqs= []                            # Internal variable.

  local def binarySearch(x):
    # PRE: sqs is sorted (from data-type invariant)
    ...                      ← Fill this in later (Sec. 12.2).
    # POST: sqs[:n]<x<=sqs[n:] and 0<=n<=len(sqs)
    return n                                                      (10.7)

  def makeEmpty: sqs= []

  def add(s):
    n= binarySearch(s)
    if n<len(sqs) and s == sqs[n]: return
    else: sqs= sqs[:n]+[s]+sqs[n:]     # ... or sqs.insert(n,s)

  def isIn(s):
    n= binarySearch(s)
    return n!=len(sqs) and sqs[n] == s
```

two pieces of code have exactly the same effect then that is equality, a trivial kind of refinement.[11] An example is that the sorted-sequence sqs class is equal to the original (unordered) sequence qs class which, in turn, is equal to the original set ss version of the Set class: equality is in the sense that no surrounding program can tell the difference.

Adding a data-type invariant to a data-type *always* results in a refinement of it, no matter what that invariant might be. (Remember that being equal is a special case of refinement.)

But the array-based implementation ar of the class on the right in Fig. 10.4 is *not equal to* the fixed-size set ss specification on the left — it is actually *better*, because the ss version can fail if add is called when |ss| ==N but the ar version can fail only if n==N *and* s is not in ar already. A refinement that's not equality is called a *proper*, or *strict*, refinement.

We can now give a more precise justification for the rules of data-type encapsulation, in terms of refinement: it is that

> if you follow the rules given in Sec. 8.5 earlier, for replacing an abstract data-type definition by a concrete one, and the encapsulations themselves follow the rules given in Sec. 10.3, then the concrete version will be a refinement of the abstract version.
>
> The translation of an abstract to a concrete data-type is called *data* refinement.

It is also true that imposing an extra data-type invariant, even if you don't change the local variables, produces a refinement of the original data-type. That is effectively what we did between the versions of qs and sqs — the extra data-type invariant was that the sequence was sorted, and that was the only change. (Indeed, as a final step we could rename sqs back to qs.)

10.5 More advanced techniques

Some of the "basic" rules given in Sec. 10.3 can be relaxed for more advanced situations. In this section we explain some of those situations.

More advanced rules for encapsulations and their data refinements:

(a) The encapsulation may declare variables that are *directly* accessible from the surrounding program, as long as they cannot be *assigned to* by the surrounding program, nor their declarations be changed during a data refinement. These are sometimes called *attributes*.

(b) The surrounding program may refer to the formal parameters of the encapsulation, but it may not change them. (For example, the surrounding program may read the set-size N in (10.3); but it may not assign to it.)

(c) The coupling invariant may refer to global variables, that is those in the surrounding program, provided that the surrounding program itself does not assign to those globals. (The best way to ensure that would be to use a programming language that allows declarations of

Ex. 10.11

Ex. 10.12

---

[11] In the same way, equality ($=$) is a trivial form of ($\leq$). And the *strict* form of ($\leq$) is "strictly less than" ($<$).

constants, say labelled `const`, so that an assignment to a `const` is a syntax error.)

The same applies to the special case of imposing a further data-type invariant, without changing the variables. It too may refer to global constants.

Ex. 10.13

(d) The precondition(s) for the encapsulation (the assertions before the initialising statements in `local`) can refer to variables outside the encapsulation, with no restrictions. They do not have to be constants.

(e) An extended version of the encapsulation may have more procedures/functions than the old; but they must use the same coupling invariant.

See Appendix C for a concise summary of the above rules, in their most basic form.

10.6 Exercises

Exercise 10.1 (p. 103) ⇓ Suppose we tried to implement the ss-based (10.1) *without* adding a precondition PRE `|ss|!=N` to its `add(s)`. According to our remarks above, the rules we are following should prevent that from checking: an unbounded-in-length sequence cannot be implemented by a fixed-size array. But where is the failed check?

As you read further, keep "Where does the check-failure occur?" in mind.

Exercise 10.2 (p. 104) The assertion `|ss|!=N` at the beginning of the abstract `add(s)` in (10.1) is stronger than it needs to be. The reason it's there at all is that `add(s)` is obliged to preserve the data-type invariant `|ss|<=N`, and it does so. But let's look at it more closely.

According to our rules, the place that `|ss|<=N` must hold is actually at the *end* of `add(s)` — so let's put the assertion there instead (as an `assert`). That gives

```
def add(s):
  ss= ss∪{s}                                            (10.8)
  assert |ss|<=N
```

Then we use the program equality

$$\texttt{x= } expr\texttt{; assert } cond \quad = \quad \texttt{assert } cond'\texttt{; x= } expr$$

where $cond'$ is $cond$ with x replaced by $expr$. It's an example of "program algebra" — an equality is asserted between programs rather than, as in normal algebra, between numbers.

Use the program equality just above to rewrite (10.8) in the form

```
def add(s):
  assert ???                                            (10.9)
  ss= ss∪{s}       .
```

Do it by first using program algebra to find out what `???` is, and only then simplifying it. What do you get? Does it make sense?

Exercise 10.3 (p. 104) ⇓ Use the data-type invariant and your answer to Ex. 10.2 to explain why the assertion at the beginning of `add(s)` can be just $s \notin ss \Rightarrow |ss| \mathrel{!}= N$.

Exercise 10.4 (p. 104) Is `add(s)` allowed to break the data-type invariant if it is called when `n==N` (i.e. when the `assert n!=N` at its beginning is not true)?
   Discuss both the abstract and concrete cases.
   Hint: Think carefully about what "allowed to" means.

Exercise 10.5 (p. 104) ⇓ In condition (c) in Sec. 10.2, there is the reservation "… provided that only procedures in the class can assign to its variables." Why is that necessary?

Exercise 10.6 (p. 105) ⇓ In (10.3) the final statement of `find(s)` is `return n`. Would it not be clearer to have `return i` instead, to match the `return` in the loop body?
   Hint: See App. G.3 and App. B.4.5.

Exercise 10.7 (p. 105) ⇓ Add a `remove(s)` procedure to the abstract `Set` type of (8.7). Then add a corresponding `remove(s)` procedure to the concrete `Set` type of (10.3). Make sure the data-type invariant is respected.
   What should the specification of `remove(s)` do if `s` is not in `ss`?

Exercise 10.8 (p. 106) What does the concrete code (10.4) do when adding `s` to set `ss` in the case that $s \in ss$ already?

Ex. 10.14 **Exercise 10.9** (p. 110) ⇓ Exercise 10.7 added an extra procedure `remove(s)` to the set data-type. Is it all right in general to add new procedures? How do we decide in this case what should be done if the element to be removed is not there?
   Is it all right to remove existing procedures in a data-type?

Exercise 10.10 (p. 110) Add a procedure `remove(s)` that removes `s` from the concrete `Set(N)` of Fig. 10.4's right-hand side if `s` is there but does nothing if it's not.

Exercise 10.11 (p. 112) Take any data-type, and impose on it an additional data-type invariant Dᴛɪ `False`.
   If the rules of this chapter have been followed by the data-type, the new version is at least as good as the old: that is, any surrounding program that used the old successfully would also succeed with the new. Yet the *implementor* of that new version can now assume `False` at the beginning of every procedure, and so can place any code at all in the procedure body: infinite loops, array indices out of range, divisions by zero… or simply `skip`!
   Is there something wrong with our rules for imposing data-type invariants?

Exercise 10.12 (p. 112) ⇓ The left- and right-hand sides of Fig. 10.4 look wholly unrelated: the left-hand one is in terms of so-called "sets", which we are assuming our programming language doesn't even implement; the right-hand one uses an "array", and doesn't have sets –whether implementable or not– anywhere. How can we say that they might be "equal"?

Exercise 10.13 (p. 113) In Sec. 10.5, what is the difference between a variable in the encapsulation that is accessible (but cannot be altered) from outside, as in (a), and a variable outside the encapsulation, as in (c), that can be referred to by the coupling invariant but cannot be altered by anything?

Exercise 10.14 (p. 114) Suppose that the hidden procedure `binarySearch` in (10.7) of Fig. 10.5 were changed to be visible. Does that break the encapsulation rules?

No, it does not break the rules, because that procedure was not there before and so could just be considered to be a new procedure. Or. . .

Yes, it does break the rules, because it reveals the inner structure of the representation: searching for some "s" could reveal its position in `sqs`, which a surrounding program could then depend on. In fact you could search for all the possible values of `s`, one by one, and so deduce the exact value of `sqs`.

Which statement is correct? Either? Both?

Exercise 10.15 In (10.4), it would probably be clearer to put the `assert` just before the `if`, rather than within it. What would that look like?

Why, however, is the "behaviour is unpredictable" still important?

Exercise 10.16 ⇓ In spite of the fact that the concrete version (10.6) of the `Set` datatype does not need an explicit `assert`, it is still a good idea to write explicitly the `assert n==N` ⇒ `s∈ar` there.

Can you think of reasons other than those we mentioned, reasons that would apply at checking time?

Ex. 10.17

Exercise 10.17 (p. 115) ⇓ In spite of Ex. 10.16, it might be that there's no point in adding the assertion explicitly, as suggested, because no one would ever see it. Is that true?

Case study: the Mean Calculator [1]

11.1 Requirements and specification of the calculator

This case study in data-type encapsulation models a pocket calculator with a "find the average" function:

> First you `clear` it, then you `enter` a collection of numbers, and then you press `mean` — the calculator will display the mean (average) of the numbers you entered.
>
> After that, you can go further –enter more numbers– or clear and start again. You can also remove a number if you decide, along the way, that it should not have been included. (11.1)

The paragraph above is presented as a unit of its own, set off from the surrounding text, because it serves as an "advertisement" for this calculator, written in English so that it can be understood by anyone who is likely to want to calculate averages. It gives the *requirements*, in our earlier sense, explaining the operation of the device sufficiently enough to indicate whether it might be useful, but not covering every small detail. (For example, it does not say what happens if you try to take the mean of no numbers, or try to remove a number that you did not enter.)

The program text at (11.2) below is similar, but it is written in our `Python`-like programming language. We say "`Python`-like" because it uses the "multiset", or "bag" data-type, which we assume our whatever-like[2] programming language does not have or, at least cannot compile directly to running code. (multisets use "bag brackets" $\langle\cdots\rangle$ rather than set braces $\{\cdots\}$, and allow elements to occur more than once. That will be explained in more detail below.) But –again– it is not "pseudocode" (Sec. 8.4); again, it is more than that.

The code (11.2) below agrees with our requirements –as it is supposed to– but it says quite a bit more, and it is more precise too. Think of requirements as being used to decide whether to buy a thing, and the more detailed specification as being a

---

[1] This case study appeared earlier in Morgan, *Programming from Specifications* [43, Sec. 17.6].

[2] We could just as well give a *C*-like or a *Java*-like specification, and the following comments would also apply.

description of how it is to be used once you have bought it:

```
class MeanCalculator:              # Abstract version.
  local: nb= ⟅⟆                   # Initialise to empty.

  def clear: nb= ⟅⟆                  # Empty bag.
  def enter(n): nb= nb+⟅n⟆       # Add a single element.      (11.2)
  def del(n): nb= nb-⟅n⟆      # Remove a single element.

  def mean():                     # Calculate the mean.
    assert nb!=⟅⟆
    return ∑nb / |nb|
```

If our programming language has a precise meaning, as this one does, it can –and should– be used for writing specifications in the style above. Because it is simple (no complicated control-structures are used) and has powerful and intuitive data-types (such as multisets), it can be clear and precise at the same time. As such, it serves a dual purpose: it serves the customer/analyst, allowing the latter to answer detailed questions such as "What happens in this-or-that unusual situation?" And it serves the programmer, who ultimately must create code that behaves as the specification says it should (or better, if it's a proper refinement).

For example, answers to questions like "What happens when I press **mean** but haven't entered any numbers?" should not be part of the requirements (11.1). It's too detailed, a distraction, and is dealing with something that might never happen and which –if it does– will probably not cause a disaster. For "What happens if I delete a number that I did not enter?" the same applies.

Both those questions are answered in any case by the program text at (11.2). In the first case, there is **assert nb!=⟅⟆** , a statement which means (as we have seen) "If the condition nb!=⟅⟆ is not true, then the calculator (i.e. program) might crash at this point, or behave arbitrarily."

To answer the second question, we use the properties of multisets. A *multiset*, or *bag* is like a set except that it can have a given element more than once. (Alternatively, it is like a sequence where you have forgotten the order.) Specific multisets, like ⟅n⟆ above, are written with bag brackets "⟅−⟆" rather than set braces "{−}", and for example ⟅1, 2, 3, 2⟆ has 1 once, 2 twice, 3 once and therefore overall size 4, whereas the set {1, 2, 3, 2} has one each of 1, 2 and 3 –in spite of the repetition of 2– and so has size 3. (The repetition of "2" is ignored in the set case.) For a bag nb and potential element n, we write n∈nb for the number of times n occurs in nb: thus if n is not in nb at all then n∈nb is 0. The sum of two bags takes the sum of the memberships, so that n∈(nb1+nb2) is (n∈nb1)+(n∈nb2), and the difference is similar except that membership cannot become negative:

$$
\begin{aligned}
& n \in (nb1-nb2) \\
== \quad & n{\in}nb1 - n{\in}nb2 \quad \text{if} \quad n{\in}nb1 >= n{\in}nb2 \quad \text{else} \quad 0 \quad .
\end{aligned}
$$

A notational convenience is to be able to write n∈nb where a Boolean is expected, in which case we understand it as shorthand for (n∈nb)!=0; and if we write n∉nb for a bag nb we always mean (n∈nb) == 0.

With bags now understood, we can see how (11.2) answers the question "What happens if I delete a number n that I did not enter?" In that case, the bag nb is unchanged, because n∈nb cannot become negative.

11.2 Implementation of the calculator

It is not hard to implement the `MeanCalculator` using sequences (if the programming language provides them), since a sequence (concrete) represents a bag (abstract) if you ignore the order. But actual pocket calculators might not do that. Instead they might be able to keep only the sum of the numbers entered, giving the following as a possible concrete implementation:

```
class MeanCalculator:   # Concrete version,
                        # using a running total.
  local: s,c= 0,0 # Natural numbers.

  def clear: s,c= 0,0
  def enter(n): s,c= s+n,c+1                       (11.3)
  def del(n): s,c= s-n,c-1        # Hmm... See below.

  def mean():
    assert c!=0
    return s/c    .
```

It has been designed using the coupling invariant $\mathtt{s}{==}\sum\mathtt{nb}$ and $\mathtt{c}{==}|\mathtt{nb}|$ and the | Ex. 11.1 | methods of Sec. 8.5. But as part of that design process for `del(n)`, we would have found ourselves checking the hybrid fragment

$$\{\,\textsc{Pre}\colon\ \mathtt{s}{==}\textstyle\sum\mathtt{nb}\ \text{and}\ \mathtt{c}{==}|\mathtt{nb}|\,\}\qquad\leftarrow\ \textit{coupling invariant assumed}$$
$$\mathtt{nb,s,c}{=}\ \mathtt{nb}{-}\lbrace n\rbrace,\mathtt{s}{-}\mathtt{n},\mathtt{c}{-}1 \qquad\qquad (11.4)$$
$$\{\,\textsc{Post}\colon\ \mathtt{s}{==}\textstyle\sum\mathtt{nb}\ \text{and}\ \mathtt{c}{==}|\mathtt{nb}|\,\}\ \leftarrow\ \textit{coupling invariant re-established}\quad.$$

The fragment is "hybrid" because it contains both the abstract `nb` and the concrete `s,c`, with its pre- and postcondition expressing that the coupling invariant is maintained; and it would not have checked *unless* $\mathtt{n}{\in}\mathtt{nb}$, because only then does the number of instances of `n` in the abstract `nb` actually decrease; but the concrete `c` is decreased unconditionally. A gross failure of the check occurs for example when some `n` is removed from the empty bag: in the abstract calculator `nb` remains empty; but in our concrete calculator the count `c` becomes -1. A natural question –faced with the check failure– is to try to fix the implementation, or the coupling invariant or both, so that the check succeeds. But in fact that's not possible: if the implementation is recording only the sum and count of the entered numbers, there is no way in general that it can remove a specific number. Instead, we have discovered an oversight in the abstract *specification*, and that is what we must fix.

One way to repair the specification would be to remove the `del` button on the calculator altogether. Another would be to replace it with an `undo` button that would remove the most recently entered number (but could be used only once). A third way (which we will now take) is to alter the specification so that it *requires* the deleted number to be one that was entered at some point (but not necessarily the most recent one). We'd add that as an assertion to the abstract version

```
def del(n):
  assert n∈nb                                      (11.5)
  nb= nb-⌊n⌋    ,
```

and the effect would be (just as for "adding too many elements to the set" in (10.1)) that a calling program that violated that requirement would not itself check.

When the coupling invariant and concrete variables are added to that we'd have this hybrid instead, the code

```
def del(n):
    { s==∑nb and c==|nb| }              ← Can assume this.
    assert n∈nb
    nb= nb-⌊n⌉                                          (11.6)
    s,c= s-n,c-1
    { s==∑nb and c==|nb| } ← Must re-establish this if del terminates.
```

Ex. 11.2 which does check — even though it does *not* re-establish the coupling invariant when n∉nb: instead, in that case, it fails to terminate, because the assert condition is false. (Recall the qualification "on successful termination" from Sec. 10.2(b).)

To remove the abstract nb= nb-⌊n⌉ from (11.6), however, we need nb to be auxiliary — yet it is used in the assert n∈nb, and we cannot express that n∈nb in terms of the concrete s and c. The solution is to remove the whole assert: first weaken its condition to True (App. C.3(a)), and then remove it altogether (e). Once it is gone, variable nb *is* auxiliary, and so we can remove nb= nb-⌊n⌉ as well. That gives us the simple code

```
def del(n):
    # This works only if n is still in the bag:
    # consult the abstract specification!                (11.7)
    s,c= s-n,c-1
```

for the concrete implementation — which, remarkably, is just what we had before in (11.3)! (There is an added comment, however.) But it checks now, because what it
Ex. 11.3 checks *against* –that is, the abstract (11.5)– has changed.

In fact it's the comment itself which plays the star role: why *must* it be included? Again, it is defensive programming: without the comment, the justification for a runtime failure here would be found only in the abstract specification. It cannot be explained, or even *expressed*, in terms of the variables s,c actually in the code. So, in this case, the careful development procedure we follow has told us not only what kind of comments we should use ("What's true here.") — it has also told us whether there needs to be a comment at all. Here, it's absolutely needed.

11.3 Exercises

Exercise 11.1 (p. 119) ⇓ Is the assert c!=0 necessary in mean() in (11.3)?

Exercise 11.2 (p. 120) In the discussion of the failed check at (11.4), it was suggested that the del operation be replaced by an undo. Do that, and give both the bag version and the sum version of the MeanCalculator class.

Then explain what happens (is "allowed" to happen) if undo is (i) pressed twice in a row, or is (ii) pressed when the bag is empty.

Hint: You might have to add extra variable(s).

Then give the coupling invariant that you've used to connect your specification and implementation.

Another hint: The coupling invariant might have to refer to the extra variable(s) you could have added.

Exercise 11.3 (p. 120) In the code of (11.7) it's clear that calling `del` "too often" could make the variable `c` negative. Yet `c` is supposed to be the number of elements in the bag, whose mean will eventually be asked for. How can a bag have a negative number of elements? What's going on? Is the code of (11.7) correct?

12

Summary of Part II

12.1 What is obvious

Part II has been about organising the *data* in your programs. (Part I was about "organising" the programs themselves.) The main point was that it is good style to group conceptually related variables, to encapsulate them and their associated procedures and functions, together in one place: it's as simple as that.[1]

For example, when the programmer is *thinking* about a "set-valued" variable which the algorithm relies upon conceptually, the program code which *implements* that set within an array can then be considered easily, all at once, without having to search through a file or leaf through a printout.

It would be silly, for example, in (10.6) to put the declaration of our set-implementing array `ar[0:N]` in one place, and yet to put the `n`, which indicates how many values are currently stored in the set, in some other place, and then maybe the initialisation `ar= [0]*N` somewhere else again. It's common sense *not* to do that.

Much of "common sense" however turns out to have sound engineering principles behind it. In this case, the grouping together of the related data and procedures enables systematic and *practical* techniques that simplify the understanding, checking and maintenance of large programs: we separate their components into portions that can be dealt with one at a time. In particular, one of the main themes of Part II has been the way in which the implementation of a sophisticated data-type can be altered "behind the scenes" by taking advantage of an absolute guarantee that such alterations won't invalidate an already-checked program "unaware" of those alterations.

We will return to that issue of "already checked" in Sec. 12.3 below. In between, however, we examine some interesting possibilities of abstract vs. concrete and specification vs. implementation that have been suggested by the way we have been organising our data-types.

---

[1] And such encapsulation is one part of the "why" of object-oriented programming — which we don't treat in this text. (See however App. G.4.) Further features of object-oriented programming include "inheritance", where more specific types can be derived from others, and "instantiation" (where a single class definition can serve as a template for many realisations of it).

12.2 Specifications vs. implementations: how are they connected?

In Fig. 10.4 we showed two version of the Set data-type: the left-hand one was in terms of size-limited sets directly, using a set-valued variable ss; and the right-hand one used *two* variables: an array ar and a "How full is it?" variable n.

The left-hand "abstract" version in Fig. 10.4 made it clear what could be done with the set, and it could also answer more obscure issues like "What happens if you try to remove an element that is not there?" (after we have added a remove() procedure as well, as in Ex. 10.7).

The larger issue here is, however, that the abstract version allows a programmer to check a surrounding program, using that abstract version, *even though* the abstract, set-valued variable ss might not be supported directly in the programming language being used. That was the point of our example (8.9), and it is again an example of "more than (just) pseudocode". It's an astonishing advantage of abstraction, and –at least at first– it might not be obvious that it's even possible.

The right-hand "concrete" version in Fig. 10.4 shows how to write the Set data-type in the programming language we actually have. That is, the left-hand side "specifies" and the right-hand side "implements". That they correspond is precisely what the rules for encapsulation in Sec. 10.3 achieve: indeed, the rules were *designed* to make that possible.

Inside the right-hand version, however, we find another opportunity for specification vs. implementation. The find(s) function is local, not accessible from outside the encapsulation, and we used it in two places to see whether element s was already in the set. (Remember, the set is ss on the left and ar[:n] on the right.) While coding that implementation, it was a bit of a nuisance to have to "take time out" to write the body of find(s), the linear search of ar, with its for-loop, where really all we wanted to do was to say what find(s) was for, what it was supposed to do. We had to get even *more* concrete there, temporarily, deciding whether to search the array from its beginning (range(n)) or its end (range(n-1,-1,-1)) because sought-for elements are perhaps more likely to have been added recently — or even to implement binary search if we had decided to keep the array ar in ascending order.

Having to dive briefly into those details is distracting and, because distraction is energy-sapping, it is also error-prone. Much better would be to be able to say what find(s) must do *without* (at this stage) having to say how it does it. Chapter 10 has a nice example of that in its Fig. 10.1, where it would have been nice not to have to give the array-searching code just then: it's a "we can do that later" moment...[2] just as in (10.7), where rather than write out the code of binarySearch, we wrote "···" but at the same time gave a pre- and a postcondition that would be checked later, when the dots ··· were actually filled in. (They could even be supplied by someone else, say a more junior programmer: we would use the Pre and the Post to check the code of our class, in effect looking outwards; the junior programmer would use the very same Pre and Post to check the code replacing the "···", but looking inwards.)

---

[2] There is also a nice example in Sec. 17.10 of Part III to come, where a "count the black-coloured nodes" specification is introduced, which we don't bother to implement until we have checked that counting those black nodes actually does the job that the surrounding program requires it to do.

In Fig. 10.4, using the same technique could mean that we would write

```
local def find(s):
  # PRE: 0<=n<=N
  ...
  # POST: ar[i]==x if 0<=i<n else x∉ar[:n]
return i   ,
```
(12.1)

and we wouldn't have to write the actual for-loop until later. The postcondition on its own is all we need to know in order to use function find correctly within add and isIn.

We will now –finally– introduce an abbreviation that makes all that easier. We have been writing

```
# PRE: pre
prog
# POST: post
```
(12.2)

for some specific precondition *pre*, postcondition *post* and program *prog* and then asserting "This program works." if whenever *prog* is started in a state satisfying *pre* then it will finish in a state satisfying *post*. But we have been saying that "after the fact", when we have our program *prog* already and we want to check it.

Yet now we are seeing that it would also be useful to be able to write "We will supply a program *prog* such that (12.2) works." in a similar way, when we know what *pre* and *post* are but (of course) not yet *prog*: for that, we have been writing

```
# PRE: pre
...
# POST: post
```
(12.3)

with the dots indicating where our code must be put in order to check it.

The "streamlining" is to introduce this abbreviation for the whole of (12.3). By x:[*pre*,*post*]   we mean "some code that, when replacing ··· just above, will make (12.3) work while changing only variable(s) x in the process." Thus x can be a list if we want: it is called the *frame*, and the whole thing is called a *specification* — it has a frame, a precondition and a postcondition. Although we don't know (and at this stage, don't care) what that code actually is, because we know what "(12.3) works" means, we *do* know that the code –whatever it turns out to be– will have these properties:

(a) If its initial state does not satisfy *pre* then the code can do anything at all. Given that the specification says clearly what is expected of the initial state, that seems fair.

(b) If the initial state *does* satisfy *pre*, then the code must ensure that its final state satisfies *post* while changing only variable(s) x. The specification says that clearly too.

As an extra convenience, however, we introduced the convention that

(c) The code can change only variables in the list x — and that allows us to introduce some useful further abbreviations:

(d) The specification [*pre*,True] (with no x:) that insists on the initial state's satisfying *pre*, but changes no variables at all, must do nothing if indeed *pre* holds; but if *pre* does not hold, it can crash — and its meaning is exactly what we have been using "assert *pre*" for already.

Ex. 12.1

(e) The specification x:[*post*], where the precondition is missing, takes a default
    precondition of True. And furthermore...

(f) For the specification x:[*post*], allowing *any* initial state but establishing *post*
    while changing only x, we can write   assume x:*post* . (For more about assume
    see App. B.6.3.)

    If it is allowed to change *no* variables at all then we leave the x: off, writing
    just   assume *post*.

Once we put (c)–(f) all together, we have a nice vocabulary for specifying what
programs must do, and writing their specifications at the moment we realise we need
them. We do that *before* we go on to find the code. And so our motivating example
(12.1) can be replaced by the simple code fragment

```
local def find(s):
  i:[0<=n<=N , ar[i]==x if 0<=i<n else x∉ar[:n] ]
  return i    .
```

It could also be written

```
local def find(s):
  assert 0<=n<=N
  assume i:(ar[i]==x if 0<=i<n else x∉ar[:n])
  return i    .
```

Ex. 12.2

Ex. 12.4

Ex. 12.5

Ex. 12.6

Now that we have a concise way of writing specifications, we can even give rules
for using them directly in checking programs (App. B.6.3).

12.3 What is *not* obvious

It might not be obvious why the rules of Sec. 10.3 work, that is *why* they guarantee
that for all possible surrounding programs a concrete implementation data-type will
be as good as the abstract data-type that it came from. How could we ever check *all*
possible surrounding programs?

The coupling invariant is the key, and it works in a similar way to a loop invariant
which, after all, guarantees that once the loop has finished the invariant will still be
true — no matter how many iterations have occurred (even none).

For the loop invariant, you reason "If there are no iterations, the invariant is true
after the loop ends because it was true just before the loop would have begun — but
the loop was not entered at all." And "If there is just one iteration, then it's true after
the loop because we have checked that a single iteration preserves the invariant."
    And if there are two iterations, then it's still true because that's just one more than
one iteration, and we already know (just above) that the invariant is still true after
just one iteration. So it's still true now, as well." And from three on, it's the same
argument again, each time referring to the one before.[3] (Recall Sec. 3.6.)

For the abstract and concrete data-types, the reasoning is similar. You imagine
both of them executing in parallel, as in Sec. 8.5.2 where we (temporarily) had both
the abstract and the concrete variables together, and then you see that no matter

---

[3] This is a proof by induction, written out in words.

how many times the operations of the data-type are called, and with no matter what parameters, the abstract and the concrete version will give the same answer (if they are functions) and will result in final states whose abstract and concrete parts correspond according to the coupling invariant. In more detail:

- At the beginning, both the abstract initialisation and the concrete initialisation are executed (in parallel). If the abstract initialisation terminates then the concrete initialisation must terminate too. And the rules say that executing the two of them together must establish the coupling invariant. So the coupling invariant is true after (a terminating) initialisation.

- When, for the *very first* time, an operation on the data-type is called, the data-type invariant is true (as stated just above). And so (1) the two operations, the abstract and the concrete, return the same answer (if they are functions), and (2) the coupling invariant is re-established afterwards.

- When, for the *second* time, an operation on the data-type is called, the data-type invariant is still true from the first time, because the scope rules do not allow the surrounding program to invalidate it between the two calls.[4] And so again the two operations, the abstract and the concrete, return the same answer (if functions), and the coupling invariant is re-established afterwards — ready for the *third* operation.[5]

- And so it continues, using an inductive argument in a way similar to the description we gave for loop invariants in Sec. 3.6.

Some of the rules for encapsulation are necessary to make the argument above work. The remaining rules –mainly to do with certain variables not being assigned to– are what make sure that the surrounding program cannot falsify the coupling invariant. (Recall our earlier comment in Sec. 9.6 about encapsulation being like "putting the internal state in a locked box".) If it could, we would not be able to string the constructs together as we did, with each operation able to assume the coupling invariant at its start, because it was (re-)established by the operation before, at its end. Specifically, the encapsulation rules are:

- We don't allow the surrounding program to assign to the encapsulation's local variables, because we have no way of checking that those assignments will preserve the coupling invariant. (Remember — we don't even know what the surrounding program is.)

- And –in the other direction– we don't allow the coupling invariant to refer to non-constant variables in the surrounding program because, again, that surrounding program might change them and so falsify the coupling invariant.

---

[4] That is, the surrounding program cannot change the encapsulated variables because it cannot even refer to them.
[5] Again... This is a proof by induction, written out in words.

12.4 Exercises

Exercise 12.1 (p. 125) ⇓ Can the specification [*pre*,True] change the program variables if executed when *pre* is false, i.e. if the program is allowed to crash? There is no x: written there...

Exercise 12.2 (p. 126) The code below is from add(s) in the right-hand encapsulation of Fig. 10.4, but replacing the code i= find(s) with its actual body, assuming that body has been written as a specification, as in

> \# Code of add(s), with find written as a specification.
> \# PRE: (s∉ar[:n] ⇒ n!=N) and *dti*
>
> i:[0<=n<=N ,   ← *specification of* find
>   ar[i]==x if 0<=i<n else x∉ar[:n]]⁶   (12.4)
>
> if i==n: ar[n],n= s,n+1   ← *implementation of* add(s)
>
> \# POST: s∈ar[:n] and *dti*   ,

where *dti* is the data-type invariant, viz.

> \# DTI: Array ar[:n] has no repeats.
> \# DTI: 0<=n<=N   ,

of the right-hand encapsulation in Fig. 10.4 that we are starting from.

We have surrounded (12.4) with PRE and POST, so that we can check that add(s)
Ex. 12.3 really does add s to the set.

Using only the specification of find(s) *(i.e. as in-lined in the code above), check that (12.4) works.*

Remember though that this is only an *exercise*, because add in its concrete version does not *have* to be checked: we know already that it works — because it has been constructed, using a coupling invariant, from the abstract version while following the rules of Sec. 12.3.

Hint: To get the best from this exercise, you should check *every detail.* Once you have more experience, in similar work you will be able to skip the simpler steps with less risk of error.

Exercise 12.3 (p. 128) ⇓ In Ex. 12.2, the PRE for our proposed check contains the condition s∉ar[:n] ⇒ n!=N. But that happens to be precisely the condition required for termination of the concrete code for add(s) — if it does not hold then add(s) will attempt to access ar[N], which gives an index-out-of-range error.

Doesn't it seem like cheating, therefore, to include that condition in the PRE? It's like assuming the very thing you need for the check to go through, which surely defeats the whole purpose of the check.

Where does the condition really come from, and why isn't it cheating to include it?

---

⁶ The specification's postcondition "ar[i]==x if 0<=i<n else x∉ar[:n]" is a Python *conditional expression*. In general A if C else B has value A if C has value True, otherwise value B.

Exercise 12.4 (p. 126) ⇓ Go all the way back to (3.12) ("Length of the longest run" within "Find the strict majority") and insert a specification where the comment says "Put a 'sort sequence A' program fragment here." How precise do we need to be?

Exercise 12.5 (p. 126) ⇓ As they are used in this text,[7] what is the difference between these notations?

(a) *# cond*

(b) *{cond}*

(c) Either of the above, beginning with an annotation PRE, POST, INV... etc?

(d) assert *cond*

(e) assume *cond*

Exercise 12.6 (p. 126) ⇓ Explain informally why x: [*pre, post*]   is the same as

    assert *pre*
    assume x: *post*   .

---

[7] These are not by any means universal conventions, and you can invent your own. What's important is to understand the various uses to which conditions *cond* can be put, and to be consistent.

Part III

Concurrency — and how to check it

What is "concurrency"?

13.1 Introduction to concurrent programs

Concurrent programs are *groups* of conventional programs ("conventional" as in "like those we have considered so far") that execute *all at the same time* and *interact with each other as they execute.* Up to now, we have been considering only programs executing alone. The kinds of interactions we will see here however, with groups executing together, are those where simultaneously executing programs can share variables between them, and can read and update those variables independently of each other.

Here is perhaps the simplest possible example:

```
# Initially, i.e.  what's true at the very start:
  { PRE: x==0 }
```

```
# One (conventional) program:     call it Thread 1
  x= x+1
                                                    ← concurrent
                                                      system
# Another (conventional) program:  call it Thread 2
  x= x*2
```

The individual programs running concurrently, also described as "in parallel", are sometimes called "threads", as for Thread 1 and Thread 2 above, which we will abbreviate *Th*1 and *Th*2. A typical way of indicating that two (named) threads are executing together in parallel is to write

$$Th1 \ || \ Th2 \quad , \tag{13.1}$$

with the symbol "||" suggesting "in parallel"; and the effect is to allow each of the two programs to execute as it usually would... except that at any moment its variables might be altered "behind its back" by the other program.

In the case above, we might ask "What will the final value of x be if the concurrent system in (13.1) is run from an initial state x==0?" The answer is not determined:[1] it depends on which of the two threads goes first. If *Th*1 goes first then x will be (0+1)*2 == 2 afterwards; but if *Th*2 goes first then x will be (0*2)+1 == 1.

---

[1] The technical term for that is "nondeterministic".

That uncertainty –obviously– can be quite tricky to deal with, especially if the programs are complicated even on their own. The "interleaving" style of computation allows the threads' individual statements to execute in any order that respects their individual coding, and there can be many, indeed very many, possibilities for that interleaving. For example if each of our threads *Th1, Th2* had *two* statements instead of just one, say A then B in the first and C then D in the second, then the possible interleavings of their individual statements would be ABCD, ACBD, ACDB, CABD, CADB, CDAB, that is six possibilities in all. (If they were not run in parallel, there would be only two possibilities: first one then the other or vice versa, that is ABCD or CDAB. But when there are six possibilities, checking the program would –in principle– require checking all six of those interleavings.)

But before going on to show that checking concurrent programs is not (quite) as bad as the above makes it sound, we should at least make it clear why we need concurrent programs at all. In the next section we give a simple reason: it is that most activities (in the world) go on concurrently, and although many do not interact with each other very much, in some cases there is intense interaction — as we are about to see: thousands of automated teller machines throughout a whole country are active at the same time; and they interact with each other through the bank accounts to which they share access. If they were kept separate, it would be as if every bank transaction had to be done at head office, where there was exactly one bank teller and a (very long) single queue.

At the other extreme, in Chapter 17 we give another motivating example: concurrent activities within a single computer, deep in its operating system. Here the activities are not physically separated from each other but, for efficiency, they must both be active most of the time: it's not practical (as we explain there) to make each one execute alone.

So –since we must live with concurrent programs– we must learn how to check them. This Part III of our text shows one way that is done, mainly in Chapters 14 and 15.

13.2 A small example: automatic teller machines

Suppose there are two automated teller machines that can be used simultaneously. We imagine that their code is something like (13.2) below, where we're using bb to represent your bank balance (stored centrally), and c1 and c2 to represent the amount of cash you ask for, and cc to represent the cash you have with you (say in your wallet):

```
# ATM1 -- Withdraw c1.
if c1<=bb: # Examine balance.
  bb,cc= bb-c1,cc+b1 # Cash withdrawn at ATM1,
                     # now with you.
                                                              (13.2)

# ATM2 -- Withdraw c2.
if c2<=bb: # Examine balance.
  bb,cc= bb-c2,cc+c2 # More cash withdrawn, at ATM2...
```

Each *ATM* examines your balance, whether you have sufficient funds and, if you do, delivers your cash c1, c2 respectively into your wallet cc. If you use one *ATM* and then the other (and you have at least c1+c2 in your account), which you could call *serial* use, then afterwards you will have bb-c1-c2 in your account, and cc+c1+c2 in your wallet. If initially you have nothing in your wallet and BB in your bank account, that is cc==0 and bb=BB, then BB == bb+cc is an invariant of the whole system, you and the bank considered together, and it is maintained no matter which *ATM* you visit first.

Provided BB>=0, a second invariant is bb>=0 — meaning that you cannot withdraw more than you have in your account.

But suppose now that you and a friend visit the two machines at the same time, which we could call *concurrent* use, and that each *ATM* communicates with the bank twice: first it examines your balance, and then it notifies the bank that it has dispensed cash to you. Let's say that your account has $100, that is initially BB==bb==100, and both you and your friend ask to withdraw the whole $100 from your account — that is c1==c2==100. Each *ATM* asks the bank whether you have $100 in your account, one then the other, and each receives the answer "Yes." Those are the first two actions.

The third and fourth actions are that you and your friend *both* withdraw $100, and your balance is finally *minus* $100 — so that you are overdrawn. Although the first invariant BB == bb+cc is maintained (assuming your friend hands over your cash), the second invariant bb>=0 has been broken.

That simple example, and others like it, motivates the first three of the several interesting issues that concurrency introduces: they are "atomicity", "locks" and (as we saw earlier) "threads".

We begin with *atomicity*. What went wrong in the concurrent scenario above is that the step-by-step separate activities of the two friends occurred in an unexpected order: it was

```
    if c1<=bb:                       #  ATM1 examines c1<=bb.
                if c2<=bb:           #  ATM2 examines c2<=bb.
    bb,cc= bb-c1,cc+c1               #  Withdrawal at ATM1.    (13.3)
                bb,cc= bb-c2,cc+c2   #  Withdrawal at ATM2.
```

If the visits had instead been serial –that is, all of one before any of the other– then the order might have been

```
      if c1<=bb:                     #  ATM1 examines c1<=bb.
        bb,cc= bb-c1,cc+c1           #  Withdrawal at ATM1.
              if c2<=bb:             #  ATM2 examines c2<=bb.
                  skip               #  Denial at ATM2.
```

where we remember that an if whose conditions are false can be thought of as executing else: skip. Each of those smaller pieces is called *atomic* because it is executed by the bank in one piece: it cannot be further subdivided. In general, we indicate that a statement is atomic by writing it on a single line.

The second issue introduced by the *ATM* example is the use of *locks*, which is how we fix the problem illustrated by (13.3) just above. Obviously what real banks must do, instead of (13.2) in Fig. 16.2, is something like this:[2]

---

[2] In Python there are function calls acquire() and release() corresponding to the (fictitious) commands lock and unlock that we're using here for these examples. There many different schemes for concurrency and locks: we are concentrating just on the essentials.

```
# ATM1                           # ATM2
lock bb # Lock the account.      lock bb # Lock the account.
if c1<=bb:                       if c2<=bb:                        (13.4)
  bb,cc= bb-c1,cc+c1               bb,cc= bb-c2,cc+c2
unlock bb # Unlock the account.  unlock bb # Unlock the account.
```

The effect is to convert the whole of the program text shown for *ATM1* into a single atomic action (and the same for *ATM2*) — thus *ATM2* cannot "interrupt *ATM1* in the middle of its action" (or vice versa).

The third issue is *threads*. As we said above, the two programs *ATM1* and *ATM2* above are called "threads" and, in general, a thread gives a guaranteed execution order for its *own* constituent atomic actions only. Thus the code of *Th1* guarantees that `if c1<=bb:` will occur before `bb,cc= bb-c1,cc+c1` (or the `else`); but it has nothing to say about the `if c2<=bb:` and `bb,cc= bb-c2,cc+c2`. That's the concern of *Th2*.

We'll now look the first two of those issues in more detail.

13.3 Atomicity of expressions and assignments

As mentioned above, we indicate that a statement is *atomic* by writing it on a single line: thus our writing `x= y-z` on one line expresses *our* conviction that, while a thread is executing it, interruption from *another* thread between this thread's reading `y` and reading `z`, or between its having read both and then assigning their difference to `x`, is not possible. In some cases however that might be unrealistic, and then a finer grain of atomicity should then be considered — together with the more detailed reasoning it will require.

Suppose for example that arithmetic operations cannot be done on variables directly: instead, their constituent values (such as `y, z`) must first be loaded into machine registers, then the operations carried out there, and finally the result stored back into a variable (e.g. into `x`) — with (only) the loads, the subtraction and the store-back each being atomic on its own. In that case the `x= y-z` above might actually be an abbreviation of the four, smaller and separate atomic steps

```
r1= y          # The r variables are machine registers.
r2= z
r0= r1-r2                                                          (13.5)
x=  r0   ,
```

where variables `r0, r1, r2` are accessible only to the thread that is notionally executing `x= y-z`[3] — that is, they can neither be read nor written by other threads. Those other threads however could still execute statements referring to `x, y` or `z` *between* the statements above, in which case the overall effect might *not* be the `x= y-z` intended.

To respect the likely reality of (13.5) –and similar– being what "actually happens", we will usually indicate (and therefore assume) atomicity only for statements in which at most a *single* variable is accessed that is not local to the thread executing the statement, where multiple (read) accesses on the right-hand side (to the same variable) count as just one access, but a (write) access on the left-hand side is counted separately from read access(es) on the right.

Ex. 13.1

Ex. 13.2

---

[3] They could be *CPU* registers, for example.

13.4 What simple locks guarantee

The `lock bb` / `unlock bb` combination introduced in (13.4) just above works by guaranteeing that there cannot be more than one `lock bb` executed in a row, that is without an `unlock bb` in between. Usually that means that `lock` and `unlock` execute in alternation, as in `lock, unlock, lock, unlock`... although that can be disturbed if an `unlock` executes twice without a `lock` in between. (If that does happen, it means there is probably a programming error somewhere.)

The simple scheme above separates the behaviour of the locks themselves from the goal that using the locks is supposed to achieve, a conceptual advantage; but it *does* mean that the programmer has to put the locks in the right place. We now look at how a programmer can check that, with simple locks like these.

With each variable that can be locked, say `bb` (which is here an integer, but it doesn't matter what it is) we associate a special extra "lock variable" `$bb` whose possible values are thread names (or abbreviations for them) plus a special value $\perp$ that means "no thread". The command `lock bb` executes `$bb=` *Th* , where *Th* is the name of the thread executing it, but only if `$bb==`$\perp$ beforehand. (What `lock bb` does in the other case, that is when `$bb!=`$\perp$, we will see in a moment.) However the command `unlock bb` executes `$bb=` $\perp$ unconditionally.

Ex. 13.3

With that procedure, we can add assertions to (13.4) as follows, using names `atm1` and `atm2` for the two threads. (We can use any names we like, even say integers `1` and `2`: all that matters is that different threads have different names.) That gives

```
# ATM1                              # ATM2

{ $bb!=atm1 }                       { $bb!=atm2 }
lock bb # Lock account bb.          lock bb # Lock account bb.
{ $bb==atm1 }                       { $bb==atm2 }
if c1<=bb:                          if c2<=bb:                      (13.6)
  { $bb==atm1 and c1<=bb }            { $bb==atm2 and c2<=bb }
  bb,cc= bb-c1,cc+c1                  bb,cc= bb-c2,cc+c2
  { $bb==atm1 and bb>=0 }            { $bb==atm2 and bb>=0 }
unlock bb # Unlock account bb.      unlock bb # Unlock account bb.
{ $bb!=atm1 }                       { $bb!=atm2 }
```

and we now see that the invariant `bb>=0` is maintained, because the *ATM1* assertion

Ex. 13.4

  { PRE: `$bb==atm1 and c1<=bb` } `bb= bb-c1` { POST: `$bb==atm1 and bb>=0` }

achieves local correctness (as does `atm2`) — except that we must explain why *ATM2* cannot falsify the precondition { `$bb==atm1 and c1<=bb` } in *ATM1*. Here is the explanation, in which we deal with the two conjuncts `$bb==atm1` and `c1<=bb` separately.

- First — to falsify `$bb==atm1` in *ATM1*, an assignment to `$bb` must occur, either `$bb=` `atm2` from `lock bb` in *ATM2*, or `$bb=` $\perp$ from `unlock bb` in either thread. But `lock bb` can execute only when `$bb==`$\perp$ (and here `$bb` is not $\perp$; instead we have `$bb==atm1`). And `unlock bb` in *ATM2* has precondition `$bb==atm2`, so it cannot execute either — because `$bb==atm1`. So *ATM2* cannot falsify `$bb==atm1`. (And, trivially, `unlock bb` in *ATM1* can't falsify it either, because it is not at that point in its own program code.)

- Second — for *ATM2* to falsify `c1<=bb` in *ATM1*, it must execute an assignment to `bb` or to `c1`, and only `bb,cc=` `bb-c2,cc+c2` assigns to `bb` in *ATM2* (and there are no assignments to `c1` anywhere in *ATM2*). Like `unlock` in *ATM2*, that assignment has precondition `$bb==atm2`, so it cannot execute. Thus *ATM2* cannot falsify `c1<=bb` in *ATM1*.

We have now checked that the problems in (13.3) can no longer occur — if we use locks in the right way. But what do locks actually do?

13.5 What simple locks actually do

Actual implementations of locking usually depend on a built-in hardware instruction that reads *and* writes as one atomic action. A typical example is the "compare and swap" instruction, abbreviated *CAS*, which assigns a new value to a variable only if its current value equals one that is given in the instruction itself; if the current value does not equal the one given then no assignment occurs.[4] Thus *CAS* must read the current value and (only) then, if it's equal to the given value, overwrite that current value with the new value *without* being interrupted in between. It reads, compares, then (possibly) writes — all executed as a single atomic action on the hardware level.

Thus we could implement `lock bb` in some thread *Th* by using a tight loop

> `while $bb!=`*Th*`:`
> $\quad$"Read `$bb` and, without interruption, $\leftarrow$ *CAS, atomic in hardware.* (13.7)
> $\quad\quad$assign *Th* to `$bb` if `$bb` was $\perp$."   .

It "keeps trying" to assign *Th* to `$bb`, going around the loop again (and again) until it succeeds. It's sometimes called a *spin lock* implementation, because of the way the thread *Th* "spins" around the loop until it acquires the lock.[5] The key observation is that even if some other thread *Th'* is trying to lock bb at the same time, only one of *Th, Th'* can succeed: if the code above sets `$bb` to *Th* then `$bb` cannot be changed to *Th'* by a *CAS* in *Th'*, because the comparison of `$bb` with $\perp$ (by *Th'*) will fail, and no assignment of *Th'* to `$bb` will be made at that point.

Ex. 13.5

Ex. 13.6

13.6 Where simple locks came from

Locks in computer programming were originally called "semaphores", an idea motivated by the need to restrict a single-track section of a railway trajectory to one train at a time: a semaphore indicating "open" at one end of the section would ensure that "closed" was indicated at the other end.[6]

Their utility as a concept for computer programs (or processors) was recognised in the 1960s as an instance of the same "one user at a time" requirement as for railways: the need for what is now called "mutual exclusion" (one train at a time) between "critical sections" (single-track portions). In computer applications, that becomes portions of code (trains) accessing a shared resource (a track section) without interfering with each other while doing so (without colliding in the middle), as in our earlier *ATM* examples. It inspired a search into how mutual exclusion could be programmed on computers that did not have anything like semaphores "built in" (such as *CAS* from Sec. 13.5 just above).

The first solution to "mutual exclusion without *CAS*" was discovered in the 1960s,[7]

---

[4] Written out in full, it would be something like *CAS x old new* , which would assign *new* to *x* if *x* were equal to *old*, but would leave *x* unchanged otherwise.

[5] If it contains no *CAS* or similar then we call it a spin *loop*.

[6] Figures 13.1–13.3 show the first three pages of *EWD74*, held at the Dijkstra Archive [12] of the University of Texas at Austin (written in approximately 1964, translated by Carroll Morgan in 2021 and included with permission of Rutger Dijkstra). It is where the idea of *computer-program* semaphores, nowadays called "locks", was first published. (The Dijkstra "typewriter font" used in the figures is copyright 2019 Darren W. Ringer.)

[7] It was found by the Dutch mathematician Theodorus Dekker, but not published by him.

— and it was followed by many others (one of which is the topic of Chapter 16): but a major step beyond that was the recognition of the "mutual exclusion and critical section" -combination as a "design pattern" whose properties should be explored in a more abstract way, with reasoning tools induced from that. (Earlier, for example, the 1960s-style `goto`-statement implemented[8] the design pattern "do something; test whether it's been done enough; if not, `goto` (back to) its beginning and do it again; repeat until done"[9] eventually became a `while`-loop, with its own syntax, and the reasoning tool induced from that was of course *invariants*. Similarly, the pattern of "group your data and its manipulation together" eventually became data encapsulation, again with its own syntax and the reasoning tool of *data refinement*.)

Thus `lock` and `unlock` were explored as programming primitives on their own, but their original names were "`P()`" and "`V()`": based on Dutch words, the first stood for "passing" (Dutch `P()` *assering*), and the second for "release" (Dutch `V()` *rijgeven*). But as Fig. 13.1 shows, there are other proposed origins for their names as well.[10] In any case, they have been renamed many times since.

More important than their names, however, is that the original `P()` and `V()` were slightly more general than the modern `lock` and `unlock` — something perhaps not so well known. Rather than expressing a Boolean "it's locked" or "it's open", they were applied to *semaphores* that could take any non-negative integer value, and they could be incremented or decremented in tandem (the latter only if they remained non-negative). For example, in Fig. 13.3 it's shown how a circular buffer shared by many processes can be safely managed by the adroit use of just four of those more general semaphores, no matter how many processes might be involved. And the capacity of the buffer is used only once, in the initialisation of one of the semaphores. The `lock` and `unlock` that we used earlier in this chapter then become a special case: they are "binary" semaphores whose only values are `0` (locked) or `1` (unlocked).

The generalisation and exploration of those then led to the `await`-statements –another design pattern– which we introduce in Chapter 15, and further to many other higher-level design-pattern motivated approaches to controlling concurrency. Here we concentrate however on how to *reason about* concurrency, for which one of the most important steps is the method to be explained in our next chapter.

13.7 Critical sections and other techniques

Locks are typically used to provide "critical sections" within threads: as we saw in Sec. 13.6, a *critical section* is usually a small code fragment appearing within one thread that must never be active simultaneously with a similar fragment in any other thread; and that is precisely what the code fragments `if c1<=bb:` ⋯ and `if c2<=bb:` ⋯ are taking advantage of in their threads *ATM1* and *ATM2* at (13.6) above. A group of critical sections is easily implemented with locks by associating a lock `lk` (for a fresh name `lk`, say) with each group, and enclosing each individual critical section with `lock lk` ⋯ `unlock lk` .

Introducing a critical section group is similar to making the enclosed fragment atomic, but it is not quite the same: critical-section fragments from *different* groups

---

[8] Programs full of `goto`'s were often derisorily referred to as "spaghetti coding".

[9] In contrast, the "then repeat" on shampoo bottles describes an infinite loop.

[10] In Fig. 13.1 they are related instead to the words *verhoog* and *prolaag*, the second of which is not listed even in the principal Dutch dictionary. In both cases, the letter chosen is from the prefix of the word only, not its more significant portion, so avoiding any mnemonic connection with its intuitive meaning.

Perhaps it was a deliberate step away from any temptation to indulge in operational reasoning.

Figure 13.1 First page of *EWD74: Concerning semaphores* (translated)

EWD74-1

Concerning semaphores.

We consider a number of mutually "weakly coupled" processes of which each one separately is sequential. By "weak coupling" I mean that they must at certain points take account of each other. For example, if a number of processes must now and then make use of some facility or other that however can serve only one process at a time, then this means that the processes might indeed occasionally have to wait for each other. If one process is processing information that must be delivered by another, then it is also clear that the former might have to wait for the latter. In other words, the processes might have to be synchronised to a certain degree with respect to each other.

In order to arrange the situation so that the processes can exchange information with each other about their progress, a shared memory is included. The elements of this memory are non-negative integers, which we name <u>semaphores</u>.

The important synchronisation points are marked within the individual processes, and it is required that in passing such a point a certain operation must be carried out. The individual processes have here the choice between two operations, the so-called V-operation and the so-called P-operation. We describe them below.

In the following we assume that S1,S2,S3 etc. are the names of accessible semaphores (although not all semaphores need to be accessible from every process!); the V- and the P-operations we will write as procedure calls.

The V-operation ("Verhoog, to increase").

The V-operation concerns at least one semaphore, thus for example "V(S1)" or "V(S1,S2,S3)". If one of the individual processes carries out the V-operation, then the effect is that all the semaphores referred to are increased by one <u>in a single indivisible operation</u>.

<u>Remark 1.</u> The inclusion of "in a single indivisible operation" in the above is intended to express the following. Suppose that the value of S1 is 3 and that for example two of the (simultaneously active!) processes would like to carry out V(S1) "at the same time". As a consequence of the indivisibility of the procedure we can then imagine that these two V-operations on the same semaphore occur in an arbitrary order, so that at the conclusion S1 is 5 and in particular that neither of the updates is lost.

<u>Remark 2.</u> The V-operation with more than one argument is actually not logically necessary, but it is elegant. In the statement V(S1,S2) one is asking for a simultaneous increase of both semaphores; but if we replaced this in one of the individual processes by "V(S1);V(S2)" then we have very explicitly asked for the increments to occur in a certain order. It would be unpleasant to be forced into such a choice if one would rather increase a number of semaphores, simultaneously, in a "neutral" way.

<u>Remark 3.</u> If we do use V-operations with more than one argument, we will for the moment limit ourselves to the case that all those semaphores are different.

The P-operation ("Prolaag, attempt to decrease").

In an individual process the P-operation marks a tentative transition through that point. The P-operation concerns one or more semaphores, thus for example "P(S1)" or "P(S1,S2,S3)". If the P-operation is initiated in one of the individual processes,

EWD74 contains eight pages in all. It dates from the early 1960s.

Figure 13.2 Second page of *EWD74: Concerning semaphores* (translated)

EWD74-2

then an operation has begun that can end only at a moment when all of the semaphores concerned are [non-negative]. Ending of a P-operation implies that all the semaphores mentioned have been decreased by 1 and that this operation is (again) a single indivisible operation. With the P-operations as well we limit ourselves to the case that all the semaphores mentioned are different.

Remark 1. The P-operation with more than one argument is logically necessary.

Remark 2. Many semaphores in fact take only the values 0 and 1. In that case the V-operation serves as "open the railway section (to passage)"; the P-operation, the tentative passage, can then be completed only if the semaphore (or semaphores) concerned indicate "open", and beginning (and during) the passage it (or they) are set to "closed". They are called "binary semaphores".

Some examples of the use of semaphores.

Example 1. If we have a collection of machines (alias processes!) Xi (that is X0, X1, X2 etc.) and in each process a critical section occurs, critical in the sense that no two critical sections may be active at the same time, then we can achieve that with a (binary) semaphore SX, say, that in this simple case has only two values:

SX=0 shall mean:
        one of the machines Xi is active in its critical section.
SX=1 shall mean:
        none of the machines Xi is active in its critical section.

The description of each of the processes is now of the form:

"LXi: P(SX); TXi; V(SX); remainder of process Xi; GOTO LXi."

If we start all of the processes Xi at the LXi-labelled point (that is, "at the beginning of the line") with the initialisation SX=2, then we will have achieved, irrespective of the environment of the collection of processes Xi, that there will never be more than 2 of them simultaneously active in their critical sections TXi. This is clearly a generalisation of the problem of mutual exclusion. (It is precisely the situation for example of n tape decks on 2 channels.)

We emphasise that the formulation of the individual processes Xi is independent of the extent of the class of all Xi's, something that is much to be wished for when we consider the possible dynamic variability of that environment. Also the maximum allowed simultaneous use of the critical sections does not intrude on the formulation of the individual processes.

Example 2. We now consider a group of machines Xi and another group Yj, each with their critical sections TXi,TYj respectively. Execution of a critical section excludes execution of all other critical sections, but as well we demand that the execution of TX-sections and TY-sections must alternate.

We can accomplish this with two binary semaphores, say SX,SY.

SX=1 means that it is now the turn of a TX section, and
SY=1 means that it is now the turn of a TY section.

The machines' programs are now

"LXi: P(SX); TXi; V(SY); remainder of process Xi; GOTO LXi"
"LYj: P(SY); TYj; V(SX); remainder of process Yj; GOTO LYj" .

If the processes are all started at "the beginning of the line" then we must have SX=1 and SY=0 or vice versa.

Figure 13.3 Third page of *EWD74: Concerning semaphores* (translated)

Example 3. Finally, we consider a class of machines Xi that place units of
information into a cyclic buffer with a capacity of N units, and a class of
machines Yj that remove and process units from the buffer.

Because filling the buffer involves administrative operations with the
"capacity indicator" etc. and mutatis mutandis the same holds for emptying, we
demand in addition that filling can be carried out by at most one Xi at a time,
and similarly that removing can be carried out by only one Yj at a time.

For this we make use of four semaphores:

SX1 is the number of free places in the buffer (initially N).

SX2 is 0 if one of the machines Xi is currently filling (otherwise 1).

SY1 is the number of filled places in the buffer (initially 0).

SY2 is 0 if one of the machines Yj is currently removing (otherwise 1).

Invariant is that N-1 <= SX1+SY1 <= N.

The machines themselves are now

```
        LXi:    P(SX1,SX2);
                fill the next available place in the buffer;
                V(SY1,SX2);
                etc;
                GOTO LXi.
and

        LYj:    P(SY1,SY2);
                empty the next available place in the buffer;
                V(SX1,SY2);
                etc;
                GOTO LYj.
```

/ continues

(i.e. different "lk" names) can be active simultaneously, and that is important for efficiency. If for example we simply made if cn<=bb: bb= bb-cn atomic, then every *ATMn* for the bank would have to take turns *even if accessing different accounts*: only one withdrawal could be taking place at a time among *all* the bank's *ATM*'s. To avoid that, a separate lock is associated with each bank account.

Critical sections are therefore an example of a typical approach to concurrency problems; and the description at the start of this section is indeed a design pattern for solving them with locks. Another example of a pattern is "synchronised methods" where data that requires serial access (one thread after another, not interleaved) is collected within a class, and access to it is via methods that act as critical sections for each particular instance (object) of the class: it's a mixture of locks and encapsulation.

13.8 Concurrency and interference

The example in Sec. 13.4 above, with its final assertions given at (13.6), shows how seriously we must take into account the extra work that can be involved in checking concurrent programs, even quite small ones. As well as the usual checks we have already learned in Part I, we now have an extra set of checks to do: that atomic program fragments in one thread do not "interfere" with assertions in another. That is precisely what we did at the end of Sec. 13.4. In more detail:

(a) *Local correctness* — To show that invariant bb>=0 was maintained by the assignment bb= bb-c1 in *ATM1*, we needed to refer to the assignment's precondition c1<=bb. That will be called *local* checking (or checking for *local* correctness), and is what we did in Part I of this text where –effectively– there was only one thread.

(b) *Global correctness* — Even though the precondition c1<=bb was established (as a postcondition) by the conditional if c1<=bb preceding it, it might be invalidated by execution of bb= bb-c2 in *ATM2 before* execution of (the now inevitable) bb= bb-c1 in *ATM1* has had a chance to execute, which would be an example of interference — Thread *ATM2* is interfering with (an assertion in) *ATM1*. Thus, more precisely,

> *interference*   concerns one assertion and one statement,[11] occurring between threads when a *statement* in one thread invalidates (changes its value from True to False) an *assertion* in another thread.

Note in particular that interference is not merely one thread's changing a variable that another thread accesses: indeed that is normal, for without that the threads could not cooperate at all. To interfere, you must actually falsify an assertion.

Making sure that interference does not happen is *global* checking (or checking for *global* correctness), and is the main new feature of this chapter.

(c) To show that such interference cannot happen, we relied in our examples on the fact that all the potentially interfering statements in *ATM2* could execute only when $bb==atm2, and that as well as c1<=bb we had $bb==atm1 (i.e. that $bb was *not* atm2) at the point we were checking for interference.

---

[11] ...and not, in particular, two *statements* where one "interferes with" the other.

In the next chapter we draw all that together, discussing how our ordinary (local) checks and our (global) checks for noninterference fit together. The method is called "Owicki–Gries", named after its inventors.

Ex. 13.7

13.9 Exercises

Exercise 13.1 (p. 136) ⇓ Suppose the assignment x= x+1 is written on a single line of one thread, and x can be *read* –but not written– by other threads. That is sometimes described as that thread's *owning* x.

Having written the assignment on one line, we are stating that it is atomic; and any checking we do here will depend on that. But is it *reasonable* to assume that x= x+1 is atomic within a thread that owns x ?

Exercise 13.2 (p. 136) ⇓ Recall Ex. 13.1, but now assume that another thread can *write* to variable x — which makes it a *global* variable, no longer owned by this thread alone.

Is it still reasonable to assume that x= x+1 is atomic?

Exercise 13.3 (p. 137) Is the \$bb introduced "behind the scenes" in Sec. 13.4 an auxiliary variable (Sec. 8.5.1), since it does not appear in the actual code anywhere?

Exercise 13.4 (p. 137) Check the reasoning about (13.6) by applying the actual substitution rule (Sec. 5.2) for assignments.

Hint: Use the substitution

$$(\$bb==atm1 \text{ and } bb>=0)[bb,cc\backslash bb-c1,cc+c1] \quad ,$$

and then an implication, to check that

```
{ PRE: $bb==atm1 and c1<=bb }
bb,cc= bb-c1,cc+c1
{ POST: $bb==atm1 and bb>=0 }
```

works.

Exercise 13.5 (p. 138) ⇓ The spin lock in (13.7) is inefficient because in a multiprogramming environment (i.e. a single core), where interrupts are used to share a single *CPU* between threads, the time the lock spends "spinning" is time that could have been used by other threads for something more important. Even in a multi-core environment, the spinning is still using (extra) electricity and possibly contributing to bus contention. What is usually done to prevent that?

Exercise 13.6 (p. 138) ⇓ We have learned that infinite loops are to be avoided, and that variants are used to show that they do not occur. Yet the loop in (13.7) appears not to terminate, and has no evident variant. Does it terminate? Does it have a variant?

Exercise 13.7 (p. 144) In (13.6) the extra variable $bb took one of three possible values: ⊥, atm1 and atm2. But the only tests of that variable in the code were whether it was ⊥ or not: there was no test "Is it atm1?" or "Is it atm2?" So we could perhaps merge those two values into a single one, having now ⊥ for "unlocked" and ⊤ for "locked". The program would still work.

But there is a *disadvantage* of merging atm1 and atm2 into a single value ⊤. What is it? (See also Sec. 15.2 to come.)

Exercise 13.8 In (13.6), the `unlock bb` in *ATM1* sets $bb to ⊥, so establishing $bb==⊥ ; but the assertion written there is only the weaker { $bb!=atm1 }. Why?

Hint: You might look ahead at Sec. 14.5 for this.

14

The Owicki–Gries method

14.1 Introduction

In Sec. 13.1 we saw just how difficult it is to check concurrent programs that are sharing variables: the reason was the very large number of "interleavings" in which their statements could execute. And because we cannot predict which of those interleavings will actually happen –it could even be different on each run– the techniques of Part I would have had to be used to check every single one of them.

Luckily, the techniques of Part I *can* be carried over into the concurrent setting, once we concentrate not on "what happens" when the program executes, but rather on *what is true* as it executes. That is the difference we have been emphasising so much, between thinking "What does this statement do?" and "What does this statement make true?", between "What did the previous iteration of this loop do?" and "What truth does *every* iteration of this loop maintain?"

Thus in this chapter we will examine how the activities of other threads (i.e. their atomic statements) affect the *checking* of this thread (i.e. its assertions), rather than the execution of it. The main innovation –global correctness– is introduced in Sec. 14.5 below.

14.2 Controlled interleaving

Assume we have a collection of threads *Th1*, *Th2*, ..., *ThN*, such as those in Sec. 13.2 where there were only the two threads *ATM1* and *ATM2*. All those programs will run concurrently, which means that their atomic program fragments will be interleaved arbitrarily *except* that –as we mentioned before in Sec. 13.1– within each thread individually, the fragments execute in the order determined by the code of the thread itself.

Further, each of the threads has assertions

(a) at every point within the thread at which program control can pass from one atomic fragment to the next.[1]

(b) at the thread's very beginning;

---

[1] For us, those points are usually *between* lines of code: recall Sec. 13.3.

(c) at the thread's very end.

And for the whole collection of threads there is

(d) a single overall precondition at the very beginning of them all, and

(e) a single overall postcondition at the very end of them all.

As we saw in Part I, each assertion indicated in (a) is a postcondition for the program fragment immediately before, and a precondition for the one immediately after. And finally

(f) there can be "global" invariants that apply to all the threads together.

Much of the above can be seen in Fig. 15.2 further ahead. (Have a look.)

How exactly do we check a concurrent system set out like that? We will explain it in the next three sections, Secs. 14.3–14.5.

14.3 Checking *local* correctness: what's *old*

For "local correctness" we check each thread separately, entirely on its own — and, while that is being done, we have only "local" concerns. That is what we have already learned: it is exactly what we did in Part I for sequential programs (i.e. not concurrent) — because a sequential program is a special case of a concurrent system, one with only a single thread.

Here are the three steps for local correctness within a single thread.

(a) We check every program fragment and its adjacent assertions

$$\{\textsc{Pre: } pre\} \; prog \; \{\textsc{Post: } post\} \qquad,$$

where we recall that the "Pre" and the "Post" indications are there just to remind us of the role that those assertions play. In the actual thread code we would possibly find simply $\{pre\} \; prog \; \{post\}$. This is called *local correctness*, abbreviated *LC* and, as was said above, the checking is done just as in Part I for programs on their own.

Assertions *within* a line are checked for local correctness too: for example

$$\{pre\} \; prog1; \; \{mid\} \; prog2 \; \{post\}$$

would induce two checks, one for each of *prog1* and *prog2*. But we do not need to consider any of the other threads here: they cannot interfere with *mid* because –Sec. 13.3– the single line is assumed to execute atomically.

Ex. 14.1

(b) We also must show that the (global) precondition of the whole system implies the very first (local) precondition of each thread.

(c) Finally, we must show that the conjunction of all the local postconditions, that is of all threads taken together, implies the global postcondition.[2]

If we wish, we can use as many (or as few) of the global invariants (mentioned at (f) in the previous section) while doing those checks: that is, for (a) above we could use global invariants *gInv1* and *gInv2* to check

$$\{\textsc{Pre: } pre \text{ and } gInv1 \text{ and } gInv2 \cdots\} \; prog \; \{\textsc{Post: } post\}$$

which, because it has a stronger precondition, might be slightly easier.

---

[2] If however the individual threads contain non-terminating loops, as we will see in later examples (e.g. Sec. 15.2), this last check does not apply: there is no overall postcondition in that case.

14.4 Checking global invariants: what's obvious

To check that the global invariants really *are* invariant, however, we need to make sure that each one is established initially, and that it is preserved by every atomic fragment in the whole system, no matter which thread that fragment might be in. That is, for this part we ignore the thread structure altogether and simply consider each (atomic) statement separately.

In more detail: we check that the global precondition implies each global invariant,

$$
\begin{array}{lll}
gPre & \Rightarrow & gInv1 \\
gPre & \Rightarrow & gInv2 \\
& \vdots &
\end{array}
\tag{14.1}
$$

and we can even use one invariant to help with another, as in

$$
\begin{array}{lll}
gPre & \Rightarrow & gInv1 \\
gPre \text{ and } gInv1 & \Rightarrow & gInv2 \quad ,
\end{array}
\tag{14.2}
$$

provided we don't do so circularly. For example

$$
\begin{array}{lll}
gPre \text{ and } gInv1 & \Rightarrow & gInv2 \\
gPre \text{ and } gInv2 & \Rightarrow & gInv1
\end{array}
\tag{14.3}
$$

is obviously not allowed.[3]

Then for every atomic fragment *prog* in the system, whichever thread it might be in, we check *gInv*'s invariance with

$$\{\text{PRE: } pre \text{ and } gInv \} \ prog \ \{\text{POST: } gInv \} \quad .$$

Just as in (14.2), if there are several global invariants then we can use some of them to help check others — and here we can do that even if it looks circular. For example

$$
\begin{array}{ll}
& \{\text{PRE: } pre \text{ and } gInv1 \text{ and } gInv2 \} \ prog \ \{\text{POST: } gInv2 \} \\
\text{and} & \{\text{PRE: } pre' \text{ and } gInv2 \text{ and } gInv1 \} \ prog' \ \{\text{POST: } gInv1 \}
\end{array}
\tag{14.4}
$$

are both allowed.   Ex. 14.2

14.5 Checking *global* correctness: what's *new*

The idea of "global correctness" is the principal innovation of the Owicki–Gries method; it is –as mentioned in Sec. 14.1– how the *checking* of a thread (its assertions) must take into account the activities of atomic statements in other threads.[4]

Thus *global* correctness is achieved by checking that the activity of those "other" threads does not interfere "too much" with the *local* reasoning we have already checked (i.e. as in Secs. 14.3 and 14.4 above).

Let us consider assertions including some pre- or postconditions between, but not within, atomic fragments. Wherever they are, as long as they are not the global precondition, nor the global postcondition, nor a global invariant, the global-correctness   Ex. 14.3

Ex. 14.4

---

[3] Circular reasoning is sometimes called "begging the question", i.e taking as a premise the very thing one is trying to prove. (That's not the same as newsreaders' more recent usage "making one want to ask the question whether. . ."). Compare "one foul swoop".

[4] The Owicki–Gries method was invented in 1975 by Susan Owicki in her Ph.D. thesis *Axiomatic proof techniques for parallel programs* [47]. Her supervisor was David Gries [48].

checks are

$$\{\,\textsc{Pre:}\;\; assn\;\text{and}\;pre\,\}\;\; prog\;\;\{\,\textsc{Post:}\;\; assn\,\} \tag{14.5}$$

for every atomic $\{\,\textsc{Pre:}\;\; pre\,\}\;\; prog\;\;\{\cdots\}$ in any *other* thread. (We do not care about the postcondition of that other-thread *prog* here.) Obviously we need only consider a *prog* that assigns to variables that actually occur somewhere in the *assn* we are checking, since otherwise (14.5) checks trivially — and often that cuts down the work considerably. Also, we might appeal to global invariant(s) by checking the easier

$$\{\,\textsc{Pre:}\;\; assn\;\text{and}\;pre\;\text{and}\;gInv\,\}\;\; prog\;\;\{\,\textsc{Post:}\;\; assn\,\}\qquad.$$

The above fragment (14.5) is *global correctness*, abbreviated *GC*.

And that –amazingly– is all the Owicki–Gries method entails. In the next chapter, we will see examples of how it works. $\boxed{\text{Ex. 14.5}}$

14.6 Exercises

Exercise 14.1 (p. 148) ⇓ We are following the convention that statements written all on one line are atomic, i.e. that *stmt1*; *stmt2* cannot be "interrupted at the semicolon" (Sec. 13.3). Suppose however that there is an assertion there, for example

$$stmt1;\;\{\,assn\,\}\;\; stmt2\qquad.$$

Must *assn* be checked for local correctness (*LC*), i.e. that it is established by *stmt1*? Does it have to be checked for global correctness (*GC*), i.e. that it cannot be falsified by a statement in another thread? Do global invariants have to be checked against *stmt1* on its own (or *stmt2* on its own)?

Exercise 14.2 (p. 149) The situation in (14.4) certainly *seems* circular: it looks as if we are using *gInv1* to prove *gInv2* and similarly *gInv2* to prove *gInv1* — precisely what we disallowed in (14.3). But here it *is* allowed. Why?

Exercise 14.3 (p. 149) ⇓ Why do we *not* have to check global correctness (14.5) when *assn* is the global pre- or postcondition?

Exercise 14.4 (p. 149) Why do we not have to check the global correctness of *assn*, in (14.5), when *assn* is a global invariant?

Exercise 14.5 (p. 150) ⇓ In Sec. 14.5 we allow the precondition *pre* of an assignment in another thread to be used when we are checking *GC* for an assertion *assn* in this thread — and vice versa. That is, for the two threads

# *Th1*	# *Th2*
$\{\,pre1\,\}$	$\{\,pre2\,\}$
stmt1	*stmt2*

the *GC* of $\{\,pre1\,\}$, i.e. its noninterference from *stmt2*, would be checked with

$$\{\,\textsc{Pre:}\;\; pre1\;\text{and}\;pre2\,\}\;\; stmt2\;\{\,\textsc{Post:}\;\; pre1\,\}\qquad, \tag{14.6}$$

assuming *pre2*; but, in the other direction, for the *GC* of { *pre2* } we would check

$$\{\,\text{Pre:}\quad pre2 \text{ and } pre1\,\}\;\;stmt1\;\{\,\text{Post:}\quad pre2\,\}\qquad,\qquad\qquad(14.7)$$

assuming *pre1*.

Why is that not circular reasoning?

Hint: In any interleaving concurrent execution of the two threads, one of (14.6), (14.7) must occur before the other.[5]

---

[5] If the two threads were executed truly in parallel, e.g. a multi-core system, the hint does not apply.

15

Critical sections with Owicki–Gries

15.1 Introduction

In Sec. 13.4 we introduced some ad hoc techniques for locks (e.g. using variables $bb), to explain how locks work and to show how they can be used to implement critical sections. In this chapter we show how to implement critical sections with "await" statements, which are more expressive than locks, as a first step towards a more general use of the Owicki–Gries method.

15.2 Using `await` statements with a single Boolean

Consider two threads, each implicitly in a never-ending loop,[1] as in Fig. 15.1. *"Other business"* is arbitrary code; the *"critical section"* must eventually terminate; and neither of those accesses the variable c (nor any other variable that we might later introduce to control access to the critical section). *Mutual exclusion* is what we say we have achieved if the two critical sections here can never be active simultaneously.

The system in Fig. 15.1 below uses "await" to implement an abstract version of the "compare and swap" that we encountered earlier in Sec. 13.5. The await construction, in this case

$$\text{await not c: c= True} \quad , \tag{15.1}$$

means "Wait here until c (re-)evaluates to False, and then set c to True without interruption in between." Here, the variable c means intuitively to us that "Some thread is in its critical section." and so the await statement prevents a thread from entering the critical section when another thread is already there, just as *CAS* did in Secs. 13.5 and 13.7. But the code in Fig. 15.1 does not (yet) contain enough information for us to *check* that it achieves mutual exclusion (although in fact it does achieve it). We will come back to that.

In general, an `await` *cond*: *awaitBody* causes execution in one thread to pause –so that other threads can be scheduled instead– unless (or until) the condition *cond*

---

[1] Imagine there is a `while True:` enclosing each thread.

Figure 15.1 Mutual exclusion with `await` and single Boolean

{ PRE: not c }   ← *overall precondition*

```
# Th1 repeats this forever        # Th2 repeats this forever
"other business 1."               "other business 2."
await not c: c= True              await not c: c= True
   "critical section 1."             "critical section 2."
c= False                          c= False
```

is made true by activity in one of those other threads. The condition is evaluated atomically and –if it is true– execution proceeds to *awaitBody* without any potential interruption from other threads and, furthermore, the entire *awaitBody* is then executed without interruption (i.e. atomically) as well.[2] On the other hand — if execution *was* paused then when the thread is rescheduled the condition is evaluated again (and again... until it becomes true).

By analogy with `if`-statements (as in Sec. 5.4 but without `else`), to check the `await` code

{ PRE: *pre* }   `await` *cond*: *awaitBody*   { POST: *post* }

we check only

{ PRE: *pre* and *cond* }   *awaitBody*   { POST: *post* }   ,   (15.2)

where –crucially– there is no implication to check in an `else` branch — because there is no such branch. (Checking `else` was explained in Sec. 5.4 as well.) That's the difference between `if` and `await`: if an `if` condition is false, then the `else` branch (default `skip`) is taken and must itself be checked; but if an `await` condition is false, the thread simply waits until that condition becomes true, which (of course) must be achieved by some *other* thread. An `await` never "takes else" — because it doesn't *have* an `else`.[3]

In Fig. 15.2 we've extended Fig. 15.1 by adding an auxiliary variable "t" (for "thread") and, with that, we *can* use Owicki–Gries to show that mutual exclusion is achieved. The reason that t is auxiliary here is (as usual) that it does not affect the program's behaviour in any way: the participation of t in the assertions, however, does affect what we can *say* about the program's behaviour, in this case that mutual exclusion is achieved at runtime.

Here's how the checking procedure works in this case: referring to Chapter 14, we recall that we must check both local and global correctness. For local correctness we use the "how to check `await`" at (15.2) just above to check that the `await` in *Th1* respects its pre- and postcondition: that is, for

{ PRE: True }   `await` not c: c,t= True,1   { POST: c and t==1 }

we check the `await` body with

{ PRE: True and not c }   c,t= True,1   { POST: c and t==1 }   ,

Ex. 15.1

Ex. 15.2

---

[2] Even if *awaitBody* is on multiple lines (in Python, indented), it cannot be interrupted between those lines.

[3] An `if` *cond* without `else` is very polite: if *cond* is false, it says "OK, I won't bother." and just carries on. *With* an `else` it says "OK, I'll try something else instead." An `await` however says "I insist — and I'm going to stand here and keep trying until I can."

Figure 15.2 Mutual exclusion with `await` and auxiliary variable t

$\qquad$ {PRE: not c}   ← *overall precondition*

```
# Th1 repeats this forever.           # Th2 repeats this forever.

"other business 1."                   "other business 2."
await not c: c,t= True,1              await not c: c,t= True,2
{ c and t==1 }                        { c and t==2 }
    "critical section 1."   ←t==1 and t==2→   "critical section 2."
{ c and t==1 }                        { c and t==2 }
c= False                              c= False
```

Because we cannot have `t==1` and `t==2` true at the same time, mutual exclusion is checked — provided of course that we successfully checked the local and global correctness of all the assertions.

The variable "`t`" is auxiliary, and therefore is not used in the actual running program: it's used only to *check* the program, that is to *reason about* it.

---

which is obvious. In fact we don't need the `await`-condition `not c` for that; and the same applies for *Th2*. (What is the `await` condition used for, in that case? We will find out below.) And the assertions `t==1, t==2` (continue to) hold because we have assumed that the critical sections do not refer to them.

The difference is that for global correctness we check assertions, rather than whether or not statements respect their pre- and postconditions (as we did just above). For the assertion `{ c and t==1 }` in *Th1*, recalling (14.5), our check for noninterference from the `await` in *Th2* (whose precondition is `True`) is

$\qquad$ { c and t==1 and True } await not c: c,t= True,2 { c and t==1 }   (15.3)

where surprisingly the assignment `t= 2` occurs in the `await` body... but the `await`'s postcondition contains `t==1`! Carrying on regardless, thus holding our breath and using (15.2) to check (15.3) anyway, we see that in fact we must check this:

$\qquad$ { c and t==1 and True and not c } c,t= True,2 { c and t==1 }   .

And that check *succeeds* because the precondition's conjuncts –that is `c` and `not c` together– imply `False`, meaning that *any* postcondition, even `t==1`, will be established by the assignment `t= 2`. Operationally what that means is simply that the conjunct `not c` prevents the execution of *Th2*'s `await`, for now: it must wait until *Th1* is no longer at its assertion `{ c and t==1 }`, i.e. that it is no longer in its critical section. (And *there* is where we used the `await`'s condition `not c`.)

The second global-correctness check in *Th1* is against `{ c and t==2 }` `c= False` in *Th2*, that is

$\qquad$ { c and t==1 and c and t==2 } c= False { c and t==1 }   ,

and it too, with precondition `False`, checks successfully. (Variable `t` can never be both 1 and 2.)

Yet still the above programs are indeed slightly mysterious: the program at (15.3) for example did seem to be saying that we must show that $\cdots$ t= 2 $\cdots$ establishes t==1. But actually it does *not* say that. It says in the first check that

If c and t==1 is true

and `await not c: c,t= True,2` executes   (15.4)

then c and t==1 will still be true.

The key to understanding (15.4) is to realise that when c and t==1 is true, the `await not c: c,t= True,2` *cannot* execute. And so the in-English implication (15.4) holds trivially: its antecedent (the first two lines "If... and...executes then") are together false.

In the second check, we know that c= `False` in *Th2* cannot execute because –given the assignment's precondition– *Th2* cannot be at that point in its execution.

And so now we know we have checked mutual exclusion — because if both *Th1* and *Th2* were in their critical sections, that is at the same time then the assertions located there show us that we would have t==1 and t==2 , which cannot happen. (Recall $\leftarrow$ t==1 and t==2 $\rightarrow$ in Fig. 15.2.)

There is a clear conceptual connection between this auxiliary t and the lock values atm1, atm2 assigned to the variable $bb used in (13.6). But the difference is that those lock values are used in the actual running code of (13.6), whereas neither t nor its possible values will appear in the actual running code of Fig. 15.2 (because t is auxiliary).

Ex. 15.3

15.3 Deadlock, livelock and starvation

It probably seems obvious that establishing critical sections must rely ultimately on hardware locks, at least at some level: as we saw in Sec. 13.5, typically it is a special lock-like instruction that both reads and writes *and* is guaranteed to be atomic while it does so. We mentioned compare-and-swap (*CAS*) there, as one example, where the "critical section" is between the comparison with the existing value and its (possible) replacement by a new one.

Similarly, a general `await` *cond*: *awaitBody* can be implemented with (spin) locks in the style of (13.7) by

```
# --- Implement await cond: awaitBody .

while True:
  lock
  "Set local variable c to cond."  # Might take several lines,
  if c: break # Still locked →
  unlock
  # Go back and try again.
# ← at this point.
awaitBody                                # ...as might this.
unlock
```
(15.5)

where the `lock` guarantees that the evaluation of *cond* is atomic, no matter how complicated it might be, and that the execution of *awaitBody* begins –without interruption– only when *cond* is found to be true, and is itself carried out atomically as well.

But it is actually not true that critical sections must rely ultimately on hardware locks, at least not in the obvious way. The following code "almost" implements a critical section without using locks at all — for no `await` here has a body, and the conditions are single Boolean variables. There's no need to lock anything:[4]

The Safe Sluice[5]

{PRE: not c1 and not c2}

Th1 repeats this forever. # *Th2* repeats this forever.

"other business 1."	*"other business 2."*	(15.6)
c1= True	c2= True	
await not c2:	await not c1:	
"critical section 1."	*"critical section 2."*	
c1= False	c2= False	

Indeed `await not c2` is easily implemented by the simple loop `while c2: skip`, which requires neither `lock` nor *CAS*. We'll call those "spin *loops*" because they have no interior atomicity — that is, they do not require any protection at all from interference.

There is nevertheless a serious problem with (15.6), which is why we wrote "almost" just above the program, and why that program would never be used in practice: if both threads set their Booleans to `True` and then both `await`, they will wait forever. That is called *deadlock* — the system doesn't crash; it just... stops. If however the `await` is implemented as suggested just above, that is with underlying spin locks (or loops), then instead the whole system might be "busily stuck", executing those two loops forever (though in a sense at a lower level), each one in its own thread checking a Boolean that will never change: that is an example of what is called *livelock*. Thus whether it's called deadlock or livelock depends on how deep you look. Either way, it's bad; and so we must figure out how to check not only mutual exclusion, but also that neither deadlock nor livelock occurs.

That the critical sections are indeed mutually exclusive is called a *safety* property — the dangerous (i.e. "unsafe") situation, in which both threads are in their critical section at the same time, cannot occur. Yet (15.6), while safe with respect to the mutual exclusion, is unsafe in another sense: it can deadlock by reaching a state in which both threads wait forever.

All the above is enough on its own to make (15.6) unsatisfactory; and so for practical use perhaps we do after all need hardware locks at some level. Yet even the simple implementation of critical sections in Fig. 15.1, where implicitly hardware locks are used to implement `await not c: c= True`, and deadlock does *not* occur, has another problem — although it might not be so obvious yet. We will now take a closer look.

Ex. 15.4
Ex. 15.5

Ex. 15.6

---

[4] Actually, it is not *quite* true that no locking is ultimately required: at a very low level, it often is. Here it would be at the hardware level where a single memory location (e.g. containing `c1`) is not read-from and written-to at the same time. See however Leslie Lamport's *Bakery Algorithm* [35], which accommodates even that [34, Item 12].

[5] This program is called "The Safe Sluice" by Feijen and van Gasteren in their text *On a Method of Multiprogramming* [18], which is devoted entirely to Owicki–Gries reasoning.

Suppose for example that the two threads of Fig. 15.1 interleave as below:

Th1	*Th2*	
{PRE: not c}		# initially
OB1	*OB2*	# other businesses
await not c: c= True		# *Th1* enters CS1
{c}	await not c	# *Th2* must wait
CS1		# *Th1* in CS1
c= False		# *Th1* leaves CS1
	{not c}	
OB1	{not c}	# But *Th2* doesn't notice...
	{not c}	
await not c: c= True	{not c}	# *Th1* enters again
{c}	await not c	# *Th2* waits again
CS1		# *Th1* in CS1 again
c= False		# *Th1* leaves CS1 again
⋮	⋮	# Repeat indefinitely

(15.7)

Ex. 15.7   This system is safe (respecting the critical sections and avoiding deadlock), but it is unsatisfactory in the sense that, as the above interleaved code illustrates, it is possible for one of the threads to "starve" the other: that is, *Th1* can execute *CS1* repeatedly, while *Th2* is never able to execute *CS2* even though it "wants to" (indicated by executing the await not c repeatedly).

The above is essentially a problem of "fairness", where the scheduler's interleaving of the threads is *unfair* in the sense that *Th2* is scheduled to execute its await –to "have another go" – only when its await condition not c –at that particular moment– is again false. That is, while it is *possible* above for *Th2* to be allowed to retry its await c while *Th1* is in its *OB1* (and *Th2* is not rescheduled), there is not necessarily any *guarantee* that it will be. It's unfair in the same sense as it would be unfair to phone a colleague at work, repeatedly, but only on days where you know she is working from home — and then claiming that "She is never there."

In the next chapter we will see how to avoid all those problems for mutual exclusion, achieving its safety (including the absence of deadlock), as well as the absence of livelock and the absence of starvation — at least for two threads.

The program that does that –Peterson's algorithm– took 15 years to find.

15.4 Exercises

Exercise 15.1 (p. 154) If the program of Fig. 15.2 and (13.6) were executed in lock step with each other, there would be a correspondence between the values of c,t in the first and $bb in the second. What is the strongest condition (over all three variables) that describes that correspondence?

Consider the two situations "critical section occupied by a thread" and "critical section empty".

Exercise 15.2 (p. 154) ⇓ Explain why simply *knowing* that the use of a lock in (13.6) has established critical sections in the two threads (in the sense of Fig. 15.2) allows you to conclude that the invariant bb>=0 is maintained.

What role does atomicity play?

Exercise 15.3 (p. 156) Why don't we need "bottom" ⊥ as a possible value for t in the Owicki–Gries version Fig. 15.2 of critical sections?

Exercise 15.4 (p. 157) We saw that (15.6) implements mutual exclusion safely (but, remember, it might deadlock even so); yet in its current form its safety cannot be shown by the Owicki–Gries method. Or can it?

Why couldn't we just place assertions just after the await statements

$$\begin{array}{ll}
\cdots \quad \texttt{c1= True} & \cdots \quad \texttt{c2= True} \\
\quad \texttt{await not c2:} & \quad \texttt{await not c1:} \\
\quad\quad \{\,\texttt{c1 and not c2}\,\} & \quad\quad \{\,\texttt{c2 and not c1}\,\} \\
\quad\quad \textit{"critical section 1"} & \quad\quad \textit{"critical section 2"} \quad\quad (15.8) \\
\quad \texttt{c1= False} & \quad \texttt{c2= False}
\end{array}$$

and then argue that if both critical sections are active we must have   c1 and not c2 and   c2 and not c1   simultaneously true — which cannot happen?

That is, why doesn't (15.8) check (15.6) successfully for mutual exclusion?

Exercise 15.5 (p. 157) By introducing auxiliary variables b1 and b2 into threads *Th1* and *Th2* of (15.6) respectively, overcome the problem in Ex. 15.4 and show how to check (15.6) (with those extra auxiliaries) for mutual-exclusion safety.

Can the await statements still be implemented by simple spin loops, as remarked just after (15.6)?

Hint: To show mutual exclusion in (15.6), the approach of Ex. 15.4 is the right idea; but a problem is that its Booleans c1 and c2 do not correspond exactly to their threads' being in their critical sections: either Boolean can be True over too wide a section of the program.

Attach a new b-auxiliary to each await directly, and thus arrange that it has value True *exactly* when the corresponding thread is in its critical section.

You will need a global invariant as well.

Exercise 15.6 (p. 157) One way to prove absence of deadlock is to show that it's not possible for every await to be waiting on false at the same time — i.e. that if *all* the await *pre* conditions are true then *at least one* of the await "waiting for" conditions must be true as well.

In Fig. 15.1, however, the await (implicit) preconditions are (both) true, and the two "waiting for" conditions are (both) not c. Can you prove absence of deadlock here?

Exercise 15.7 (p. 158) ⇓ Figure 15.2 has a similar problem to Fig. 15.1: how do we prove absence of deadlock? Here again the conjunction of all the await *pre* conditions does not imply that at least one of the await *waiting-for* conditions must be true.

This time however it *is* possible to add preconditions that are both locally and globally correct, and that will allow proof of absence of deadlock.

What are those preconditions, and why are they locally and globally correct?

Yet this implementation of critical sections is still not satisfactory. Why not?

Peterson's algorithm for mutual exclusion

16.1 Introduction

In Sec. 13.7 we began the discussion of critical sections and mutual exclusion: recall that a *critical section* is a portion of code that must be allowed to execute *without* being interrupted by other threads that are executing code of the same kind. That is, all those code fragments in the whole system must be *mutually excluded* from each other, so that no two can be active simultaneously. As we saw in the rest of Chapter 13, that is such an important programming tool that there are special hardware instructions (like CAS) for doing it. It can also be done by controlling interrupts directly (i.e. by turning them on and off).

Later, in Sec. 15.3, we described some of the issues that can complicate the implementation of mutual exclusion: specifically deadlock, livelock and starvation. And we will encounter a further issue soon.

It might be surprising therefore that it is possible to program mutual exclusion *without* using special instructions (like CAS) or the direct manipulation of interrupts. Although it isn't much done in practice, the "puzzle" of figuring out *how* to do that is a very good showcase for many of the techniques we have spent the earlier part of this book learning and practising: assertions, invariants, data abstraction... and careful checking. As a special case, we will set it as Ex. 16.1 right here: do try it for yourself before looking at the (partial) answer!

Exercise 16.1 ⇓ Using only single-assignment statements to simple variables (i.e. no multiple assignments, no expressions referring to more than one global variable, no sequences or other non-basic data-types) and only body-free `await`-statements that can be implemented using spin loops, that is by an "`await` *cond*" with no body and no atomicity needed to evaluate `cond`, as in (15.6), ...

... program a two-thread mutual-exclusion protocol that is safe (the two threads cannot be in their critical sections at the same time), cannot deadlock (the two threads cannot both be "stuck", trying to enter the critical section), that does not allow one thread to overtake the other indefinitely (i.e. allows no unfair "queue jumping") and does not stop one thread from entering the critical section simply because the other thread is not participating in the protocol at all (i.e. because it is busy elsewhere).

Figure 16.1 A framework for the "no locks" critical-section program

Some initialisation outside of both threads.

Th1 repeats this forever.

other business 1.
simple assignment statement(s). # Indicate that *Th1* wants to enter CS1.

await *cond1* # with no body.
  critical section 1.

simple assignment statement(s). # Leave CS1.

Th2 repeats this forever.

other business 2.
simple assignment statement(s). # Indicate that *Th2* wants to enter CS2.

await *cond2* # with no body.
  critical section 2.

simple assignment statement(s). # Leave CS2.

The last of those is the "further issue" referred to above.

The structure should be as in the code skeleton in Fig. 16.1 and, when complete, should not have more than, say, eight statements in each thread. And the solution should be symmetric, that is the code for *Th2* should be the same as for *Th1* except for swapping 1 and 2 in the obvious way (i.e. *mutatis mutandis*).

16.2 Implementation based on a queue

Peterson's algorithm will solve Ex. 16.1 above, achieving mutual exclusion between two threads (safety) while avoiding all the issues above. We approach it however from a more abstract level.

That is, our key idea is to think abstractly about what we really want, and then to build it with the tools we have: so we begin by imagining that the two threads cooperate by using a *two-place queue* to decide which of them enters the critical Ex. 16.2 | section, and when. That scheme is shown in Fig. 16.2.[1]

---

[1] The idea of starting here, at this abstract level, is due to Jayadev Misra [41, pp. 26–31] , and we will follow his development. So far, it is not the answer to Ex. 16.1 that we are looking for, because it uses a sequence variable which *itself* requires mutual exclusion if it is to be manipulated safely: remember that, in Ex. 16.1, only simple variables were allowed. To reach a more concrete program, i.e. *without* queues (or sequence variables), Misra used coupling invariants, one of the topics of our earlier Part II. As we will.

Figure 16.2 Peterson's algorithm implemented with a queue

```
{ qs==[] } # Queue qs is initially empty.

# Th1 repeats this forever.

"other business 1."
qs= qs+[1]              # Th1 joins qs at rear.
await qs[0]==1:    # qs[0] is the head of qs.
   "critical section 1."
qs= qs[1:]         # qs[1:] is the tail of qs.              (16.1)


# Th2 repeats this forever.

"other business 2."
qs= qs+[2]              # Th2 joins qs at rear,
await qs[0]==2:         # waits until at front,
   "critical section 2."
qs= qs[1:]                 # and now leaves qs.
```

Informal checking for *safety* relies on the fact that qs[0] is always the name of the current thread in the critical section (if indeed one of the threads is there) — thus that fact must be invariant. Since qs[0] cannot have more than one value at the same time, there cannot be more than one thread there.

Ex. 16.3

Absence of deadlock relies on the fact that if each thread is at its await then the queue is full — and so they cannot *both* be not at the head of the queue.

And *absence of starvation* relies on the fact that once *Th1*, say, has joined qs it must eventually reach the head of the queue, provided *Th2* does not stay in its critical section forever (which must always be assumed — otherwise there is no hope of achieving "liveness" at all).

Yet the reason that we don't immediately take (16.1) as "the solution" is precisely that it *is* (too) abstract: the manipulations of qs itself need protection from interference. To join the queue, for example, a thread must write its identity into the queue *and* increase an index — and it must not be interrupted by another thread between those two actions. So using the scheme (16.1) "as is" would simply be pushing the critical-section requirement to a lower level.

To get from abstract to concrete, we will use the data-abstraction techniques of Part II to implement the sequence qs in terms of more elementary variables: we introduce a coupling invariant that links the "abstract" qs to a "concrete" representation as three simple Booleans t1, t2 and t.

Our first step towards that is to realise that qs can have only five values: either it's empty, or it has just 1 or 2 in it, or it has both 1 and 2 but in either order. (This is a global invariant, easily checked: but checked it must be!) Our coupling invariant is then that t1 means that 1 is in qs (somewhere); and similarly t2 means that 2 is in qs. And t (an "honorary" Boolean, so-called since it has only two values, which we could call True and False) applies only when *both* 1 and 2 are in qs — and it indicates which of the two is in qs[0], i.e. is at the head of the queue. (If qs is not

Figure 16.3 Encoding queue qs as three Booleans t1, t2 and t.

```
                not t1 and not t2        # initialisation

    # Th1                                # Th2

    OB1                                  OB2
    t1,t= True,2        # atomic         t2,t= True,1        # atomic
    await not t2 or t==1                 await not t1 or t==2
      CS1                                  CS2
    t1= False                            t2= False
```

The two multiple assignments, and the "or" in the await conditions, look like they might themselves need critical sections. But we will discover that they do not.

---

full, then t has no significance.) With that coupling invariant we convert (16.1) into the program shown in Fig. 16.3, using the translations that the coupling invariant determines and following the techniques of Part II for the manipulations of qs, and the tests on it, to show us how to express them in terms of the three Booleans:

(a) Initially the queue is empty: so we have t1==t2==False. (And t has no significance.)

Ex. 16.4

(b) Abstract qs= qs+[1] "*Th1* joins the queue at its end." becomes the concrete t1,t= True,2.

(c) Similarly qs= qs+[2] becomes t2,t= True,1.

(d) await qs[0]==1 "*Th1* waits until it is at the head of the queue." becomes await not t2 or t==1.

(e) Similarly await qs[0]==2 becomes await not t1 or t==2.

(f) qs= qs[1:], that is leave the queue (either thread), becomes t1= False in *Th1* and t2= False in *Th2*. (And t need not be changed.)

Using those translations gives us Fig. 16.3, where there is no longer a queue variable qs. We have made progress but have not yet eliminated the possible need for "lower level" critical sections: there are still multiple assignments. Further, although no await has a body here (as we require), their conditions refer to two global variables. Those are the topics of Secs. 16.3 and 16.5 to come.

16.3 Eliminating multiple assignments

The code in Fig. 16.3 has two multiple assignments: they are `t1,t= True,2` and `t2,t= True,1`. Each is written on a single line, which is how we indicate that it's atomic; and because of that (1) we could check the local correctness with a single multiple substitution, and (2) we would not have to check for interference *between* the two assignments — they have no "between".

But to implement that "at runtime" where we have only single-assignment atomicity, we would have to put the two statements in a critical section of their own: in the first case, for example, we would have to write

$$
\left.
\begin{array}{l}
\texttt{lock} \\
\quad \texttt{t1= True} \\
\quad \texttt{t= 2} \\
\texttt{unlock} \quad ,
\end{array}
\right\} \rightarrow
\text{Indentation documents the critical section that the \texttt{lock/unlock} establishes.}
\tag{16.2}
$$

where the two statements in the critical section –between the `lock` and the `unlock`– can be in either order precisely because the locking is there.[2]   `Ex. 16.5`

If we remove the lock, however, which is what we would like to do, then the order of the two statements becomes very important — because interference might happen between them. It is even possible that neither order works (but luckily we will discover that one of them does).

Thus when we split those multiple assignments in Fig. 16.3, we have only two possibilities: `Ex. 16.6`

$$
\begin{array}{ll}
\begin{array}{l} \texttt{t= 2} \\ \texttt{t1= True} \end{array} & \qquad
\begin{array}{l} \texttt{t= 1} \\ \texttt{t2= True} \end{array}
\end{array}
\tag{16.3}
$$

$$
\text{or} \quad
\begin{array}{ll}
\begin{array}{l} \texttt{t1= True} \\ \texttt{t= 2} \end{array} & \qquad
\begin{array}{l} \texttt{t2= True} \\ \texttt{t= 1} \end{array} \quad .
\end{array}
\tag{16.4}
$$

The first of those possibilities (16.3) is however not safe: mutual exclusion is no longer guaranteed. The second possibility (16.4) however *is* safe, as we will see.   `Ex. 16.7`

Employing "operational reasoning" here would mean that, to show that the second alternative (16.4) is safe, we would argue that (on the left, between the two assignments) Thread *Th1* is "about to" execute `t= 2` and that, if it is, variable `t1` cannot be set to `False` before it does so — because setting `t1` to `False` can be done only by *Th1* itself, and *Th1* is "here" (between the assignments) and not "there" (at the end of *CS1*).[3]

And the problem with the first alternative is now clear: it is that `t` *can* be set to 1, falsifying `t==2`, while *Th1* is between the assignments, because the assignment `t= 1` is done by *Th2*.

But "operational" is only helpful, not conclusive: it gives insight — but it is terribly unreliable, especially for concurrency. (See Sec. 17.11.1 below for an example of just that.) To check carefully, we add a label-like auxiliary variable as follows. In the two program fragments below, the "L:" –which is designed to look like a label– is

---

[2] A more `Python`-like syntax for this might be `lock` *lockName:* then indentation and finally outdenting instead of an explicit `unlock`. But we will stick with the above because it is more familiar generally.

[3] Purely "operational" reasoning is in the style "This happens, then that happens." exclusively, rather than the "If this is true then that is true." reasoning that we promote in this text. Relying only on the former is precisely what we are trying to avoid in the general "What's true here?" approach. For concurrency in particular, operational reasoning is especially risky.

Figure 16.4 Peterson's algorithm completed.

```
              not t1 and not t2        # initialisation

   # Th1                               # Th2

   OB1                                 OB2
   t1= True                            t2= True
   L1: t= 2                            L2: t= 1
   await not t2 or t==1                await not t1 or t==2
   { not L1 and t1 and                 { not L2 and t2 and
     (not t2 or L2 or t==1) }            (not t1 or L1 or t==2) }
     CS1                                 CS2
   t1= False                           t2= False
```

The atomic double assignments from Fig. 16.3 have been split into single assignments.

The two assertions before *CS1* and *CS2* are inconsistent, and so establish mutual exclusion between the critical sections.

---

shorthand for introducing an auxiliary Boolean variable L that is true in between the two statements, and nowhere else. In other words, the left-hand statements are abbreviations for the right-hand statements:

```
        stmt1                stmt1; L= True  # atomic
   L:   stmt2                stmt2; L= False # atomic    .
```

With that we can be more precise with the "about to" above, and introduce two auxiliaries L1, L2 in that style, giving Fig. 16.4 based on Fig. 16.3. In effect (the appropriate) L is True just when the thread is "poised" between two statements.

Ex. 16.8

Although the assertions in Fig. 16.4 are long (three conjuncts, the third one itself a triple disjunct), they are easy to motivate: on the left, the conjunct not L1 is true there because *Th1* is not at its L1 "label" (and it is globally correct, since only *Th1* can affect L1); the Boolean t1 is true from the earlier assignment t1= True (and is globally correct, because *Th2* does not assign to t1), and not t2 or L2 or t==1 is *implied by* the await condition, that is by the not t2 or t==1 alone. We weakened that assertion by including the extra "or L2" precisely in order to make it globally correct — for these reasons:

- if not t2 is falsified by the assignment t2= True in *Th2* still the disjunct as a whole is true, because L2 is now True;

- and if L2 is falsified by *Th2*'s moving beyond the label L2: then the disjunct as a whole is still true because t==1 becomes True;

- and t==1 cannot be falsified by *Th2*, since *Th2*'s only assignment to t is t= 1.

Ex. 16.9

Figure 16.4 is Peterson's algorithm; and we have now established that it is safe.

16.4 No deadlock, no starvation in Peterson's algorithm

It is easy to check that Peterson's algorithm cannot deadlock, a safety property: if both `await` conditions are false, we have `t!=1 and t!=2`, which is impossible because 1 and 2 are the only values assignable to `t`: its value must be one or the other. (More precisely, we have that `t==1 or t==2` is a global invariant.)

Ex. 16.10

For absence of starvation, a liveness property, we must show that `not t2 or t==1` must eventually become –and remain– true if *Th2* continues to execute (and vice versa): and here is where we assume that *Th2* cannot execute indefinitely in its critical section.

Once *Th2* leaves its critical section, it must eventually reach *OB2*; and while it remains there `not t2` is true, so that *Th1* can enter the critical section. But if *Th2* leaves *OB2* then eventually `t==1` must become true and remain true — and again *Th1* can enter the critical section. Thus *Th1* cannot be starved by *Th2*.

16.5 Peterson's algorithm without locks

In Fig. 16.3 it was remarked that there were two places where Peterson's algorithm might need locks for its implementation: one was the atomic multiple assignments, but we dealt with that in Sec. 16.3. The other was the multiple tests in the two `await` statements, which we look at now.

For the "multiple tests" we recall from (15.5) in Sec. 15.3 that an `await` can be implemented with a lock, no matter how complicated the condition, because the lock can be used to make evaluation of the condition atomic. In (15.6) however it was shown that if the condition is based on only a single variable, a lock is not necessary: a spin loop will do.

The full truth lies between those two extremes: an `await` can be implemented without a lock provided its condition refers only to a *single* variable from another thread: that variable is read once, and then the calculation of the condition is based on the value read. But if two (or more) variables must be read from other threads, there is a risk that the thread performing those two reads could be interrupted between one read and the other.

Now Peterson's *Th1* `await` does read two variables, both `t2` and `t` — and unfortunately both can be written-to by *Th2*. Yet it *can* be implemented without a spin lock, because the condition `t==1` is *stable* in *Th1*, meaning that *Th2* cannot falsify it. A lock-free, that is spin loop (not spin lock) implementation of `await not t2 or t==1` in *Th1* is therefore possible: it is

Ex. 16.11
Ex. 16.12
Ex. 16.13
Ex. 16.14
Ex. 16.15

```
while True:
    if not t2:
        break
    if t==1:                                    (16.5)
        break # t==1 is stable, preventing starvation.     ,
```

where we have used separate lines to show precisely where interruption is tolerated. (Recall Sec. 13.3.)

16.6 Exercises

Exercise 16.1 is on p. 161.

Exercise 16.2 (p. 162) Add assertions to (16.1) in Fig. 16.2 that are sufficiently detailed to check its safety carefully. Remember that manipulations of qs must have preconditions that ensure the absence of "everyday" errors: if the queue is empty, for example, you can't examine its first element, nor can you take its tail.

Exercise 16.3 (p. 163) Explain in detail why deadlock cannot occur in the Peterson's-algorithm system of Fig. 16.2, i.e. that qs[0]==1 and qs[0]==2 can never both be false. How do we know that qs[0] is defined?

Exercise 16.4 (p. 164) In Sec. 16.2 (b), (c) –where one thread joins the queue qs at its end– the variable t is set to the identity of the *other* thread — even though that thread might not be in the queue at all.
    Why?

Exercise 16.5 (p. 165) ⇓ Using (16.2) as inspiration (or other ideas of your own), suggest a nice syntax for critical sections. Propose a checking rule (in the style of Appendix B) that could be used for it.

Exercise 16.6 (p. 165) Are there really only two possibilities for splitting the double assignment in Peterson's algorithm? Can you think of a third?

Exercise 16.7 (p. 165) Set out a schedule in the style of (15.7) showing that the first alternative at (16.3) above for splitting t1,t= True,2 is *not* safe.

Exercise 16.8 (p. 166) Check that the two assertions mentioned in Fig. 16.4 are indeed inconsistent, so establishing that *Th1* and *Th2* cannot simultaneously be in their critical sections.
    Hint: See Appendix D.

Exercise 16.9 (p. 166) Consider just one "run" of each of *Th1* and *Th2* in Fig. 16.4; ignore the *OB* and *CS*, so that each thread is just four lines long. If you checked mutual exclusion for every single execution path possibly arising from running the two threads in parallel, how many paths would you have to check? Since each path is four lines long, how many pre-post checks (i.e. Hoare triples) would that checking require altogether?
    Hint: Recall "ABCD" from Sec. 13.1. Here it is more than 500.

Exercise 16.10 (p. 167) Check that the *negations* of the two await conditions mentioned in Fig. 16.4 are indeed inconsistent, so establishing that *Th1* and *Th2* cannot deadlock.
    Hint: Remember to consider global invariants; and see De Morgan's law (E.23) in particular (App. E.2.2).

Exercise 16.11 (p. 167) ⇓ Why do we know that (16.5) is a correct implementation of `await not t2 or t==1`?

Exercise 16.12 (p. 167) What are the differences between a condition's being *stable*, being *globally correct* and being *globally invariant*?

Exercise 16.13 (p. 167) Why would

```
while True:
  if cond1:
    break
  if cond2:
    break
```
(16.6)

not be a correct implementation of `await` *cond1* `or` *cond2* if neither *cond1* nor *cond2* were stable?

Exercise 16.14 (p. 167) ⇓ Why don't we simply write `while t2 and t!=1: skip` for program (16.5)?

Exercise 16.15 (p. 167) Give an implementation of `await` *cond1* `and` *cond2* that is lock-free, assuming *cond1* is stable and that each of the two conditions refers to at most one shared variable (but not necessarily the same one). Be sure to take starvation into account. (Note it's and here, rather than `or` .)

17

Garbage collection on the fly

17.1 Introduction

In Sec. 13.1 we observed that concurrency occurs "in the large", for example between many customers each using a *separate ATM* to access potentially the *same* bank account, and from widely separated locations — but also that it can occur "in the small", deep within the operating system of a single isolated computer. The latter is the subject of this chapter.

We will explain below what "garbage" is (in a computer), and what "on the fly" means (concerning its collection) — but in broad terms the issue here is that for efficient execution of some computer programs it's convenient not to force them to "clean up after themselves" as they go, because the clean-up might turn out not be necessary anyway. But sometimes it *is* necessary, especially if the program runs for a long time. In that case the clean-up *is* necessary; and a straightforward solution is to pause the program temporarily and, while it is paused, clean up everything at that point. Then the program is allowed to resume.

An alternative solution, but much more complicated, is to have an extra "clean-up" program running separately in parallel, all the time, so that the main program does not have to pause. But if those two things are active at the same time, then you are dealing with concurrency; and you must make sure that the extra program does not interfere with the main program. Here is an "everyday" example.

Think of empty coffee cups you might leave around your office at work, because you are too busy to take them to the kitchen yourself. When you finish work for the day –your job is "paused"– someone else collects all of them: from your desk, from your bookshelves, from the floor next to your seat... Because you are not in your office (i.e. paused), you are not interfered with by that collection. It's simple and efficient, both for you and for the cup collector — until, one day, you go the kitchen to make your next coffee and find that there are no clean cups there at all. (They are all somewhere in your office and will be collected all at once, but only after you have gone home.)

The more complicated "on the fly" alternative is to have a separate "parallel" person whose sole job during the day is to search continually for used almost-empty cups, take them to the kitchen, clean them and return them to the cupboards there. Interference –which we must prevent– would in this case be the situation where you turn away from your nearly-but-not-quite-empty cup, just for a moment — yet when you turn back to take that very last sip... the cup has disappeared.

This chapter is about how to implement an on-the-fly, collect-in-parallel algorithm for computers in a way that allows it to be checked rigorously that only real garbage is collected: never items that are still potentially in use. And we will see just how challenging a problem that is.

17.2 What "garbage" is — in a computer

Garbage is an issue for computer programs that use "pointer variables" either explicitly, or implicitly behind the scenes. The pointer variables refer to other variables indirectly, that is to their location and not directly to their value. The simplest example of a pointer (here in C rather than Python) is the variable p below, which refers indirectly to another variable n :

```
int n= 0;            // Declare integer n; initialise it to 0.
int *p;                      // Declare pointer-to-integers p.
p= &n;                       // Assign "the address of n" to p.
*p= *p+1;       // Increment the integer (n) that p points to.
// Because p was pointing to n, it is n that was incremented.

{ POST: n==1 }
```

Pointers are however not very often used in the above way, that is to access variables (like n) that are available directly by name already (that is, are "on the stack"): we could have achieved the same effect much more simply with just n= n+1.[1] Instead pointers are combined with "dynamic memory allocation", where rather than declare an integer at compile time (say via int n as above, so that it can be referred to directly), instead space is allocated for the integer at runtime: the space comes from an area called "the heap", which is reserved precisely to allow such runtime allocations. The integer has no name but does have an address; and then the above program becomes

```
int *p;                     // Declare pointer-to-integers p.
// Allocate space from the "heap" for an integer;
// and make p point to it.
p= malloc(sizeof(int));
*p= 1;             // Assign 1 to the integer that p points to.
```
$$(17.1)$$

Typically, the heap (and pointers) are used where the amount of memory that a program will use is not known until it is run (because for example it might depend on how much data the program is given). And that is where the "garbage" problem comes from: it occurs when a program allocates space (using malloc()) but then loses access to it by "losing the value" of variables (like p) that point to it. If for

---

[1] Pointers are used also for parameters that a function must alter: in that case, a pointer to the actual parameter is passed, not its value.

example we used the same p to allocate a *second* integer in (17.1), something like

```
int *p;                         // Declare pointer-to-integers p.
p= malloc(sizeof(int));
*p= 1;              // Assign 1 to the integer that p points to.

p= malloc(sizeof(int));              // Garbage created here.
*p= 2;          // Assign 2 to the integer that p points to now.    ,
```

then the first integer is still 1 (somewhere on the heap) but the program cannot find it: its address *was* in p but is no longer. The "1" has become garbage, an integer-sized space the program has taken from the heap but can no longer access.

The garbage problem above is avoided by returning the no-longer-needed space to the heap, before there is a subsequent assignment to p. The result would be

```
int *p;
p= malloc(sizeof(int));
*p= 1;

free(p);                  // Return the integer-space to the heap.

p= malloc(sizeof(int));          // This makes no garbage now.
*p= 2;      .
```
(17.2)

That is precisely the "clean up your coffee cup as you go" scenario from above.

17.3 Why garbage needs to be collected

If all programs were written as carefully as (17.2) was, then garbage would not need to be collected: in effect, `free()` is "putting the garbage in the bin" instead of just dropping it onto the floor. But knowing when something is garbage, and when it is not, can be tricky. For example, although

```
p= malloc(sizeof(int)); *p= 1; free(p)
```

is fine (i.e. the garbage is properly "tidied up", not just thrown away), the related

```
p= malloc(sizeof(int)); *p= 1; q= p; free(p)
```

is *not* fine: when p is freed here, it is not garbage — the address formerly in p is still available in q, and so the integer returned to the heap can be accessed via *q even though in the meantime it might have been allocated (`malloc()`'d) to something else.

Because of that (and other complications), applying `free()` to no-longer-needed space is often not done even when it should be... which is the lesser of two evils; and so the garbage builds up. It's invisible but unreachable, yet still occupying memory. That is known as a "space leak", and eventually the program might run out of memory — even though the memory to which it needs access is actually quite small.

17.4 How garbage is collected

There are two principal ways in which garbage is collected; we mentioned the first one in Sec. 17.1.

That first way, called *mark–sweep*, is to pause the execution of the program, and then let a "Scanner" go through the heap, marking all reachable nodes: if the Scanner finds a marked node pointing to an unmarked node then it marks the latter also, and continues. That Scanning process is repeated until there is a complete scan in which no marks are propagated. Then the Scanner stops, and a "Collector" sweeps through the heap, moving all unmarked (hence unreachable) nodes to a "free chain", from where "`malloc()`" takes them when and if the program needs them (again). That process is illustrated in App. F.1.

The "marking of a node" requires of course that at least one extra bit –for each node– is devoted to recording whether the node has been marked.

In more detail: the program is paused and all nodes are set to unmarked, therefore considered as *potential* garbage. Then the "root nodes" that are explicit, named program variables (like p in (17.1) above) are marked as "reachable". At that point the Scanner's mark–propagation process begins, and is repeated, marking more and more nodes as reachable from other reachable nodes until no new nodes are marked. At that point, everything (still) unmarked is garbage, unreachable, and the Collector sweeps through the whole heap, moving all those unmarked nodes to the free chain. Once that is done, the program can be resumed.

The main disadvantage of the above mark–sweep method is the pausing of the program: anything *using* the program –a self-driving car for example– is likely to be at risk while its controlling program is paused for garbage collection.

The second main way of collecting garbage is *reference counting*: a newly allocated item from the heap is marked with a reference count of 1; every time its address is copied into another pointer the item's reference count (stored with it) is increased by 1; every time a pointer is reassigned to point elsewhere, the reference count of what it *used* to point to is decreased by 1, and the count of where it *now* points increased by 1; and when any count reaches 0, the item pointed to is `free()`'d, as p was in (17.2), but automatically.[2]

The main disadvantage of reference counting is that circular structures, those that point to themselves although nothing else does, will never be collected even though taken together they are garbage. Figure 17.1 illustrates the following example (still in *C*):

```
typedef struct node {struct node* ptr;} Node;
Node *p,*q;
p= malloc(sizeof(Node));        // *p's reference count is 1.
q= malloc(sizeof(Node));        // *q's reference count is 1.
p->ptr= q;                      // *q's reference count is now 2.      (17.3)
q->ptr= p;                      // *p's reference count is now 2.
p= NULL;                        // *p's reference count is back to 1.
q= NULL;                        // *q's reference count is back to 1.

// Both *p and *q are garbage, but their reference counts are not 0.
```

Ex. 17.1

Garbage collection "on the fly", this chapter's topic, is not so much a third method as it is a variation on the first — yet (astonishingly) it *can be* carried out without

---

[2] `Python` uses reference counting. Here of course more than one extra bit is required for keeping the reference counts.

Figure 17.1 Reference-counting misses some garbage

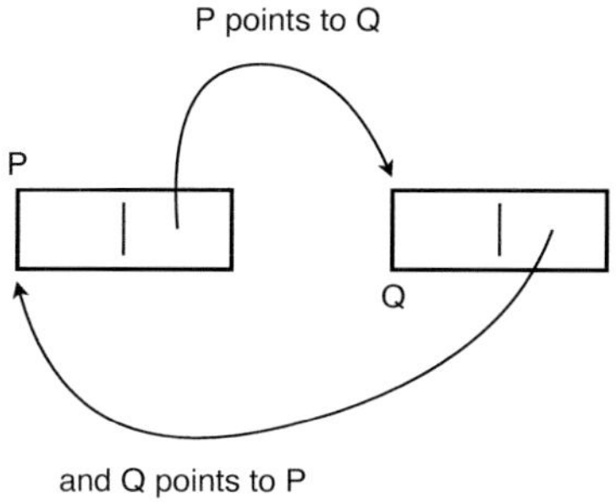

P points to Q

P

Q

and Q points to P

Both nodes P, Q above are "pointed to", and so their reference counts will be (at least) 1 in each case. But if they are *exactly* 1, that is not pointed-to from anywhere else, then they are both garbage.

Yet looking for reference counts of 0 won't find them.

---

pausing the program. That is, the marking and propagating –the scanning– occurs *concurrently* with the continuing activity of the program itself: the program might slow down slightly, but it does not at any time stop altogether. The challenge of on-the-fly collection however is to make sure that the "Mutator" (the application program, which changes the pointers) and the Scanner (which marks non-garbage) do not interfere with each other. An example of such interference is shown in Fig. 17.2. (There is less danger of interference between the Mutator and the *Collector*, however, since the portions freed by the Collector cannot (by definition) be reached by the Mutator.[3])

Ex. 17.2

17.5 Origins of this presentation

Pointer-generated garbage is not itself the problem: indeed in Sec. 17.4 we saw some solutions to collecting it.

The issue here is *concurrency*. What we present in this chapter concerns finding a concurrent program that solves an easy-to-understand but still very difficult problem, *and* to check that the program works. Ideally, the "finding" and the "checking" go together, each one supporting the other. We quote:

> ONE OF THE PROBLEMS that have to be dealt with is organising the cooperation of . . . concurrent processes so as to keep exclusion and synchronisation constraints extremely weak, in spite of very frequent manipulations (by all processes involved) of a large shared data space. The problem of garbage collection was selected as one of the most challenging problems in this respect (and hopefully a very instructive one). Our exercise has not only been very instructive, but at times even humiliating, as we have fallen into nearly every logical trap possible.[4]

---

[3] The original article [16, p. 969] discusses this point.

[4] This quote comes from the original article by Dijkstra, Lamport, Martin, Scholten and Steffens

Figure 17.2 Why garbage collection on the fly needs mark bits

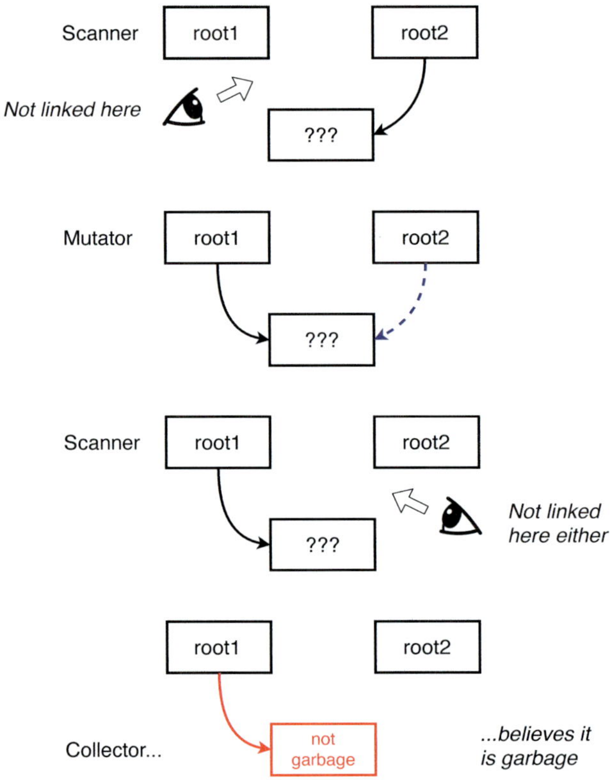

The four diagrams above show actions of the Scanner, then of the Mutator, then of the Scanner again and finally of the Collector.

When the Scanner looks from root1 (top diagram), the bottom node ??? seems inaccessible: but in fact it is reachable from root2.

The Mutator (second diagram) then introduces a pointer from root1 to ??? and deletes the pointer from root2. (Note that the Mutator must first use the pointer from root2 to find ???, so that it can make root1 point to it.)

When later the Scanner looks from root2 (third diagram), however, the bottom node still seems inaccessible: but now it is reachable from root1, because the Mutator changed the pointer between the Scanner's two visits, "behind the Scanner's back" so to speak.

Then (last diagram) the Collector, believing the unfortunate node ??? to be garbage because it found no link to it from either side, collects it — in error, because it is not garbage.

That is, although concurrent garbage collection "on the fly" is a real, practical problem, it was chosen by the authors of the above mainly as an exercise in writing *any* (complicated) program and being sure that it worked. (That is of course the point of this book!) And our first step –following those authors– is to be very clear about the context, in this case the behaviour of pointers and what programs do with them. So let us begin with that.

A *node* is a structure containing pointers (and possibly other data, which we won't worry about); if a node is declared directly in a program, it is called a *root* node because the program does not need to follow pointers to find it. (Figure 17.1 shows two (non-root) nodes; each is a structure with two components. Figure 17.2 shows two root nodes.) But nodes can be allocated at runtime as well (as with "`malloc()`" in (17.1) above), and "pointed to". A node is said to be *reachable* just when it is either a root itself, or it can be found by following a chain of pointers from a root.

Below is what programs can do with pointers, where a "null" pointer (c), (d), (e) is a value of pointer type (i.e. that *could* point to a node), but does not point to one at the moment:

(a) A reachable pointer p (see below) can be "swung", that is changed from pointing to "this" node to pointing instead to "that" reachable node. (Note the "reachable" — a pointer cannot be swung unless the target of the swing –the node it is *about* to point to– is reachable already: see Sec. 17.8 for why that's important.)

(b) A reachable pointer can be changed from pointing to "this" node to pointing instead to a new node (`malloc()`). (Remember that `malloc()` is the *C*-name for the procedure by which new nodes are allocated at runtime.)

(c) A reachable null pointer can be changed to point to an already reachable node.

(d) A reachable null pointer can be changed to point to a new node.

(e) A reachable pointer can be set to null.

It's cases (a), (b) and (e) that can create garbage.

Following the original authors (see footnote 4), we now simplify the problem by reducing those five cases above to just one. Instead of having a "null" pointer, we have a special root node called N that points to itself: all other previously called "null" pointers will now point to N instead. And the "free" nodes are themselves in a chain starting from a special root node F, whose last element points to N. With those modifications, the single operation on pointers we must consider is just (a) alone. That's how the original five cases are reduced to just one.

The other original cases (b)–(e) of course sometimes become *several* instances of the single remaining case (a), done one after the other: to implement (b) for example we would replace p with the pointer within F that points to the head node h say of the free chain (provided it is not N, in which case we are out of memory); then F's pointer would be updated to point to the tail t of the free chain (found within node h); then the pointers within h would both be set to point to N; and finally p would be set to point to h, the newly allocated node. $\boxed{\text{Ex. 17.3}}$

---

[16], later modified by van der Snepscheut [50]; our presentation here comes from the latter. None of those authors used Owicki–Gries reasoning, though, because it had only just been invented and was not yet widely known. Later, however, Gries himself did [21]: but our presentation is based mainly on van de Snepscheut's, which –in turn– referred to a solution by Ben-Ari [7].

17.6 Using a Boolean *mark-bit* to control scanning

One point of the example in Fig. 17.2 was to justify our conclusion that the Scanner will need to mark the nodes somehow, because otherwise it could not possibly notice the interference of the Mutator that occurred there — and so we cannot escape marking altogether. But it turns out that we will need only one extra bit per node: we assume every node is given a colour, either white W or black B and, during scanning, white will mean "not yet reached by the Scanner" and black will mean "reachable from a root". *Marking* a node means "making it black".

The *scanning* phase goes through all nodes in some fixed order (directly in the heap, not following pointers; say in ascending order of machine address). Call the nodes pointed to by a given node its "successors". We start however with a preliminary "whitening" phase as follows:

(a) Go through the heap, one node at a time (in any order — just make sure that all of them are examined). Set the colour of every node to white W.

And then we have the "scanning" phase:

(b) Set the colour of every root node to black B. That includes N and F, but also any node that is declared explicitly as a variable in the Mutator program, like p and q in (17.3).

(c) Propagate the B markings by scanning through all the nodes again (and again); each time, for every B-marked node encountered, set its successors –the nodes it points to– to B as well. (Note: after that, however, do not follow the pointer to *its* successors; instead just carry on scanning nodes in the original order.) When all nodes have been scanned on this pass...

(d) If during (c) some node was changed from W to B, that is a B-propagation occurred, go back to the start of (c) and propagate again: that is repeat the propagation step until an entire scan is completed in which no W nodes were changed to B.

In the program below, we will use a Boolean flag c to record whether any W nodes were changed to B.

Once the whole scanning process is complete, there should be no B-marked nodes that point to W nodes any more, anywhere; and, since all roots are B, we know that all W nodes are not reachable, that is are garbage, and so the scanning can stop. The *Collector* phase then begins, and goes through all the nodes, again in some fixed order, transferring all W nodes to the free chain which begins at root F. (See footnote 3 above.)

Sometime later, the whole process begins again, starting with whitening as at (a) above.

But –remember– while all this scanning and collecting is going on, the *Mutator* –our application program that is possibly *creating* the garbage– is "out there" potentially messing things up by executing pointer-swing operations of type (a) from Sec. 17.5 above. It is (potentially) *interfering* with the scanning/collecting activity: in Owicki–Gries terms, it is potentially interfering with the *assertions* that we will be using to check the garbage-collection thread.

The postcondition that we need for scanning, in order that its garbage collection is safe, is "White nodes are garbage." But "garbage" means "not reachable from a root", and all the roots are black. So we can take as our postcondition "No black node points to a white one." The variant for the inner loop (the list item "(c) Propagate..."

above) will be the number of nodes left to scan; the variant for the outer loop (in list item "(d) Go back to the start of (c)...") we will see further below.

Ex. 17.4

17.7 Ensuring local correctness of the Scanner

We now look at the scanning phase in more detail. For simplicity, we assume each node contains exactly two pointer-valued variables called `left` and `right`, and a one-bit W/B-valued variable `colour`. For *local correctness*, the Scanner code will use a "Boolean" c to note whether any "black node pointing to a white target", abbreviated B↦W, was removed by propagation.[5] For now, as we're concerned only with local correctness, we imagine that our Scanner will execute on its own, in particular without the Mutator running at the same time. Our code is[6]

Ex. 17.5

```
# Scanner (Version 1): Find and remove all B↦W's.
c= W # Used for the variant.
# INV: If c==B then no black node in Nodes points to a white node.
repeat
  c= B
  # INV: If some node in Nodes scanned so far is B↦W then c==W.    (17.4)
  for n in Nodes: # In some order: doesn't matter what.
    if n.colour == B:  # Needs propagation?
      if n.left.colour ==W: n.left.colour, c= B,W
      if n.right.colour ==W: n.right.colour,c= B,W
until c==B
```

The inner (`for`-)loop's variant is "the number of nodes not yet examined in `Nodes`". The variant for the outer (`repeat`-)loop is "the number of W-marked nodes *including whether* c is W".

Ex. 17.6

Now we consider the two invariants. Since for the outer loop we want postcondition "No black node in `Nodes` points to a white node." we simply take as our invariant

If c==B then no black node in `Nodes` points to a white node.   (17.5)

Finding an invariant for the inner loop is in the style of "iterating up" (Sec. 3.3.1), where the iteration is from "no nodes scanned" to "all nodes scanned". Writing that a B node is B↦W if either or both of its pointers target(s) a W, our invariant is

If some node in nodes scanned so far is B↦W then c==W.   (17.6)

On termination of the `for`-loop, "nodes scanned so far" will be "all nodes", and so the postcondition of the inner loop is simply

If there is any node in `Nodes` at all with B↦W then c==W.   (17.7)

(That is an application of the "split a conjunct" style of invariant synthesis from Sec. 3.2.) With (17.7), the `until` condition c==B of the outer loop gives the following overall postcondition:[7]

There is no node anywhere in `Nodes` with B↦W.

---

[5] We call it "Boolean" because it is two-valued, and because of what it means. For convenience in checking, however, we make it a colour, either B or W. It's an "honorary" Boolean.

[6] `Python` does not have a `repeat` loop; but they are easily implemented with `while True:` and `break`.

[7] This is an example of simple propositional reasoning, that (A⇒B) and not B ⇒ not A. See (E.30) in App. E.2.4.

Finally, we return to the inner invariant (17.6) — and here is perhaps the only bit of checking that is not routine. The assignment `n.left.colour=` B can *introduce* a B↦W into the "nodes scanned so far" because `n.left` (rather than `n` itself) might already have been scanned. If the node `n.left` was white then any white successor(s) *of it* would not have been blackened: but now we have made it black, and those white successors –if there were any– might still be there — and so we might have introduced a B↦W into the already scanned portion of `Nodes`. Thus to maintain the inner-loop invariant, we must now set c to W.

The above effect is supported by our intuition that the only reason we must make *multiple* scans is that some blackened nodes might "point backwards" into the already scanned portion of `Nodes`; and so another scan is needed to go back and repair those, that is to change those new B↦W nodes to B↦B nodes; but those repairs might in turn introduce B↦W nodes even further back, and so on. That's why the Scanner must keep scanning until c remains B.

We have now checked the local correctness of the Scanner.

17.8 Ensuring global correctness of the Scanner

Although we now see (from above) that our proposed Scanner is locally correct, that is, in isolation, we must check its global correctness too. Remember that in reality the Mutator is active at the same time... and so we must now imagine that pointer-swings in the Mutator might occur as the Scanner in (17.4) executes. Although we wrote the Scanner's inner-loop conditionals on single lines (for neatness), we will in fact allow interference between `if` conditions and their "then" branches; multiple assignments however, also on one line, will for now remain atomic.

Ex. 17.7
Ex. 17.8

As we saw in Sec. 17.5(a), the Mutator can at any time swing a reachable pointer so that it points to some other reachable node. If however the pointer's source is black and has been scanned, but the pointer's (new) target is white, then additionally that target must be blackened as part of the swing operation — for otherwise the inner-loop's invariant (17.6) "If some node in nodes scanned so far is B↦W then c==w." will be interfered with, that is changed from `True` to `False` (unless c==w already). Thus we assume the Mutator's action (a) in Sec. 17.6 is "Swing a reachable pointer p to any other reachable target node, *and blacken that target*." and that the action is atomic. Note that our reason for doing that is to prevent interference with the `for`-loop invariant: that is, the definition of global correctness, and our obligation to ensure it, *is helping us to design our program*.

Unfortunately however, the above suggestion for enhancing (a) is not enough: there is a more subtle issue. If the Mutator's new target was white and itself points to a further white then the Mutator's blackening it (as above), to avoid falsifying the invariant in one place, might actually break it in another place: from the new target to that target's even further target.

We will leave that for the moment, and consider possible interference with the outer-loop's invariant (17.5). In fact it *is* globally correct: the Mutator cannot make its antecedent c==B true, because the Mutator cannot assign to c at all. Can it make its consequent false: that "no black node points to a white node"? It cannot, at least not when c==B — for if c==B then *all* white nodes are unreachable, and so the Mutator cannot swing any pointer to one of them. (This is where Sec. 17.5(a) is important.)

Returning now to the inner invariant, in Fig. 17.3 we illustrate the (subtle) issue we discovered above when the Scanner and the Mutator are executing in parallel,

Figure 17.3 Failure of Program (17.4)

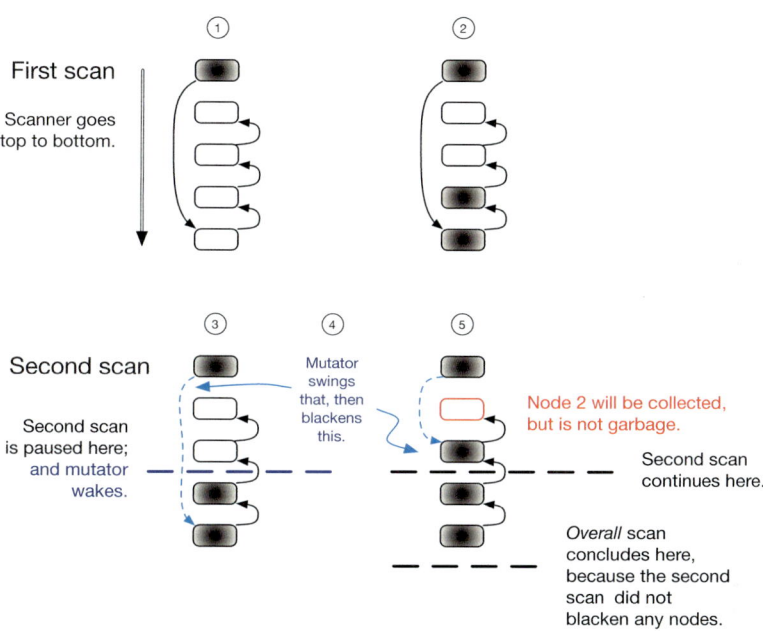

Here is an example for which (17.4) fails — even when the Mutator's swing-then-blacken is atomic. The first scan begins (Step 1) with a single black root node, node 1, and concludes having blackened nodes 4 and 5 (Step 2). Because it *did* blacken nodes, it starts a second scan.

The second scan returns to node 1 (Step 3), but pauses after having examined node 3. The Mutator then swings node 1's pointer from node 5 to node 3 and blackens node 3 (Step 4).

When the Scanner resumes, in Step 5, it finds node 4 is black — but the node it points to, node 3, *is already black* and so cannot be blackened again: the scan simply carries on. And when the second scan completes (Step 5), no node has been blackened *by it*, so the overall scan terminates. node 2, not garbage, will subsequently be collected in error.

The problem revealed by the above is that the Scanner does not "notice" any node-blackenings done by the Mutator, and so the overall scan might terminate before it should. That's the motivation for the approach taken in Sec. 17.9.

that is at the same time: it's a counter-example to our efforts so far. Step 5 in the figure shows that when the Mutator swings the pointer $1\mapsto5$ so that it becomes $1\mapsto3$ (and blackens node 3 as it does so), it introduces a $B\mapsto W$ pointer $3\mapsto2$ into the nodes scanned so far by the Scanner — but it had no way of informing the Scanner that it had done so.

The essence of our problem is that the Scanner "does not notice" blackenings done by the Mutator, because the Mutator has no access to the Scanner's variable c and thus no way of saying to the Scanner "I have just blackened a node, so you must scan at least one more time."

Because of the failures above, clearly we will have to do something more sophisticated than the straightforward "Use a 'Has anything changed?' flag." for termination of the outer loop. That's the topic of the next section.

17.9 Using a *count* to control scanning

The "more sophisticated" remark just above is encouraging: it is so much better than "start again from scratch". And the problem illustrated by Fig. 17.3, that the Scanner stopped too soon, suggests a possible remedy. Because the change of node 5 from W to B was done by the *Mutator*, and therefore did not update the Scanner's Boolean flag c, we look for a different way for the Scanner to control its outer loop's termination.

For that we introduce "B-counting" below: it's insensitive to whether the Scanner or the Mutator blackened a node: they are both detected. And –as we will see- the invariants and variants we tried in Secs. 17.7 and 17.8 earlier will suggest similar invariants and variants that we can use for this new "counting" version: we will not have to discover them from scratch.

With B-counting we rewrite the Scanner so that it controls termination simply on the basis of whether the number of black nodes has increased, irrespective of whether the Scanner or the Mutator caused the increase. For that we introduce two variables nB, oB for "new blacks" and "old blacks" respectively, and assume –temporarily– that the expression |blacks| gives atomically the exact number at that moment of B-marked nodes in all of Nodes.[8][9]

As mentioned above, the intuitive reason for this approach is that part of our earlier problem (with Scanner Version 1) was that the Mutator could not access the Scanner's "Boolean" variable c in order to indicate that –by its blackening a node– it might have introduced a $B\mapsto W$ "behind the scenes" into the already scanned portion of Nodes. Our counting approach here gets around that because a newly blackened node, whether caused by the Scanner *or by the Mutator*, will be detected automatically in the Scanner because |blacks| will have increased. In that way the Mutator is communicating with the Scanner implicitly.

So we write just |blacks| for "the number of black nodes in Nodes at this moment", and –as stated above– we assume for now that it is evaluated atomically. And we continue as well to assume that the Mutator swings-and-blackens atomically, so that a Mutator swing is guaranteed to increase |blacks| only if it blackens its target.[10] Our new Scanner (Version 2) is shown in Fig. 17.4. The assertions we introduce

---

[8] The idea of counting rather than "flagging" comes from Ben-Ari [7], but was implicit in the approach of Dijkstra *et al.*, because their outer loop was controlled by a count rather than by a Boolean as we did here. Counting was also used by van der Snepscheut [50], on which our presentation is based. We remove the temporary "magical" |blacks| in Sec. 17.10 below.

[9] Dijkstra *et al.* [16] adopted a different remedy: they introduced a third colour, "grey", meaning (roughly) "will be blackened, but hasn't been yet". It would therefore require two bits for the marks. Gries [21] applied the Owicki–Gries method to its proof.

[10] That will be relaxed in Sec. 17.11.

Figure 17.4 Scanner Version 2

```
             # Scanner (Version 2): Find and remove all B↦W's.
Atomic →  nB= |blacks| { |blacks|>=nB }
             repeat

                 oB= nB # oB is how many blacks before this scan.
                 for n in Nodes: # In some order: doesn't matter what.
                   # INV1: |blacks|==oB ⇒ no B↦W's in scanned.
                   # INV2: |blacks|>=oB.
                   if n.colour == B:                          # Ensure n is B↦B.
                     n.left.colour=  B          # This can't decrease |blacks|.   (17.8)
                     n.right.colour= B                             # Nor this.
                 # POST: |blacks|==oB ⇒ no B↦W's anywhere in Nodes.
Atomic →     nB= |blacks| # nB is how many blacks after this scan.

                 # INV3: nB==oB ⇒ no B↦W's anywhere in Nodes.
                 # INV4: |blacks|>=nB.
             until nB==oB # No new blacks were created.
             # POST: No B↦W's anywhere in Nodes.
```

Note that the two inner **if**'s of (17.4) from Sec. 17.7 have been removed in (17.8). With a blacks-counting scheme they are not necessary.

---

include two invariants INV1, INV2 for the inner (**for**-)loop, and two more INV3, INV4 for the outer (**repeat**-)loop.

Here is our reasoning for the assertions' local correctness:

(a) |blacks|>=nB is trivial.

(b) INV1 (inner loop) is true initially (i.e. before the first iteration) because nothing is (yet) scanned: **scanned** is empty.

(c) INV2 (inner loop) is true initially because of the assignment oB= nB just before it, and the assertion |blacks|>=nB that precedes the outer loop's first iteration, and INV4 for the outer loop's subsequent iterations.

(d) INV1 is maintained because, from INV2, its antecedent |blacks|==oB can never change from false to true; and if INV1's consequent is made false by an assignment n.--.colour= B in the inner-loop body, then |blacks| strictly increases and INV1's antecedent becomes false as well.

(e) INV2 is maintained because oB is never changed, and |blacks| can never decrease in the inner-loop body.

(f) INV3 (outer loop) is true at the end of the outer loop because of the inner loop's INV1, the (inner) **for**-loop termination condition that "already scanned" has become "anywhere" and the assignment nB= |blacks| just before.

(g) INV4 is established unconditionally by the assignment nB= |blacks| just before.

(h) The overall (outer-loop) postcondition is true because of INV3 and the outer-loop `until`-condition.

So far, so good — but now, to address global correctness, we must again consider possible interference from the (still atomic) Mutator, which can introduce a B↦W anywhere simply by swinging a pointer to a new target that it changes (at the same time) from W to B. (The possibly introduced B↦W would be from the newly-blackened target to some other W node: the same effect was discussed at the end of Sec. 17.7.) If it does that, however, it must increase |`blacks`| at the same time (atomically, for now): the Mutator can never decrease |`blacks`|.

Here is our reasoning for *global* correctness (*GC*) of the assertions we just above checked for *LC*:

(i) INV1 is globally correct for the same reason given at (d) above. There the "interference" was from within the body of the `for`-loop in the Scanner itself; but now it is from the Mutator.

(j) INV2 and INV4 are globally correct because the Mutator cannot change oB, cB, and it can only blacken, never whiten, nodes: its interference can only increase |`blacks`|.

(k) INV3 and POST are globally correct first, because the Mutator cannot change oB, nB and second, because if "No B↦W nodes anywhere." holds then all reachable nodes are B already, since the roots are all B. So if the Mutator swings a pointer, it must be to a node (already) B, because that node is reachable: thus the swing itself does not introduce a B↦W, and setting the new target to B has no effect, that is does not falsify "No B↦W nodes anywhere."

And yet... when checking global correctness, we have to be careful of possibly ignored intermediate assertions *between* atomic fragments, ones that we might have skipped over while doing local correctness — perhaps they were so obviously *LC* that we didn't even write them down. Are *they GC* too?

Indeed in this case there is an assertion, important in retrospect, that we skipped during *LC*-checking (an error of process, because we *should* have written it down so that the subsequent *GC* would be sure to check it). Shown in (17.9), it is

```
if n.colour == B:              # Ensure n is B↦B.
  n.left.colour= B
  n.right.colour= B
{n is B↦B}    .
```
(17.9)

Clearly "n is B↦B" holds at that point, because it is exactly what the `if` statement is intended to establish. But n is going to be moved from unscanned to scanned at the *end* of this iteration of the inner loop, and it must *still* be B↦B when that happens. Can Mutator interference change it back to B↦W between here and there?

Perhaps it could, if the Mutator were to swing either pointer `n.--` after this code but just before the end of the inner loop; luckily however the target of that swing must have colour B once the swing has been carried out, because the Mutator blackens the target atomically (for the moment) at the same time as the swing occurs — and so in fact the Mutator cannot change any n from B↦B back to B↦W.

Thus Scanner Version 2 (with its magically atomic |`blacks`|) and the Mutator (with its magically atomic swing-and-blacken) is both locally and globally correct. It works! And yet...

...we still have two things to do, in order to reach a practical and efficient solution: we must count the blacks non-atomically, that is without using |blacks| (which we accomplish in Sec. 17.10 just below); and we must allow the Mutator to swing-and-blacken in two separate steps, that is non-atomically (accomplished in Sec. 17.11).

Here incidentally is another example of "outside-in design": we begin by assuming temporarily that large-ish parts of our preliminary design are atomic (which simplifies things); and then we relax those assumptions one-by-one, that is by splitting the larger atomic fragments into smaller ones that have the same effect locally — but each of those newly exposed splits now requires global-correctness checking of the assertion revealed there. Doing them one at a time is what helps to prevent the *GC*-checking from becoming too overwhelming. (We did precisely that, earlier, for Peterson's algorithm in Sec. 16.3.)

17.10 Counting blacks non–atomically

One way to "count the blacks atomically" would be to impose a critical section around a black-counting loop, which (as we've already mentioned) is *exactly* what we're trying to avoid: that would hardly be "on the fly". But –we remember– the Mutator cannot decrease |blacks|: that number can only be increased. And that turns out to solve the problem: it will be enough to count the blacks *approximately*.

Instead of using nB= |blacks| to establish nB==|blacks| after the inner scan-loop, we might consider establishing only the weaker nB>=|blacks|, which is an over-estimate, because in that case the until-condition oB==nB of the outer loop would still imply that |blacks| itself has not increased — which is all that is needed for the overall postcondition.[11]

But the approximation nB>=|blacks| would conflict with the |blacks|>=nB of Inv4, which goes in the opposite direction and is necessary for the outer loop's next iteration where, instead, at the oB= nB we will need (only) that oB becomes an *under*-approximation. We escape that dilemma by introducing an auxiliary variable cB (for "current blacks"), to capture the actual value of |blacks|, and we set nB to be at least that cB — but then we allow |blacks| itself to increase further, consistently with Inv4.

Rather than write that approximate black-counting code now, we will *specify* it and then use (only) its properties, that is its specification, to make Scanner Version 3. Only if this Version 3 works will we bother to *implement* our specification of approximate black-counting (so constructing in effect a Version 3a). The "approximate counting" program fragment is shown at (17.10) in Fig. 17.5, where the specification stands for some code (to be written later) that would check if placed between that pre- and postcondition pair. (See App. B.6.3 for more about specifications.)

Using a specification, in program (17.10) of Fig. 17.5 we re-write Scanner Version 3 as (17.11) in Fig. 17.6. Our key insight –remember– is that if the under-approximating black-count "before" (oB, possibly too low) is *equal to* the over-approximating black-count "after" (nB, possibly too high) then in fact the *actual* black-count is equal to both — and so cannot have changed.

Many of our checks for the earlier Version 2 still go through; but we will check them all again anyway.

Local correctness

(a), (b), (c), (d) are unchanged.

---

[11] In fact we would then have oB==|blacks|==nB; but we do not need that.

Figure 17.5 "Approximate" black-counting specification

```
Auxiliary → cB= |blacks|        # Actual value of |blacks|...
Specification → nB:[ cB<=|blacks|,cB<=nB<=|blacks| ]              (17.10)
                      # ...but allow nB<=|blacks| afterwards.
```

The point of having a specification here is that we can use it to check carefully that the surrounding program will work, given this tentatively proposed approximate-count program fragment, without actually having to code it up yet.

If later we find out that in fact the approximate count is not sufficient to check the surrounding program then there would have been no point in implementing it now — and we would have saved ourselves some work by avoiding a blind alley.

Figure 17.6 Scanner Version 3

```
# Scanner (Version 3): Find and remove all B↦W's.
nB= 0 {|blacks|>=nB}
repeat
  oB= nB
  for n in Nodes:
    # INV1: |blacks|==oB ⇒ no B↦W's in scanned.
    # INV2: |blacks|>=oB.
    if n.colour == B:
      n.left.colour= B
      n.right.colour= B
    # POST: |blacks|==oB ⇒ no B↦W's anywhere.              (17.11)
Auxiliary → cB= |blacks|    # Capture |blacks| exactly into auxiliary cB.
    New → { oB<=cB and (cB==oB ⇒ no B↦W's anywhere) }    # LC and GC.
      nB:[ cB<=|blacks|, cB<=nB<=|blacks| ]        # specification.
      { oB<=cB<=nB }

    # INV3: nB==oB ⇒ no B↦W's anywhere.
    # INV4: |blacks|>=nB.
  until nB==oB
  # POST: No B↦W's anywhere.
```

(new) The new assertion's first conjunct oB<=cB comes from `Inv2` and the assignment cB= |blacks| just before. The second conjunct

$$\text{cB==oB} \;\Rightarrow\; \text{no } B{\mapsto}W \text{ nodes anywhere}$$

is true because of `Inv1` and the **for**-loop termination condition that "already scanned" is now "anywhere", and the assignment cB= |blacks| just before. (Similar reasoning was used for `Inv3` at (f) in Version 2; recall Sec. 17.9.)

(f) `Inv3` now depends on oB<=cB, from the first half of the new assertion, and cB<=nB from the postcondition of the specification: taken together they give nB==oB ⇒ cB==oB. Then the second half of the new assertion can be used.

(g) `Inv4` is true because of the specification's postcondition.

(h) Unchanged.

Global correctness

All the global-correctness arguments are unchanged.

And so we have checked that Scanner Version 3 works; and all that's left (for this version) is to implement the specification for approximate counting of blacks, since with its specification we have established that approximate counting is good enough. It is the straightforward program | Ex. 17.9 |

```
# PRE: cB<=|blacks|        ← precondition of specification (17.10)
nB= 0
for n in Nodes:
    if n.colour == B: nB= nB+1                              (17.12)
# POST: cB<=nB<=|blacks|  ← postcondition of specification (17.10)
```

which does not contain the auxiliary cB in its code. (It should of course be checked | Ex. 17.10 | for local and global correctness with respect to its specification; but we do not need to refer to the program that contains it.) Since cB is no longer in the code, it can be removed.

And so now, finally, we deal with the (impractical) atomicity of the Mutator.

17.11 Atomicity of the Mutator, in two steps

17.11.1 Step 1: the main part of the scanning loop

This –the very last issue we must deal with in this chapter– is that currently our Mutator swings one of the pointers of some node s (for "source"), that is either `s.left` or `s.right`, to a new node t ("target") and blackens that t *at the same time*. That is, the Mutator's sole (and atomic) action is " swing s to t, and blacken t ", as follows:

```
# s,t are both reachable nodes.
s.left,t.colour= t,B   # ...or s.right .                    (17.13)
```

Our final task therefore is to break (17.13) into two *separate* assignments, either

```
t.colour= B            or          s.left= t
s.left= t                          t.colour= B    ,         (17.14)
```

where the left alternative is "blacken *then* swing", and the right is "swing *then* blacken". (In both cases "and" has become "*then*". Recall that we had a similar situation in Sec. 16.3 for Peterson's algorithm.) At first sight, since the motivation for doing the two assignments atomically was to preserve the Scanner's inner-loop invariant

$$\text{INV1: } |\text{blacks}| == \text{oB} \Rightarrow \text{no B} \mapsto \text{W's in scanned. } , \tag{17.15}$$

it seems safer to blacken first (as at left above), so that if indeed `t.colour` was W then the Mutator would have increased $|\text{blacks}|$, thereby falsifying the antecedent $|\text{blacks}| == \text{oB}$ of INV1 *before* the subsequent swing that would falsify its consequent — and so INV1 as a whole would remain true all the way through, that is even if the Mutator were suspended between the two actions.

Yet that turns out to be a mistake, as the original designers of this algorithm discovered the hard way — and described as follows:[12]

> TO KEEP INVARIANT that there are no B$\mapsto$W's in the scanned nodes, during the marking cycle, we at first made our Mutator atomic.
>
> Encouraged by that success, we then tried to maintain the invariant with a *non*-atomic Mutator, that is, one in which the Mutator's action was split into two separate atomic operations: one for redirecting the pointer and another for blackening the new target. To be sure of maintaining that invariant, the Mutator had to blacken the target first, and only then swing the pointer.
>
> This non-atomic "finer grained" solution –although presented in a way sufficiently convincing to fool ourselves– contained a bug...

Ex. 17.11

The bug is essentially that if the target is blackened *before* the pointer is swung (as above), and the Mutator is suspended at that point, then an entire "whiten everything" process might be carried out during that period by the first phase of the Scanner. When control is returned finally to the Mutator and it swings the pointer –the second of the two assignments it must carry out– its target will now have been whitened (by the Scanner), its blackening lost — and so the Mutator's swing threatens

Ex. 17.12

to create a B$\mapsto$W in scanned after all.

And so we must try the other alternative, the right-hand "swing then blacken" in (17.14). Before looking more closely, we make a further restriction and then an observation:

(a) RESTRICTION: We now assume there is only *one* Mutator. (There are however extensions of this approach that work for multiple Mutators.) The practical implication of the restriction is that we can now assume that the Mutator's interference strictly alternates, that is swing, blacken, swing, blacken... In particular, there is never more than one swing in a row.

(b) OBSERVATION: When the (single) Mutator carries out a swing, the (new) target must be reachable — remember "reachable" in (a) of Sec. 17.5, and the assertion in (17.13). That means that if the target `t` is W (which is the "problem case", where the swing might create a B$\mapsto$W from s to t), there must be a B$\mapsto$W step somewhere on the path to that `t` from a root node.[13]

---

[12] This quote is freely adapted from the article by Dijkstra *et al.* [14] (with italics added), and the bug was discovered by Stenning and Woodger. An analogue of the bug, adapted to our current presentation, is shown in Fig. F.2 of App. F.2.

[13] It's the reachability of `t` that implies the existence of a path from a root node to it. It doesn't matter which root node it is: what matters is that the root node is B, yet the path from it to `t` ends in W. There must therefore be a change from B to W somewhere along the way.

But if the swing occurs during the inner Scanner loop, invariant `Inv1` ensures that the above B↦W step cannot be in `scanned` (unless `|blacks|>oB`, in which case `Inv1` is maintained trivially). And so it must be unscanned: the Scanner when completing its inner loop (later) will find it, and will propagate that B↦W node's colour B eventually, even if the Mutator doesn't. At that point `|blacks|` will be increased — and the Scanner's outer loop (its `until nB==oB`) will be forced to scan again. That "saves the day", as we will see below.

We exploit the restriction (a) above, introducing a label-like Boolean auxiliary `P` into the Mutator (for "poised", as in Sec. 16.3 for Peterson's algorithm, but this time "about to blacken") that is usually `False`. It becomes briefly `True` just (and only) when the (sole) Mutator has swung but not yet blackened. (Recall our earlier use of a similar labelling technique, in Sec. 16.3.) That is, the Mutator –in (17.14) above, its right-hand alternative– with the (auxiliary) `P` added, becomes

```
# Atomic multiple assignments, with auxiliary label-Boolean P.
```
{not P and s,t both reachable}
s.left= t   # Swing.
```
{P}          # P holds iff swung but t not yet blackened.
P: t.colour= B                       # t now blackened.
{not P}    .
```
$$(17.16)$$

Our new version of the earlier invariant Inv1 (17.15), taking advantage of `P` and OBSERVATION (a) above, we call Inv1A. It refers to the Mutator's `P`:

```
# This Inv1A adds a disjunct
# to the consequent of Inv1 from (17.15).
```
|blacks|==oB ⇒   # Invariant Inv1A .   (17.17)
         no B↦W in scanned
    or   P and B↦W in unscanned   .
```

Inv1A says essentially "The original Inv1 holds *unless* (·) the Mutator is poised between its two statements, i.e. that `P` is true, and (·) there is a B↦W in `unscanned`." We look first at the local correctness of Inv1A.

The first local-correctness check is that Inv1A holds at the beginning of the inner scanning loop: no node has been scanned yet, and so "no B↦W in scanned" holds trivially.

The second is that Inv1A suffices for "`|blacks|==oB` ⇒ no B↦W anywhere", the postcondition of the inner loop. It does so because at that point it's `unscanned` that is empty, and `scanned` is `anywhere`.

The final local-correctness check is that Inv1A is invariant, i.e. it is *maintained* by the inner loop. But the only update the inner loop can make is to change some node's colour from W to B, which trivially falsifies Inv1A's antecedent. So the invariance is pretty clear too — *except* for the hidden transfer at the very end of the loop of the current node `n` from `unscanned` to `scanned`. (Recall (17.9).) We will come back to that tricky transfer in Sec. 17.11.2 below: we leave it for now, and turn to global correctness of Inv1A.[14]

(†) Sec. 17.11.2

For *global* correctness of Inv1A, we must check *both* statements in the Mutator *separately* (because the Mutator is no longer atomic). For the `swing` we have from its

---

[14] By "hidden" is meant that it happens, but (in Python's for-loop) there is no source text like "`choose the next n for the loop`" that can be annotated with assertions.
```

precondition both **not P** and **t** reachable , and from INV1A itself (given **not P**) we have **|blacks|==oB** $\Rightarrow$ **no** B↦W **in scanned**. After the swing, however, we will have **P** — and so we show that **swing** under these circumstances has re-established (17.17). There are two cases: if the swing was to an already-B node, then the first disjunct **no** B↦W **in scanned** is preserved; but if the swing was to a white node –**t** say– then, because of **swing**'s precondition that **t** is reachable, there must be a B↦W somewhere on the path from a root to **t** and, from our precondition **Inv1A** for **swing** in this context, that B↦W cannot be in **scanned**: thus we have B↦W **in unscanned**. That deals with the first step of the Mutator in (17.16).

For the other **blacken** step in the Mutator we again assume INV1A (since we are treating the two steps separately). If **t.colour==B** already, the assignment **t.colour=** B has no effect; if however **t.colour==W**, then the assignment will increase **|blacks|**, so falsifying INV1A's antecedent.

That completes the local- and global correctness argument for the Mutator... except for the issue we deferred at (†) above. We attend to that now.

17.11.2 Step 2: moving from one node to the next in the scanning loop

Our last check (deferred from (†) above) is of the local correctness of the (hidden) transfer of **n** from **unscanned** to **scanned**, which occurs at the end of the inner scanner-loop. We expose (i.e. "unhide") it here:

```
for n in Nodes:
    ...for-loop body...

    # Hidden at the end of the for-loop.                       (17.18)
    { Inv1A } {n is B↦B }              ←   # No longer holds?
    "Transfer of n from unscanned to scanned."   # Exposed.
    { Inv1A }                          ←   # Not maintained?
```

In fact (17.18)'s precondition *is* locally correct — but its (right-hand) conjunct is not *globally* correct. We did consider that possibility earlier, at (17.9): but there it turned out that it *was* globally correct, because the *atomic* Mutator blackened its target. Unfortunately, with the now *non*-atomic mutator, it isn't globally correct any more — the Mutator might swing **n.left** or **n.right** or both to a W target, as before, *but then pause* before blackening its target, not yet "following through". During that pause, the assertion n is B↦B has become false.

The issue is that if (17.18) is reached in the Scanner while n is B↦B *is* false (i.e. with the Mutator paused between its **swing** and its **blacken**) and the transfer of **n** from **unscanned** to **scanned** is carried out then INV1A might not be maintained: either its first disjunct afterwards could be falsified, because the (no longer B↦B but now) B↦W node n has been added to **scanned** (and **scanned** is not supposed to have B↦W's); or its second disjunct could be falsified because a B↦W is removed from **unscanned** (and **unscanned** is supposed to have at least one B↦W).

We examine first the case where the Scanner's propagation of B completed, did establish n is B↦B, but that was falsified by a *later* Mutator **swing** of n.-- . (INV1A cannot be falsified by a Mutator **blacken**.) At that moment there must be a B↦W in **unscanned**: and it cannot be n itself, because n was B↦B.

But B↦W in **unscanned** is *itself* not globally correct: the Mutator could blacken its target — but that would increase **|blacks|**. Or it could swing the B↦W to a black target, *except* that it cannot do that before blackening the original swing from n, because its uses of `swing` and `blacken` must alternate. (Remember that we are assuming there is only one Mutator.) Again |`blacks`| would increase.

Collecting all that together gives us that even with Mutator interference after the Scanner's establishing n is B↦B , then

$$\text{n in } B\mapsto B \quad \text{or} \quad B\mapsto W \text{ in unscanned-}\{n\} \quad \text{or} \quad |blacks|>oB$$

will still hold at (17.18), sufficient for INV1A to be re-established by the (hidden) transfer.

That leaves only the case where the Mutator acts *between* the `n.left.colour=`B and the `n.right.colour=`B, so that n is B↦B was never established in the first place. That is, first `n.left` is coloured B — but then it is immediately swung by the Mutator to a W node, and in particular to one that was reached via `n.right` itself. The Scanner will then set `n.right` to B, however, thereby increasing |`blacks`| because the Mutator cannot swing `n.right` away without blackening `n.left` first (again, because `swing` and `blacken` must alternate).

17.12 The completed program

The final version of the Garbage Collector is given in Fig. 17.7 below; in Fig. 17.8 the propagation part of the Scanner is given alone, without assertions, to emphasise how much careful reasoning is required even for short programs — when they are concurrent.

Ex. 17.13
Ex. 17.14

17.13 Exercises

Exercise 17.1 (p. 174) Give an example of the circular-structure problem of (17.3) in Python.

Exercise 17.2 (p. 175) A garbage-collection method is *safe* if it never collects nodes that are still in use, i.e. they are not actually garbage. Is mark–sweep safe?

Is reference-counting safe? If you believe it to be, state an invariant that establishes its safety beyond any doubt.

Similarly, a garbage-collection method is *complete* if it collects all garbage: none is left behind. Is reference-counting complete?

Is mark–sweep complete when the Mutator is paused? Is it complete "on the fly"?
Hint: See Fig. 17.3.

Exercise 17.3 (p. 177) ⇓ Why is the problem not made *more* complex by having to carry out what was originally one instance of operation (b) in Sec. 17.5 by four instances of other operations?

Exercise 17.4 (p. 179) Is "All white nodes are garbage." the same as "All garbage is white." or not? If not, does it matter?
Hint: See (E.30) in Appendix E, and Drill A.16.

Figure 17.7 Scanner Version 4: final version

```
# --- Scanner (Version 4): Set all reachable nodes to B

# Initialisation.
for n in Nodes: n.colour= W # Whiten everything.
for n in Roots: n.colour= B # Blacken roots.

# Propagation.
nB= 0
repeat
  oB= nB
  for n in Nodes:
    # Inv1A and Inv2
    if n.colour == B:
      n.left.colour=  B
      n.right.colour= B
  nB= 0
  for n in Nodes:                    }  → count blacks
    if n.colour == black: nB= nB+1   )
  # Inv3 and Inv4
until nB==oB
# Post: No B↦W's anywhere.

# Collection
for n in Nodes:
  if n.colour= W:   # Add n to free list.
    n.left= F
    F= n

# Inv1A: See (17.17).
# Inv2:   |blacks|>=oB
# Inv3:   if nB==oB then no B↦W's anywhere
# Inv4:   |blacks|>=nB
```

The specification of the count (from (17.11) in Fig. 17.6) has been replaced by its implementation (17.12); and the auxiliary cB has been removed, because it is no longer needed.

Figure 17.8 Scanner propagation alone, without assertions

```
# Propagation alone.
nB= 0
repeat
  oB= nB
  for n in Nodes: # Propagate B.
    if n.colour == B:
      n.left.colour=  B
      n.right.colour= B
  # Propagation complete: did anything change?
  nB= 0 # Recalculate nB.
  for n in Nodes:
    if n.colour == black: nB= nB+1
until nB==oB # ...until nothing changes.
```

$$(17.19)$$

Exercise 17.5 (p. 179) ⇓ The c= W just before the `repeat` in (17.4) is clearly not necessary, because c= B is executed immediately afterwards. So we can (and will) remove it. But why is it useful for now?

Exercise 17.6 (p. 179) Check carefully that the variant is strictly decreased in the outer loop of (17.4).

Exercise 17.7 (p. 180) ⇓ In (17.4) we did *not* assume that the step from evaluating the `if`-condition to the `if`-body was atomic (although we did write it all on one line). An assertion `{ n.left.colour == W }` after the `if` (and similarly for `right`) must therefore be checked for correctness. It is trivially locally correct; but it is obviously not globally correct, since the mutator might execute `n.left.colour= B` if `n.left.colour` were the target of its pointer swing. That being so, *we cannot leave that assertion in our program.* But what can replace it?

What assertion should be there? Would `{ True }` do? After all, it can't matter if `n.left.colour` is set to B when it's B already, surely. But if `{ True }` is good enough, why do we need the `if n.left.colour == W:` at all?

Exercise 17.8 (p. 180) Suppose we removed *both* `if` statements from the inner-loop code, so that the inner loop simply blackens everything. Wouldn't that be simpler?

In fact it's *too* simple: then the inner loop would run at most twice, after which the outer loop would terminate with all nodes black (and, trivially, all white nodes would be garbage — because there aren't any white nodes).

What essential property would that trivial loop *not* have, and how do we prove that the actual loop has it?

Exercise 17.9 (p. 187) ⇓ The specification

```
nB:[ cB<=|blacks|, cB<=nB<=|blacks| ]
```

is easily implemented by the simple assignment nB= cB. And we have already checked that Scanner Version 3 works if that specification is met. Yet it clearly *cannot* work in that case, because it negligently declines to count anything at all. Or does it work after all...

Can you explain?

Exercise 17.10 (p. 187) Check (17.12) for local correctness, and for global correctness with respect to the Mutator.

Exercise 17.11 (p. 188) The Owicki–Gries method requires each thread's assertions to be checked for global correctness, that is, to be checked that they cannot be falsified by assignments in other threads. Most of the concurrency-related reasoning in this chapter –at least the subtler parts– has been doing just that, checking that the Mutator does not interfere (destructively) with the assertions in the Scanner/Collector.

But don't we have to check also that the Scanner/Collector does not interfere with the Mutator? Did we do that?

Hint: See Sec. 17.11.1.

Exercise 17.12 (p. 188) ⇓ Re-do the explanation of Woodger's scenario in App. F.2, but with the Mutator (now) correctly swinging before blackening. Is the bug avoided?

Exercise 17.13 (p. 191) ⇓ We have shown that the on-the-fly garbage collector here is safe, since all white nodes are garbage. But is it complete: is all garbage white?

If not, figure out whether it is possible for a piece of garbage to remain forever uncollected. If not, for how long can a piece of garbage escape collection?

Exercise 17.14 (p. 191) ⇓ The Collector runs after the Scanner, and moves all W-nodes to the free list, which is a singly linked list starting with root node F (and using only one of its pointers). It might be something like this:

```
for n in Nodes:
  if n.colour == W:
    n.left= F
    n.colour= B
    F.left= n    .
```
(17.20)

But the Mutator is still executing while this collecting going on: might it interfere with the code above?

Further, the Mutator might be acquiring a new node from the free list at the very same time as the Collector is adding a node to the free list: the Mutator's code (corresponding to "malloc()" in C) would be something like

```
newNode= F
F= F.left    .
```
(17.21)

Discuss (informally, perhaps) how these potential problems might be avoided.

## Part IV

Machine-assisted program checking, and testing

Machine–assisted program checking

18.1 Why by-hand checking is only a beginning

Up to this point we have concentrated exclusively on the by-hand checking of fairly small programs — though in some cases they were still quite complex, however small they might have been. We did that because, generally speaking, most programmers have not been taught the basic insights needed to see how informal correctness-checking can be done cheaply and effectively, nor have they been given the opportunity to see the improvements it brings not only to the quality of their programs but in the satisfaction they experience from really, seriously understanding the good job they have done.

And being unaware of those techniques and insights is not the programmers' fault. It is the fault of their teachers.

One of the reasons that rigorous program checking was lost, became rarely taught, is that it was originally promoted in an all-or-nothing way: the cost of rigour, the "all" option, in many cases was simply too high, too hard, too complicated... even too boring. And so we –and our students– were left instead with the "nothing". The "Lost Art" referred to in the Afterword is therefore how to use a light touch, to operate *between* those two extremes, to concentrate just on the assertions you really need: write them informally at least; or even just be aware that they are there. That is what makes the difference, and that is in a nutshell what this text is intended to demonstrate: how astonishingly effective the approach can be.

But it's not the whole story, and it is not *nearly* enough in the long run.

It is of course possible for errors to occur in the *checking* process itself, even for small programs: that's one of the reasons that program *testing* remains so important (Chapter 19 to come), whether you checked your program or not. Who has not occasionally made mistakes in adding up a shopping bill by hand?

Indeed with larger, or more complex, programs, the risk of "checking-time" errors itself becomes too large to tolerate when correct functioning is vital, when even a small bug could lead to death or disaster. In those cases, we use special-purpose programs to "check our checks", and in Sec. 18.2 below we look at just one checking-checker in particular: it is an especially good one (Dafny).

An analogy worth remembering is that even when we have learned the theory of differential equations, when we apply it to electrical circuits, or apply statics and dynamics to buildings and bridges, we still use pocket calculators for doing the arithmetic.

18.2 Automated checking of assertions in Dafny

18.2.1 Compile-time vs. runtime assertion checking

Dafny is a programming language similar in style to Python and C, and it does far more than simply check assertions.[1] Given our focus in this text, however, we will concentrate mainly on that.

In Dafny, programs –and their assertions– are checked *at compile time*. We discuss below how that is done — but first we look at two implications.

The first implication is that for a computer (i.e. one running Dafny in this case) to check assertions automatically, they must be written in a language the computer "understands". Informal, written-in-English assertions are no longer sufficient: we need propositional, and possibly even predicate calculus (Appendices D, E). Thus the price we pay for automated program checking is –possibly– having to take a crash course on logic *first*, since otherwise we cannot even express what we would like to have checked in terms that the automatic checker can "understand". The reason however that the bulk of this text does *not* use (formal) logic, that it is based on Python rather than on Dafny, is that it's important to learn *in* formally first what the benefit of the (formal) logic will be. Otherwise, how can you judge whether it's worth it?

Assuming that point is understood, we'll proceed as if formal logic has been learned (or at least that we understand what it is for) and address the second implication of compile-time checking. In Dafny, a program with an assertion that *might* fail at runtime *will definitely fail* at compile time. This induces some astonishment when one sees it for the first time.

Here's an example: *if* Python had compile-time assertion checking, with assertions written as **assert** *statements* rather than as comments, then the program

```
x= 0
print("Goodbye, cruel world!")
assert x==1 # This assertion is a statement, rather than a comment.
```

would *not* print its message and then fail with an assertion error, *because it would never get that far*.[2]

Instead, a compile-time error (in the Dafny style) would appear, looking roughly like the message below[3] — where the print statement is *not* executed, because the program is never run:

```
File GoodbyeCruelWorld.py
Line 3 character 1: assertion violation.
Program verifier finished with 0 verified, 1 error.
```

---

[1] Dafny [36] was created by Rustan Leino, now at Amazon Web Services; it builds on an intermediate language *Boogie* and uses the *Z3 SMT*-solver to check assertions.

[2] Note that vertically stacked **assert** *statements* do not indicate here that the higher implies the lower: instead they must all hold.

[3] The output is edited from a run of the Dafny version of the program, whose file extension of course would be .dfy instead of .py. For now we're trying to make the point with as little syntactic distraction as possible. Further below we will see actual examples.

On the other hand, if the program were processed by Python in the normal way, that is without compile-time assertion checking, instead we would get something like this — at runtime:

```
Goodbye, cruel world!
Traceback (most recent call last):
  File "GoodbyeCruelWorld.py", line 3, in <module>
    assert x==1
AssertionError    .
```

Here we can see that the program *is* run, the message *is* printed, and only *after* that does `assert x==1` give a runtime assertion error.

That's far too late, if you're on your way to Mars.

18.2.2 Binary search in Dafny

For a more realistic example, we return to the binary-search program text given in Sec. 3.3.3 but now presented in Fig. 18.1 below; and we now use actual Dafny syntax, its having been transliterated from Python. It's a method (rather than def),[4] whose precondition (called "requires" in Dafny) is that the sequence is in ascending order and whose postcondition ("ensures") is what we discussed so extensively in Ex. 3.5. The loop invariant (three conjuncts) is given just after the while keyword, and the loop variant ("decreases") appears just after that.

We've learned by now that while binary search is a small program, it is not trivial.[5]

Yet Dafny checks it *automatically*, with no further help from the programmer, and says that it "verifies" (in Fig. 18.2). Notice that Dafny did not for example need intermediate assertions to verify the loop body, to check that the invariant was maintained and that the variant decreased: it figured them out for itself. (We'll return to that point in Sec. 18.2.3.)

Now let's experiment. Figure 18.3 shows Dafny's output when we have introduced a deliberate mistake, replacing the if-condition `A[mid]<a` by the incorrect `A[mid]<=a`. In Fig. 18.4 we instead replace `low:= mid+1` by `low:= mid`; and in Fig. 18.5 we leave off the requirement (i.e. precondition) that the sequence be sorted in ascending order beforehand. (Forgetting to mention that requirement is all too easy to do! See Secs. 19.2.1 and 19.2.2 below.)

The experiments (the errors we deliberately introduced) remind us that the virtue of checking is most evident when a check *fails*. It's then that we are saved from bad outcomes.[7]

---

[4] The difference is immaterial: it's only Dafny vs. Python syntax.

[5] In *Programming Pearls*, Jon Bentley wrote that professional programmers who were given "a couple of hours", to code binary search, in "the language of their choice", at the end –in almost all cases– reported that they had found correct code for the task. But once they tested their programs (for about half-an-hour each), apparently some 90% of them found bugs [8, p. 36].

Bentley goes on to say that Knuth, in his *Sorting and Searching*, wrote that the first binary-search program was published in 1946, but the first published *bug-free* version did not appear until 1962 [33, Sec. 6.2.1].

Bug free? Perhaps not yet: the binary-search *overflow* bug was discovered only in 2006. See Ex. 18.1.

[6] The Dafny syntax here is based on Leino's introductory text *Program Proofs* [36], except that we continue to write ":=" left-adjusted; the examples were run with Version 4.8.0.0. In Dafny the loop invariant is placed *after* the while, between it and the "{" that begins the while-loop's body. (In Python there is no "opening {" for a loop body: indentation is used instead.)

[7] An aside for the use of Dafny in practice: if your runs are showing no verification failures, introduce temporarily a deliberate error into the source code and make sure it's caught... because you might accidentally be editing the wrong file; or you might have an `assume cond` somewhere for which *cond* evaluates to `False`. Why is that latter situation a problem?

Figure 18.1 Dafny binary-search program

```
method BinarySearch(A: seq<int>, a: int) returns (n: nat)
```

precondition →   `requires forall i,j:: 0<=i<j<|A| ==> A[i]<=A[j]`

        `ensures n<=|A|`

postconditions →   `ensures forall i:: 0<=i<n   ==> A[i]<a`

        `ensures forall i:: n<=i<|A| ==> a<=A[i]`

```
{   var low,high:= 0,|A|;
    while low!=high
```

        `invariant 0<=low<=high<=|A|`   ← *"housekeeping"*

[6] *loop invariants* →   `invariant forall i:: 0<=i<low   ==> A[i]<a` ← `A[:low]<a`

        `invariant forall i:: high<=i<|A| ==> a<=A[i]` ← `a<=A[high:]`

loop variant →   `decreases high-low`

```
    {   var mid:= (low+high)//2;
```

loop body →   `if A[mid]<a { low:=  mid+1; }`

```
        else         { high:= mid;    }
    }
    n:= low;
}
```

Figure 18.2 Dafny checking of Fig. 18.1

```
Running dafny BinarySearch.dfy
Dafny program verifier finished with 2 verified, 0 errors
```

Figure 18.3 Figure 18.1 with incorrect test `A[mid]<=a`

```
Running dafny BinarySearch1.dfy
BinarySearch1.dfy(10,12): Error: this invariant could not be proved
                                 to be maintained by the loop
BinarySearch1.dfy(10,12): Related message: loop invariant violation

Dafny program verifier finished with 1 verified, 1 error
```

Figure 18.4 Figure 18.1 with incorrect assignment `low:= mid`

```
Running dafny BinarySearch2.dfy
BinarySearch2.dfy(8,1): Error: "decreases" expression might not decrease

Dafny program verifier finished with 1 verified, 1 error
```

Figure 18.5 Figure 18.1 with missing precondition

```
Running dafny BinarySearch3.dfy
BinarySearch3.dfy(10,12): Error: this invariant could not be proved
                          to be maintained by the loop
BinarySearch3.dfy(10,12): Related message: loop invariant violation
BinarySearch3.dfy(11,12): Error: this invariant could not be proved
                          to be maintained by the loop
BinarySearch3.dfy(11,12): Related message: loop invariant violation

Dafny program verifier finished with 1 verified, 2 errors
```

18.2.3 Some limitations... but also some pleasant surprises

To use Dafny effectively, one obviously must supply pre- and postconditions for the code that is to be checked — because, otherwise, how do we know what it's supposed to do? (Recall Sec. 1.3.) One limitation, therefore, is what we mentioned above: that the specification cannot be written (just) informally, not any more, at least not if it is to be checked automatically: Dafny does not understand English, no matter how carefully it is written.[8] The pre- and postconditions must therefore be written in Dafny's language of assertions, which is more-or-less standard predicate calculus (Appendix D), with however some concessions to the use of a reasonable character set, for example "forall" rather than "∀": see for example the "is sorted" precondition/requires in Fig. 18.1 which says that, for any two values A[i],A[j] within A, their relative order must be <= if their positions i,j are ordered <. Thus –to use Dafny– one must learn at least a little bit of formal logic first. Luckily, most of its users will have learned that already: it's the language of Booleans that they use in Dafny's if and while conditions. And this issue is common to all computerised program-checking tools: it's a price you have to pay, but not a very big one when you consider the benefit.

A more interesting question however is "How many of the *intermediate* assertions must the programmer supply?" The answer is "It depends." For anything non-trivial, the programmer is usually responsible for finding at least the loop *invariants* and adding them to the program text. In many cases, however, Dafny can find the *variant* itself: and that *is* a pleasant surprise. Not so much because the programmer couldn't figure it out; it's more because it does not have to be typed in. If it's simple, it's probably also boring. (And that might be why Jack from Sec. 1.2 did not look for a variant: in his opinion, perhaps, termination was so obvious that he didn't need one.) Dafny however has no "opinions" and *would* have looked for a variant, no matter how boring it might have turned out to be. Its failing to find one would have alerted Jack to the potential problem.)

Another pleasant surprise is that many assertions need no longer be hand-generated by working backwards through assignment statements and/or conditionals (as we have practised in so many places, e.g. Sec. 5.2). They might be found by Dafny itself, so they need not be written down explicitly: it's just substitution, and even a text editor can do that. (For example, Dafny can figure out the tedious intermediate assertions in Sec. 5.2(h) all by itself, just as it figured out the intermediate assertions in the loop body of Fig. 18.1.) Not only does that –again– save some tedious typing, it

---

[8] ...nor how loudly and slowly it is spoken.

means that those assertions do not need to be kept as documentation of the program: they can be (re-)generated as needed. You *do* however need to write down the more significant assertions, especially invariants for example, because you'll need them to help you *write* the program.

There does remain one problem, however, that even `Dafny` cannot solve automatically. Whether the assertions are found by `Dafny` itself or are programmer-introduced, there remains the issue of showing that the assertion holds, i.e. that it would evaluate to `True` during a program run. That is not necessarily a program-checking problem *per se*: it might for example just be a problem in, say, arithmetic. In other words, `Dafny` transforms *your* problem of program correctness into *its* problem of proving theorems in arithmetic (or other mathematical theories), using essentially the rules of Appendix B for that transformation.[9]

And so a second, and major, limitation is here: even if you have overcome your aversion to formal logic (Did you have one?), `Dafny` still cannot prove all the implications that you might need — no matter how much time you give it. Remarkably, it has been shown that *no* computer program (as we currently understand them) can be sure of finding all such proofs, neither `Dafny` nor any other program.[10] Even so, the scope of things that *can* be proved automatically is constantly being extended, and each advance there leads to "spin off" advances in the program-checking tools that use them.

18.2.4 The payoff

In spite of the limitations above –the need to learn (some) logic, and the inescapable presence of some truths that no tool can ever prove– the overwhelming payoff of a "machine-checked check" is that you can trust it, provided you are clear about the assumptions you are making: that the requirements (pre and post) are correctly formulated, that the hardware on which you run your program is functioning correctly, that the compiler you use to translate your program to machine code is itself error-free... and of course that the checker itself is correct. That is quite a few provisos! We address some of them in Chapter 19.

But the main source of error in computer applications remains the bugs introduced by the programmer during coding, perhaps due to a programmer's *opinion* that something need not be checked, because it is so simple that it is "obviously" correct. Sometimes however it is inherent in (what turns out to be) incorrect algorithms — or indeed badly formulated requirements — perhaps because of their complexity.

Those last potential errors are greatly reduced by even the *informal* application of formal methods that we have been studying here and –as we have just seen– even more so if backed up by computer-assisted proof-checking.

It really is worth it.

---

[9] The technique it uses for that is "satisfaction modulo theories" (*SMT*), which is an advanced topic worth reading about if you are interested in "under the bonnet" (or "-hood") material on machine assistance for mathematical proof.

[10] This is Gödel's (first) incompleteness theorem –from almost a century ago– before there were any electronic computers at all: see his *On Formally Undecidable Propositions of Principia Mathematica and Related Systems* from 1931 [37]. It states (roughly) that any (consistent) formal system within which non-trivial arithmetic can be carried out is "incomplete" in the sense that there must be truths about arithmetic that it cannot prove.

A wonderful feature of Gödel's demonstration is that if you tried to "patch" the incomplete system –adding as a new axiom the very arithmetic truth it could not prove– then for that updated system there would be another, different arithmetic truth that *it* could not prove. It's a meta-mathematical analogue of moving the goalposts, a "Tantalus construction" in logic. (In more modern terms, it would be "Whack-a-mole".)

18.3 Exercises

Exercise 18.1 (p. 213) ⇓ The binary-search code in Fig. 18.1, repeating (3.5), contains the assignment `mid:= (low+high)//2`, the infamous "overflow bug" where even if `low` and `high` were themselves within range of the computer's representation of non-negative integers (say $2^{31}-1$), their sum –the intermediate expression `low+high`– might overflow and become negative, leading later to an indexing error.

Why did `Dafny` not flag that as an error?

19

Program testing

19.1 Why is testing *always* necessary?

Testing is always necessary because

> A computer system[1] is truly correct *only* when its *actual* behaviour meets the expectations of the person who commissioned it. (19.1)

The techniques of this text cover only a very small part of the overall enterprise of producing reliable computer-based systems, and just *how* small is illustrated in Fig. 19.1 below. But note we have just written "reliable" rather than "truly correct" — the latter is often unobtainable, and many systems justify their cost by being "good enough", working "most of the time". Testing is especially necessary for those; but so is careful reasoning, and assertion-based checking (the subject of this text).

In the following sections we will look at Fig. 19.1 from top to bottom, beginning with the expectations mentioned in (19.1) just above. (They are not at all the same as a pre- and postcondition pair.) Our intention here is to reassure the reader that we do understand that the main topic of *this* text is far from the whole story.

19.2 From expectations to actual behaviour, in five steps

The person with expectations –call her "the customer"– is (probably) *not* the programmer, *not* the systems analyst, *not* the salesman... It's the person who ends up using the system, and who paid for it.[2] That is where we begin.

---

[1] ...or any artefact, of course.
[2] The connection might be indirect: the customer herself might sell her product to her own clients: for our purposes, they are "the customer" too — and also *their* expectations must be met.

Figure 19.1 Why testing is essential

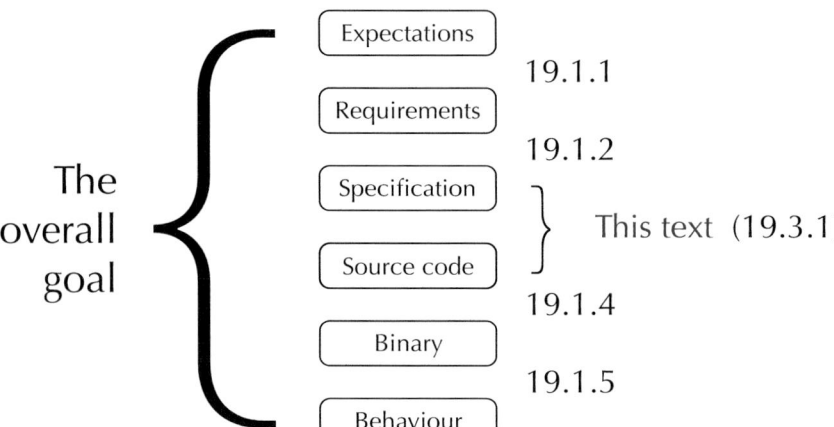

Figure 19.1 shows that the topic of *this* text, careful reasoning about the program code as it is developed, is just one of the many steps a successful software project must go through.

19.2.1 From expectations to requirements

The example for our first step is not computer related, but we hope it will be a reminder to you that the potential for misunderstanding, error and disappointment is not at all limited to computer programs.

Our customer, we assume, is an expert in her own business, its particular practices and constraints, and she hopes to be working with a systems analyst who is familiar with at least the most obvious, everyday practices and constraints: that's why she chose him. If she notices that the requirements being developed between the two of them are missing something important, perhaps (unconsciously? optimistically?) she thinks it's only because the missing piece is self-evident, something "everybody knows" — and so she doesn't call it out.

Our example comes from the *Relocation Project* on the island of Fiji, where whole villages were moved to higher ground to escape the rising sea levels caused by global warming: the incident concerns the first village to be moved, where the customer (in our analogy) was the whole population of the village, and the systems analyst was the group/committee responsible for articulating the requirements of its move.

The failure in this example was that *none of the houses in the new, relocated village were equipped with kitchens* (at least, not initially and not for some time afterwards).

What could be called a "major unarticulated assumption" here, abbreviated in the trade as "*MUA*", was that the customer (the whole village) knew that houses require kitchens, but the analysts (a smaller, perhaps self-appointed group) seemed not to appreciate that or, at least, not to take it into account. And because the need for kitchens was so obvious ("major"), it was not thought that it needed to be mentioned (i.e. it was "not articulated"). Perhaps the remaining villagers (customers) thought this was so obvious (their "assumption") that they did not say anything; perhaps the analysts assumed that they had been told everything (or knew everything).

Testing would have discovered the *MUA*, if done early enough, and it would have been a *simple* test: "Actually let someone spend a whole day in one of the new houses."

19.2.2 From requirements to specification

This example concerns computers, but not really a computer program. Remember that (at least in our usage here) "requirements" are informal but somewhat abstract descriptions of what the system is supposed to do, enough for a potential user to decide whether it is likely to meet her needs. A "specification" is an elaboration of those requirements, consistent with them, but with enough further detail added that a program can be developed from it.

A 1980s popular desk-top computer operating system provided a command for copying files from one directory ("folder") to another, as most operating systems do; and it could even copy whole directories at once. The *requirements* would have been something like "Copy a file or directory from 'here' to 'there'. " — requirements sufficient (as pointed out in Sec. 1.2, and recalled just above) for a user to find this command, its name and its syntax, but not so detailed that extensive reading would have been required to understand its fine points.

The *specification* of the copy command, however (if there was one), was not precise enough for a program developer to be sure she was designing a program that was correct: in particular, it did not seem to say that "In the target directory there should for every source file be a corresponding file with the same name and the same contents."[3] (It's reasonable though to consider that to be too detailed for requirements. There is even a case for considering it to be an *MUA*.)

And it turned out that the actual copy program did not copy *empty* files: after all (perhaps some programmer thought), if a file is empty what's the point of making a copy of it? The requirements were vague enough (deliberately so) that one could argue (and perhaps the analyst would have argued) that a file with no data was not actually information that needed to be copied. The specification (we are imagining) did not say "Do it anyway."

The failure here occurred when a large database had been constructed in its initial state in a single directory, at some effort and expense and, and was ready to be tried out. Before experimenting with it, a copy of that directory –all its constituent files– was made as a backup, so that several experiments could be carried out from an initial, fresh version each time without having to (re-)construct the database from scratch again and again. Some files in the (initial) directory however were "log files", there to record the sequence of operations carried out on the database. (That is normal practice in database and transaction systems generally.) And initially, before any operations *had* been carried out, those log files were empty because no operations had yet occurred. But those empty files were there.

When the database was restored from that backup copy –ready for the second experiment– it was missing the empty files: not because they were not copied by the restore, but because they had not actually been copied into the backup in the first place. And the database program would not start with the restored copy because it

---

[3] At this remove, we do not know what the specification actually was or even whether there actually was one. But this incident really occurred.

could not find and open its log files. They weren't "there but empty", as they should
have been: they were not there at all, and so information about the initial transactions
could not be appended to them. The whole database had to be reconstructed from
scratch, another day lost.

Here the point is that the specification *must* exist *and* be as precise as possible,
even to the point that it contains too much detail for the customer to assimilate. It's
the job of the analyst and the programmer to make sure the requirements and the
specification are consistent.

Testing would have discovered that error, if done early enough: "Try restoring the
database into a second copy, and opening it, before beginning the experiment on the
first copy."

A good example of the difference between requirements and specification is given
by comparing (2.1) and (2.2) in the *Bad* subsegment example of Sec. 2.2.

19.2.3 From specification to program's source code

Here is what we cover in this text, just one step out of the five overall in Fig. 19.1.
Our use of assertions and what's-true-here reasoning is designed to avoid mistakes in
that step — as much as possible.

For programs of any realistic size however –that is, even small programs if they
are complex– it is still possible that our informal approach can lead to programs
that do *not* meet their specifications. Simply being careful with your pen-and-paper
developments is not enough: for serious work, computer assistance is required to check
that the *reasoning* –about your program– that you are carrying out itself is correct.
Chapter 17 is complex enough to benefit from mechanical checking, and Chapter 18
gives just one example of how it might be done, but it is a particularly good one –for
our purposes– because the reasoning it carries out uses the *actual source text* of the
program being checked.

Other, more comprehensive approaches check mathematical reasoning directly (interactive theorem provers, for example) and are more versatile; or they simulate the
program's behaviour as exhaustively as possible, looking for errors (model checkers).
That is a successful strategy provided there are not too many possible behaviours and
the simulation itself is accurately constructed.

19.2.4 From source code to binary

The path from source code to binary is often overlooked, at least for commercial
non-safety-critical applications. (For safety-critical systems, on the other hand, it's
sometimes the *binary* that is checked directly; the compiler and other utilities that
take source to binary might themselves contain errors.)

The issue here is that the programmer writes code in a programming language and
applies checks as we have explained in this text or verifies the code with an automatic
checker as in Sec. 18.2 — and yet what is actually executed is not that code. In the
case of `Python` it's a `Python`-interpreter that is executed, with (a translation of) that
code as its input; or it might have been developed in `Python` but then transliterated
into say C. Even if the code was C originally, there's then an assembly-code compiler
that carries out a *second* translation from the C-compiler's output to machine-code
binary. How do we know there are no errors in the interpreter, or the transliteration
or in compilations?

We don't know that there are no errors. If those steps themselves have not been
proved correct, all we have left is testing.

A good example is binary search from Sec. 3.3.3. In spite of footnote 5 (in Chapter 18), almost all implementations of binary search were discovered to be incorrect as late as the early 2000s. How could that be? (The `Dafny` version in Fig. 18.1, verified in Sec. 18.2.1, *is correct* however — provided it is run in `Dafny`. Why might it not be correct if it were transliterated into C or `Java`?)

Binary search is not (just) a program — it's an algorithm, and source code for it is to found in countless different applications and their accompanying programming languages. For example the translation (probably by hand) from `Dafny`'s assignment `mid:= (low+high)//2` to say C's `mid= (low+high)/2` is incorrect *precisely* in the case that overflow occurs in the C code. `Dafny`, and incidentally `Python` as well, carry out integer arithmetic to arbitrary size: their integers do not overflow. To be quite specific: in `Python` half of the sum `1+2147483647`, the "mid", is `2147483648/2`, that is `1073741734`; but for a C program on a 32-bit machine using signed two's-complement integers, that same expression evaluates to `-1073741734`.

Thus in this case what the source code appears to do is not necessarily how the binary actually behaves.

One approach to reducing the risk in this step is to check (i.e. "verify") the compilers, to prove that they are correct, and that is indeed what is done in situations where its high cost is justified by the importance of the application's correctness. But for more everyday situations, where the program is small or the risk is considered to be negligible ("Binary search has been around for decades: if there were an error, it would have been discovered hundreds of times over by now!"), testing is needed, and is probably cheaper (and thus more likely to be carried out) than compiler verification.

19.2.5 And finally: from binary to behaviour

Even this very last step –loading and running your program– contains risks: the hardware on which our program is installed might itself contain errors. The manufacturer's manual might say that one thing happens, but in fact in some circumstances it does not.

In 1994 it was discovered that the floating-point calculations of a widely distributed processor chip, for some floating-point values of numerator `N` and denominator `D`, would calculate –at the hardware level– the wrong answer for their quotient `N/D`. All those processors, worldwide, had to be recalled and replaced.[4]

Obviously the processor manual did not include the fact that it occasionally gave the wrong answer; but even in less spectacular cases it can be hard to discover what a complicated piece of hardware actually does in some unlikely –but still possible– situations. That might be because it's too hard to explain; or it might be that the manufacturers are not absolutely sure themselves; or it might be that they are protecting their intellectual property from competitors.

In this case (and others that are similar), testing alone cannot solve the problem: there are too many instances of `N` and `D` to be able to check all the divisions `N/D`. The best we can do at the moment is (of course) to test some of the behaviours, hoping to catch as many errors as possible.

---

[4] A major competitor determined at the time that *they* would not have had the financial resources to survive such a recall — and therefore they turned to formal methods *before* the horse had bolted.

19.3 How assertions and testing can work together

A major concern with testing is determining *how to test.* Here we will concentrate on the step from specification to program source (Sec. 19.2.3), since that –unlike the other steps– is the one that has largely been neglected.

The contribution of assertions (including pre- and postconditions together, that is to say *specifications*) is that they determine *what should be true.* Why not use "what should be true" to help determine "how to test"? There are at least two ways of doing that.

19.3.1 "As you go" assertion checking

Typically a beginning programmer will test her program by providing some input and then, looking at the output, decide whether it is what she expected. If it is not, what then? There are many approaches: look carefully at (i.e. review) the "edge cases"; print out variables' values while the program is running; single-step the program, possibly with breakpoints, and check at each stage that the variables' values "now" are what you expect given their values the last time you looked;[5] "binary chop" the program's source code, narrowing down by halves the part of the program in which the error seems to be occurring. . .

If the programmer had used assertions to write the program, she could print out not the variables' values but instead the **True** or **False** values *at runtime* of the assertions she used. Indeed, many programming languages (including **Python**) have runtime **assert** statements that do just that. But how do you decide what to assert?

Often, assertions are placed at "cannot happen" locations in the code, for example at default cases that should never occur, or loops that should never "fall through" instead of executing an early **break**. Why not, as well, place runtime assertions at the very places where the what's-true-here assertions occurred during the program's construction?

Binary search (again) provides an example. The "choose **mid** halfway between **low** and **high**" is often specified as **mid= (low+high)//2** , that is as the code itself. But it's enough at that point simply to specify what is *actually needed*, and that is only **low<=mid<high**. The search will succeed as long as that holds. Suppose then that a runtime assertion (based on that design-time reasoning) had been placed just there, stating clearly what the assignment just before is supposed to achieve:

```
mid= (low+high)//2
assert low<=mid<high
if A[mid] < x:  ...  .
```

If the overflow error occurs, the program will be halted *right there* by the assertion, at the very point of the error, and the programmer will focus on "How could **(low+high)//2** not lie between **low** and **high** ?"

Without that assertion, the program would fail instead with "Indexing error." and –in more complicated cases– that failure might occur later, not here where the problem actually lies. (Even here she might waste time wondering whether **low** or **high** were incorrect.) The programmer –misled by the fact that it's an indexing error into a sequence of size **N**– will then wonder perhaps "How could **(low+high)//2** not lie between **0** and **N**?". . . and it would take several further debugging steps to discover first, that the index had become negative and second, *why* it did.

---

[5] That requires executing the code between last time and this time "in your head". How much simpler it would be if you needed only to check whether the variables satisfied an assertion *right here.*

If, for example, it's a loop that is misbehaving (although the programmer might not know that yet), a runtime `assert` *invariant* at the end of the loop body (i.e. still within the loop) would catch the *very first* iteration in which the loop did not do what it was supposed to. Similar runtime asserts at the beginnings (preconditions) and ends (postconditions) of code blocks, or procedure calls, would focus attention immediately on the problem. There are many programming environments that encourage that, and provide support for it.

Similarly, edge cases would be caught immediately by introducing an `assert` that the invariant is established initially ("even when the sequence is empty") and is still true finally.

19.3.2 Automatic overall test–case generation

A second way in which assertions can be used in testing programs is to use their specifications to generate test cases randomly. Often the specifications will give the types of the important variables and, in simple cases, easily processed relations between them: not necessarily as precise as "satisfies the postcondition", but certainly more useful than "What do I test next?" Moreover, automatically generated test cases will often capture the edge-cases that humans miss — because computers don't think "That will never happen."

Further, once a failing case has been found, many of the automatic testers will systematically look for smaller examples that lead to the same error, with luck discovering one simple enough that its characteristics will help the programmer see what caused it.[6]

19.4 A cautionary tale

If testing is so important, so effective, why do we here concentrate only on reasoning?

This text concentrates on reasoning –only one of the five steps illustrated in Fig. 19.1– simply because *most other elementary texts do not* — at least not those that can be used by non-formally-inclined programmers. (See however the Afterword and the Bibliography.)

My own[7] initial experience with "real world" programming was in industry, just after leaving university, and it was the first time I had to write a program that took longer than just a few days to complete, start to finish. (As a tutor, that had been the typical time I needed to prepare a student exercise for undergraduates.) I was to write a front-end program for a new piece of hardware, exploiting capabilities that the existing hardware did not have. I asked my manager "How long do you think it will take?" He said "About six weeks." — and I was astonished: that was many times longer than I had ever needed before. I asked "What's the specification?" He replied by dropping a 1cm-thick program listing on my desk. "Make it do that." he said.

It took three months.

Appointed at the lowest level of my company's programming pyramid, I saw the actual code being written by my colleagues. *It was appalling* — and nobody higher up knew about it. Nobody checked. When something failed, the very person whose failure it was had to fix it. Nobody else ever saw the mess that was there.

---

[6] Many of the programs in this text were tested in that way, by for example trying "All strings of length up to ten characters made from the letters "A", "B" and "C". The edge-cases "string of length 0" and "all characters the same" are automatically included, precisely because the computer never thinks "That will never happen." Python's "`hypothesis`" tester was used for that.

[7] i.e. the author's

When later I had moved up the ladder somewhat, and was managing other programmers in a small team, I dealt with that mess –having seen it "from below", first hand– by designing a simple pseudocode notation that forced (gently) a more structured approach to the code my programmers wrote: they had to use *my* notation for it, rather than writing in `FORTRAN` directly. (One of my programmers complained however that doing so "impeded his creativity".)

But they could not compile or test it, because it was only a made-up language: instead, they had to *think* about it. Once they had done that, I would take perhaps one-in-three programs home, and go through all of it with a fine-toothed comb. (I could not take *all* the pseudocoded designs home, because there was not enough time for that: I stayed home to go through those designs perhaps one day per week. But my programmers never knew in advance whose code I would pick.)

Once I had checked their code (or they had a "bye"), they were allowed to transliterate it into `FORTRAN` by hand, following by themselves a "transliteration" guide I had written: and even then I would occasionally spot-check their transliterations.

What is the point of that "war story"? It is not simply reminiscence, because all of it is still going on. It is that *none* of those people had ever been taught to reason about their programs, had heard ever of an assertion, an invariant or a variant. And it wasn't because those ideas did not exist yet (for I had heard of them). It was because they *weren't taught*.

If instead those programmers *had* been taught how to reason about their code, that code would have been considerably improved, of course — but, more importantly, I would not have had to spend 20% of my (more expensive) time checking every line of what they wrote. They would do that on their own, developing personal quality standards which *they themselves* would then strive to meet.[8]

That is the true cost of not teaching beginning programmers to ask "What's *true* here?" rather than "What *happened* over there?" — to *think* before they code and test. Otherwise, the small programs they write could well be the sand their grander computer systems are built on,[9] instead of firm foundations; and no amount of higher-up post-hoc management will ever fix that. If your nail is bent, no amount of hammering will drive it in.[10]

Teaching "What's true here?" to beginning programmers *does not take more time*. It simply requires presenting the material in a different, more effective way.

---

[8] The company became insolvent not long after I left, about two years later. And I had already seen first-hand why that was inevitable: most of our programmers spent a large portion of their time on the phone to customers who had already had our software installed, and they were trying to debug those systems remotely. They had no time to concentrate properly on their next project, and that fed back to even less reliable deliveries further down the line.

[9] Gospel according to Matthew 7:26 — *... a foolish man, which built his house upon the sand: and the rain descended, and the floods came, and the winds blew, and beat upon that house; and it fell: and great was the fall of it.*

[10] "For want of a nail..." The "Jack" responsible for the music-player bug could easily have been one of my programmers, his tiny mistake –the missing variant– the topic of Sec. 1.8 in the very first chapter of this text. The massive consequence was that his coding of (1.1) "lost the kingdom" — a worldwide failure of millions of portable devices.

19.5 Exercises

Exercise 19.1 In Sec. 19.3 we mentioned that `Dafny` verified the program of Fig. 18.1, and yet if simply syntactically transliterated say into C or Java, at runtime it might not give the right answer. So the program *did* check, that is `Dafny` verified it; but in traversing the further steps in Fig. 19.1 it *became* incorrect in spite of that earlier verification.

On which of the five steps in Sec. 19.2 was the error introduced?

Ex. 18.1

Exercise 19.2 ⇓ In one software-system company, when a product was finished and thought to be ready for delivery, the company's *CEO* would attend a dry run of its official hand-over presentation (but still within the company's offices). After all, at the *real* presentation at the client's site, she would be the one in the front line.

One of her tests was to go to the keyboard and run her elbow up- and down the keys, sending who-knows-what control characters, punctuation, excessively long inputs etc. to the program expecting the input.[11] Sometimes the whole system would fail at that point, even before the dry run had properly started.

In terms of the "paths" mentioned above, what kind of failure was that, and how might it have been prevented?

---

[11] Literally the elbow: this is a true story.

Afterword

The "Lost Art" — *What* was lost, and why?

Most of the program-checking techniques explained in this text were invented from the late 1960s, throughout the '70s and into the early '80s, then vigorously proselytised in the '80s and '90s. For a while, it looked as though methods based on them would change radically the way in which introductory programming was taught. But it has been more than 40 years since then and –generally speaking– the teaching of introductory programming has *not* changed. Indeed nowadays those techniques are taught very rarely, are part of very few curricula: the opportunity has been lost...

Hence the "Lost Art".

Why are those self-evidently beneficial techniques not taught, now, in every introductory programming course in the world?

One possible reason is that, when formal methods was new, there was an exuberance, a feeling that finally program development could be "done properly" — with rigorous mathematical-style reasoning right from the very start. It was also believed by some –or at least hoped– that programs would no longer have to rely so much on extensive testing to help ensure their correctness. (Recall however our Part IV.)

But that excitement was far from universal –indeed there was much scepticism, dissent, even hostility– because the mathematical rigour that "proper" formal methods required turned out to be beyond the reach of most programmers, whether they were just beginning or had already been programming for some time. For not every programmer wants to be a mathematician, and they all knew –or believed– that, even if they were not already, they would *become* reasonably good programmers anyway.

And indeed most of them did: they are our IT professionals today. For those programmers, the utility of this text is to show how their computer science learning trajectory could have been improved *right from the very start*. For beginning programmers, this text might help them *right now*.

It's terribly important, either way, because today our dependence on computers in everyday life is far greater than it was 50 years ago; the consequences of programs that don't work, or only "nearly work", are correspondingly far greater than they used to be; and yet programming seems to be taught with far less rigour than ever before. That is why explaining formal methods *informally*, communicating the basics in a way that does not require formal logic, nor even elementary propositional calculus,[1] is such

---

[1] Actually, as the presence of Appendix D in this text confirms, at least *propositional* logic *is* needed. But it should be introduced gradually, once students see the need for it in the programs they are reasoning about: a good example is De Morgan's laws, (E.22), (E.23) in Appendix E, used to deduce the assertion that is true, once a `while`-loop has terminated, from its compound (i.e. conjunction-

a cost-effective way of inducing now –and for the future– an immense improvement in the reliability of programs and the processes by which they are constructed. It's a real opportunity for us to reach the large group of programmers, including the "next generation", who otherwise *would never know* how easily they can learn to think much more carefully and effectively about what they create.

Of course there is and always will be a smaller group, fascinated by the whole idea of formal methods and inclined to study it for its own sake: we would like to reach them too, even though they are not our main target. But without an "informal" lure like this one, they might never know that formal methods exists, that programs *can* be checked rigorously[2] — yet we need them to know that, for they will become the highly sought-after specialists, the experts who develop, check and implement the more-critical programs and systems whose failure would be too expensive to tolerate.

Although we might never see that smaller group, we do depend on it: we might not be riding in the spaceship, but we will have paid for it. Those specialists not only check their programs, but they use *other* programs to "check their checks", to verify that they haven't made mathematical mistakes (Chapter 18). And some of them even write *those* programs, the ones that check the checks. (And then those programs, that check the programs that check the checks, must themselves be checked: it really is "mathematics all the way down".[3]) For that smaller group, the utility of *this* text is *recruitment* because, in some cases, they might become aware of their aptitude for "formal" formal methods only because they saw it informally first. And if only we can capture their interest, they will then help us teach the rest.

The primary purpose of this text therefore, the one you are now reading, is to rescue the general principles –the "informal" formal methods arising from the discoveries of the 1970s and '80s– that could make so much difference, for so many people, for so little cost.[4] It lifts the bar for what "reasonably good" programming means, and shows today's programmers that using those pioneering experts' methods won't make their programming more difficult.

Instead, it will make it *easier* — and more effective.

Background, evolution, experience and prospects

Background and initial presentation

This text grew out of –and now accompanies– the course "(In-)Formal Methods: The Lost Art", first delivered in 2010 at the University of New South Wales (UNSW). Originally its format was real-time whiteboard (no slides), to a small class of only about 20 students: the trajectory of each lecture was therefore able to be somewhat fluid (and as a result great fun!) But overall there still was of course a well-defined target of topics and skills to achieve by the end of term.[5] Lectures were *not* recorded for later viewing, and in-person attendance was usually 100% — or more (i.e. with some attending just out of interest, not for credit).

---

containing) guard. See for example program (8.6).

[2] Indeed this approach sprang (in 2009) from a casual conversation with a top-ranked final-year undergraduate who was explaining a program he was proud of. His response to "Cool! What's the invariant?" was "What's an invariant?" [44, Sec. 1.2]

[3] *Quis custodiet ipsos custodes?*

[4] The further extensive –and exciting– developments of formal methods, in the decades since then, do not appeal to most *beginning* programmers: that is why they are not our topic here.

[5] At the time the term comprised 12 weeks of three one-hour lectures.

Pitched at approximately second-year undergraduate level, the enrolment never-theless included some higher-year computer science students, plus a small number of postgraduates from other (technical) disciplines. There were no separate tutorials (since the lectures were effectively in that style anyway), and no teaching support staff (all marking done by the lecturer); assessment was based on three two-week assignments. They were handed-in program printouts (i.e. as a PDF, not executable as such), returned to the students individually with comments hand written as if for essays.

Each assignment was a small project building a program which the students would have met already (but not known how to construct) — for example using the course's methods to develop "The longest up-sequence", and then building around it, with shell scripts (`sort`, `join`, etc. . .), a prototype `diff` utility. In that way some of the "magic" of the mysterious programs –the ones they could not write for themselves, but used every day– would rub off (one hoped), enhancing therefore the attraction of the "informal" formal-methods techniques that were used, in the assignments, to build them.[6] The idea was to make those techniques themselves a bit magical too.[7]

The course had *no formal written exam* (and still does not) because, for material of this kind, it just does not seem right to encourage people to program "under pressure". Careful thought, stress-free musing on the bus, in the shower, while falling asleep. . . is an essential component of reliable, robust and –in the end– simple and evidently correct solutions to complex problems.

Evolution and its consequences

A significant challenge, however, accrued from the year-by-year increasing success and popularity of this informal approach — that it really should be available the for whole computer science cohort, possibly integrated into or just after the traditional "Here's your first programming language, your tools." first-year course as "Now you *have* your basic tools: here's how you *use* them." But assessment becomes a problem for a larger enrolment: many computer science courses now attract more than 1,000 students into their first year; and students often do not attend lectures, instead watching them offline later (perhaps at double speed). How do you assess the work of so many in a course like this one? How do you reach the students individually, adapting your presentation to their needs?

Running their exercises against many test inputs –the traditional "auto-marking" approach– will not teach them to think "statically" about what the program makes true, to consider assertions, invariants, variants, rather than "operationally" about what the program is doing. The latter is *much* less effective. A poorly written program might still receive 100% if it passes all tests, no matter how clumsily it is expressed.[8] At the other extreme, mandating computer-checkable assertions etc. in homework, although now technically achievable (e.g. as in Sec. 18.2) is not going to work for first-year students, as the decades since the 1970s have shown again and again: beginning programmers as a rule do not enjoy having to learn formal logic first (or even *ever*); they don't understand what it's for, nor why they should be forced to take an interest in it. They just want to get on with coding and –paradoxically– with debugging their *own* errors, getting satisfaction from repairing failures they themselves have caused. Only later, with deadlines and responsibility (and sometimes humiliation?), do they

---

[6] Another example is the optimal-paragraph-layout algorithm of TeX (and hence of LaTeX).

[7] One of the students' anonymous comments, collected as part of UNSW's post-delivery course-evaluation process: "After taking the course I felt as if I was privy to a powerful ancient magic."

[8] Style checkers can mitigate that, but they address a different problem: neatness of code-layout does not ensure neatness of thought.

discover how unpleasant and energy-sapping that can be. We want to reduce that "later" as much as possible — by acting "sooner".

And sometimes, formality applied too early, or excessively enforced, can even lead to students' protests being supported by their other teachers too, an uncomfortable situation in any academic environment[9] — and then the formal methods approach, or anything like it, becomes inaccessible to the bulk of students, is again reserved for the higher-year "theoretically inclined", is once more an "art", lost to all the rest.

Part of the approach in this text therefore has been to *induce* an interest in (elementary but rigorous) logic, not to compel it.

At UNSW, from 2010 until 2023 (the time of writing), the course format and size has varied: while 2011 and 2012 remained at 20 students, in 2014 there were ∼40 students, an experiment: they were divided into small groups of size 4–6 each, and three theoretically inclined teaching assistants were engaged to meet with each group for an hour every week, with explicit instructions to make sure that every student in the group would participate: no "silent observers" were allowed. The lecture format however remained the same — whiteboard, full attendance, no recordings.

The point of the small groups was that, by then, it was realised that one of the problems with informal approaches generally is that people *think* they understand them, can apply them, when in fact they do not and cannot: not immediately. As they sit there, they see what a teacher is doing, can follow every step — but afterwards, on their own, they don't even know where to begin. A good way to get past that is to ask them small questions, in a non-threatening small-group context, thus letting them experience *for themselves* that when they open their mouths to give the answer to what seems an easy question... sometimes nothing comes out.

The three assistants in 2014 also marked the assignments (with the lecturer a fourth marker), and it was then possible to have four assignments rather than three: still hand-marked, but dependent on there being assistants who themselves were "formal methods capable". Unfortunately, that approach is perhaps unsustainable in many institutions (though perhaps not all): for example, 1,000 students would require 75 course assistants, all of them understanding assertion-based reasoning.

In 2019 the course returned to its original size and format (no assistants), and was similarly successful.[10] In 2020-2, however, COVID mandated a completely different approach (for all courses, naturally). The (In-)Formal Methods course became entirely online; instead of a whiteboard, there was a tablet, and the lectures –delivered remotely– were live-streamed as well as recorded. One (disappointing) surprise was that the whiteboard "writing as you go" approach did not carry over well to the remotely presented tablet: the extra bandwidth of the in-person presence –the lecturer's gestures, timing of delivery, walking here and there, seeing and reacting to students' facial expressions (ranging from delight to bewilderment)– was all gone. It seemed necessary to compensate by preparing the "slides" (tablet screens) at least partially beforehand, then perhaps writing a small amount of extra information onto them during the lecture itself. And flexibility, adapting the lectures to students' progress anew each year, became very time-consuming, sometimes intensely deadline-driven: "last year's slides", now available on the tablet, not erased from the whiteboard, could *almost* always be improved and tailored to this year's progress-so-far, a serious and beguiling temptation for the lecturer — and it is so difficult to resist doing that just the day (or even late at night) before they are needed. The original whiteboard-presentation style, on the other hand, was "on the fly" –took no extra time– and is

---

[9] This course however did not attract such protests: instead the main issue was that it did not have enough capacity for people wanting to enrol in it.

[10] For administrative reasons, the course was not available in the years 2015–18.

very rewarding both for the lecturer and the students. In short, on-the-fly is not only more effective: it's also more fun.

One mitigating advantage however of the tablet approach was that the whiteboard became infinite, capturing not only what had been prepared beforehand but also any student-inspired annotations collected as the lecture progressed: and those real-time annotated slides, that is including their extra remarks written on the slides during the lecture itself, could be posted on the course website afterwards, later the same day. "Afterwards" is important here: if the students have the lecture notes beforehand, it is difficult to engage their attention directly; and they might even use them to justify (to themselves) not needing to come to the lecture at all. But posting "the same day" also matters: catch them while they are still engaged, while they still remember that afternoon what had aroused their curiosity only a few hours before.

Once COVID restrictions were relaxed, the course size was expanded to 50 — a first step towards seeing whether it might be possible after all to increase the enrolment to perhaps several hundred, making it available at least to the whole of UNSW's Software-Engineering stream.[11] By that time, however, the policy

> Lecture attendance is *not* mandatory,
> and lectures *will be* recorded (even if not streamed).

had become the university's norm, a legacy of the lockdown: of those 50 students in 2021, fewer than 10 actually came to lectures. (Many other courses, at other universities also, had a similarly low ratio... or even worse.)

Prospects and challenges: what now?

At the moment, given the policy above, expanding the course to hundreds of students would require careful planning. The principal barriers are three: for this kind of material, in-person attendance at lectures would seem to be very important but is not yet again the norm; the logistics of assessment-via-assignments (and no exam) are still experimental for large groups; and we have not yet "taught enough teachers".

For the first: encouragement to attend lectures is of course a matter of university (or at least faculty) policy. We can only hope that eventually full in-person attendance will return. In-person is important because we are not trying (only) to communicate facts and formulae: we are aiming to alter a mind-set. Personal contact is how that's done.

For the second, however, two approaches have so far been tried (in 2022 and 2023). In 2022, instead of three assignments there was only one, taken from a previous year and expanded so that the step-by-step partial solutions (program fragments) were extended with `assert` statements supplied in the assignment text, included within a program "skeleton" that the students had to complete themselves. And it was split into two parts. During auto-marking with test inputs,[12] the assertions were checked at runtime, but were adjusted so that they merely reported whether they were satisfied (or not) rather than terminating the program at that point if they failed. A log was kept automatically for each program, recording which assertions passed and which ones failed. Marks were calculated automatically (no hand-marking), mainly on the basis of satisfying the assertions, and those could be given different weights. That was mostly successful, but a small problem was that sometimes the rigidity of an assertion's being true or false inhibited a student's progression in the assignment past

---

[11] The Software-Engineering stream was an integrated path through the whole UNSW Computer-Science curriculum, from start to finish, set up by Ken Robinson and based on J.-R. Abrial's *B method* and its *Rodin* tool.

[12] For this `Python`'s *hypothesis* package was used.

that point: that is, stuck at the assignment's part 1 because of an assertion failure that was not understood, some students could not proceed to part 2; and –for them– that was a significant, and perhaps unfair, disadvantage.

As well as the (single) assignment (and making up for there being only one), in 2022 there were for the first time *weekly multiple-choice quizzes*[13] concentrating on the basic skills: substitution, and assignment statements etc. as they appear in the Drills section of this text (Appendix A). They accounted collectively for 50% of the overall assessment; the assignment was 40% and the remaining 10% was a subjectively determined "participation" mark, that last to encourage interaction in class, the interaction that had been such an attractive and important feature of the earlier, smaller setting.

Finally, in 2023, the assignment was split into one-piece-per-week (and had no assertions inline), nine pieces overall, with its overall goal being again a "magic" program (in the sense above) that was revealed only in the very last piece, that is at the very end of term. All the earlier weekly components before were steps in that direction, larger and larger fragments taking the students towards the final program — the goal that they would then be proud of having reached "by themselves". *And testing was encouraged at every stage.* Answers to the assignment pieces became multiple choice, again auto-marked; but only the *questions* were released at the beginning of each week (not the possible answers), leaving four days to try to discover the needed assertion, or invariant or code fragment before the possible answers were revealed at the end of the week — with very limited time (≤ 30 minutes) to choose from those answers. The idea was to encourage independent, exploratory thinking (rather than "Which of these possibilities could it be?") between the Monday and the Friday and, by limiting the time available for answer-selection, to make a "Let's just wait and see what the possible answers are." -strategy much less effective.

The above "spread-out" piece-by-piece assignment strategy has seemed to be very effective; but more experimentation is required. And it is not easy to come up with a new "magic program" target every year for an assignment in that style.

Finally, again in 2023 one of the four lecture hours[14] was converted to a tutorial session, where students would sit around small tables, be given a collection of questions (usually drills or exercises from the this text, but of course chosen only from those whose answers were not supplied); and they were encouraged to attempt them in those small groups together; the tutorial was not assessed except as possibly contributing to "participation". (The assignment and quizzes, assessment together 90%, were to be attempted alone, not collaboratively.) Two teaching assistants (former students, from 2022, the beginning of a group of "taught teachers") circulated through the room, with the lecturer, responding to questions and giving help generally. Here there was perhaps 40% attendance, and the students' post-course evaluation was extremely positive about the extra tutorial hour.

Support and suggestions for teachers

The assignments, quizzes and other materials for a course based on this text can be shared with accredited instructors elsewhere, and –in the other direction– advice and

---

[13] They were implemented by `Moodle`.

[14] UNSW converted from two 12-week terms to three 9-week terms in 2018: in the first there were three lecture-hours per week; in the latter there were four, making the "stolen" tutorial feasible. In both cases, beginning the week with a two-hour lecture, then one (or two) one-hour sessions, was a good format: two hours is a long time, but generates more interactions throughout the remaining days of the week –say via the course's on-line forum– than a one-hour lecture would.

suggestions from them is very welcome. For instructors, a complete set of answers to the exercises and drills is available: see the book's website.

Here as well are a few small, perhaps quite specific, issues that might be worth considering:

- Do the program examples first, even with operational reasoning — and only *then* present the rules showing that the programs work. The examples will build the intuition for "what's going on", and that intuition will help the students understand the reason that those rules make sense and are worth understanding. (Chapter 2 is an example of that, and it is also discussed in an earlier *(In)-Formal Methods* article [44, Sec. 2.3 "Roll up your sleeves... actually *roll them up.*"].)

- The rules for conditionals, that is for `if`-statements, are particularly sensitive to being introduced at the right moment, not too soon: perhaps even more sensitive than loops are. That is because the *rules* for conditionals are sometimes more complicated than the increased confidence they actually achieve at that early stage. Until then, let the students think of them operationally, intuitively — and entice the clever ones to wonder "If there's a rule for assignment, and for loops, why isn't there one for conditionals?" Make them *want* it before you give it to them.

- Present conventional programs as well as their celebrity cousins,[15] and use invariants for *both*. That diminishes the "novelty" of assertion-based reasoning and so reinforces the idea that it can be used very widely, even for everyday programs.

- Give examples of actual runs. `Python` is widespread, and easy to use: tempt the students to try out their own assertion-based ideas by actually writing programs that way and then running them. Do not however get into input and output (in `Python`): it's a distraction. Keen students will do that for themselves anyway — and one must absolutely avoid any suggestion that we are talking about "programming in `Python`".

- Try not to talk too much about "verifying" and "correctness" — indeed, use those words only sparingly, at least at first. Students already know that they must check their programs: it's just that they are so often doing it in an inefficient way. Pretend you are teaching them a better way to do what they already do, rather than advising them to discard something they have learned and replace it with what you claim is better.

  Indeed early-stage programmers don't do verifying/proving at all, at least not by that name. Many of them will be unfamiliar with (and wary of) proofs of *anything*, of *any* kind. "Proving a program" might not make sense, not at all, from their perspective. And "proving a theorem" might be something they did not entirely enjoy at school.

  Instead, emphasise that they are *checking* their programs: stick to that nomenclature (for now). It's what they do already, although they haven't learned yet how to do it in any other way than "executing the program in their heads", tearing their hair out because they can't find the bug and then, finally, choosing good test cases and hoping for the best.

---

[15] The "celebrity cousins" are the programs that you've never heard of, very tricky to program even though usually quite short, that are used by formal methods proselytisers to dazzle their audience. It's a mistake: it gives the impression that formal methods is just for fancy stuff.

Show them there's a second, complementary approach — this one.

- **And remember** — many (most?) of the people we are trying to reach here are the ones who don't believe that programming can be done this way... but they are about to find out that it can. And they will be out there, eventually, programming things that the rest of us use: so we *need* them to know that.

The others, the "high fliers" (who *did* enjoy proving theorems at school) will take flight anyway: for those, we are helping them fly in the right direction.

Sources, literature, future directions

Seminal research papers: where it started

The three main research "quantum leaps" that led to *reasoning* about programs in the style of our Part I (i.e. beyond their construction and testing alone) were, in chronological order, Robert Floyd's *Assigning meanings to programs* in 1967 [19], C.A.R. Hoare's *An axiomatic basis for computer programming* in 1969 [25] and Edsger W. Dijkstra's *Guarded commands, nondeterminacy and formal derivation of programs* in 1975 [13]. The last of those led to a short –but highly influential– text in 1976 [14] (about which more below).

Two more ground-breaking research contributions, in this case building the foundations to our Part II, were Robin Milner's *An algebraic definition of simulation between programs* in 1971 [40] and Tony Hoare's *Proof of correctness of data representations* in 1972 [26], which laid the basis for our informal presentation of encapsulating datatypes (Part II), and led to work by many others subsequently on "data refinement" (for which see e.g. Abrial and Jones below) and its completeness.

A further step was Niklaus Wirth's *Program development by stepwise refinement* in 1971 [52], whose influence in this text (and elsewhere) is pervasive, particularly for "writing your program from the outside in". It too led to a text: his *Algorithms + Data Structures = Programs*, in 1976 [53]. The link from "refinement", as Wirth informally recommended it, and the more rigorously expressed approach of Floyd, Hoare and Dijkstra (particularly the *weakest preconditions* of the last), was then provided by R.-J.R. Back in his Ph.D. thesis in 1978 [3], the origin of the "refinement calculus".

Particularly in the 1980s there were several notable approaches to *specification* in its own right (from which a program development was expected to follow): they were the *Z* specification method of J.-R. Abrial *et al.* [2] and *VDM*, the Vienna Development Method from IBM in Austria. Principal contributors to *VDM* were Cliff Jones [29] and Dines Bjørner. Abrial's *Z*-approach was that a program's behaviour should be specified in terms of simple set theory, taking advantage of "exotic" constructions only for concision and clarity... but then simplified, refined (in the sense above) with mathematical rigour until the set theory used was elementary enough that it corresponded almost directly (i.e. almost within reach of transliteration) to the syntax of some actual programming language. The subtitle of Abrial's *The B Book* in 1996 [1] was "Assigning programs to meanings", reflecting its complementary approach to Floyd's annotated flowcharts 30 years before [19] — which assigned meanings to programs.

Early and accessible texts on *Z* include Ian Hayes' *Specification Case Studies*, in 1987 [23], Mike Spivey's *Understanding Z : A Specification Language and its Formal Semantics* [51] and Jim Woodcock *et al.*'s *Using Z — Specification, Refinement, and Proof* [55].

The major innovation on which we rely for our Part III is Susan Owicki's approach to interference between shared-state concurrent threads, explained in her Ph.D. thesis, supervised by David Gries [47]. Wim Feijen and Netty van Gasteren later wrote an introductory text based on it, and emphasised case studies [18].

"Formal" formal-methods texts: going further

After the foundational work mentioned above, during the 1980s and '90s there were many teaching texts that contributed to the further spread of formal methods, in most if not all cases giving recommended practices and examples of how the methods could be used. In effect the theory was "hidden", and procedures, almost recipes, were given that –if carefully followed– would result in programs satisfying their specifications, that is which would do what they were supposed to do. Any one of those is a good "second stage" for any reader seeking more formality in formal methods, as well as a guide book to its application; and each author takes his or her own approach to "spreading the word". Many (if not most) of our examples here are drawn from those texts or, in some cases, from their authors directly. And most of them suggest that logic and set theory (and discrete mathematics) be studied either beforehand or in tandem.

Relative recommendations won't be given here, as different texts will suit different readers; and we do concentrate here on techniques for imperative programs (only), as that is the topic of this text. (There are many more recent languages, with associated texts, that support correctness-oriented programming in astonishingly sophisticated ways: but they require familiarity with those languages as a first step and thus are beyond our scope here.)

This author is happy to correspond directly with readers seeking advice on which of the texts below might suit them best. They are (in order of publication, showing only the first author if there are several)

Dijkstra	*A Discipline of Programming*	1976	[14]
Gries	*The Science of Programming*	1981	[22]
Reynolds	*The Craft of Programming*	1981	[49]
Meyer	*Object-Oriented Program Construction*	1988	[38]
Kaldewaij	*Programming: The Derivation of Algorithms*	1990	[30]
Morgan	*Programming from Specifications*	1990,4	[43]
Cohen	*Programming in the 1990s*	1991	[10]
Meyer	*Applying "Design by Contract"*	1992	[39]
Hehner	*A Practical Theory of Programming*	1993	[24]
Broda	*Reasoned Programming*	1994	[9]
Abrial	*The B Book*	1996	[1]
Backhouse	*Program Construction and Verification*	1996	[5]
Back	*Refinement Calculus:*	1998	[4]
	A Systematic Introduction (two volumes)		
Backhouse	*Program Construction:*	2003	[6]
	Calculating Implementations from Specifications		
Jackson	*Software Abstractions:*	2006	[27]
	Language, Logic and Analysis		

Texts or papers concerning *concurrent* programming in the (Owicki–Gries) style of Part III are fewer in number, but include[16]

Owicki	An axiomatic proof technique for parallel programs	1975	[47]

---

[16] Although our Chapter 17 uses the Owicki–Gries approach, the papers on which it relies do not [16, 7, 50]. As mentioned in that chapter, Owicki–Gries at that stage was not yet widely known.

| Gries | An exercise in proving parallel programs correct | 1977 | [21] |
| Feijen | *On a Method of Multiprogramming* | 1990 | [18] |

A significant step beyond Owicki–Gries for concurrency was the "rely guarantee" method proposed by Cliff Jones [28] where, instead of checking for one thread's statements' interfering with other threads' assertions, some enhanced reasoning about threads is gained by grouping in effect "all the interferences" and "all the reliances" (vulnerabilities to interference) on a thread-by-thread basis. That can improve the modularity of concurrent-program development considerably, since one can then reason about the threads to some extent separately rather than having to re-examine the internal assertions of one thread every time some potentially interfering assignment is added in another.

Finally, shared-state concurrency (which is all we have considered in this text) is just one of many (other) quite different approaches to concurrency that do not use states and assignment to variables at all, most notably process algebras, message passing and transactions.

Informal, formal and machine assistance: where we are now

For those who have been introduced to formal methods "informally", in the style of this text, the first surprise is often that one can "reason" about programs at all! Most are delighted to discover that it is indeed possible and, in particular, without having to learn formal logic first. The approach here shows just how far you can go with *in* formal reasoning — provided it's used effectively: not "What did that statement do?" but rather "What did that statement establish?"

As explained in the previous subsection, however, to some extent the possibility of error might seem merely to have been moved from one place to another: instead of being unable to keep in one's head all the possible paths a program might take (e.g. Exs. 1.1, 16.9), one must reason in the extremely precise setting of a logical calculus (as in Appendices D, E) where a single missed symbol might wreck everything.

Where we are now is in a much better position than that, because, as explained in Chapter 18, it's now possible to have the logical reasoning about your program's correctness checked for you automatically by a compiler enhanced with that capability: your program contains assert statements as part of its text and, rather than running against a test case and failing at runtime if an assertion evaluates to False, instead the compiler will check *for you* –and *in advance*– whether a false assertion could ever occur. That reduces considerably the reliance on exhaustive testing — though testing *still* must be rigorously applied (Chapter 19).

There are many sources for "advanced", say "formal" formal methods, some appearing in the first (optimistic) decades since the beginnings in the 1970s and, indeed, even since 2000. A disadvantage of listing those is however –first– that there are too many, and so a (biased?) selection would have to be made and –second, but less obviously– the later works almost always build-in a particular recipe, or at least a "point of view", inherited and then passed on by that text's author. That risks a "soap-box effect", which is not helpful for people trying to learn the essence of this programming approach without getting "baked in" to a *particular* author's style, intellectual toolkit or even prejudice.

Thus only three (of the many) recent texts will be mentioned here, for those who would now like to go further. They are

2014 *Concrete Semantics with Isabelle/HOL* (Nipkow and Klein [46])
    The "Isabelle/HOL" of the title is a sophisticated interactive theorem prover

for mathematics generally, at least mathematics that can be rendered in logic.[17] If however a particular programming language's semantics, its "meaning", can be encoded in mathematics then an interactive theorem prover can be used to prove properties of programs in that language, after they have been translated into mathematics.

The above text shows how to do that in a particular case.

2023 *Program Proofs* (Leino [36])   To the title here could be added "in **Dafny**", the topic of Sec. 18.2 above. Its topic includes ours here (and goes further, into other programming styles); but it does require some knowledge of the logical calculi beforehand because, otherwise, there is no way of "telling the compiler" what specification your program must satisfy.

There is however the more-than-compensating exhilaration of, first, learning how to reason informally about programs using assertions (this text's topic) rather than simulations "in your head"; then, second (and after some time having learned to take the "first" for granted, self-evident), experiencing how with more complicated programs the *assertions themselves* can become too complicated for comfort; and finally, learning that many of those assertions (but alas not all of them) can be proved automatically in push-button style.

2023 *Effective Theories in Programming Practice* (Misra [42])   Here is found a combination of informal and formal reasoning, with many more examples than in this text (and more challenging too). The style is a combination of intuition, formality and (sometimes remarkable) insight into how one can know when to be formal, when to be clear (not always the same thing) and when to take an unexpected reasoning path (as for example Misra showed us in our Sec. 16.2).

---

[17] Isabelle/HOL was for example used to prove the Kepler Conjecture, concerning the most efficient stacking of spheres. That's mathematics, discrete geometry, not a computer program.

Appendices

Drill exercises

The drills in this appendix are best attempted *without* consulting the text as you do them (or looking at the answers, if given). By all means however consult the text beforehand (to refresh your memory) and afterwards (to see whether you were right or, if not, why you were wrong).

Only then are you testing yourself in order to discover what you *don't* (yet) know.

A.1 What are "drills"? And what are they for?

Drills are exercises of simple skills that need to become second nature, to be "bedded in", before attempting real-world problems.

Times tables and addition tables in primary school are not drills in the sense we intend here; rather they are analogues of our Appendix E below, because for many (most?) they are meaningless and boring rote-learning: just patterns, equalities to be learned by heart and recited on demand. Why do it? What's the point?

Once the tables are absorbed, however, study moves on to more intricate (but still boring?) manipulations with those tables as a basis: complicated calculations using numbers comprising many digits rather than just singles as earlier. There, the practice might consist of doing long divisions followed by "multiplying back" to check your answer. Again, it's not a favourite activity for everyone. But they *are* drills.

And university students learning "discrete maths" or "elementary logic" as a pre-requisite to computer programming might be asking the same question. "What do we need this stuff for? I already know how to program." *Are they drills*?

The moment of truth for primary-school students is when they realise that *using* those single-digit tables, and the algorisms[1] built on them, they can solve real-life problems like "How long is the diagonal of a football field?" knowing only the lengths of its sides, without having to pace across it. Or "How deep is this well?" using a stopwatch to time the interval until the "plonk". Suddenly it all starts to make sense, at least for some.

The moment of truth for programmers might be when they realise that writing programs is one thing, but writing *correct* programs is a serious challenge. And for many, their only recourse by then –but depending on what they have been taught– is to begin debugging *after* the program has already been written. Its primary-school analogue is the tedious multiplying-back done *after* the long division has already been attempted.

---

[1] The word "algorisms" is derived from the same Al-Khwārizmī who gave us "algorithms": but it refers specifically to arithmetic.

The drills in this appendix are intended to exercise the "algorisms" of reasoning about your programs *as you are writing them*. For example, substitution is easily enough explained: it's an (almost) purely textual replacement of one string by another. As a concept on its own, it's hardly interesting: it's a "times table". But its *use* is crucial to reasoning about assignment statements and the programs that contain them. And doing it correctly should become second nature.

"Learning to do these rote operations correctly", saving your neurones for application to the program itself, is what these drills are about. You don't want to falter over a simple substitution when your actual concern is preserving an invariant; you don't want to wonder what the product of a zero-length sequence might be when your actual concern is initialising a loop; you don't want to worry about simple iterate-up or iterate-down invariants when the problem's actual invariant is much more subtle, the essence of the algorithm.

That's what these drills are for, to make the routine, but still essential parts of program construction become second nature, automatic... so that you can concentrate on the interesting and important parts. They are a useful source for "in class" exercises/tutorials in an (in-)formal methods course as it progresses, and are presented here more or less in increasing order of difficulty, to reflect the amount of material already learned.[2]

A.2 Substitution

Substitution is the key operation for checking whether assignments work. But in these drills we practise substitutions on their own. (See App. E.3.1.) Each of the following exercises should be done in two stages: first, perform the substitution *exactly as it is*, but putting additionally parentheses $(\cdots)$ around the "replacing" text. Second, use "ordinary" reasoning (e.g. arithmetic) to simplify the result. Here are two examples, written in ordinary mathematical style:

1. Substitute 1 for x in $x + 1$.[3] *Answer:* First $(1) + 1$ and then simplify to 2.

2. Substitute $y + 1$ for x in $2x$. *Answer:* First $2(y+1)$ and then (if you want to) simplify to $2y + 2$. Note that without the parentheses the substitution would have given the incorrect expression $2y + 1$.

Drill A.1 (p. 9) ⇓ Do these substitutions, using **Python** syntax — first write down the literal result, and then simplify it if you can. When simplifying, assume x is an integer.

(a) Substitute x+1 for x in x==0.

(b) Substitute x//2 for x in x==2.

(c) Substitute 2 for x in x==2.

(d) Substitute 2 for x in 0==x.

(e) Substitute x-y-1 for y in x-y>=3.

---

[2] We are skipping altogether the issue of calculators vs. pencils for school students, interactive development environments (*IDE*'s) vs. the command line for first-year university students, and *SMT*-solvers vs. Appendix D for more serious program developers.

In each case, it's a question of how much you should know about what a button actually does *before* you start to rely on being able to push it: and opinions do vary.

[3] You could also say "Replace x by 1 in $x + 1$." ("Substitute x by 1 in $x + 1$." is not normal usage.)

Drill A.2 (p. 9) Do these substitutions, using `Python` syntax, and simplify them if you can. When simplifying, assume that `x` is an integer.

(a) Substitute `x*x-2*x+1` for `y` in `y==0`.

(b) Substitute `x*x-3*x+2` for `y` in `y==0`.

(c) Substitute `t` for `y` in `x==Y and y==X`.

(d) Substitute `y` for `x` in your answer to (c).

(e) Substitute `x` for `t` in your answer to (d).

A.3 Sequences and operators on them

A *sequence* `A` has some length `N>=0` and (in `Python`) is indexed from `A[0]` *in*clusive to `A[N]` *ex*clusive: thus its elements are `A[0]`, `A[1]`, ... ,`A[N-1]`. Usually all the elements have the same type. (That's not always true; but we will assume it here.)

`Python`'s subsegment notation `A[lo:hi]` means (again in the inclusive/exclusive style) `A[lo]`, `A[lo+1]`, ... ,`A[hi-1]`, and there are various conventions for "default" range values: a missing `lo` is 0; and a missing `hi` is `N`. Just `A` on its own is the same as `A[0:N]`, and `[]` is the empty sequence. The first element is `A[0]`; and all elements *except* the first (i.e. the "tail" of the sequence) is `A[1:]`.

`Python` allows also *negative* sequence indices, which "count backwards from the end" so that for example `A[-1]` is `A`'s last element and `A[:-1]` is all but the last element.[4]

Now speaking mathematically, for a moment: for associative binary operators on the sequence's type, such as $(+)$ for numbers, there are corresponding general operators that act on a whole (sub-sequence) at once, such as $\sum$; and the drill exercises below are about that. Some of the mathematical operators are implemented directly in `Python` (for example $(+)$ which becomes `+` of course, and $\sum$ which becomes `sum()`). And some are not: but that doesn't stop us from using them in assertions — as long as we know what they mean.

Assume in the exercises that all indices have "sensible" values: thus in Dr. A.3(a), for example, we assume `0<=lo<=hi<=N`.

Drill A.3 ⇓ Suppose that `A` has length `N`, and that `0<=lo<=hi<=N`.

(a) How long is `A[lo:hi]` ?

(b) Simplify $\sum$`A[lo:mid]` + $\sum$`A[mid:hi]` .

(c) Simplify $\sum$`A[lo:mid]` + `A[mid]` , assuming `lo<=mid<N` of course.

(d) How many elements does `A[n:n]` have? (Assume `0<=n<=N`.)
    Does it depend on `n` ?

(e) What is the value of $\sum$`A[n:n]` ?

---

[4] Note however that "out of order" indices in `Python` give the empty sequence, not an error, as do subsegment selectors that are out of range. Since the conventions in other languages might differ, it's best not to rely on those behaviours.

Drill A.4 Suppose that A has length N, and that 0<=lo<=hi<=N.

(a) Why is it sensible to write the empty sequence as just [], without mentioning any A?

(b) If for all 0<=n<N we have A[n]==n, what is $\sum A$?

(c) How many elements does A[:] have?

(d) Write $\prod$ for the product of all elements in a sequence. With the same element values for A as in (b), what is $\prod A$, where A written alone means "the whole thing A[0:N]"? What is $\prod A[1:]$?

(e) Are [] and A[0:0] and A[1:1] and ... A[N:N] all equal? If not, explain why they differ. What then is $\prod A[n:n]$ for any 0<=n<=N?

Drill A.5 Continue to assume we are working over sequences of numbers, and that mathematically we have both positive and negative infinity, i.e. both ∞ and $-\infty$. Write MAX for the whole-sequence generalisation of the binary operator max.

(a) Simplify MAX A[lo:mid] max MAX A[mid:hi] .

(b) Simplify MAX A[lo:lo] max MAX A[lo:hi] .

(c) Given your two answers just above, what must MAX A[lo:lo] be? And therefore also MAX [] ?

Drill A.6 Repeat Dr. A.5 for MIN, the whole-sequence generalisation of the binary operator min.

A.4 Invariants

Drill A.7 ⇓ Suppose that A[0:N] is an array of integers. Try to do each of these exercises *without* looking back at the text until you have tried them all.
     Then check the whole lot afterwards, once you've finished.

(a) What would be a good invariant for a loop that summed A from low-to-high index? (Make up your own variable names, but keep them simple.)

(b) What would be a good invariant for a low-to-high loop that found the largest element in A, assuming A is not empty?

(c) What postcondition should be found at the end of your program for (a)?

(d) What precondition should be found at the beginning of your program for (a)?

(e) What would be a good invariant for a loop that sets Boolean b to whether the integer a occurred somewhere in A?

(f) What would be a good invariant for a loop that set integer n to the index of the first occurrence of a in A, if a is there at all? (And what would therefore be a good value for n when there is no a in A?)

Drill A.8 Suppose (as in Dr. A.7) that `A[0:N]` is an array of integers.

(a) What would be a good invariant for loop that summed `A` from high-to-low index?

(b) What would be a good invariant for loop that found the smallest element in `A`, assuming `A` is not empty and moving from low to high?

(c) What precondition should appear first in your answer to (b)?

(d) (Tricky.) What would be a good invariant for a loop that found the index of the first element of `A` that was strictly greater than the *average* of all (other) elements before it?

Could that program have precondition `{ PRE: 0<=N }`? What answer should it produce if *no* element is greater than the average of all others before it?

What answer should the program produce when `A` is empty?

What answer should the program produce if `A` has exactly one element `A[0]`, i.e. when there are *no* elements before `A[0]`?

A.5 Variants

In these drills we will re-use the invariant questions from App. A.4, concentrating this time however on the *variant*.

Drill A.9 ⇓ Suppose again that `A[0:N]` is an array of integers. Remember that variants (for now) must be integer valued and either strictly decreasing or strictly increasing (but not a mixture) on each loop iteration — and they must be bounded below or above in the direction in which they are moving.

(a) What would be a good variant for the loop in Dr. A.7(a), which summed `A` from low-to-high index?

(b) What would be a good variant for the loop in Dr. A.8(a), which summed `A` from high-to-low index?

(c) What would be a good variant for the loop in Dr. A.7(b), which found the *largest* element in `A`, assuming `A` is not empty? Do you rely on the precondition for the correctness of your choice?

(d) What would be a good variant for the loop in Dr. A.8(b), which found the *smallest* element in `A`, assuming `A` is not empty?

Drill A.10 Again `A[0:N]` is an array of integers.

(a) What would be a good variant for the loop in Dr. A.7(e), which set Boolean `b` to whether integer `a` occurred in `A`?

(b) What would be a good variant for the loop in Dr. A.7(f), which set integer `n` to the index of the first occurrence of `a` in `A`, if there is one?

(c) (Harder.) What would be a good variant for a loop that set integer `n` to the index of the first occurrence of `a` in `A` *when it is known* that there is one? The program's precondition would be `{ PRE: "Element a occurs in A." }` and the loop guard would probably be `while A[n]!=a: ····`.

You must be sure to establish that the variant is bounded (probably bounded above).

A.6 Propositions, sets and predicates

In these drills we will use mainly `Python` syntax for logic (as elsewhere in the main text) except for "implies" $\Rightarrow$.

Drill A.11 State for each of the following implications whether it is equivalent to `True` or to `False`:

(a) `True` $\Rightarrow$ `True`   (c) `False` $\Rightarrow$ `True`

(b) `True` $\Rightarrow$ `False`   (d) `False` $\Rightarrow$ `False`

Drill A.12 ⇓ It's a simple rule of elementary set theory that for two sets A, B their intersection $A \cap B$ is a subset of each of the two sets A, B separately: that is, we have both $A \cap B \subseteq A$ and $A \cap B \subseteq B$.

But is that still true when A and B have no elements in common, that is when their intersection is empty (i.e. they are *disjoint*)? If yes, say why; if no, give a counter-example.

Drill A.13 Consider the statement (in English) "If A is true then also B is true." where A, B stand for any claims at all. In logic (e.g. in an assertion) we could write it $A \Rightarrow B$. Which of the following are equivalent to $A \Rightarrow B$?

(a) $B \Rightarrow A$ (c) `not` $B \Rightarrow$ `not` A (e) `not` $A \Rightarrow$ `not` B

(b) `not` A `or` B (d) A `or` B (f) A `and` B

Drill A.14 ⇓ For each of the following statements (in English), give the correct logical equivalent using $\Rightarrow$ or its related $\Leftarrow$ and $\Leftrightarrow$. (You might need "`not`" in some cases.)

(a) if `A` then `B`   (d) `A` if and only if `B`   (g) `A` iff `B`

(b) `A` if `B`   (e) `A` just when `B`

(c) `A` unless `B`   (f) `A` only if `B`

Drill A.15 State for each of the following implications whether it evaluates to `True` for all values of integers `x,y`:

(a) `x<=y and y<=x` $\Rightarrow$ `x==y`   (c) `x<y and y<x` $\Rightarrow$ `x!=y`

(b) `x<y and y<x` $\Rightarrow$ `x==y`   (d) `x<y or y<x` $\Rightarrow$ `x!=y`

Note that the first three are `and` but the last is `or`.

Drill A.16 Consider the statement "If you can't see my mirrors, then I can't see you." Which of the following are equivalent to that?

(a) If I can't see you,
    then you can't see my mirrors.

(b) You can see my mirrors,
    or I can't see you.

(c) If I can see you,
    then you can see my mirrors.

(d) You can't see my mirrors,
    or I can't see you.

(e) If you can see my mirrors,
    then I can see you.

(f) You can't see my mirrors,
    and I can't see you.

Hint: Consider using the contrapositive law (E.30), and (E.26).

A.7 Thinking outside the box

Drill A.17 ⇓ When people were figuring out how to reason with negative numbers,[5] a typical question arising about multiplying two negative numbers was this:

> If $-1 \times 2 = -2$, i.e. multiplication by -1 takes $+2$ down to -2, shouldn't multiplication of an (already) negative number by -1 be "even more negative"?

Give a *rigorous* argument that the product of two negative numbers should be positive. You can use any general algebraic facts about *non-negative* numbers in order to do so.

A.8 Hoare triples "in the small"

Drill A.18 Which of the following Hoare triples are correct? For those that aren't correct, explain why they are not.

(a) `{x==0} x= x+1 {x==1}`

(b) `{x==1} x= x+1 {x==0}`

(c) `{True} x= x+1 {x==1}`

(d) `{True} x= x+1 {x==0}`

(e) `{False} x= x+1 {x==1}`

(f) `{False} x= x+1 {x==0}`

Drill A.19 ⇓ Fill-in the missing assertions ???, making them as weak (i.e. as general, as permissive) as you can. Simplify them arithmetically, afterwards; but

> *do the substitution first.*

Assume in all cases that x is an integer.

(a) `{???} x= x+1 {x==1}`

(b) `{???} x= x//2 {x==4}`

(c) `{???} y= x*x-2*x+1 {y==0}`

(d) `{???} y= x*x-3*x+1 {y==0}`

(e) `{???} y= x*x+1 {y==0}`

Drill A.20 ⇓ As for Dr. A.19, fill in the missing assertions ??? , making them as weak (i.e. as general, as permissive) as you can. Start from the bottom one, then substitute and simplify as you work towards the top.

(a) *Hint*: Recall Ex. 9.4.
```
{???}
x= x+y
{???}
y= x-y
{x == X+Y and y==X}
```

(b)
```
{???}
x= x+y
{???}
y= x-y
{???}
x= x-y
{x==Y and y==X}
```

---

[5] "As for negative numbers... most mathematicians of the sixteenth and seventeenth centuries did not accept them... Pascal regarded the subtraction of 4 from 0 as utter nonsense." [32, p. 252]

Drill A.21 As for Dr. A.19 and Dr. A.20, fill in the missing assertions ???, making them as weak (i.e. as general, as permissive) as you can.

(a) { ??? }
    s= x
    { ??? }
    s= s+y
    { ??? }
    s= s+z
    { s == x+y+z }

(b) { ??? }
    p= 1
    { ??? }
    p= p*x
    { ??? }
    p= p*y
    { ??? }
    p= p*z
    { p == x*y*z }

A.9 Hoare triples in the large(r)

Drill A.22 ⇓ Here is a "schematic" loop, including some assertions:

```
# PRE:  pre
init
# INV:  inv
while  test:
    { test and inv}
    body
    { inv }
# POST:  post
```
(A.1)

Assume the assertions are correctly placed, which means that if (A.1) starts in a state where *pre* is true then every time the program's flow of control reaches an assertion, that assertion will be true as well.

What are the individual implications and Hoare triples that ensured the correct placement of those assertions?

Drill A.23 Here's the same loop as in Dr. A.22,[6] but this time with "unknown" general assertions called A, B, C, D, E :

```
{ A }
init
{ B }
while  test:
    { C }
    body
    { D }
{ E }
```
(A.2)

Which of the following Hoare triples and implications must be correct in order for (A.2) to have been correctly annotated?

---

[6] That is, whatever the program fragments *init*, *test* and *body* might be, they are the same in both cases: only the assertions might be different.

(a) $\{A\}$ *init* $\{B\}$ (c) B and not *test* $\Rightarrow E$ (e) D and *test* $\Rightarrow C$

(b) B and *test* $\Rightarrow C$ (d) $\{C\}$ *body* $\{D\}$ (f) D and not *test* $\Rightarrow E$

Drill A.24 ⇓ Here is a "repeat" loop: it enters unconditionally, and it terminates just when *done* holds at the end of an iteration.[7] Again we suppose "unknown" general assertions called A, B, C, D, E:

$$\{A\}$$
init
$$\{B\}$$
repeat:
   $\{C\}$ (A.3)
   body
   $\{D\}$
until *done*
$$\{E\}$$

Which of the following Hoare triples and implications must be correct in order for (A.3) to have been correctly annotated?

(a) $\{A\}$ *init* $\{B\}$ (c) $\{C\}$ *body* $\{D\}$ (e) D and *done* $\Rightarrow E$

(b) $B \Rightarrow C$ (d) D and not *done* $\Rightarrow C$

Drill A.25 (p. 53) Give invariants that could be used to annotate each of the following loops correctly for establishing their (partial) correctness. You may write the invariants in English if you wish, as long as they are precise and clear. You do not have to write out the loop again: just give the invariant for each one; but you might want to include extra assertions as well, to help your reasoning.

Give also for each program a variant that could be used to establish its successful termination, which –together with its partial correctness– would establish total correctness for the postcondition given.

In each case A is a sequence of length N, and we assume # PRE: N>=0.

(a)

```
n= N
while n!=0:
  n= n-1
  if A[n]==x: {···} break
# POST: "If x is in A at all, then its last occurrence is at A[n]."
```

You might consider placing an extra assertion just before the break, to justify your reasoning.

(b)

```
n,c= N,0
while n!=0:
  n= n-1
  if A[n]==x: c= c+1
# POST: POST "c is the number of occurrences of x in A."
```

---

[7] Python does not have repeat loops, but they can be simulated with while True and break.

(c)

```
# Variable x is fixed beforehand.
n,ℓ,e= 0,0,0
while n!=N:
  if A[n]==x: e= e+1                          (A.4)
  else: e= 0
  n,ℓ= n+1,ℓ max e
# Post: "ℓ is the length of a longest run of consecutive x's in A."
```

A.10 Whole-program drills

Drill A.26 ⇓ Use your invariant from Dr. A.25's program (A.4) to suggest an invariant for a program that establishes "ℓ is the length of a longest run of *almost*-consecutive x's in A." where a run has "almost-consecutive x's" just when it never contains two or more consecutive non-x's. For example, these are almost-consecutive x runs:

$$\text{[], x, xx, y, xy, yx, xyx, yxx, xxy, yxyxyxyxyxy} \dots$$

These are examples of runs that are *not* almost-consecutive x:

$$\text{yy, xyy, yyx, xxxxxxxxxxxxxxxyyxxxxxxxxxxxxxxx} \dots$$

Do not *write the program yet!* Wait until Dr. A.27, and then use your invariant to help.

Drill A.27 Use your answer to Dr. A.26, i.e. the invariant you discovered there, to change *only* the if-statement in (A.4) to make a program that establishes the post-condition "ℓ is the length of a longest run of *almost*-consecutive x's in A."

Drill A.28 ⇓ Suppose B gummy bears (*Gummibären*) are to be handed out to C children.[8]

If C divides B exactly, then each child should receive B/C (whole!) bears. But if the division is not exact then some children must receive more bears than others; even so, no two children should have numbers of bears more than one apart.

Let constants bL (for "low") and bH be $\lfloor B/C \rfloor$ and $\lceil B/C \rceil$ respectively, where $\lfloor \cdot \rfloor$ and $\lceil \cdot \rceil$ are the floor and ceiling functions from arithmetic. If every child receives only bL bears, then clearly B bears *will* be enough overall — but some bears might be left over. On the other hand, if every child receives bH bears then B bears might *not* be enough. So the solution is to give each child c some (whole) number b_c of bears with bL <= b_c <= bH, making sure however that the sum of all the b_c's equals B exactly.

But how do we decide when to "go low" (with bL), or "high" (with bH)?[9]

Below is the framework of a program that does that (working outside-in, as usual):

---

[8] This program is based on an exercise of Jeffrey Kingston [31].
[9] Do you suffer from "indexitis"? Did you feel the urge to write "child c_i" and "bL <= b_{c_i} <= bH" here? Or to number the children from 1 to some C?

```
b,c= B,C # Number of bears; number of children.
while c!=0:
    "Set r to some integer such that ⌊b/c⌋ <= r <= ⌈b/c⌉ ."
    "Hand out r bears to the next child."        # (A.7) below.
    b,c= b-r,c-1                    # Now one child fewer.
# Each child got between bL and bH bears; no bears left over.
```
(A.5)

We want to show that (A.5) checks, that indeed

$$\text{exactly B bears are handed out overall; and} \tag{A.6}$$

$$\text{each child receives between bL and bH bears.} \tag{A.7}$$

(Remember that bL and bH are fixed, and are no more than one apart.)

Hint: Consider an invariant resembling[10]

```
    bL<=⌊b/c⌋ and ⌈b/c⌉<=bH
and B == b + "the number of bears handed out already"   .
```
(A.8)

---

[10] You might have to alter it slightly...

Summary of rules
for checking programs

In this appendix we gather all the program-checking rules together in one place, for easy reference.

Remember that one strategy, for an already written program, is to apply checking rules to the smallest pieces of it (the assignment statements, principally), and then use the combining rules –the rules for sequential composition, conditionals and loops– to work your way outwards towards having checked the program as a whole.

On the other hand, if you are using these rules to help *design* programs then the order is reversed: you work your way inwards. Figure out what the pre- and postconditions (and invariants) might be that would make your overall program work, and then use checking rules, starting at the outside, to fill in the smaller –and smaller– pieces, until there are none left unchecked.

In either direction, if some of the actual Boolean reasoning for the checks turns out to be intricate in detail (even if simple in principle), it might help to refer to the rules in Appendix D for working with Boolean expressions.

We start with the basic programs, following –for this presentation– the inside-outwards strategy.

B.1 The basic programs

"Basic" programs are those that do not have other programs inside them: for us so far, there have been effectively only two. (But there are in fact three further, more specialised basic programs: they are treated separately, in App. B.6.)

B.1.1 Assignment statements

Assignment statements –of course– update a variable with a new value: that's what they *do*. But *checking* them provides the complementary view, the focus of this text: not what do they do, but what do they achieve. For that, first we carry out a substitution into the postcondition (as if with a text editor) and then we check a Boolean implication with respect to the (unaltered) precondition: that is, the assignment

$$\{\textsc{Pre}: \ pre\} \ \mathtt{x=} \ expr \ \{\textsc{Post}: \ post \ \}$$

checks just if $pre \Rightarrow post'$, where the implication's consequent $post'$ is the original $post$ but with all (free) occurrences of its x replaced by $expr$. We write that act of substitution as $post[\text{x}\backslash expr]$, adding parentheses if necessary.[1] For multiple assignments, the replacements are done simultaneously.[2]

The program (1.12) in Sec. 1.5 gives an example.

B.1.2 The "do nothing" statement skip

The skip program literally does nothing, and is not often used in actual code. But –as for zero in arithmetic– it is helpful to understand how skip is checked and –furthermore– skip helps to understand other checking rules later on, for example the else-less conditional (App. B.3.2), and multiple assertions on separate lines (App. B.2.2). The rule is that

$$\{\,\text{PRE: } pre\,\} \text{ skip } \{\text{POST: } post\,\}$$

checks successfully just when $pre \Rightarrow post$. In Python, skip is written "pass". See p. 67 and p. 69 for examples.

B.2 Assertions: "What's true here?"

Assertions are how we record what we expect to be true about variables' values. Sometimes we write them as comments, for example # *What's true here.* in Python; at other times we put them between braces { What's true here. } The two styles are equivalent, but often the choice between them is influenced by how precise they are: the less formal assertions might at first be in English; and later, as we learn more about the program we are making, we might change to Boolean formulae between braces.

A second convention we are following is that assertions "helpful along the way" are written with {···}, whereas assertions we would like to be retained in the program's code, because they are important or hard to regenerate, are written with # ··· and could well become part of the program's documentation. Whether they are in English or are Boolean formulae is irrelevant, for that decision. Typical "keep for later" assertions are preconditions, postconditions and invariants.

Assertions however *are not themselves program fragments*: they are *about* program fragments. (On the other hand, the assert *statement* is a program: we come to that later, in App. B.6.1.)

Usually assertions have executable program fragments on either side, so that they sit on the arcs between program-fragment boxes in flowcharts like the one in Fig. 1.1 — but sometimes we find it's useful to write assertions *without* program fragments in between. Below we explain how they are checked in that case; we'll use the {···} format.

---

[1] See App. D.11.4 concerning α-conversion.
[2] There is also occasionally the issue of so-called "α-conversion", sometimes necessary if *expr* itself contains bound variables (App. D.11.4).

B.2.1 Multiple assertions on one line

Two (or more) assertions $\{\mathit{assn1}\}$ $\{\mathit{assn2}\}$ on the same line are treated as a single assertion $\{\mathit{assn1}$ and $\mathit{assn2}\}$, that is as the conjunction of the two.

Thus if the assertion is a postcondition then *both* $\mathit{assn1}$ and $\mathit{assn2}$ must check from the statement before; if it's a precondition, however, then *either* $\mathit{assn1}$ and $\mathit{assn2}$ may be used to check the statement after. (See (E.37) and (E.40) in App. E.2.4 for more motivation of "both if after" vs. "either if before".)

B.2.2 Multiple assertions on successive lines

If assertions occur one after the other vertically, that is they are on separate lines, then they are not conjoined (unless there is specific text saying that they should be, because for example they are too long to fit together on one line as in (B.1) of App. B.4.1 below). Instead, it must be checked that each one implies the one that follows it. The very first one should be checked from the program statement before; and the last one may be used to check the statement after. Thus

$$\begin{array}{ll} \{\mathit{assn1}\} & \\ \{\mathit{assn2}\} & \leftarrow \textit{Imagine a } \mathtt{skip} \textit{ here.} \end{array}$$

checks just if $\{\mathit{assn1} \Rightarrow \mathit{assn2}\}$. It is exactly as if there were a $\mathtt{skip}$ in between, as in

```
{PRE:  assn1}
skip
{POST: assn2}    ,
```

and you applied the $\mathtt{skip}$ rule from App. B.1.2 above. A common pattern for multiple assertions mixes both arrangements: it is

$$\begin{array}{l} \{\mathit{inv}\}\ \{\mathtt{not}\ \mathit{cond}\} \\ \{\mathit{post}\}\quad, \end{array}$$

which is often found at the end of a loop. (See App. B.4.1 below for examples of that.) The required check in that case, as explained above, must be

$$\mathit{inv}\ \text{and not}\ \mathit{cond}\ \ \Rightarrow\ \ \mathit{post}\quad,$$

so that the first two are conjoined to make the antecedent and that conjunction must imply the consequent.

B.2.3 Assertions for expressions: are they well defined?

When evaluating an expression (say in an assignment statement or in a condition) could possibly cause an error, it must be checked that the *precondition* of the statement implies that the expression is *defined*, that is does not cause an error. Thus for example the use of division $\mathtt{n/d}$ in an expression requires that d is not zero, that $\mathtt{d!=0}$ occurs in (or is implied by) the precondition of the statement in which the division occurs.

Another example is the use of $\mathtt{A[n]}$ for indexing into a sequence $\mathtt{A[0:N]}$ — it requires $\mathtt{0<=n<N}$ in the precondition, ensuring that the index is applied within range.

See Ex. 16.2 from Sec. 16.6 for examples.

B.3 Rules for checking larger program fragments

B.3.1 Sequential composition

The sequential composition of two programs *prog1* and *prog2* is the program that first executes *prog1* and then executes *prog2*.[3] That means that the postcondition of the first one must imply (or be equivalent to) the precondition of the second: thus the composition

> {PRE: *pre*}
> *prog1*
> *prog2*
> {POST: *post*}

checks just if there is (or could be[4]) an assertion *assn* "in between" so that

> {PRE: *pre*}   *prog1* {POST: *assn*}
> and {PRE: *assn*} *prog2* {POST: *post*}

both check on their own. When used in annotating a program with assertions, instead of writing {*assn*} twice, as above, it can be written just once, between the two program fragments, as here:

> {PRE: *pre*}
> *prog1*
> {*assn*}
> *prog2*
> {POST: *post*}   .

See p. 8 in Sec. 1.5 for examples.

B.3.2 Conditional without `else`

The simple "without-`else`" conditional requires a separate check of its body, but the precondition of that `if`-body will include the `if`'s condition — which of course makes the check easier. But it must also be checked that the precondition with the *negated* `if`-condition implies the overall postcondition directly: thus

> {PRE: *pre*} if *cond*: *prog* {POST: *post*}

requires *two* checks: the first is for the implicit "`then`"

> {PRE: *pre* **and** *cond*} *prog* {POST: *post*}   ,

and the second is for the implicit "`else`", the implication

> *pre* **and** **not** *cond* ⇒ *post*   .

See p. 68 in Sec. 5.4 for examples, and Ex. 5.3.

---

[3] In Python, sequential composition is either newline or semicolon, In *C* it is just writing the two programs next to each other, because semicolons in *C* are mandatory.
[4] By "could be" is meant that you do not necessarily have to write the in-between assertion, especially if it's trivial: but you should be confident that you could if someone asks for it... for example, yourself later, when you have forgotten why you thought that code was correct.

B.3.3 Conditional with else

We've just seen that the conditional without else (just above) is a special case of the conditional *with* else, one where the else-branch is actually skip. (That is an example of where skip is useful in understanding other checking rules.) If the else-branch is *not* skip (or even if it is skip), then the following rule is used: that

> {Pre: *pre*}
> if *cond*: *prog1*
> else: *prog2*
> {Post: *post*}

checks if

> {Pre: *pre* and *cond*}   *prog1* {Post: *post*}
> and {Pre: *pre* and not *cond*}   *prog2* {Post: *post*}

both check.

See p. 68 in Sec. 5.4 for examples.

B.4 Rules for checking loops: while and for

In general, loops have two things to check: their partial correctness, that they establish the postcondition *if* they terminate; and that they actually *do* terminate. Partial correctness and termination are together called *total* correctness.

B.4.1 Partial correctness for while-loops

To check the partial correctness of

> {Pre: *pre*}
> while *cond*:
>   *body*
> {Post: *post*}   ,

an *invariant* (assertion) must be found, a condition that is true before and after each iteration of the body, including being true just before the very first iteration (even if there *isn't* a "first one", because the loop is not entered even once), and after the very last iteration (again, even if the loop was not entered). That was explained in Chapter 2, and finding those invariants was the subject of Chapter 3. Once found, the invariant would probably become part of the program's documentation, as here:

> {Pre: *pre*}
> # Inv: *inv*
> while *cond*:
>   {*inv* and *cond*}
>   *body*
>   {*inv*}
> {*inv* and not *cond*}
> {Post: *post*}   .

Thus to check the loop above we must find a what's-true condition *inv* (or comment, if written, less formally, in English), and then check these three things:

$$pre \Rightarrow inv \qquad \text{\# The invariant is true initially.}$$

and $\left.\begin{array}{l} \{\,\text{PRE: } \textit{cond} \text{ and } \textit{inv}\,\} \\ \textit{body} \\ \{\,\text{POST: } \textit{inv}\,\} \end{array}\right\} \rightarrow \text{\# The invariant is maintained.}$ (B.1)

and $\quad inv$ and not $cond \Rightarrow post$
   \# The invariant and the negated condition...
   \# ...imply the postcondition.

Ex. B.1

Note that this `while`-check generates a "sub-check", so to speak, of the loop body: it conjoins the loop guard *cond* to the precondition because the body is entered only when the condition is true. The sub-check will in turn be carried out by using the (other) rules here, each according to its own structure: it's a sort of hierarchical progression down towards the basic cases.

Because the invariant is usually the key to the loop's correctness, we usually write it as a comment "# INV: *inv*" (i.e. rather than as {*inv*}), so that it will remain as part of the final program's documentation.

B.4.2 Termination for `while`-loops

To check the termination of `while` *cond*: *body* , we must find an integer-valued variant (not *invariant*) expression *expr* which the loop body is guaranteed to decrease, but not below zero. (Variants were the subject of Chapter 4.) Often the `0<=`*expr* part of the loop body's postcondition will come from the loop's invariant.

We have to show that

$$\{\,\text{PRE: } inv \text{ and } cond \text{ and } expr == \texttt{V}\,\}$$
$$body$$
$$\{\,\text{POST: } \texttt{0} <= expr < \texttt{V}\,\}$$

checks, where *expr* is an integer expression and `V` is a variable not assigned-to by *body*: typically `V` will be auxiliary (but does not have to be).

For examples, see Chapter 4.

B.4.3 `while`-loops with `break` statements

Sometimes a loop can "terminate early", using a `break` statement. To check for example

$$\{\,\text{PRE: } pre\,\}$$
`# INV:` *inv*
`while` *cond1*:
   body 1
   `{` *assertion* `}`
   `if` *cond2*: `{` *assertion* and *cond2* `}` `break`   (B.2)
   body 2
$$\{\,\text{POST: } post\,\} \qquad ,$$

where the *body* contains one or more `break` statements, the usual technique from App. B.4.1 is followed *except* that after the loop one can assume only the invariant and the negated guard *or* an assertion that held immediately before any of the **break** statements — and the latter might *not* include the invariant. The loop's postcondition *post* must be implied by *each* of those disjuncts separately.

Thus (B.1) from above is modified so that the third check in program (B.2) would be

$$(inv \text{ and not } cond1) \text{ or } (assertion \text{ and } cond2) \quad \Rightarrow \quad post$$

```
or        # The invariant and the negated while-condition,       (B.3)
in        # or the break condition(s)
English   # imply the postcondition.
```

Note that **break** statements need not decrease the variant, since they ensure the loop's immediate termination. (The variant must still be decreased however for normal exits from the loop, those occurring only because its guard is false.)

B.4.4 Total correctness

Checking total correctness of a loop means checking both its partial correctness *and* its termination. As we saw just above, that is usually done by checking partial correctness first, and then termination separately.

B.4.5 Correctness for for-loops

Particularly simple **while**-loops can be written as **for**-loops, with the initialisation, incrementing (or decrementing) and exiting the loop all "built in" — and the rules are as a result similar to the **while**-loop rules: in particular, you will need an invariant.

It is best however not to check **for**-loops at all, not directly: instead, develop your program as a **while**-loop, and then transliterate it into a **for**-loop and "inherit" its correctness.

If you must, however... To check a (**Python**) **for**-loop of the form[5]

```
{PRE:   inv("initial iterator value")  }
for e in "iterator":  # INV: inv
    body
{POST:  inv("last iterator value")  }
```

we must check this:

```
{PRE:   inv("iterator values so far")  }
body
{POST:  inv("iterator values so far and value e as well")  }   ,
```

where e is the variable, mentioned just after the **for** keyword, that holds the current value for the iteration.

A common example of an iterator is **range(N)** for some integer N.

Note however that (in **Python**) it is *not* true in general that the assertion *"the iterator value is the last one"* is true after the **for**-loop has ended. For example, if we are using n to iterate through the sequence **range(N)**, then we would have that

initial iterator corresponds to n==0, and

---

[5] Although **while**-loops are more or less the same in all languages, the **for**-loops might differ. See App. G.3.

iterator so far corresponds to n, and

iterator so far and... as well to n+1 and

last iterator value to n==N.

See Sec. 1.7 for some examples of for-loops. More detail about for-loops is given in App. G.3.

B.4.6 Termination for for-loops

A for-loop usually doesn't need a variant, because its exiting is built in. But –as mentioned just above– we must be careful about the *final* value of the iterator, i.e. once the for-loop has finished. At the end of the (Python) for-loop described just above, we have n == N-1, not n==N as you might expect.

Even worse, if the range happens to be empty then the iterator will be empty too, and the index variable will not have been assigned-to at all (!) when the loop has terminated (which it does immediately, i.e. after no iterations). Again, more detail about for-loops is given in App. G.3.

B.5 Concurrency: await, and global correctness

Reasoning about concurrency (the principal subject of this text's Part III) adds two ingredients to what we have already seen above: the await statement, and checking *global* correctness.

B.5.1 The await statement

The "await *cond*: *prog*" construction, introduced in Sec. 15.1, is used to make one thread wait until *cond* is made true by some other thread. (If *cond* is true already then await can simply proceed: it does not have to wait in that case.)

It is like an else-less if, but one that does not skip over its then-part if the condition is false: instead –ever hopeful– it just waits there until that condition becomes true. The rule is that

$$\{\,\text{PRE: } pre\,\}\ \text{await } cond:\ prog\ \{\,\text{POST: } post\,\}$$

checks just if { PRE: *pre* and *cond* } *prog* { POST: *post* } checks.

Just "await *cond*" on its own (i.e. without *prog*) is treated as await *cond*: skip so that what must be checked in that case is only *pre* and *cond* $\Rightarrow$ *post* .

B.5.2 Global correctness and interference

The other ingredient in checked *concurrent* programs is having to ensure that assertions in one thread are not *interfered with* by (assignment) statements in other threads: interference was first mentioned in Sec. 13.8, and we returned to it in more detail in Sec. 14.5.

To check that assertion { *assn1* } in say Thread 1 is not interfered with by the statement { *assn2* } *prog* in Thread 2, we check that { *assn2* } *prog* cannot change *assn1* from True to False: that is, we check

$$\{\,\text{PRE: } assn1 \text{ and } assn2\,\}$$
$$prog$$
$$\{\,\text{POST: } assn1\,\} \leftarrow \text{Note this is } assn1 \text{ again, not } assn2.$$

The precondition *assn2* of Thread 2's possibly interfering *prog* is included in the precondition of the check, because (assuming { *assn2*} has itself been checked) the statement *prog* cannot execute at all if the assertion *assn2* does not hold — it can't interfere with anything, or indeed do anything else either.

As a convention, we are indicating atomicity by whether several assignment statements are written on the same line (Sec. 13.3): if they are then assertions *between* them do not have to be checked for global correctness. Assertions on their own lines, between program components, *do* have to be checked for global correctness.

Expressions on the right-hand side of an assignment, however, are usually *not* assumed to be atomic if they refer to two or more "non-local" variables, that is variables that can be accessed by other threads (Sec. 13.3 again). In our presentations we have not used special notations for that; rather we have pointed it out in the surrounding text, and in the final version of the program made sure that assignments refer to at most one non-local variable.

| Ex. B.2 |

B.6 Exotica: assert and assume statements, and specifications

There are three basic programs (beyond the two discussed in App. B.1) that are used mainly in checking, but the latter two do not usually appear in the final code. They are used "temporarily" to make the program construction and its checking easier.

B.6.1 The assert statement

The assert statement is used mainly, at least for us here, to express the connection between abstract and concrete data-types (the subject of Part II), and to help to specify not-yet-written code. In particular, an assert is used to state a condition that "must be true at this point" if the program is to check (and thus work correctly) and –furthermore– if executed at runtime checks that it indeed evaluates to True. The rule is that

$$\{\text{PRE: } pre\} \text{ assert } cond \{\text{POST: } post\} \tag{B.4}$$

checks just when

$$pre \quad \Rightarrow \quad cond \textbf{ and } post \quad . \tag{B.5}$$

Such assert statements are sometimes available in programming languages as executable code, where they are used for debugging and defensive programming.[6] In that case, an assert evaluates its condition and halts the program (usually with a message) if the condition is not met. Checking it (as above) is then equivalent to making sure it will never halt the program *and* that it will establish its postcondition: implication (B.5) says that (B.4) checks just if *pre* implies both that *cond* (no halt) and *post* (the postcondition is already true) hold.

Unlike { *cond*}, the statement   assert *cond*   *is* a program fragment: if executed at runtime when *cond* is false, it will abort the program; but if the program is checked automatically *before* being run –for example, by Dafny (Sec. 18.2)– then it will fail the check if it *could* be false at runtime.

---

[6] Python has assert statements.

B.6.2 The `assume` statement

The `assume` statement is a program fragment as well but is used mainly while developing programs, for checking them. It is usually considered to be "non-compilable" and so must somehow be removed from the program before the program can be compiled and run.

The statement `assume` *cond* can be thought of as "forcing" the program to make *cond* hold at that point — in the sense that if *cond* does not hold then the program cannot proceed beyond that point: one could think of its being "suspended" there.

In spite of that, it has a checking rule, that

$$\{\textsc{Pre:}\ pre\}\ \texttt{assume}\ cond\ \{\textsc{Post:}\ post\,\}$$

checks just when

$$pre\ \textbf{and}\ cond\ \Rightarrow\ post\quad.$$

Ex. B.3

The checking rule forces us to do one (or possibly both) of two things, encountered later in App. C.4 below on the "essence" of data refinement.

The first is illustrated in App. C.4.3(b). The concrete variables `ar,n` are up to this point declared but not initialised (or initialised to `???`, which we regard as the same thing). We interpret that as their having an arbitrary value, but we don't know what — which in turn means that when we decide to *give* them values, that is initialise them, we can pick any value in their type. In this case we choose `ar,n= [0]*N,0` precisely because those values make the condition in the following `assume` evaluate to `True`, and so we can remove it.

The second thing is that in App. C.4.3(d) we add code that assigns values to the concrete variables (again) that make the assumption there true. It is that second coding requirement that forces us to do the actual work of implementing `Add(s)` with `ar,n` rather than the original `ss`...

...because, until we do that, the `assume` cannot be removed. And, until it is, our program cannot be compiled and run: the only way to get rid of that `assume` is to show that its condition is identically true, because `ar,n` have been set to suitable values.

B.6.3 The specification statement $x:[pre, post]$

A specification statement is like an `assert` followed by an `assume`, and is used to describe the effects of "not yet written" code in a way allowing the surrounding program to be checked *now*, rather than only after that "not yet written" code *has been* written. It can be thought of as a kind of procrastination: we say that we *will* provide code here that takes a precondition *pre* to a postcondition *post* while changing only variable(s) x... but we will do it tomorrow, not today.[7]

Since specifications, like `assume` statements, cannot be executed directly, when "tomorrow comes" we are obliged to replace the specification with code that takes its precondition to its postcondition while changing only the allowed variables.

Between now and tomorrow, however, the program text *containing* our specification can be checked even though the specification's (eventual) code is not yet there. The

---

[7] The "cras" in procrastinate is Latin for "tomorrow", thus its meaning to "put off until tomorrow". Similarly, "perendinate" means to put off until the day *after* tomorrow. Tombstones from the Middle Ages were often inscribed *hodie mihi, cras tibi*: "Today it's me; tomorrow it will be you."

rule is that

$$\{\text{PRE: } pre\} \; \text{x:} [pre1, post1] \; \{\text{POST: } post\}$$

checks just when

$$pre \quad \Rightarrow \quad pre1 \text{ and } (\forall \text{x} \cdot post1 \Rightarrow post) \quad ,$$

where an "empty $\forall$", that is one in which no x is given, can simply be removed. $\boxed{\text{Ex. B.4}}$

A very common case is when *pre* and *pre1* are the same, and *post* and *post1* as well, in which case there is nothing to check. But –like `assume` statements– in general specification statements cannot be compiled. The only way to "get rid" of them is to supply the missing code.

A specification statement is used for example in (17.10) of Sec. 17.10. And in (3.5) of Sec. 3.3.3 there is a opportunity to use a specification statement in the binary-search program: making the selection of p lie "halfway between" the bounds m and n is not necessary for the program to work (though it is necessary to achieve logarithmic-time efficiency). Instead, at that point we could have written

$$\text{p:} [\text{0<=V==(n-m)} \; , \; \text{m<=p<n and 0<=(n-m)<V}] \quad , \tag{B.6}$$

where V is an auxiliary variable, then carrying on with the rest of the program and leaving the code for fragment (B.6) to be supplied later.

B.7 Exercises

Exercise B.1 (p. 246) $\Downarrow$ Explain why with App. B.2.2 above it's sufficient to be able to check the partial correctness of `while`-loops with the single rule below, instead of needing all three clauses given in App. B.4.1:

$$\begin{array}{l} \{\text{PRE: } inv\} \\ \text{while } cond\text{:} \\ \quad body \\ \{\text{POST: } inv \text{ and not } cond\} \end{array} \quad \} \text{ checks if } \{\text{PRE: } cond \text{ and } inv\} \; body \; \{\text{POST: } inv\} \text{ does.}$$

For examples, see Chapters 2 and 3.

Exercise B.2 (p. 249) Why is it reasonable to assume that "only one non-local variable" on the right-hand side of an assignment allows the statement to be considered atomic? What if that non-local variable appears more than once on the right-hand side? What if it appears on the left- and on the right-hand side?

Exercise B.3 (p. 250) $\Downarrow$ What is the difference between `assume` *cond* , that is with no variable x, and `await` *cond*, that is with no following statement?

Exercise B.4 (p. 251) What is the difference between x:[*pre, post*] and

```
assert pre
assume post   ?
```

Data refinement: the real story

C.1 Introduction

Section 8.5 ("Coding concrete data-types") went through the steps –a "recipe" in effect– for changing the internal implementation of a data-type encapsulation from abstract to concrete: what we called data refinement. It set out three steps there, but we will present them here as four, and at a more general level. They are: introduce concrete variables as auxiliaries, to make a hybrid encapsulation containing both abstract and concrete; impose a data-type invariant on the abstract and concrete variables together, in this case called a coupling invariant; alter (in fact "refine") the code of the hybrid encapsulation so that –swapping their roles– the abstract variables become auxiliary and the concrete become "real" (while respecting the coupling invariant); and finally remove the (now-) auxiliary abstract variables.

To explain how those steps are validated at a more basic level, we use `assert` statements (which we have already seen), and `assume` statements, mentioned in App. B.6.2 above. Doing that gives more insight into why those steps are the right ones and, further, it might help to answer some tricky and sometimes subtle questions about what is valid and what is not. We'll use `aa` for the abstract variable(s), and `cc` for the concrete variables and –where necessary– `gg` for global variables, those in scope from within the encapsulation but declared outside of it, that is in the surrounding program.

C.2 Step-by-step from abstract to concrete

C.2.1 Step 1: Add auxiliary "concrete" variable(s)

Within an encapsulation, you can always[1] add a fresh local auxiliary variable `cc` say, and code that manipulates it, in any way you like — provided the existing code's behaviour is not affected. *Fresh* means any variable (name) that is not already in scope from within the encapsulation: i.e. is not the same as any (local, abstract) `aa` already there in the encapsulation , and is not the same as any external (global) `gg`

---

[1] "Always" here means exactly that: you can add a local variable as explained below, whether or not you are using it for data refinement; one is always allowed to do that. The significance here is that we add it –because– we want to use it for data refinement, and that's the only reason we call it "cc".

accessible from the encapsulation. In particular, "not affected" means:

(a) The new code (concrete, with the cc) terminates whenever the existing code (abstract) would have.

(b) The new cc-code does not assign to any abstract variables aa or globals gg in a way that would introduce dependencies on cc, and there can be no cc-controlled conditionals or loops whose bodies assign to anything other than cc itself.

The first constraint, that is (a), would be violated if for example we added the assignment cc= 1/0 or the loop while cc==cc: pass or even assert cc!=cc , because it might introduce non-termination that was not there before.

The reason we write "concrete", that is within quotes, is that this Step 1 is valid no matter what the new variable cc is going to be used for: its being added does not necessarily have to do with data refinement. But that is what we will use it for here. The easiest way to satisfy criteria (a),(b) above is to add local cc= ??? to the encapsulation's initialisation and cc= ??? anywhere you like, but usually in parallel with assignments to aa — where the "???" means "any value at all, not yet decided". It is an example of "demonic" nondeterminism.

The above corresponds to Sec. 8.5.2 from earlier.

C.2.2 Step 2: Impose a data-type ("coupling") invariant

This is the new step, the second in sequence. Again the quotes ("coupling") indicate that we can impose any data-type invariant we like, for any purpose, but that here in particular our purpose is to couple abstract and concrete variables together.

That is, you can impose *any* data-type invariant *dti* you like *provided* its truth cannot be affected by code executed outside the encapsulation.

To add a data-type invariant *dti*, instead of writing DTI: *dti* at the beginning of the encapsulation –as we did before in Sec. 10.2– instead we use assert and assume statements directly (App. B.6) as follows:

(a) Add assume *dti* to the end of the encapsulation's initialisation.

(b) Add assert *dti* at the beginning of every *externally accessible* procedure or function in the encapsulation.

(c) Add assume *dti* at the end of every *externally accessible* procedure or just before every **return** of any *externally accessible* function (more generally, at every exit point).

The statement assert *cond* causes the program to "crash" if *cond* is false at that point. If *cond* is true, it has no effect.

The statement assume *cond*, on the other hand, *forces* the program to establish *cond* at that point: it does not crash. As perhaps the simplest example, consider the code x= ±1; assume x>=0 , where by the ±-assignment we mean that at runtime x will be set either to +1 or to −1, but we don't know which. (It's again an example of demonic nondeterminism.) The assume statement immediately afterwards, however, forces the program to have established x>=0 — and the only way it can do that is by having chosen +1 earlier (rather than −1). And so the effect of the two statements together is the same as x= +1 would have been on its own.

C.2.3 Step 3: "Tweak" the encapsulated code

This third step resolves the **???** nondeterminism, choosing particular values that make the *cond* conditions of `assume` statements true.

We return to (a) above, where we added variable `cc` to the encapsulation, say with a declaration `local cc= ???`. How is it initialised? The conceptually simplest answer to that is "initialised to any value consistent with its type" and, because you don't know –that is cannot in any way depend on– what that value is, it is effectively the same as `cc`'s being "undefined" in the sense that you don't know anything about its value. If however the `local cc` were followed by `assume` *cond* –and *cond* might refer to `aa`– then the program would be forced to have resolved the nondeterministic **???** assignment to `cc` by having chosen some value that makes *cond* true, in particular a value that respects the coupling invariant (which is what *cond* expresses).

An example of that is the set-as-sequence data-refinement example from Sec. 8.2: we can now see the initialisation as two steps rather than just one. First introduce `local qs= ???` as a new variable, initialised to anything in its type; then impose the data-type invariant `ss == set(qs)` by adding `assume ss==set(qs)` just afterwards. The overall effect is then –for the moment–

```
local ss:  ss= {}
local qs:  qs= ???; assume ss == set(qs)     .
```

But then, because the `assume` forces the condition `ss == set(qs)` to be established by the program, it has the overall effect of resolving the earlier **???** to `[]`, giving `ss,qs= {},[]` — just what we did before but in a more intuitive way.

Now we look at (b), continuing with our `ss/qs` example. Having added variable `qs` (which is the "`cc`" of this running example), and the *dti* as described by (b), we would first have for procedure `add(s)` the fragment

```
class Set:  # Both ss and qs together.
  ...
  def add(s):
    assert ss == set(qs)
    ss,qs= ss∪{s},???
    assume ss == set(qs)
  ...
```

in which the `assume` forces the **???** here to resolve to `qs+[s]`, sufficient to establish the *dti* immediately following *provided* the `assert` immediately before did not crash. That gives

```
class Set:  # Both ss and qs together.
  ...
  def add(s):
    assert ss == set(qs)
    ss= ss∪{s}
    qs= qs+[s]                        #  ←Originally was "Set qs to ???."
    assume ss == set(qs)
  ...
```

in which `qs= qs+[s]` has replaced the original "Set `qs` to anything." by making the one choice `qs+[s]` that satisfies the condition `ss == set(qs)` of the `assume` immediately following.

Now that both the concrete cc and the assert and assume statements have been added (but the abstract aa is still there) the code in the module is altered by adjusting the assignments and conditions that use cc to ensure that the new checking constraints –maintaining *dti*– are met, and that any return values (or assignments to "result" formal parameters, if the programming language allows it) contain only expressions in which aa does not appear — they will be replaced by expressions containing cc instead. Usually that is done using *dti*, the coupling invariant, reasoning that the (old) aa-expression is equal to the (new) cc-expression precisely because the coupling invariant holds.

The point is that the encapsulation's behaviour is not altered by this "tweaking" — it's just that its dependence on aa is removed. Earlier we described that behaviour as "maintaining *dti*". Now however we see it as "making sure that all assume statements' conditions are true.

Once we have checked that the assume statements' conditions are all indeed equivalent to skip (that is assume True), they can be removed.

C.2.4 Step 4: making the "abstract" variables auxiliary

In the previous step we resolved the occurrences of ??? by choosing values to be assigned to cc so that the *dti* holds between aa and cc throughout the procedure bodies: they are "coupled together". In this last step we use the *dti*, that coupling, to replace all uses of aa by equivalent uses of cc — which equivalence is shown by appeal to the *dti*.

Any assert statements containing aa should be replaced by weaker versions in which aa does not appear; if as a result they become assert True they can be removed altogether.

Once all occurrences of aa are auxiliary, they too can be removed from the code altogether.

C.3 Other manipulations of assertions, assumptions and specifications

At this point we mention other ways in which one can manipulate assert statements, assume statements and specifications at *any* time, that is not necessarily within an encapsulated data-type:

(a) You can weaken any assert *cond*, because that makes it easier to meet for any code preceding it. If you weaken it to assert True, you can remove it altogether (as (e) below).

(b) You can strengthen any assume *cond*, because that makes its effect more useful in any code following it. If you strengthen it too much, however, you will not be able to remove it from your program text: it can be removed only when its condition is True (as in (e) below) and, if you don't remove it, your program will not be accepted for compilation to code. (It will however be accepted for checking.)

(c) You can resolve nondeterminism, replacing for example a specification such as m:[l<h,l<=m<h] by a simple assignment m= (l+h)//2, since if the surrounding program checks with *any* m satisfying l<=m<h then it will also check with the particular value (l+h)//2 given that indeed l<= (l+h)//2 <h holds whenever the specification's precondition l<h held.

(d) You can replace equals by equals, using context provided by assertions {—} you have checked, or explicit **assert**- or **assume** statements.

(e) You can add or remove whole **assert**- or **assume** statements whenever context makes their conditions equivalent to **True**.

C.4 An example: add(s) to a size-limited Set

In the following subsections we apply the methods outlined just above to the **Add(s)** procedure of the **Set** example we have already considered (Sec. 10.2), and see how we end up in the same place but by more fundamental means. We'll start with the fragment

```
class Set(N)
  local assert N>=0; ss= {}

  def add(s):
    ss= ss ∪{s}
    assert |ss|<=N     ,
```

in which we have placed the size constraint at the very end of **add(s)**, that is where its purpose is clearest. For we will (of course) know that |ss|<=N holds when the procedure is called; but where that matters is when the procedure *returns*, and making that true should be clearly identified as an obligation on the *caller* of **add(s)**. She must make sure her calling program cannot cause the **assert** to fail in the abstract version... *if* she intends to implement **Set(N)** concretely as an array of size **N**.

C.4.1 Step 1: Add auxiliary (to become "concrete") variables "ar,n"

We now recall that we replaced the abstract set **ss** by two concrete variables **ar,n**, intending to represent **ss** by the first **n** elements of **ar**. Here we (re-)do it at a more basic level, using the principles set out above. When we add **ar** and **n**, it is *they* that are auxiliary — and we add them with "choose anything" assignments, which cannot affect the encapsulation's behaviour in any way; we get

```
class Set(N)
  local: assert N>=0; ss= {}
  local: ar,n= ???,???        # ← Arbitrary values... for now.

  def add(s):
    ss= ss ∪{s}
    ar,n= ???,???
    assert |ss|<=N     ,       # ← This assert was already here.
```

where in the style of this more basic explanation they now appear with nondeterministic assignments ??? explicitly given, both in the initialisation and in the procedures (i.e. not only **Add(s)** but all the others we have not shown, as well). They have no effect on the encapsulation at all (yet): simply adding their declarations, and "set them to anything" is all we have done in this first step. Note however that the **assert** at the end is *not* part of that first step: it was there in the *abstract* definition already, and states that it is the *user*'s responsibility not to add "too many" elements to **ss**.

Those modifications have not affected the external behaviour of **Add(s)** in any way.

C.4.2 Step 2: Add the "coupling" data-type invariant

Now we introduce the data-type invariant, aka the coupling invariant *dti* that will link (i.e. "couple") the abstract ss and the concrete ar,n. Although this is Step 2, obviously we had a particular *dti* in mind for coupling even in Step 1: otherwise we would not have known which auxiliary ("concrete") variables to introduce there.

Our *dti* is first that 0<=n<=N==len(ar), that ar has non-negative length N, and second that ss == set(ar[:n]), that ss is represented by the first n elements of ar. That implies –we notice– that |ss|<=N, which we will be depending on further below.

But now we go further by using the rules of App. C.2.2, instead of the earlier DTI-notation of Fig. 10.4:[2] we insert assert and assume statements and get

```
class Set(N)
  local:
    assert N>=0
    ss= {}
    ar,n= ???,???
    assume 0<=n<=N==len(ar) and ss == set(ar[:n])       #  dti
  def add(s):
    assert 0<=n<=N==len(ar) and ss == set(ar[:n])       #  dti
    ss= ss ∪{s}
    ar,n= ???,???
    assert |ss|<=N                 #  ← Here already: see Exercise C.1.
    assume 0<=n<=N==len(ar) and ss == set(ar[:n])       #  dti   ,
```

$$(C.1)$$

where the assert and (two) assume statements replace our earlier use of DTI. (Remember however that the assert |ss|<=N was there already.)

Ex. C.1

Remarkably –and perhaps surprisingly?– the encapsulation (C.1) *already* represents ss with the pair ar,n, because the two assume statements *force* it to do so — that is what assume statements do. Here, they force their condition to hold by constraining assignments of ??? that occurred earlier. The "only" problem is that in general an assume statement cannot be compiled into running code; instead, we have to resolve the "anything" assignments ??? ourselves, doing so in a way that allows all assume statements to be removed. Most current compilers are not "smart enough" to do that for us.

---

[2] That earlier Fig. 10.4 uses a less tolerant (abstract) specification than the one here: Fig. 10.4 can reject adding an element s when |ss|==N even if s is already in the set; we are just illustrating the specification choices that are possible. Also interesting is that the (concrete) implementation in Fig. 10.4 will fail with an index error if too many items are added, and it has no documentation pointing that out. Again, we are just making a point: good practice –defensive programming– demands that such documentation *should* be there (and we will see it later); but strictly speaking it does not *have* to be there, because the specification allows arbitrary behaviour if too many elements are added.

C.4.3 Step 3: "Tweaking" the encapsulated code"

(a) Our first step in this particular tweaking is to move the final (already present) assert forward. That gives

```
class Set(N)
  local:
    assert N>=0
    ss= {}
    ar,n= ???,???
    assume 0<=n<=N==len(ar) and ss == set(ar[:n])

  def add(s):
    assert 0<=n<=N==len(ar) and ss == set(ar[:n])
    assert |ss∪{s}|<=N          # ← Moved forward to here.
    ss= ss∪{s}
    ar,n= ???,???
    # Was here.
    assume 0<=n<=N==len(ar) and ss == set(ar[:n])     ,
```

where the new assert condition |ss∪{s}|<=N is given by substitution, induced by the assignment ss= ss∪{s}.

(b) We now make the first assume, just after the initialisation, into an assume True by resolving the ???-assignments just before it to ar,n= [0]*N,0. The initial fragment is now

```
local:
  assert N>=0
  ss= {}
  ar,n= [0]*N,0                               # Was ???,???.
  {0<=n<=N==len(ar) and ss == set(ar[:n])}
  assume 0<=n<=N==len(ar) and ss == set(ar[:n]) # Now True.
```

The {···} checks because of the statements before it (including assert N>=0), and it allows us to remove the assume that follows it, because its condition is now identically True.

(c) We now turn to the remaining assume, first introducing a local procedure find –a big step, but one we have done before, at (10.3)– and resolving the ??? occurrences in ar,n as shown:

```
local def find(s):  # As before.

def add(s):
  assert 0<=n<=N==len(ar) and ss == set(ar[:n])

  i= find(s);
  assert i<N, "Full" # Fails if "i<N" is not True.
  {s∈ar or |ss|<N} # Must hold if we reach here.          (C.2)
  assert s∈ar or |ss|<N # Equivalent to |ss∪{s}|<=N .

  ss= ss ∪{s}
  if i==n: ar[n],n= s,n+1
  {0<=n<=N==len(ar) and ss == set(ar[:n])}

  assume 0<=n<=N==len(ar) and ss == set(ar[:n]) # Now True.
```

Note that {s∈ar or |ss|<N} checks not only because of the assignments we chose for ar,n but also because of the **assert** at the beginning of add(s) and the **assert** i<N just after the use of i= find(s); assert i<N,"Full" .

Remember however — even after all the work we have just done, this procedure is still maintaining *both* ss and ar,n. The small steps taken in this appendix are only to explain the fundamental process, not to recommend or enforce a snail-like pace.

C.4.4 Step 4: Removing auxiliary variables

(d) Now, finally, we can remove the final **assume**, because the assertion just before it shows it to be true at this point; and we can remove the **assert**'s because **assert**'s can be removed at any time. That is what makes ss auxiliary, and allows us finally to remove it as well, leaving only the concrete ar,n: our removing all of the intermediate working in (C.2), that is

```
def add(s):
    assert 0<=n<=N==len(ar) and ss == set(ar[:n])
    i= find(s);
    assert i<N, "Full"
    {s∈ar or |ss|<N}
    assert s∈ar or |ss|<N
    ss= ss ∪{s}
    if i==n: ar[n],n= s,n+1
    {0<=n<=N==len(ar) and ss == set(ar[:n])}
    assume 0<=n<=N==len(ar) and ss == set(ar[:n])    ,
```

leaves just

```
def add(s):
    i= find(s);
    assert i<N, "Full"
    if i==n: ar[n],n= s,n+1    .
```
(C.3)

Although overall we have carried out the same data-refinement process as before, what we have done here is in much more primitive steps so that we could see exactly what was going on. In practice, the DTI-and-check approach that we used earlier is fine; but the detail of this section allows more sophisticated manoeuvres when occasionally they are needed.

C.5 Postscript on justification of *dti*'s and their rules

In Appendix C.2.2 it was stated that "In any encapsulation, you can impose any data-type invariant *dti* you like provided its truth does not depend on any variables outside the encapsulation." The three steps (a)–(c) there showed how such a *dti* is to be added.

Ex. C.4

But why does it work? And what exactly does you can mean?

"You can", for us, has a very precise meaning: you can "do something" to a program if (and only if) any check the program passed *before* you do the something will still check *after* you have done it. The technical term for that, that is for the preservation of successful checks, is *refinement*.[3]

App. C.2.2's steps (a) and (c), that is adding `assume` statements, constitute a refinement because adding an `assume` is *always* a refinement: it can only reduce the possible results of a program to a possibly smaller subset of the values that were already acceptable before. In App. C.2.2 for example we added an `assume x>=0` just after an assignment x=±1, and the overall effect was to change that program fragment to x= 1. The reason that's allowed is that if the program checked before with x=±1 then it must have checked in *both* possible cases: the case where x was set to 1 and the other case where x was set to -1. And so –trivially– it must still check in the case where we set x to +1 (only).

For `assert` statements, however, the opposite is true: you can always *remove* them, because the only thing an `assert` can do is crash the program (if its condition is false) — and a crash will fail any check. Thus removing an `assert` can only make the program pass more checks, never fewer.

Why then can we *add* an `assert` *dti* at the beginning of every procedure when imposing a data-type invariant? The reason is that, because of the rules for choosing *dti*'s in particular, their variables cannot be altered outside the encapsulation — and so the *dti* will be true at the beginning of every procedure. That is, the last reference to it can only have been at the end of (perhaps another) encapsulated procedure (where the `assume` there will have forced it to be `True`), or perhaps at the end of the initialisation (also with `assume` *dti* there). No activity of the surrounding program "in between" can change *dti* from being true to being false... because that surrounding program cannot access the variables of the *dti* at all. They are out of scope.

In effect, the truth of the *dti* is passed from the end of each procedure (or the encapsulation's initialisation) to the beginning of the next procedure, and it cannot be changed in the meantime. (The analogy with loop invariants is that their truth is passed from the end of one iteration to the beginning of the next: it's just that in that case there is no "other program" to worry about.)

C.6 Exercises

Exercise C.1 (p. 258) ⇓ What would happen if we left out the `assert |ss|<=N` in program (C.1)?

Exercise C.2 ⇓ Suppose we removed the `assert` in the concrete program (C.3). The remaining code would get an index-out-of-range error if it is called when n==N and with an s that does not already occur in `ar`. How can such code be correct?

Exercise C.3 ⇓ Replace the initial and final occurrences of {···} in (11.6) with an `assert` for the first and an `assume` for the second, and then see whether you can remove them from the program using the rules of this Appendix C.

---

[3] An important point, but one we will not examine here, is that your checks' *vocabulary*, that is the things you are allowed to check *for*, must be carefully determined beforehand. In this text we are not checking e.g. for programs' running time, or use of space: what we check is only that a precondition's truth before a program guarantees its postcondition's truth afterwards.

Exercise C.4 (p. 260) In Ex. 10.11 we asked what would happen if one imposed a *dti* of False. Adapt your answer to Ex. 10.11 to the more basic approach here: explain what happens to a *dti* False if we follow the method of App. C.4.

The "arithmetic" of conditions [1]

D.1 Introduction and rationale

We have so far seen "conditions" in two places mainly: the first is as Boolean-valued, true- or false-valued expressions that control whether the **then-** or the **else**-branch of an **if**-statement is taken, or whether a **while**-loop is (re-)entered. Readers who have got this far are probably very familiar with those uses already: the conditions are evaluated as the program runs, and so contribute to the answer that the program finally gives.

The second place we have seen conditions is as assertions: preconditions, postconditions, invariants, or sometimes just commented by "**#** $\cdots$" or enclosed by "**{** $\cdots$ **}**", placed between statements as if they were on the connecting lines of a flowchart (Fig. 1.1), and sometimes labelled with "Pre:" etc. if they are of especial importance. Those conditions are *not* evaluated as the program runs: their only (but crucially important) role is to help us to *understand* the answer which the program finally gives, or is supposed to give — and to increase our confidence that it does so correctly. Ex. D.1

In this appendix we make the connection between those conditions, as they appear in our programs, and mathematical logic as it *really* is — that is we will concentrate on their second use, making sure that programs are correct, and indeed even helping to *design* programs, because sometimes the conditions-as-assertions tell us what the **if-** and **while-** conditions-to-execute should be.

Sometimes those conditions –soon to be called *formulae*– have to be extracted from the program text and thought about on their own, a bit like grabbing a bit of scrap paper to do a complicated bit of arithmetic "on the side" which –though having no intrinsic interest itself– might say be important for your tax return. Your copied-out calculations are carried out in a different state of mind: you forget temporarily *why* you need to know what 15% of $1,234.56 is (although you might continue to resent having to know it). Instead you are focussing only on getting the right answer.

When you do that with logic, you are in effect using scrap paper for conditions rather than for numbers, for computer programs *containing* those conditions rather than for tax returns containing those numbers. Again, in that state of mind it does not matter *why* you need to simplify some complicated logical/Boolean condition: what's important is that you do it correctly: in this analogy, a failing program would correspond to failing a tax audit. Both are unwelcome.

---

[1] Some of Appendix D appeared in the author's earlier work *Programming from Specifications* [43].

That is what we are studying in this appendix: *logic*, the distillation of correct reasoning about conditions, wherever they might have come from. For us here, they come mainly from computer programs.

D.2 Why is my program correct?

Recalling *where* our conditions come from, in programming, is therefore how we begin. This example is from Sec. 5.2(h) (on p. 67):

```
# --- Swap the values of x and y.
t= x
x= y
y= t    .
```

As we all know, the effect of the program is that variable x finally will have the value that y had initially, and for y vice versa. But in what sense can we *prove* that to be true? And why do we bother?

To answer the second question first: for a program of this size, and indeed one you might have written many times, we probably wouldn't bother with a proof. (Still, it's easy to get it wrong: especially if you're in a hurry.) But for *big* programs, it becomes much more valuable to be able to prove that even the *little* bits of them are doing what they should — it's a double-check, while coding is in progress, that might save hours of debugging later once coding is done.

Now for the first question: how do we prove correctness? We have seen that we can show that a program "works" by inserting carefully chosen comments that simply say (with an assertion, whether in English or in logic) what is supposed to be true at that point in the program. For the program above, we introduce (auxiliary) variables X,Y which we suppose have captured the initial values of x,y, and we add a comment, at the very beginning of the program, that shows clearly what X and Y are for; and then, at the end of the program, we insert another comment that says that those values have been swapped. Thus the comment at the beginning of (D.1) below says "*Here*, let x,y be some X,Y respectively." And the comment at the end says "In that case, *here* we will find that they have been swapped, that now x==Y and y==X."

Note that the assertions/comments are not executed, that there is no assignment to a variable or even expression evaluation going on while the program is running. They merely state "What's true here." (or what we *hope* will be true) at that point in the program as it runs. It's the program's assignment statements that "do stuff", and it's the program's comments that "assert stuff". And if those comments are right (about the program), then indeed the program swaps those two variables.

Of course there will be other comments in your program (one hopes); and they might be of the form "This is why I did it this way." or "The following steps do more-or-less as follows." Those are helpful, even necessary; but they do not contribute *directly* to proof. Only the "What's true here." comments do that.

So how do we know the comments are right? That's what we discussed earlier, that is, with the "how to check parts of your program" techniques we have explained already (e.g. in Sec. 5.2 and App. B.1.1). We wrote

Ex. D.2

```
# --- Swap the values of x and y.
# PRE: x==X and y==Y
t= x
{ t==X and y==Y }
x= y
{ t==X and x==Y }
y= t
# POST: y==X and x=Y      .
```
(D.1)

Each comment-like assertion says what's supposed to be true at that point. But how do we know the assertion *is* true at that point? We look at just one step in the program... and apply a bit of magic:

```
     ⋮
{ t==X and y==Y } # Get this by substitution.
x= y          ↕
{ t==X and x==Y }
     ⋮      .
```

The "magic" is that you can be sure an assertion *before* an assignment is saying what it should if you can obtain it by carrying out the substitution, induced by the assignment, on the comment *after* the assignment: that is the x in x==Y is replaced by y because of the assignment x= y, giving y==Y. (The other half, the first conjunct of the after-comment, has no x, so it carries through unchanged.) Remember that you "go backwards", from the after-comment to the before-comment.

It's as simple as that (as in App. B.1.1).

D.3 How do I write my program in the first place?

Now recall our exponential-calculating program in Sec. 3.4.1 that set p to the value B**E, that is base B to the power of exponent E. A straightforward, linear-time solution was (3.9), reproduced here:

```
# PRE: 0<=E
p,e= 1,0
# INV: p== B**e and 0<=e<=E
while e!=E:
  { p== B**e and 0<=e<E }
  p,e= p*B,e+1
  { p== B**e and 0<=e<=E }
{ p== B**e and e==E }
# POST: p== B**E      .
```
(D.2)

But a much faster, logarithmic-time exponential program was given at (3.10) — this one:

```
# PRE: 0<=E
p,b,e= 1,B,E
# INV: B**E == p*b**e and 0<=e<=E
while e!=0:
  if e%2==0: b,e= b*b,e//2
  else:       p,e= p*b,e-1
{B**E == p*b**e and e==0}
# POST: p == B**E      .
```
(D.3)

Do you remember how logical calculations with conditions helped us to *write* this program?

Forget that you have just seen (D.3). Suppose instead that you have begun by realising *only this*: that in the special case where E is a power of 2, say E == 2**N for some N, it would be enough to set p to B initially and then to square it N times. That is a typical starting point for thinking about this problem (and where we all begin, with writing a program to solve it): but getting the details right is tricky. And getting the details *wrong*, even at this early stage, can consume nights and weekends later as you try to debug your best attempt to flesh out the intuition above. Details like these...

- What do you do when E==0? There is no 2**N for that. Would your (not yet written) program just go into an infinite loop, dividing 0 by 2 again and again, forever?

- What do you do when E!=0 but still is not a power of 2? You'd have to fiddle something... But what? And how, exactly?

If you brush those worries aside (temporarily), still you might be able to exploit your intuition, to take a first step, getting as far as the incomplete program

```
p,e= B,E
while e!=1: # But what if E was zero?
  if e%2 == 0: p,e= p*p,e//2 # This works...
  else: # ...but what do I do when e is not even?
```
(D.4)

Clearly we are developing this program from the outside-in instead of from front-to-rear: always a good idea.

But *now* what? This is where logic, and our "What's true here." comments, help us to get our weekends back. Instead of "guessing" our first step (D.4) as just above, we'll take a *different* first step instead, to a still-incomplete program — but one that at least handles E correctly even when it is zero:

```
# PRE: What must be here, to make B**E = p*b**e be true at the start?
while e!=0:
  if e%2==0: {e is even}
    e= e//2
    # What code must be here, to make B**E = p*b**e be true again?
  else: {0<e}
    e= e-1
    # What code must be here, to make B**E = p*b**e be true again?
{How do I know B**E = p*b**e is still true here?}
{And what else is true here?}
# POST: And what therefore is true here, finally?
```

In this program it's *already* clear that it will terminate (that eventually e will reach zero) even if you're not sure (yet) what to do with p and b along the way. So that's one problem solved — and no more worries about E==0 initially.

And now... we realise that we can use B**E = p*b**e as the invariant of the loop. (Notice that it occurs at the end of both if-branches.) Remember that it's called "invariant" because it is true just before the loop guard is evaluated, every single time and whether or not the loop is entered; and it remains true no matter how many times the loop iterates. That means it must be true the first time (which is therefore the job of the loop initialisation) and it is true the last time (and so describes what the loop has established).

So, finally... What then is the role of the formulae, and where is the "magic"? It's that, with them, you can use the substitution technique from Sec. 5.2 (or App. B.1.1) to check that your "what's true" comments are correct. And you can do it mechanically, almost without thinking. (Moreover, there are even computer programs that can check them for you — mostly. See Sec. 18.2.)

Finding those comments can be hard, however, particularly for a tricky program (or a sneaky one — not quite the same thing). But if you use logic, it's much easier to be sure you have the right ones: so now –finally, with motivation reinforced and renewed by the above– let's look at logic, the conditions themselves, more closely.

D.4 *Calculating* with conditions: we start with sets

We begin our discussion of logic and conditions by looking at elementary set theory, and how it can be related to logic.

Sets contain *elements*, and $x \in S$ is how we write that some element x is contained in some set S. Similarly we write $x \notin S$ for the opposite, and so the "$\in$" means "is an element of". A particular set can be written by listing its elements between set braces,[2] called a set *comprehension*, as in $\{1, 2, 3\}$ just below. (The ordering in the list does not matter.)

That's all there is to it — for example we have $2 \in \{1, 2, 3\}$ and $0 \notin \{1, 2, 3\}$. What more could there be?

Not too much, actually, at least not for our purposes here. But sometimes we have to "calculate" with sets — usually to figure out when two sets written in *different* ways are actually the *same* set. It's more than just $\{1, 2, 3\} = \{3, 2, 1\}$, however. A better example is $A \cap B = B \cap A$, where "$\cap$" is set intersection; and in fact set intersection has a precise definition that does not rely on pictures. It is

$$x \in A \cap B \quad \text{just when} \quad x \in A \text{ and } x \in B \quad . \tag{D.5}$$

From (D.5) we can easily see that $A \cap B = B \cap A$ holds, because "$x \in A$ and $x \in B$" means the same as "$x \in B$ and $x \in A$". That's not so much a "set fact", however: it's more a "logic fact". Swapping the two sides of "and" is about *logic*, not about sets *per se*: "this" and "that" is the same as "that" and "this", no matter what "this" and "that" might be. But for that set-based example we can bolster our intuition by seeing the equality from Fig. D.1 directly, because the drawing is symmetric. | Ex. D.3 |

---

[2] These set braces have no connection with the assertion braces we use in programs — it's an accidental collision of notation.

Figure D.1 Intersection of sets: a Venn diagram

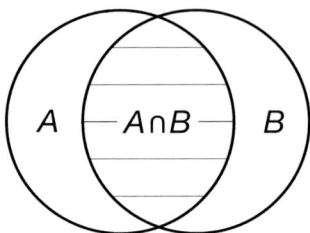

The set intersection $A \cap B$ is the lens-shaped region in the middle above, filled with the hatching $\equiv$. It is obvious that it lies inside the circle of set A (and similarly of set B).

Ex. D.4

Here are two other common notations used with sets, and their definitions:

$$
\begin{array}{llll}
(\cup) \text{ — union} & x \in A \cup B & \text{just when} & x \in A \text{ or } x \in B \\
(\subseteq) \text{ — containment} & A \subseteq B & \text{just when} & x \in A \text{ implies } x \in B
\end{array} \tag{D.6}
$$

Using those, we can now ask for example whether $A \cap B \subseteq A$ is true in general. But how would we prove that? Actually, *why* do we have to "prove" it? Isn't it, too, obvious from the "Venn" diagram in Fig. D.1: just as obvious as $A \cap B = B \cap A$ was?

Well, maybe it isn't. What about when A and B have no elements in common? The corresponding figure (where Fig. D.1 becomes Fig. D.2) is not much help now — and *that* –in a nutshell– is why we need logic and proofs.[3] In this case the proof is simple: it is

$\quad x \in A \cap B$
$\equiv \quad$ "by definition (D.5) of $A \cap B$"
$\quad x{\in}A \ \wedge \ x{\in}B \quad$ [4]
$\Rightarrow \quad$ "since $\mathcal{A} \wedge \mathcal{B} \Rightarrow \mathcal{A}$ for any propositions $\mathcal{A}, \mathcal{B}$"
$\quad x{\in}A \quad$,

so that $A \cap B \subseteq A$ by definition of $(\subseteq)$ from (D.6) above. (For now, think of "$\equiv$" as "if and only if (iff)" and "$\Rightarrow$" as "implies".)

But what are those "propositions" $\mathcal{A}$ and $\mathcal{B}$ mentioned above? And what do we mean by $\mathcal{A} \wedge \mathcal{B} \Rightarrow \mathcal{A}$? In general –and that is the point of this introduction to logic– you can often find a set-like analogue for your reasoning steps in logic (as just above). And it does help with the intuition. But over time it becomes exhausting and indeed unreliable to think in terms of little circles and how they overlap, or don't:[5] you would rather be writing programs. And getting them right.

That's where logic steps in.

---

[3] E.W. Dijkstra once began a lecture by showing a slide with nothing on it at all: it was completely blank. "This is a picture of a graph," he said, and paused. "It is the *empty* graph."
  The two sets shown in Fig. D.2 have empty intersection: but where is that "empty" in the picture?
[4] The symbol $\wedge$" means **and** ; the symbol "$\vee$" (not yet used here) means **or** .
[5] Imagine aerospace engineers who bring Cuisenaire rods to work every day, to help with their arithmetic — or worse, who count on their fingers.

Figure D.2 Intersection of *disjoint* sets, i.e. with no elements in common

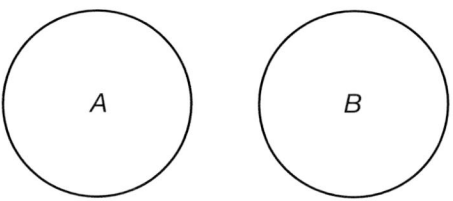

Where is $A \cap B$ now?

Where do we put the "intersection" lines now? Since there is no picture corresponding to the intersection of A and B, we cannot "see" whether it is inside of A (or B).

D.5 Simple calculations in logic

From here on we will use the usual symbols from logic, rather than their programming-language (e.g. `Python`) equivalents. Thus **not** is now "$\neg$", and **and** is "$\wedge$" and **or** is "$\vee$".

Logic is the arithmetic of computer science. In this section we start by just looking at how it works, and how you can use it. (Later –but not here– you can study *why* it works, if you want to.) It's a bit like differentiation d/dx in calculus. You don't need all those *epsilons*, *deltas* and limits tending to 0 (from introductory calculus) to do it: you just follow the rules in the back of your maths book. *Later* (and only if your interests incline that way) you can study *why* the differential calculus works.

Similarly, only if your interests incline that way do you need to know *why* logic works. Here we are just looking at what it is, how to read it, how to write it — and how to "follow its rules".

Our main aim therefore is to be able to work out whether our logical reasoning is correct or incorrect:[6] it's quite easy (with some practice) and, furthermore, it is fundamental to computer programming. So this is a "fast forward" introduction to help you get started.

Indeed you don't need to learn very much at this point: your skill will increase "by osmosis", as you get more and more used to reasoning carefully about your programs. Being able to refer to a more comprehensive list of "logical facts" will help (Appendix E), just as referring to a dictionary of words' meanings helps when reading in a new language. But you don't have to learn them all by heart right from the start! Just knowing that they are there is enough.

We start with "propositional" logic, and we present it of course in the context of programming — where there is a "program state" containing "variables" that have "values", and there are "functions" that you can apply to them.

---

[6] The technical terms applied to logical arguments are "valid" and "invalid". But we'll stick with "correct" and "incorrect".

D.6 Terms in logic are like expressions in programming

Terms in logic are like the expressions you find on the right-hand side of assignment statements in a program: they are built from the program's variables, plus constants and functions from mathematics or elsewhere. Thus x on its own is a term (a variable); and 1 is a term (a mathematical constant); and $x+1$ is a term (formed by applying the two-place function $+$ to the two terms x and 1).[7] Note that the definition of "$+$" comes from arithmetic: you have (probably) not defined it in your program somewhere.

The *program state*, which maps variables to their values, determines also the values of *terms* in that state: one speaks of a term "having some value" in a state. (In a more traditional introduction to logic, e.g. as part of a maths course, the state would be called a *valuation*.) For example, in a state that maps x to three, the term x has value three (trivially), and 0 has value zero (in every state, not only this one — which is why it is called a constant). And $x+1$ has value four in this state, because x has value three there and –in *every* state (by convention)– we know that "$+$" is to be interpreted as addition and "1" has value one (because it is a constant).

Our *variables* will have short lower-case *italic* (maths font) names, drawn from the Roman alphabet.

Our *constants* will have their usual mathematical symbols, such as 0 and π. (The real-number constants e (for Euler) and i ($\sqrt{-1}$) are special cases, not to be confused with variables.) And $\mathbb{R}$ is a set-valued constant, meaning "all the real numbers". Constants' values do not depend on the state.

Our *functions* will have their usual mathematical names too, such as square root $\sqrt{}$, plus $+$ and factorial $!$. Some functions take one argument ($\sqrt{}$ and $!$), some take two ($+$), and the position of the arguments can vary: sometimes the function is written before its argument ($\sqrt{}$), sometimes between its arguments ($+$), and sometimes after its argument ($!$). The number of arguments that a function takes is called its "arity".

We often need to introduce new (mathematical) functions, of our own, to be able to reason about a particular problem. For those, the syntax is more regular: they will have short lower-case sans-serif names, in the Roman alphabet. Their arguments follow them, separated by spaces. A special case is constants, like e and i mentioned above and in italic font, that in effect are functions with no arguments. Numerals are constants too; but we'll write them in their normal font.[8] Like constants, the meaning of functions in logic do not depend on the state.[9]

With all that, we can show how terms are constructed in general: a *term* is either

(a) a constant; or

(b) a variable; or

(c) a function applied to the correct number of other terms, depending on its arity.

Figure D.3 lists some terms. Each of them would be at home on the right-hand side of an assignment statement.

Ex. D.5

Ex. D.6

---

[7] In the earlier parts of this text we would have used "programming font" here, so that x would be a variable (and a term too) and x+1 a term (but not a variable). Here we will move to the more general mathematical conventions.

[8] A *number* is a mathematical concept; a *numeral* is how we write it. Think of the number four, written "4" in Arabic numerals and "IV" in Roman numerals. Either way, it still means four.

[9] Functions you write *in your program* however might well depend on the state. We are not discussing those here.

Figure D.3 Some (logical) terms

$$0$$
$$x$$
$$e$$
$$x + 1$$
$$e + 1$$
$$x + e$$
$$\log x$$
$$\sin(\pi/2)$$
$$(a{+}b) \times 3!$$
$$e^{i\pi}$$

D.7 Simple formulae are like (in)equalities in programming

With terms done, we now turn to formulae. *Simple formulae* are built from terms and "predicate symbols".[10] The best-known predicate symbols represent the binary-comparison relations from arithmetic: they are $(<)$, $(=)$, $(\leq)$ etc. Like functions, predicates have an arity; for binary relations, the arity is two.[11] Again like functions, predicates are applied to terms.

Unlike functions, a predicate applied to (the correct number of) terms is not another term: it is a *simple formula*. Simple formulae do not have general values as terms do; instead, in a given state, a simple formula is either True or it is False. There's no "in between".

For conventional predicates (like binary relations) we use the usual notation. Predicate symbols that we introduce ourselves will be short Roman sans-serif and their arguments will follow them, separated by spaces (as for our introduced functions).

Figure D.4 lists some simple formulae. In any particular state (that assigns values to variables, and hence to the terms containing them), a simple formula is either True or it is False. Remember however that "`True`" (in the `Python` font) is a Boolean value that a Boolean-typed *term* can denote in a given state, whereas "True" is what a whole *formula* can be in a particular state. If you evaluate the formula in that state and get `True` as your answer then the formula is True in that state. If it evaluates to `False` then it is False (i.e. not True) in that state.[12]

---

[10] Simple formulae are called *atomic* formulae in the logic literature.

[11] There is a bit of pedantry here: the predicate symbols are "interpreted" as relations: they are not relations themselves. The same applies to constants vs. constant symbols and functions vs. function symbols.

[12] An alternative would be to say that the formula "holds" in a given state, or "does not hold" there, and some texts do that — so avoiding pedantry between "True" and "`True`".

Experience shows however that no matter how carefully you try to capture those nuances of "truth", say with different fonts, different words etc., it always takes a while before the ideas settle down.

In the end, though, it all becomes clear anyway — and it doesn't matter so much what words you use. Like riding a bicycle, once those distinctions are clear in your mind, you cannot imagine how they could ever have been confusing. And –as with bicycle riding– once learned, it is never forgotten.

Figure D.4 Some simple formulae

$$1 < a \div 2$$
$$x + 1 = 7$$
$$\text{even } 6$$
$$\text{odd } 6$$
$$\pi \in \mathbb{R}$$

Figure D.5 Truth table for "and", that is conjunction $\wedge$

$\mathcal{A}$	$\mathcal{B}$	$\mathcal{A} \wedge \mathcal{B}$
True	True	True
True	False	False
False	True	False
False	False	False

D.8 Propositions, and propositional formulae

The next step is *propositional* formulae, built from simple formulae (App. D.7), using propositional connectives — that is, we regard *simple* formulae as *propositions*, and more complex propositions –propositional formulae– are made by connecting them together. The connectives are $\wedge$ (and), $\vee$ (or), $\neg$ (not), $\Rightarrow$ (implies), and $\Leftrightarrow$ (if and only if, or iff).[13]

The expressions either side of $\wedge$ are called "conjuncts"; those either side of $\vee$ are called "disjuncts".

(As nouns, they are conjunction, disjunction, negation, implication and equivalence. In `Python` they are `and`, `or`, `not`, (nothing) and `==`.) Except for $\neg$, all our connectives here have two arguments, written on either side; the single argument of $\neg$ is written after it.[14]

Like simple formulae, propositional formulae are either True or False, once a state is given. If, for example, $\mathcal{A}$ and $\mathcal{B}$ stand for arbitrary propositional formulae, then the propositional formula $\mathcal{A} \wedge \mathcal{B}$ made from them is True in a state exactly when both $\mathcal{A}$ *and* $\mathcal{B}$ are True in that same state. Note that we are writing True and False with initial capitals only, in order to avoid any confusion with the words "true" and "false" that might occur in ordinary prose.

The effect of the propositional connective "$\wedge$", or "and", is summarised in Fig. D.5 as a "truth table", showing how the Truth of $\mathcal{A}$ and of $\mathcal{B}$ in a state together determine the Truth of $\mathcal{A} \wedge \mathcal{B}$ in that same state: Each propositional connective has its own truth table, and a more extensive set of truth tables –for the six most common connectives– is given in Figure D.6.[15] In a formula $\mathcal{A} \Rightarrow \mathcal{B}$, an implication, the subformula $\mathcal{A}$ is called the *antecedent*, and $\mathcal{B}$ is the *consequent*.

Following convention, we allow the abbreviation $a < b < c$ (and similar) for the propositional formula $a{<}b \wedge b{<}c$: the "$\wedge$" is implicit.

Figure D.7 gives some propositional formulae.

Ex. D.7

Ex. D.8

Ex. D.9

Ex. D.10

---

[13] We explain in App. D.10.1 below the difference between the "$\equiv$" and "$\Rightarrow$" that we used earlier, and the "$\Leftrightarrow$" and "$\Rightarrow$" that we are using now.

[14] Again, there is scope for unnecessary confusion here between conditions in programs and propositions in logic. Is "1<2" a term, `True` or `False`, made by applying the binary function "<" to its two arguments "1" and "2"? Or is it a proposition, True or False, made by taking "<" to be a predicate applied to those arguments? For us, it will make no important difference.

[15] There are other, more exotic connectives like "nand" (not and), and "nor" and "xor" as well.

Figure D.6 Truth tables for the standard propositional connectives

$\mathcal{A}$	$\mathcal{B}$	$\mathcal{A} \wedge \mathcal{B}$
True	True	True
True	False	False
False	True	False
False	False	False

$\mathcal{A}$	$\mathcal{B}$	$\mathcal{A} \vee \mathcal{B}$
True	True	True
True	False	True
False	True	True
False	False	False

$\mathcal{A}$	$\mathcal{B}$	$\mathcal{A} \Rightarrow \mathcal{B}$
True	True	True
True	False	False
False	True	True
False	False	True

$\mathcal{A}$	$\mathcal{B}$	$\mathcal{A} \Leftarrow \mathcal{B}$
True	True	True
True	False	True
False	True	False
False	False	True

$\mathcal{A}$	$\mathcal{B}$	$\mathcal{A} \Leftrightarrow \mathcal{B}$
True	True	True
True	False	False
False	True	False
False	False	True

$\mathcal{A}$	$\neg \mathcal{A}$
True	False
False	True

Note the way in which "True" and "False" are being used here. For example, the first line of the top-left truth table says that if some formula $\mathcal{A}$ is True in a particular state, and some (other) formula $\mathcal{B}$ is True *in that same state*, then the formula $\mathcal{A} \wedge \mathcal{B}$ is True in that same state.

Figure D.7 Some propositional formulae

$$x^2 = -1$$
$$(x \leq y) \wedge (y \leq x+1)$$
$$x \leq y \leq x+1 \qquad \leftarrow \text{contains an implicit } \wedge$$
$$(x > 0) \Rightarrow (x \times y \geq 0)$$
$$(0 \leq p \leq q) \Rightarrow (0 < q)$$
$$(n! \neq n) \Leftrightarrow (n \geq 3)$$

Note! Not all of these formulae are True in every state. But they are still formulae.

D.9 Operator precedence

Strictly speaking, a term like $2 + 3 \times 4$ is ambiguous: is its value fourteen or twenty? Such questions can be resolved by parentheses, that is by writing $2 + (3 \times 4)$ vs. $(2 + 3) \times 4$, but they can be resolved also by general precedence rules. The usual rule from arithmetic is that $\times$ is done before $+$ and, for that, we say that $\times$ has *higher precedence*.

We adopt all the usual precedence rules from arithmetic, adding to them that functions have highest precedence of all: thus $\sqrt{4} + 5$ is seven, not three. When several functions are used, the rightmost is applied first: thus $\log \sin(\pi/2)$ is zero.[16] We do not require parentheses around function arguments; but note that $\sin \pi/2$ is zero, whereas $\sin(\pi/2)$ is one.

Propositional connectives have precedence rules too: for us, they are (highest) $\neg$, $\wedge$, $\vee$, $\Rightarrow$, $\Leftrightarrow$ (lowest).

D.10 Calculation with logical formulae

D.10.1 Relations between formulae

The two (simple) formulae $x{=}y \Rightarrow x{\neq}z$ and $x{=}z \Rightarrow x{\neq}y$ are "equivalent" in this sense: in every state they are both True or both False together. In general, that two formulae $\mathcal{A}$ and $\mathcal{B}$ are *equivalent* is written $\mathcal{A} \equiv \mathcal{B}$, and means that

> in every state, $\mathcal{A}$ is True if and only if $\mathcal{B}$ is True .

And that is indeed true just when "In every state $\mathcal{A} \Leftrightarrow \mathcal{B}$ is True." But it does not say that in the same way.

The important difference between "$\equiv$" and "$\Leftrightarrow$", which now –finally– we address,[17] is that the "$\equiv$", says something about how the two formulae relate to each other: that is, writing $\mathcal{A} \equiv \mathcal{B}$ is a statement *about* the two separate formulae $\mathcal{A}$ and $\mathcal{B}$; it is *not* a formula itself. On the other hand, the "$\Leftrightarrow$" *is* a propositional connective: writing $\mathcal{A} \Leftrightarrow \mathcal{B}$ says nothing about any relationship between $\mathcal{A}$ and $\mathcal{B}$ — rather it *is* a formula itself.

Here are two other relations between formulae. Writing $\mathcal{A} \Rightarrow \mathcal{B}$ means that

> in every state, if $\mathcal{A}$ is True then $\mathcal{B}$ is True .

Again, it is true just when "In every state $\mathcal{A} \Rightarrow \mathcal{B}$ is True." Similarly, the statement $\mathcal{A} \Leftarrow \mathcal{B}$ means that

> in every state $\mathcal{A}$ is True if $\mathcal{B}$ is True .

Officially, the relation $\Rightarrow$ between formulae is known as *entailment*, although in everyday speech we often say "implies" (and will continue to do so).

Those three relations *between* formulae are used to set out chains of reasoning, of logical argument, like the one just below: for any formulae that $\mathcal{A}$, $\mathcal{B}$, $\mathcal{C}$ might stand for,

$$(\mathcal{A} \Rightarrow \mathcal{C}) \vee (\mathcal{B} \Rightarrow \mathcal{C})$$
$\equiv$ "implication becomes negation with disjunction (Fig. D.6, or (E.26))"
$$(\neg \mathcal{A} \vee \mathcal{C}) \vee (\neg \mathcal{B} \vee \mathcal{C})$$
$\equiv$ "associativity, commutativity of $\vee$"
$$(\neg \mathcal{A} \vee \neg \mathcal{B}) \vee (\mathcal{C} \vee \mathcal{C})$$
$\equiv$ "De Morgan, idempotence of disjunction"
$$\neg(\mathcal{A} \wedge \mathcal{B}) \vee \mathcal{C}$$
$\equiv$ "negation with disjunction becomes implication"
$$\mathcal{A} \wedge \mathcal{B} \Rightarrow \mathcal{C} \quad .$$

Each formula in reasoning chains like the above is related to the one before it by $\equiv$, $\Rightarrow$ or $\Leftarrow$. (Above however they are all three "$\equiv$".) And each step between formulae carries a decoration, a "hint", suggesting why it is valid. The quotes "..." separate the hints from the proof itself. They are not part of the proof; they are *about* the proof.

Ex. D.11

---

[16] Without higher-order functions, the reverse does not make sense anyway.
[17] ... and which we have been ignoring so far...

The relation $\equiv$ between formulae is *transitive*, which means that whenever both $\mathcal{A} \equiv \mathcal{B}$ and $\mathcal{B} \equiv \mathcal{C}$ then we have $\mathcal{A} \equiv \mathcal{C}$ too. That is why the chain of equivalences above establishes overall that the first formula is equivalent to the last:

$$(\mathcal{A} \Rightarrow \mathcal{C}) \lor (\mathcal{B} \Rightarrow \mathcal{C}) \quad \equiv \quad \mathcal{A} \land \mathcal{B} \Rightarrow \mathcal{C} \quad .$$

The other relations $\Rightarrow$ and $\Leftarrow$ are transitive as well, but not if mixed together. Either can be mixed with $\equiv$, however; thus from $\mathcal{A} \equiv \mathcal{B} \Rightarrow \mathcal{C}$ we still have $\mathcal{A} \Rightarrow \mathcal{C}$. Finally, writing just $\Rightarrow \mathcal{A}$ on its own means that $\mathcal{A}$ is True in every state.[18]

D.10.2 Rules for calculation

To reason "in a chain" as above requires some knowledge of the rules to which one can appeal, such as "associativity, commutativity of $\lor$", that is of "disjunction", as described in App. E.2.1. Each rule can be used to justify steps in a calculation, and often there are several that will do. One soon acquires favourites.

We do not present all those rules here; indeed, it will be some time before we need many of them. Where helpful, however, we refer to them directly. The reasoning just above proved Rule (E.40) in fact.[19] Here it is again, by numbers:

$$(\mathcal{A} \Rightarrow \mathcal{C}) \lor (\mathcal{B} \Rightarrow \mathcal{C})$$
$\equiv$ "Rule (E.26) connecting $\Rightarrow$ with $\neg$ and $\lor$"
$$(\neg\mathcal{A} \lor \mathcal{C}) \lor (\neg\mathcal{B} \lor \mathcal{C})$$
$\equiv$ "Rules (E.3), (E.5)"
$$(\neg\mathcal{A} \lor \neg\mathcal{B}) \lor (\mathcal{C} \lor \mathcal{C})$$
$\equiv$ "Rules (E.22), (E.1)"
$$\neg(\mathcal{A} \land \mathcal{B}) \lor \mathcal{C}$$
$\equiv$ "Rule (E.26) again, in the other direction"
$$\mathcal{A} \land \mathcal{B} \Rightarrow \mathcal{C} \quad .$$

Note especially the use of an equivalence rule to replace a *part* of a formula, leading to an equivalence step for the *whole* formula. That is the usual rule in mathematics: we can substitute equals for equals. But some of our rules from Appendix E are entailments $\Rightarrow$, not equivalences $\equiv$, and so their substitution *within* formulae can lead either to overall entailment or to its converse $\Leftarrow$. But not always: entailment does distribute through quantification, conjunction, disjunction, and the consequent of implication; and it is reversed in negations and antecedents of implications. However it does not distribute through equivalence $\Leftrightarrow$.

Here is a slightly tricky example: the distribution of $\Rightarrow$. Suppose we know that $\mathcal{A} \Rightarrow \mathcal{A}'$, $\mathcal{B} \Leftarrow \mathcal{B}'$, and $\mathcal{C} \equiv \mathcal{C}'$. Then we can develop a reasoning chain like this one:

$$(\mathcal{A} \Rightarrow \mathcal{B}) \Rightarrow \mathcal{C}$$
$\Rightarrow$ "since $\mathcal{A} \Rightarrow \mathcal{A}'$"
$$(\mathcal{A}' \Rightarrow \mathcal{B}) \Rightarrow \mathcal{C}$$
$\Rightarrow$ "since $\mathcal{B} \Leftarrow \mathcal{B}'$"
$$(\mathcal{A}' \Rightarrow \mathcal{B}') \Rightarrow \mathcal{C}$$
$\equiv$ "since $\mathcal{C} \equiv \mathcal{C}'$"
$$(\mathcal{A}' \Rightarrow \mathcal{B}') \Rightarrow \mathcal{C}' \quad .$$

Ex. D.12

---

[18] Use == when writing equivalence between Booleans in `Python`.
[19] The "Rule number" refers to the list in Appendix E; the actual number has no other significance.

D.11 Quantifiers

"Quantifiers" will now take us beyond purely propositional logic: they are how we express "for all" and "there exist". We haven't used them very much in this text; but for completeness we give here a brief description.

D.11.1 Universal quantification

A *universally quantified* formula is written

$$(\forall x \cdot \mathcal{A}) \qquad ,^{20}$$

where x is a variable, called the *bound* variable, and $\mathcal{A}$ is some other formula, called the *body*. Variable x probably occurs in $\mathcal{A}$ somewhere. (The opposite of "bound" for a variable is "free": see App. D.11.4.)

The "$\forall$" is pronounced "for all"; and $(\forall x \cdot \mathcal{A})$ is True in a state just when $\mathcal{A}$ itself (i.e. with the "$\forall x$" stripped away) is True in *all* states, including this one, in which x may take any value at all,[21] but any other variables in $\mathcal{A}$ retain their current values.

We also allow a *list* of bound variables (i.e. rather than just one variable), as in $(\forall x, y \cdot \mathcal{A})$. There, the quantification is True in a state exactly when the body is True as well for all (other) values of those bound variables chosen independently. The order in the list does not affect the meaning.

Consider this parody of the distributive rule from arithmetic:

$$a + (b \times c) \quad = \quad (a + b) \times (a + c) \quad . \tag{D.7}$$

Although one would say informally "That's wrong!" it is in fact True in some states. (Consider the state where a, b, c are all $1/3$.) But the quantified formula

$$(\forall a, b, c \cdot \quad a + (b \times c) = (a + b) \times (a + c) \,) \quad , \tag{D.8}$$

in which a, b, c are understood to be real numbers, is False in every state, because –even though (D.7) is True for some values of a, b, c, it is not True for *all* of them.

But now consider the similar formula

$$(\forall b, c \cdot \quad a + (b \times c) = (a + b) \times (a + c) \,) \quad , \tag{D.9}$$

in which we have quantified only b and c. Its Truth depends on the value the state assigns to a, because a is not bound: Formula (D.9) is True in any state where a has value 0 but is False in every other state.

Ex. D.13

D.11.2 Existential quantification

Existential quantification is the complement to universal quantification: an *existentially quantified* formula is written

$$(\exists x \cdot \mathcal{A}) \quad ,$$

where x and $\mathcal{A}$ are as before, and it is pronounced "there exists". Again, there is probably an x somewhere in $\mathcal{A}$. It is True in a state exactly when there is at least one state, in which only the value of x has changed (perhaps), where $\mathcal{A}$ is True. So the existentially quantified formula

$$(\exists \, a, b, c \cdot a + (b \times c) = (a + b) \times (a + c) \,)$$

is True (because there do exist such a, b, c, as we saw above). Free occurrences of x in $\mathcal{A}$ are bound in $(\exists x \cdot \mathcal{A})$ just as they are in $(\forall x \cdot \mathcal{A})$.

---

[20] It's a good idea to put parentheses around the outside of a quantification: they are like the braces $\{\cdots\}$ that indicate the scope of local variables in programming languages such as C.
[21] That is, any value in its type — if it has one.

D.11.3 Typed quantifications

A *typed quantification* indicates explicitly the set from which values for the bound variable are drawn. For example, if $\mathbb{Z}$ stands for the set of all integers, and $\mathbb{N}$ for the set of all natural numbers (non-negative integers) then $(\exists x{:}\mathbb{Z} \cdot x < 0)$ is True, but $(\exists x{:}\mathbb{N} \cdot x < 0)$ is False (because there is no natural number less than 0). In general, *typed* quantifications are written

$$(\forall x{:}T \cdot \mathcal{A}) \quad \text{and} \quad (\exists x{:}T \cdot \mathcal{A}) \quad ,$$

where T denotes some set of values. The variable x then ranges over that set.

If we know beforehand the set from which values are drawn, we can use the simpler untyped quantifiers; the typing is then understood from context. But when several such sets are involved simultaneously, we use typed quantifiers.

Ex. D.14
Ex. D.15

D.11.4 Free- and bound variables; α-conversion

Formula (D.9) depends on a, but not on b or c. Variable a is a *free* variable; variables b and c are not free: they are *bound* variables, bound by the quantifier $\forall$. In fact, variables b and c are just place-holders in that formula, indicating the positions at which all possible values in the state are to be considered. Changing their names does not affect the formula (provided the new names do not conflict with existing ones). Thus

$$(\forall\, d, e \cdot a + (d \times e) = (a + d) \times (a + e)\,) \quad ,$$

where we have replaced b, c in (D.9) by d, e, has exactly the same meaning as (D.9) itself. On the other hand, formula (D.8) has no free variables at all: since a, b, c are all bound, it does not depend on the value of any variable.

In general, *bound* variables are those bound by a quantifier, as is x in $(\forall x \cdot \mathcal{A})$; all free occurrences of x in $\mathcal{A}$ itself (if there were any) become bound occurrences in the larger $(\forall x \cdot \mathcal{A})$.

Sometimes however an *expression* contains a free variable that is bound by the quantifier within whose scope it is to be substituted. Consider for example the formula $(\forall x \cdot (\exists y \cdot y > x))$, stating that whatever value the (universally bound) variable x might have, there is always a strictly bigger value (existentially bound variable y). If our state space is the set of real numbers, the formula is True in all states.

Now suppose that in a physics problem on which you are working you happen to be using variable y to represent the height of some particle. You can use the formula above to assert that, no matter how high your particle at y, there is always some particle even higher: just substitute the name y you're using to refer to your particle into the universally quantified $\forall x$ in the formula above and –voilà– you have $(\exists y \cdot y > y)$... which of course is not True in *any* state.

What's gone wrong is that your free y, which you substituted into the formula, has been "captured" by the $\exists y$ that was already there (i.e. in the formula). It's just bad luck: the problem wouldn't have occurred if whoever wrote that formula had used w instead of y.

And so the solution is simply to pretend that they did use w — first "α-convert" their formula to the equivalent $(\forall x \cdot (\exists w \cdot w > x))$, choosing any fresh variable w to replace the inconvenient y, and then your substitution gives $(\exists w \cdot w > y)$, which is True in all states, whatever value the state assigns to y: the fresh w names a position higher than the y you have.

Appendix section E.3.1 discusses the issue in more detail.

Figure D.8 Some general formulae

$$x{\neq}3$$
$$y{>}0 \Rightarrow y{\neq}0$$
$$\left(\forall x{:}\mathbb{R} \cdot \left(\exists y{:}\mathbb{C} \cdot y^2{=}x\right)\right)$$
$$a{\div}b = c \;\Leftrightarrow\; \left(\exists r \cdot 0{\leq}r{<}b \;\wedge\; a = b{\times}c + r\right)$$

The real numbers are $\mathbb{R}$; the complex numbers are $\mathbb{C}$.

D.12 (General) formulae

Now we can draw together all the above. A *formula* in general is any one of the following:

(a) a simple formula;

(b) $\neg\mathcal{A}$, where $\mathcal{A}$ is a formula;

(c) $\mathcal{A} \wedge \mathcal{B}$, $\mathcal{A} \vee \mathcal{B}$, $\mathcal{A} \Rightarrow \mathcal{B}$, or $\mathcal{A} \Leftrightarrow \mathcal{B}$, where $\mathcal{A}$ and $\mathcal{B}$ are formulae; or

(d) $(\forall x{:}T \cdot \mathcal{A})$ or $(\exists x{:}T \cdot \mathcal{A})$, where x is a list of variables, T denotes a set and $\mathcal{A}$ is a formula.

That definition allows nested quantifications, such as

$$(\forall a{:}\mathbb{R} \cdot (\exists b, c{:}\mathbb{R} \cdot a + (b \times c) = (a + b) \times (a + c)))$$

(True in all states because for any a you can choose b, c so that $a{+}b{+}c = 1$), and the application of propositional operators to quantifications, such as

$$x \neq 0 \Rightarrow (\exists y{:}\mathbb{Z} \cdot 0 \leq y \wedge y < x) \quad ,$$

which is True in all states where x is a natural number.

Ex. D.16   Figure D.8 gives some general formulae.

Ex. D.17

D.13 Exercises on propositions

Exercise D.1 (p. 263) ⇓ What about `assert` and `assume` statements? Are *they* evaluated at runtime? Do they contribute to the program's answer, or instead only to our confidence in the answer?

Exercise D.2 (p. 264) In App. D.2 it probably seems more natural that you should go *forwards* in checking (D.1) — carry out the assignment's substitution on the initial comment, work your way through, and hope to end up with the final comment.

Go on... Try it.

Exercise D.3 (p. 267) ⇓ Why does the set fact $A \cap B \subseteq A$ look so much like the propositional fact $\mathcal{A} \wedge \mathcal{B} \Rightarrow \mathcal{A}$?

Exercise D.4 (p. 268) ⇓ We've seen that intersection "$\cap$" between sets corresponds to "`and`" between propositions: you are an element of the *intersection* of two sets, say the set of women and the set of people taller than 1.75 m, just if you are a woman *and* you are taller than 1.75 m. Similarly "$\cup$" and "`or`" correspond.

In the same vein,

(a) What operator between sets corresponds to "$\Rightarrow$" between propositions?

(b) What operator on sets corresponds to "$\neg$" on propositions?

(c) What operator between sets corresponds to "$\Rightarrow$" between propositions?

Exercise D.5 (p. 270) ⇓ Which of these are terms?

(a) 17

(b) $\log^2 x$

(c) $\log \log x$

(d) $(\log x)^2$

(e) $\log x^2$

(f) $2x$

(g) $x < x{+}1$

Exercise D.6 (p. 270) Write terms for the following:

(a) The square root of the factorial of n.

(b) The factorial of the square root of n.

(c) The logarithm of the square of x.

Exercise D.7 (p. 272) ⇓ Use the truth tables of Fig. D.6 to show that these formulae are True in all states, that is for all values True/False of $\mathcal{A}, \mathcal{B}, \mathcal{C}$ in a state.

(a) $\mathcal{A} \Rightarrow (\mathcal{B} \Rightarrow \mathcal{A})$

(b) $(\mathcal{A} \Rightarrow (\mathcal{B} \Rightarrow \mathcal{C})) \Rightarrow ((\mathcal{A} \Rightarrow \mathcal{B}) \Rightarrow (\mathcal{A} \Rightarrow \mathcal{C}))$

(c) $(\neg \mathcal{A} \Rightarrow \neg \mathcal{B}) \Rightarrow (\mathcal{B} \Rightarrow \mathcal{A})$

Exercise D.8 (p. 272) ⇓ Which of these are propositional formulae?

(a) *true*

(b) True

(c) $x{<}y \Rightarrow z$

(d) $x{<}y \Rightarrow y{<}z$

Exercise D.9 (p. 272) Which of these are propositional formulae?

(a) true

(b) $x{<}y \Rightarrow z$

(c) $x{<}y \Rightarrow y{<}z$

(d) $x{<}y \Rightarrow y{>}x$

Exercise D.10 (p. 272) Supposing that all variables here denote natural numbers $\mathbb{N}$, which of these propositional formulae are True in all states?

(a) $x \geq 0$

(b) $x < y \;\Rightarrow\; x{+}1 \leq y$

(c) $x \leq y \;\vee\; y \leq x$

(d) $x \leq y \wedge y \leq x \;\Rightarrow\; x = y$

(e) $x < y \wedge y < x \;\Rightarrow\; x = y$

(f) $x < y \wedge y < x \;\Rightarrow\; x \neq y$

(g) $x < y \vee y < x \;\Rightarrow\; x \neq y$

Exercise D.11 (p. 274) ⇓ Show that $\mathcal{A} \Rightarrow (\mathcal{B} \Rightarrow \mathcal{A})$ is correct (valid).
    Hint: Recall the meaning of $\Rightarrow$.
    What about $(\mathcal{A} \Rightarrow \mathcal{B}) \Rightarrow \mathcal{A}$?

D.14 Exercises on quantifiers

Exercise D.12 (p. 275) ⇓ Justify in words the use of "since $\mathcal{A} \Rightarrow \mathcal{A}'$" and "since $\mathcal{B} \Leftarrow \mathcal{B}'$" in the example involving "distribution of $\Rightarrow$" in App. D.10.2.

Exercise D.13 (p. 276) ⇓ Show *carefully* that formula (D.9) is indeed False in *any* state where $a \neq 0$.

Exercise D.14 (p. 277) ⇓ Given that the one-place predicates even, odd mean "is an even number", "is an odd number" respectively, write general formulae for the following:

(a) Every integer is either even or odd.

(b) Every odd natural number is one more than some even natural number.

(c) There is an even integer that is not one more than some odd natural number.

Exercise D.15 (p. 277) Write general formulae for the following:

(a) Zero is the least natural number.

(b) There is no least integer.

(c) Given any positive real number, there is another real number strictly between it and zero.

Exercise D.16 (p. 278) ⇓ Recall that $(\exists x \cdot \mathcal{A})$ means "There is *at least* one x such that $\mathcal{A}$ holds." (Note that x might occur in the formula $\mathcal{A}$ stand for.) Write another formula that means "There is *at most* one x such that $\mathcal{A}$ holds."
    Make sure it holds even when there is *no* x such that $\mathcal{A}$ holds.

Exercise D.17 (p. 278) Write a formula meaning "There is *exactly* one x such that $\mathcal{A}$ holds."

Some helpful logical identities[1]

E.1 Introduction

We now look at "formal" logic on its own, exposing the conceptual infrastructure that underlies our checking of programs for their correctness — if you choose to look that deep. It is not necessary for the intended use of this text, since –the whole point– we emphasise that our program-checking applies even when the "What's true here." assertions are written in natural language: it's what they say, and where they say it, that counts.

Nevertheless, the precision of actual logic does occasionally help to sort out some tricky situations; and that is why it's probably worth having a quick look here... but with no obligation to buy.[2]

Still, that precision is *necessary* if one wants to take advantage of machine-assisted proof checking, as in Chapter 18.

This appendix can be used as an independent, that is stand-alone (though very brief), introduction to the propositional and predicate calculi in their own right. Unlike most introductions, however, the emphasis here is on *calculation* (as in the rest of this text), that is you are encouraged to reason in logic by moving from one formula to another one equivalent to it, just as confidently as you would carry out similar reasoning in mathematics, whether as elementary as arithmetic or as complex as calculus.

As in Appendix D, we use here the usual symbols from logic, rather than their `Python` equivalents. Thus "not" is "¬", "and" is "∧" and "or" is "∨". For `Python`'s `True` and `False` we write logic's true and false.

E.2 Some basic propositional rules

Throughout this section App. E.2, the symbols $\mathcal{A}$, $\mathcal{B}$ and $\mathcal{C}$ stand for propositions that can be either True or False. Variables (e.g. x, y denoting integers etc.) and quantifications over them appear only later, in App. E.3, at which point the symbols stand for predicate formulae.

---

[1] These rules were collected originally in Morgan and Sanders *Laws of the Logical Calculi* [45], but appeared also in Morgan, *Programming from Specifications* [43].
[2] That is, you do not need to learn all these rules now: just remember they are there. Think "table of integrals".

E.2.1 Conjunction and disjunction

The propositional connectives for conjunction ("**and**"), written "∧", and disjunction ("**or**") ∨, are idempotent, commutative, associative and absorptive (which terms are defined immediately below), and they distribute through each other.

As usual we write "≡" for "is equivalent to". (But see also App. E.5.)

Conjunction and disjunction are *idempotent* connectives, meaning that using them twice is the same as using them once:

$$\mathcal{A} \wedge \mathcal{A} \;\;\equiv\;\; \mathcal{A} \;\;\equiv\;\; \mathcal{A} \vee \mathcal{A} \quad . \tag{E.1}$$

Conjunction and disjunction are *commutative* connectives, meaning that they can be used in either order:

$$\mathcal{A} \wedge \mathcal{B} \;\;\equiv\;\; \mathcal{B} \wedge \mathcal{A} \tag{E.2}$$

$$\mathcal{A} \vee \mathcal{B} \;\;\equiv\;\; \mathcal{B} \vee \mathcal{A} \quad . \tag{E.3}$$

Conjunction and disjunction are *associative* connectives, meaning that you can bracket them in either direction:

$$\mathcal{A} \wedge (\mathcal{B} \wedge \mathcal{C}) \;\;\equiv\;\; (\mathcal{A} \wedge \mathcal{B}) \wedge \mathcal{C} \tag{E.4}$$

$$\mathcal{A} \vee (\mathcal{B} \vee \mathcal{C}) \;\;\equiv\;\; (\mathcal{A} \vee \mathcal{B}) \vee \mathcal{C} \quad . \tag{E.5}$$

Rules (E.1) to (E.5) mean that we can ignore duplication, order and grouping in extended conjunctions $\mathcal{A} \wedge \mathcal{B} \wedge \cdots \wedge \mathcal{C}$ and disjunctions $\mathcal{A} \vee \mathcal{B} \vee \cdots \vee \mathcal{C}$.

Sometimes terms can be removed immediately from expressions involving both conjunctions and disjunctions. That is *absorption*, allowing us to remove $\mathcal{B}$ here:

$$\mathcal{A} \wedge (\mathcal{A} \vee \mathcal{B}) \;\;\equiv\;\; \mathcal{A} \;\;\equiv\;\; \mathcal{A} \vee (\mathcal{A} \wedge \mathcal{B}) \quad . \tag{E.6}$$

The *distribution* of ∧ through ∨ is similar to the distribution of multiplication over addition in arithmetic. But in logic distribution goes both ways, so that ∨ distributes through ∧ as well:

$$\mathcal{A} \wedge (\mathcal{B} \vee \mathcal{C}) \;\;\equiv\;\; (\mathcal{A} \wedge \mathcal{B}) \vee (\mathcal{A} \wedge \mathcal{C}) \tag{E.7}$$

$$\mathcal{A} \vee (\mathcal{B} \wedge \mathcal{C}) \;\;\equiv\;\; (\mathcal{A} \vee \mathcal{B}) \wedge (\mathcal{A} \vee \mathcal{C}) \quad . \tag{E.8}$$

And finally, using "⇒" for "if ... then ... " we have

$$\mathcal{A} \wedge \mathcal{B} \;\;\Rightarrow\;\; \mathcal{A} \tag{E.9}$$

$$\mathcal{A} \wedge \mathcal{B} \;\;\Rightarrow\;\; \mathcal{B} \tag{E.10}$$

$$\mathcal{A} \;\;\Rightarrow\;\; \mathcal{A} \vee \mathcal{B} \tag{E.11}$$

$$\mathcal{B} \;\;\Rightarrow\;\; \mathcal{A} \vee \mathcal{B} \quad . \tag{E.12}$$

E.2.2 Constants and negation

In ordinary multiplication we have $a \times 1 = a$ and $a \times 0 = 0$. We say therefore that the constant 1 is a *unit*, and 0 a *zero*, of multiplication. Similarly, we now introduce the propositional constants true and false that are True resp. False in every state. The propositional constant true is the unit of ∧ and the zero of ∨ :

$$\mathcal{A} \wedge \mathsf{true} \;\;\equiv\;\; \mathcal{A} \tag{E.13}$$

$$\mathcal{A} \vee \mathsf{true} \;\;\equiv\;\; \mathsf{true} \quad . \tag{E.14}$$

The constant false is the unit of ∨ and the zero of ∧:

$$\mathcal{A} \wedge \mathsf{false} \;\;\equiv\;\; \mathsf{false} \tag{E.15}$$

$$\mathcal{A} \vee \mathsf{false} \;\;\equiv\;\; \mathcal{A} \quad . \tag{E.16}$$

Negation $\neg$ acts as a *complement*:

$$\neg\text{true} \equiv \text{false} \tag{E.17}$$
$$\neg\text{false} \equiv \text{true} \tag{E.18}$$
$$\mathcal{A} \wedge \neg\mathcal{A} \equiv \text{false} \tag{E.19}$$
$$\mathcal{A} \vee \neg\mathcal{A} \equiv \text{true} \quad . \tag{E.20}$$

Furthermore it is an *involution*:

$$\neg\neg\mathcal{A} \equiv \mathcal{A} \quad . \tag{E.21}$$

And it satisfies De Morgan's laws (which are exceptionally useful):

$$\neg(\mathcal{A} \wedge \mathcal{B}) \equiv \neg\mathcal{A} \vee \neg\mathcal{B} \tag{E.22}$$
$$\neg(\mathcal{A} \vee \mathcal{B}) \equiv \neg\mathcal{A} \wedge \neg\mathcal{B} \quad . \tag{E.23}$$

With negation, we have two more absorptive rules:

$$\mathcal{A} \vee (\neg\mathcal{A} \wedge \mathcal{B}) \equiv \mathcal{A} \vee \mathcal{B} \tag{E.24}$$
$$\mathcal{A} \wedge (\neg\mathcal{A} \vee \mathcal{B}) \equiv \mathcal{A} \wedge \mathcal{B} \quad . \tag{E.25}$$

E.2.3 Normal forms

A formula is said to be in *disjunctive normal form* if it is a finite disjunction of other formulae each of which is, in turn, a *conjunction* of simple formulae. *Conjunctive normal form* is defined complementarily.

Rules (E.7), (E.8), (E.22) and (E.23), used repeatedly, allow us to convert any propositional formula to either disjunctive or conjunctive normal form, as we choose; and rules (E.19) and (E.20) serve to remove adjacent complementary formulae. For example,

$\quad \mathcal{A} \wedge \neg(\mathcal{B} \wedge \mathcal{C} \wedge \mathcal{A})$
$\equiv \quad$ "(E.22)"
$\quad \mathcal{A} \wedge (\neg\mathcal{B} \vee \neg\mathcal{C} \vee \neg\mathcal{A})$
$\equiv \quad$ "(E.7)"
$\quad (\mathcal{A} \wedge \neg\mathcal{B}) \vee (\mathcal{A} \wedge \neg\mathcal{C}) \vee (\mathcal{A} \wedge \neg\mathcal{A})$
$\equiv \quad$ "(E.19)"
$\quad (\mathcal{A} \wedge \neg\mathcal{B}) \vee (\mathcal{A} \wedge \neg\mathcal{C}) \vee \text{false}$
$\equiv \quad$ "(E.16)"
$\quad (\mathcal{A} \wedge \neg\mathcal{B}) \vee (\mathcal{A} \wedge \neg\mathcal{C}) \quad .$

The second formula above is in conjunctive normal form and the third, fourth, and fifth are in disjunctive normal form.

The "equational" layout above, with adjacent formulae separated by some relation between them (such as "is equivalent to", "implies" etc.) and reasons given between "$\cdots$", is a nice way of reducing the likelihood of mistakes when reasoning carefully in this calculational style.

E.2.4 Implication

Implication $\Rightarrow$ satisfies the law

$$\mathcal{A} \Rightarrow \mathcal{B} \equiv \neg\mathcal{A} \vee \mathcal{B} \quad , \tag{E.26}$$

and that leads on to these rules:

$$\mathcal{A} \Rightarrow \mathcal{A} \equiv \text{true} \tag{E.27}$$
$$\mathcal{A} \Rightarrow \mathcal{B} \equiv \neg(\mathcal{A} \wedge \neg\mathcal{B}) \tag{E.28}$$
$$\neg(\mathcal{A} \Rightarrow \mathcal{B}) \equiv \mathcal{A} \wedge \neg\mathcal{B} \tag{E.29}$$
$$\mathcal{A} \Rightarrow \mathcal{B} \equiv \neg\mathcal{B} \Rightarrow \neg\mathcal{A} \quad . \tag{E.30}$$

The last above is called the *contrapositive law*. Useful special cases of those are

$$\mathcal{A} \Rightarrow \text{true} \quad \equiv \quad \text{true} \tag{E.31}$$

$$\text{true} \Rightarrow \mathcal{A} \quad \equiv \quad \mathcal{A} \tag{E.32}$$

$$\mathcal{A} \Rightarrow \text{false} \quad \equiv \quad \neg\mathcal{A} \tag{E.33}$$

$$\text{false} \Rightarrow \mathcal{A} \quad \equiv \quad \text{true} \tag{E.34}$$

$$\mathcal{A} \Rightarrow \neg\mathcal{A} \quad \equiv \quad \neg\mathcal{A} \tag{E.35}$$

$$\neg\mathcal{A} \Rightarrow \mathcal{A} \quad \equiv \quad \mathcal{A} \quad . \tag{E.36}$$

These next two rules distribute implication $\Rightarrow$ through conjunction and disjunction:

$$\mathcal{C} \Rightarrow (\mathcal{A} \wedge \mathcal{B}) \quad \equiv \quad (\mathcal{C} \Rightarrow \mathcal{A}) \wedge (\mathcal{C} \Rightarrow \mathcal{B}) \tag{E.37}$$

$$(\mathcal{A} \vee \mathcal{B}) \Rightarrow \mathcal{C} \quad \equiv \quad (\mathcal{A} \Rightarrow \mathcal{C}) \wedge (\mathcal{B} \Rightarrow \mathcal{C}) \tag{E.38}$$

$$\mathcal{C} \Rightarrow (\mathcal{A} \vee \mathcal{B}) \quad \equiv \quad (\mathcal{C} \Rightarrow \mathcal{A}) \vee (\mathcal{C} \Rightarrow \mathcal{B}) \tag{E.39}$$

$$(\mathcal{A} \wedge \mathcal{B}) \Rightarrow \mathcal{C} \quad \equiv \quad (\mathcal{A} \Rightarrow \mathcal{C}) \vee (\mathcal{B} \Rightarrow \mathcal{C}) \quad , \tag{E.40}$$

where you will notice that the conjunction/disjunction "flips over" if it is moved out of the left-hand side of $\Rightarrow$.

The following extra rules are useful in showing that successive hypotheses may be conjoined or even reversed:

$$\mathcal{A} \Rightarrow (\mathcal{B} \Rightarrow \mathcal{C}) \quad \equiv \quad (\mathcal{A} \wedge \mathcal{B}) \Rightarrow \mathcal{C} \quad \equiv \quad \mathcal{B} \Rightarrow (\mathcal{A} \Rightarrow \mathcal{C}) \quad . \tag{E.41}$$

And the next law is the basis of definition by cases:

$$(\mathcal{A} \Rightarrow \mathcal{B}) \wedge (\neg\mathcal{A} \Rightarrow \mathcal{C}) \quad \equiv \quad (\mathcal{A} \wedge \mathcal{B}) \vee (\neg\mathcal{A} \wedge \mathcal{C}) \quad . \tag{E.42}$$

E.2.5 Equivalence

Equivalence $\Leftrightarrow$ satisfies this law:

$$\mathcal{A} \Leftrightarrow \mathcal{B} \quad \equiv \quad (\mathcal{A} \Rightarrow \mathcal{B}) \wedge (\mathcal{B} \Rightarrow \mathcal{A}) \tag{E.43}$$

$$\equiv \quad (\mathcal{A} \wedge \mathcal{B}) \vee \neg(\mathcal{A} \vee \mathcal{B}) \tag{E.44}$$

$$\equiv \quad \neg\mathcal{A} \Leftrightarrow \neg\mathcal{B} \quad . \tag{E.45}$$

Also we have these:

$$\mathcal{A} \Leftrightarrow \mathcal{A} \quad \equiv \quad \text{true} \tag{E.46}$$

$$\mathcal{A} \Leftrightarrow \neg\mathcal{A} \quad \equiv \quad \text{false} \tag{E.47}$$

$$\mathcal{A} \Leftrightarrow \text{true} \quad \equiv \quad \mathcal{A} \tag{E.48}$$

$$\mathcal{A} \Leftrightarrow \text{false} \quad \equiv \quad \neg\mathcal{A} \tag{E.49}$$

$$\mathcal{A} \Rightarrow \mathcal{B} \quad \equiv \quad \mathcal{A} \Leftrightarrow (\mathcal{A} \wedge \mathcal{B}) \tag{E.50}$$

$$\mathcal{B} \Rightarrow \mathcal{A} \quad \equiv \quad \mathcal{A} \Leftrightarrow (\mathcal{A} \vee \mathcal{B}) \tag{E.51}$$

$$\mathcal{A} \vee (\mathcal{B} \Leftrightarrow \mathcal{C}) \quad \equiv \quad (\mathcal{A} \vee \mathcal{B}) \Leftrightarrow (\mathcal{A} \vee \mathcal{C}) \quad . \tag{E.52}$$

Equivalence is commutative and associative:

$$\mathcal{A} \Leftrightarrow \mathcal{B} \quad \equiv \quad \mathcal{B} \Leftrightarrow \mathcal{A} \tag{E.53}$$

$$\mathcal{A} \Leftrightarrow (\mathcal{B} \Leftrightarrow \mathcal{C}) \quad \equiv \quad (\mathcal{A} \Leftrightarrow \mathcal{B}) \Leftrightarrow \mathcal{C} \quad ; \tag{E.54}$$

and, from (E.50) and (E.51), it satisfies E.W. Dijkstra's *Golden Rule*:[3]

$$\Rightarrow \quad \mathcal{A} \wedge \mathcal{B} \Leftrightarrow \mathcal{A} \Leftrightarrow \mathcal{B} \Leftrightarrow \mathcal{A} \vee \mathcal{B} \quad , \tag{E.55}$$

where the $\Rightarrow$ alone on the left means "*unconditionally* correct" (universally valid), equivalently "True in *all* states". (Recall App. D.7.)

Ex. E.1

Ex. E.2   [3] In some texts the Golden Rule is written $\mathcal{A} \wedge \mathcal{B} \equiv \mathcal{A} \equiv \mathcal{B} \equiv \mathcal{A} \vee \mathcal{B}$, in which case the "$\equiv$" is being used as a propositional connective. Here we are using "$\equiv$" as a relation between formulae, and not as a propositional connective; and that is why we write (E.55) with "$\Leftrightarrow$".

E.3 Some basic quantifier rules

From here on our symbols $\mathcal{A}$ etc. will stand for more general formulae, and note(!) that they might contain free variables, such as "x", which refer to, say, integers or other types: in most cases we do *not* mention explicitly that "$\mathcal{A}$ might contain free x" etc. Even when they do –mentioned or not– the propositional rules of App. E.2 still apply — but now we have additional rules that deal with the variables themselves.

We begin with rules concerning the universal and existential quantifiers $\forall$ ("for all") and $\exists$ ("there exists"). Although for most practical purposes we wish the quantification to be *typed*, as in

$$(\forall x{:}T \cdot \mathcal{A})$$
$$(\exists x{:}T \cdot \mathcal{A})$$

where T gives here a type for x and $\mathcal{A}$ is a formula that probably mentions x, for simplicity we state our rules using untyped quantifications:

$$(\forall x \cdot \mathcal{A})$$
$$(\exists x \cdot \mathcal{A}) \quad .$$

(Reminder: there might be free x in $\mathcal{A}$, even though we don't mention it.)

Each of the two untyped quantifications above can be converted to a rule for typed quantification by the uniform addition of type information, *provided the type is non-empty*. These rules enable us to convert between the two styles:

$$(\forall x{:}T \cdot \mathcal{A}) \quad \equiv \quad (\forall x \cdot x{\in}T \Rightarrow \mathcal{A}) \qquad\qquad\qquad (\text{E.56})$$

$$(\exists x{:}T \cdot \mathcal{A}) \quad \equiv \quad (\exists x \cdot x{\in}T \wedge \mathcal{A}) \quad , \qquad\qquad (\text{E.57})$$

where the simple formula $x{\in}T$ as usual means "x is in the set T".

For more general constraints than typing, we have these abbreviations as well, which include a range formula $\mathcal{R}$ probably containing x:

$$(\forall x{:}T \mid \mathcal{R} \cdot \mathcal{A}) \quad \equiv \quad (\forall x \cdot x{\in}T \wedge \mathcal{R} \Rightarrow \mathcal{A}) \qquad\qquad (\text{E.58})$$

$$(\exists x{:}T \mid \mathcal{R} \cdot \mathcal{A}) \quad \equiv \quad (\exists x \cdot x{\in}T \wedge \mathcal{R} \wedge \mathcal{A}) \quad , \qquad (\text{E.59})$$

Note that (E.56) and (E.58) introduce implication, whereas (E.57) and (E.59) introduce conjunction.

E.3.1 Substitution and instantiation

We write the substitution of a term E for a variable x in a formula $\mathcal{A}$ as

$$\mathcal{A}[x\backslash E] \quad ,$$

and we write the multiple substitution of terms E and F for variables x and y respectively as

$$\mathcal{A}[x, y \backslash E, F] \quad .$$

Unless quantifiers are present, substitution $\mathcal{A}[x\backslash E]$ means *literally* replace all occurrences of x by E, so that things like

$$(\mathcal{A} \Rightarrow \mathcal{B})[x\backslash E] \quad \equiv \quad \mathcal{A}[x\backslash E] \Rightarrow \mathcal{B}[x\backslash E]$$

are true by definition (of substitution). (Note however that sometimes parentheses $(\ldots)$ must be introduced to respect operator precedence: recall App. D.9 and Ex. 1.3.)

Substitution is used in the rule which checks assignments (Sec. 5.2 and App. B.1.1), but it is also used to explain the basic properties, indeed the very purpose of the quantifiers: we have

$$(\forall x \cdot \mathcal{A}) \quad \Rightarrow \quad \mathcal{A}[x\backslash E] \qquad \text{for any term } E \qquad\qquad (\text{E.60})$$

$$\mathcal{A}[x\backslash E] \quad \Rightarrow \quad (\exists x \cdot \mathcal{A}) \qquad \text{for any term } E \quad , \qquad (\text{E.61})$$

that is $\forall x$ means "holds for *any* term E you substitute for x", and $\exists x$ means "holds if it holds for *some* term you might substitute for x". In simple cases, substitutions just replace the variable by the term.

But if the variable being replaced (for example x) occurs *within* the scope of a quantifier then we must take account of whether variables are free or bound. Suppose, for example, that $\mathcal{A}$ is the formula $(\exists x \cdot x \neq y) \wedge x = y$; then

$$\mathcal{A}[x \backslash y] \quad \text{is} \quad (\exists x \cdot x \neq y) \wedge y = y \ ,$$
$$\text{but} \quad \mathcal{A}[y \backslash x] \quad \text{is} \quad (\exists z \cdot z \neq x) \wedge x = x \quad .$$

The variable z is *fresh*, chosen *ad lib* provided it does not appear in $\mathcal{A}$ already. In the first case, $x \neq y$ is unaffected because *that* occurrence of x is bound by $\exists x$. Indeed, since we could have used any other letter (except y) without affecting the meaning of the formula –and it would not have been replaced in that case– we do not replace it in this case either. The occurrence of x in $x = y$ is free, however, and the substitution occurs.

In the second case, since both occurrences of y are free, both are replaced by x. But on the left we must not "accidentally" quantify over the newly introduced x –to write $(\exists x \cdot x \neq x)$ would be wrong– so we change (before the substitution) the bound x to a fresh variable z. Such an "accidental quantification" is called *variable capture*, and the (pre-emptive, preventative) renaming of x to z (in this case) is called *alpha conversion*.

Finally, note that multiple substitution can differ from successive substitution: continuing with the $\mathcal{A}$ from above, we have for example that

$$\mathcal{A}[y \backslash x][x \backslash y] \quad \text{is} \quad (\exists z \cdot z \neq y) \wedge y = y$$
$$\text{but} \quad \mathcal{A}[y, x \backslash x, y] \quad \text{is} \quad (\exists z \cdot z \neq x) \wedge y = x \quad ,$$

just as multiple assignment differs from successive assignment (and for the same reason).

E.3.2　The one-point rules

These rules allow quantifiers to be eliminated in many cases. They are called "one-point" because the bound variable is constrained to take one value exactly. If x does not occur (free) in the term E, then

$$(\forall x \cdot x = E \Rightarrow \mathcal{A}) \quad \equiv \quad \mathcal{A}[x \backslash E] \quad \equiv \quad (\exists x \cdot x = E \wedge \mathcal{A}) \quad . \tag{E.62}$$

If the type T in Rules (E.56) and (E.57) is finite, say $\{a, b\}$, we have the similar

$$(\forall x : \{a, b\} \cdot \mathcal{A}) \quad \equiv \quad \mathcal{A}[x \backslash a] \wedge \mathcal{A}[x \backslash b] \tag{E.63}$$
$$(\exists x : \{a, b\} \cdot \mathcal{A}) \quad \equiv \quad \mathcal{A}[x \backslash a] \vee \mathcal{A}[x \backslash b] \quad . \tag{E.64}$$

Those can be extended to larger (but still finite) types $\{a, b, \ldots, z\}$. We are led to think, informally, of universal and existential quantification as infinite conjunction and disjunction respectively over all the possible values (of the type, if given) in the state:

$$(\forall x : \mathbb{N} \cdot \mathcal{A}) \quad \text{represents} \quad \mathcal{A}(0) \wedge \mathcal{A}(1) \cdots$$
$$(\exists x : \mathbb{N} \cdot \mathcal{A}) \quad \text{represents} \quad \mathcal{A}(0) \vee \mathcal{A}(1) \cdots$$

E.3.3　Quantifiers alone

Quantification is idempotent:

$$(\forall x \cdot (\forall x \cdot \mathcal{A})) \quad \equiv \quad (\forall x \cdot \mathcal{A}) \tag{E.65}$$
$$(\exists x \cdot (\exists x \cdot \mathcal{A})) \quad \equiv \quad (\exists x \cdot \mathcal{A}) \quad . \tag{E.66}$$

Extending De Morgan's laws (E.22) and (E.23), we have

$$\neg (\forall x \cdot \mathcal{A}) \quad \equiv \quad (\exists x \cdot \neg \mathcal{A}) \tag{E.67}$$
$$\neg (\exists x \cdot \mathcal{A}) \quad \equiv \quad (\forall x \cdot \neg \mathcal{A}) \quad . \tag{E.68}$$

E.3.4 Extending the commutative rules

These rules extend the commutativity of $\wedge$ and $\vee$:

$$(\forall x \cdot (\forall y \cdot \mathcal{A})) \quad\equiv\quad (\forall x, y \cdot \mathcal{A}) \quad\equiv\quad (\forall y \cdot (\forall x \cdot \mathcal{A})) \tag{E.69}$$

$$(\exists x \cdot (\exists y \cdot \mathcal{A})) \quad\equiv\quad (\exists x, y \cdot \mathcal{A}) \quad\equiv\quad (\exists y \cdot (\exists x \cdot \mathcal{A})) \quad . \tag{E.70}$$

E.3.5 Quantifiers accompanied

Extending the associative and previous rules,

$$(\forall x \cdot \mathcal{A} \wedge \mathcal{B}) \quad\equiv\quad (\forall x \cdot \mathcal{A}) \wedge (\forall x \cdot \mathcal{B}) \tag{E.71}$$

$$(\exists x \cdot \mathcal{A} \vee \mathcal{B}) \quad\equiv\quad (\exists x \cdot \mathcal{A}) \vee (\exists x \cdot \mathcal{B}) \tag{E.72}$$

$$(\exists x \cdot \mathcal{A} \Rightarrow \mathcal{B}) \quad\equiv\quad (\forall x \cdot \mathcal{A}) \Rightarrow (\exists x \cdot \mathcal{B}) \quad , \tag{E.73}$$

where in the last case we note that the existential, when distributed in, becomes a universal $\boxed{\text{Ex. E.3}}$ on the left of the implication. This is called "contravariance".

Here are weaker rules (using $\Rightarrow$ rather than $\equiv$) which are nonetheless useful:

$$(\forall x \cdot \mathcal{A}) \quad\Rightarrow\quad (\exists x \cdot \mathcal{A}) \tag{E.74}$$

$$(\forall x \cdot \mathcal{A}) \vee (\forall x \cdot \mathcal{B}) \quad\Rightarrow\quad (\forall x \cdot \mathcal{A} \vee \mathcal{B}) \tag{E.75}$$

$$(\forall x \cdot \mathcal{A} \Rightarrow \mathcal{B}) \quad\Rightarrow\quad (\forall x \cdot \mathcal{A}) \Rightarrow (\forall x \cdot \mathcal{B}) \tag{E.76}$$

$$(\exists x \cdot \mathcal{A} \wedge \mathcal{B}) \quad\Rightarrow\quad (\exists x \cdot \mathcal{A}) \wedge (\exists x \cdot \mathcal{B}) \tag{E.77}$$

$$(\exists x \cdot \mathcal{A}) \Rightarrow (\exists x \cdot \mathcal{B}) \quad\Rightarrow\quad (\exists x \cdot \mathcal{A} \Rightarrow \mathcal{B}) \tag{E.78}$$

$$(\exists y \cdot (\forall x \cdot \mathcal{A})) \quad\Rightarrow\quad (\forall x \cdot (\exists y \cdot \mathcal{A})) \quad . \tag{E.79}$$

None of them applies generally in the opposite direction $\Leftarrow$.

$\boxed{\text{Ex. E.4}}$

$\boxed{\text{Ex. E.5}}$

E.3.6 Manipulation of quantifiers

If a variable has no free occurrences, its quantification is superfluous:

$$(\forall x \cdot \mathcal{A}) \quad\equiv\quad \mathcal{A} \qquad \text{if } x \text{ is not free in } \mathcal{A} \tag{E.80}$$

$$(\exists x \cdot \mathcal{A}) \quad\equiv\quad \mathcal{A} \qquad \text{if } x \text{ is not free in } \mathcal{A} \quad . \tag{E.81}$$

Other useful rules of this kind are the following, many of which are specialisations of Rules (E.71) to (E.73). In each case, variable x must not be free in the formula $\mathcal{N}$:

$$(\forall x \cdot \mathcal{N} \wedge \mathcal{B}) \quad\equiv\quad \mathcal{N} \wedge (\forall x \cdot \mathcal{B}) \tag{E.82}$$

$$(\forall x \cdot \mathcal{N} \vee \mathcal{B}) \quad\equiv\quad \mathcal{N} \vee (\forall x \cdot \mathcal{B}) \tag{E.83}$$

$$(\forall x \cdot \mathcal{N} \Rightarrow \mathcal{B}) \quad\equiv\quad \mathcal{N} \Rightarrow (\forall x \cdot \mathcal{B}) \tag{E.84}$$

$$(\forall x \cdot \mathcal{A} \Rightarrow \mathcal{N}) \quad\equiv\quad (\exists x \cdot \mathcal{A}) \Rightarrow \mathcal{N} \tag{E.85}$$

$$(\exists x \cdot \mathcal{N} \wedge \mathcal{B}) \quad\equiv\quad \mathcal{N} \wedge (\exists x \cdot \mathcal{B}) \tag{E.86}$$

$$(\exists x \cdot \mathcal{N} \vee \mathcal{B}) \quad\equiv\quad \mathcal{N} \vee (\exists x \cdot \mathcal{B}) \tag{E.87}$$

$$(\exists x \cdot \mathcal{N} \Rightarrow \mathcal{B}) \quad\equiv\quad \mathcal{N} \Rightarrow (\exists x \cdot \mathcal{B}) \tag{E.88}$$

$$(\exists x \cdot \mathcal{A} \Rightarrow \mathcal{N}) \quad\equiv\quad (\forall x \cdot \mathcal{A}) \Rightarrow \mathcal{N} \quad . \tag{E.89}$$

Notice again the "flipping" (contravariance) of the quantifier when moved into or out of the left-hand side of an implication.

Bound variables can be renamed, as long as the new name does not conflict with existing names:

$$(\forall x \cdot \mathcal{A}) \quad\equiv\quad (\forall y \cdot \mathcal{A}[x \backslash y]) \qquad \text{if } y \text{ is not free in } \mathcal{A} \tag{E.90}$$

$$(\exists x \cdot \mathcal{A}) \quad\equiv\quad (\exists y \cdot \mathcal{A}[x \backslash y]) \qquad \text{if } y \text{ is not free in } \mathcal{A} \quad , \tag{E.91}$$

which is another example of alpha conversion.

Finally, we recall from (E.60), (E.61), repeated here, that have for any term E,

$$(\forall x \cdot \mathcal{A}) \quad \Rightarrow \quad \mathcal{A}[x \backslash E] \qquad\qquad\qquad (E.60)$$

$$\mathcal{A}[x \backslash E] \quad \Rightarrow \quad (\exists x \cdot \mathcal{A}) \quad . \qquad\qquad\qquad (E.61)$$

If $\mathcal{A}$ holds for all x, then it holds for E in particular; and if $\mathcal{A}$ holds for E, then certainly it holds for some x.

Ex. E.6

Ex. E.7

E.4 Epilogue on logical notation and terminology [4]

Ex. E.8

Ex. E.9

Although this text –whence its point, and indeed its title– has *not* presented formal reasoning for its own sake, it remains useful at this stage for us to conclude with some explicit connections to the conventional treatments of formal logic.

To begin with, there are many (different) opinions about whether to use ($\rightarrow$) or ($\Rightarrow$) for implication,[5] or ($\equiv$) or ($\Leftrightarrow$) or ($\leftrightarrow$) for equivalence, and so on...[6] What's important of course is to be consistent within a single text, and below are the choices we have made, the conventions we use here:

implication in English (i.e. in any natural language) comes in many forms. In everyday English it's "If *this* then *that*." or equivalently "*This* implies *that*." Note however that "*This* if *that*." means the exact opposite of "implies" — instead it's "*That* implies *this*."

An alternative to "implies" is "only if", so that "*This* only if *that*." is the same as "*This* implies *that*. "

reverse implication in English From just above, we see that "*This* is implied by *that*." means "*This* if *that*."

bi-implication in English is implication both ways. It can be written "if and only if", or "just when" or (often by mathematicians and logicians) simply "iff". It can also be written "is equivalent to".

well-formed formulae Logic has very strict rules about syntax, that is about which symbol-strings are formulae and which are not. (The same strictness applies to programs in a programming language but, of course, we are not talking about the same rules.) A well-formed formula is called a *wff* (and pronounced somewhere between "wiff" and "woof").

implication as a logical connective is *in this text* written $\Rightarrow$. In some presentations of logic (especially text books on logic itself) it is written $\rightarrow$ instead. No matter how it is written, placed between one *wff* and another it makes another (bigger) *wff* whose left-hand side is the *antecedent* and right-hand side is the *consequent*.

The single-line "implies" brings with it $\leftarrow$ for "is implied by" and $\leftrightarrow$ for "iff". (In this text however we use $\Leftarrow$ and $\Leftrightarrow$.)

implication as "entails" is in this text written $\Rightarrow$. In some (probably most) presentations of logic it's written $\models$ or $\vdash$ and these two *are* different (as we explain just below) — and in this case it's *not* just a matter of whether you prefer a single- or a double line.

Whichever you use, that is $\Rightarrow$ or $\models$ or $\vdash$, it does *not* make a new *wff*. Instead it indicates a relation between the left-hand *wff* on its left (still called the antecedent)

---

[4] This section is based on Enderton, *A Mathematical Introduction to Logic* [17]. But any conventional book devoted to formal logic would do.

[5] In early texts on logic, sometimes ($\supset$) was used for implication, purely because of its rightward-pointing appearance (and lack of modern typesetting methods). If you think of propositions as describing the sets (that satisfy them), however, that symbol is oriented precisely the wrong way.

[6] It has been said that "There are two situations in which people behave like animals: one is when behind the wheel of a car; and the other is when discussing concrete syntax."

and the *wff* on its right (still called the consequent), which relation we explain just below.

In some (older) mathematical texts one can even find "$\therefore$" (therefore) for our "$\Rightarrow$" and "$\because$" (because of) for our "$\Leftarrow$". (You won't find them in more recent works. However an *advantage* is that they are harder to confuse with $\Rightarrow$ and $\Leftarrow$, the same advantage enjoyed for example by "whence", "thence" and "hence". If you spot one, do savour it: but it is better not to use them.)

Sometimes however one speaks of "assumptions" and "conclusions" instead of left-hand side or antecedent etc. And sometimes there can be several assumptions and several conclusions on either side, usually separated by commas. (We do not use that here, however.)

semantic entailment is what we are principally concerned with here, that $\mathcal{A} \Rightarrow \mathcal{B}$ or $\mathcal{A} \vDash \mathcal{B}$ (with the double bar in the latter case) means "In *every* state, if $\mathcal{A}$ is True in that state then so is $\mathcal{B}$." There are reversed versions as well.

logical entailment is what is meant by $\mathcal{A} \vdash \mathcal{B}$, that is that you can *prove by following syntactic (and very precise) rules* that $\mathcal{A} \vDash \mathcal{B}$. The difference is a bit like using a truth table (for propositions, which would be $\vDash$) or instead using the rules in this Appendix E (which would be $\vdash$). Although we list almost 100 rules, in fact fewer than 10 of them –plus a few rules of inference– are needed to be able to prove all the rest:[7] but "starting from first principles" every time is a tedious business. Far better is to become familiar with as many as you can.[8]

In this text however we are not making a distinction between semantic and logical entailment, because that is more about logic *itself* than how to use it in everyday life: and so we use $\Rightarrow$ for both. Nevertheless...

soundness (and completeness, just below) is a property of logic itself, and is absolutely fascinating. *Soundness* of the logic means that if $\mathcal{A} \vdash \mathcal{B}$ holds then so does $\mathcal{A} \vDash \mathcal{B}$, that is if we use our rules from App. E.2 to reason propositionally then a truth table would agree with our conclusion.

Usually, in presentations of logic for its own sake, the number of symbols and the rules applying to them is kept to a minimum: for propositional logic you need only three rules[9] (called propositional axioms) and only two propositional connectives, to be able to express and prove everything — provided you also allow "If you have proved $\mathcal{A}$ and you have proved $\mathcal{A} \Rightarrow \mathcal{B}$ then you have (are deemed to have) proved $\mathcal{B}$ as well." (That's called "*modus ponens*" and is a *rule of inference*, not an axiom.) The reason for keeping things small is that it makes it easier to prove things *about* the logic... for example, its soundness.

completeness is also a property of logic itself, but goes the other way: it is that if $\mathcal{A} \vDash \mathcal{B}$ holds then so does $\mathcal{A} \vdash \mathcal{B}$. In other words, if a truth table shows something to be correct (by brute force) then you could show the same thing by using the right logical rules in the right order (plus cleverness and persistence).

implication (reprise) In logic (i.e. in life) there are at least five kinds of implication, all meaning more or less "if... then... " But they apply to different things, and keeping them clearly separated is one of the crucial things that makes logic –and therefore checking program correctness– possible (and so interesting!) Here they are:

    1. Ordinary "implies" is used in everyday speech.

---

[7] Any book on formal logic explains how that's done. It's quite astonishing that it's possible [17].

[8] A mistake made by many high-school students is to learn only a few trigonometric identities, the ones with simple left-hand sides, because their right-hand sides can be derived "on the fly" as needed (for example in an exam). But they pay for that in later life, because the way those identities are used *in practice* is to recognise a complicated *right*-hand side and replace it by its simpler left-hand side.

[9] Compare the more-than-50 we have here in App. E.2.)

2. The symbol ⇒, or →, makes a bigger *wff* from two smaller ones, and that bigger *wff* is True *in a particular state unless* the antecedent is True in that state but the consequent is False in that state.

3. The symbol ⊨ relates a left-hand *wff* (antecedent) to a right-hand *wff* (consequent): it is *about* those two separately, and does not make a single, bigger *wff* itself; and it means that *in every state* if the antecedent *wff* is True in that state then so will the consequent *wff* be True in that same state.

4. Also the symbol ⊢ relates an antecedent *wff* to a consequent *wff*, but in a different way: again, it is *about* those two and not a *wff* itself. It means that if you can start with the antecedent *wff* and then –following exact and determined-beforehand logical rules (as in this appendix)– end up with the consequent *wff*, then *in every state* if the antecedent *wff* is True in that state then so will the consequent *wff* be True in that same state.

   The key thing here is the fact that there is a *proof*, following rules determined beforehand.

5. A horizontal line, with some ⊢'s above and some below, asserts that if you can prove the ones above, you are deemed to have proved the one below. Here is an example of *modus ponens* written that way:

$$\frac{\vdash \mathcal{A} \qquad \vdash \mathcal{A} \Rightarrow \mathcal{B}}{\vdash \mathcal{B}} \quad .$$

If you read ⊢ $\mathcal{A}$ as "$\mathcal{A}$ is a theorem", then *modus ponens* is in effect a rule about how to infer other theorems from theorems you already have, and that's why it's called a "rule of inference".

Interestingly enough, *modus ponens* itself must be proved: but it is a mathematical theorem *about* the logic (rather than "of" or "in" the logic), and so is called a "meta-theorem".

E.5 Exercises

Exercise E.1 (p. 284) ⇓ Why does **true** ⇒ $\mathcal{A}$ mean "$\mathcal{A}$ is True in all states"? Given that it does, it suggests that it would be convenient to make **true** the default left-hand side of ⇒. Can you suggest more concrete justifications for that?

What could the right-hand default of ⇒ be, and why?

Exercise E.2 (p. 284) If $\mathcal{A} \Rightarrow \mathcal{B}$ is correct, does it follow that $\neg\mathcal{B} \Rightarrow \neg\mathcal{A}$ is also correct? If so, can you apply De Morgan's law to your answer to Ex. E.1?

Exercise E.3 (p. 287) Prove Rule (E.73).
   Hint: Convert the implication to a disjunction, and refer to App. E.3.3.
Why isn't there a similar rule with $(\forall x \cdot \mathcal{A} \Rightarrow \mathcal{B})$ on the left?

Exercise E.4 (p. 287) ⇓ Explain in words why Rule (E.78) is correct. Couldn't the two x's that make $\mathcal{A}$ and $\mathcal{B}$ both True on the left be *different* x's?

Exercise E.5 (p. 287) Prove Rule (E.78) *without* the hand-waving that you were deliberately encouraged to do in Ex. E.4. That is, produce a line-by-line proof in the style of App. E.2.3.
   Hint: The line-by-line equational proof of (E.78), asked for here, is only three lines long: just two steps. Use (E.88) and (E.61). On the other hand, the in-English "model" answer given in Ex. E.4 involved a case analysis *and* two full paragraphs of prose.

Exercise E.6 (p. 288) Show that the following is correct, using the rules in this appendix, where $\mathcal{A}$, $\mathcal{B}$, $\mathcal{C}$ stand for any general formulae, possibly including free occurrences of x:

$$(\exists x \cdot (\mathcal{A} \Rightarrow \mathcal{B}) \wedge (\neg\mathcal{A} \Rightarrow \mathcal{C})) \quad \equiv \quad (\exists x \cdot \mathcal{A} \wedge \mathcal{B}) \vee (\exists x \cdot \neg\mathcal{A} \wedge \mathcal{C}) \,.$$

Exercise E.7 (p. 288) ⇓ Suppose $\mathcal{N}$ contains no free x, but $\mathcal{A}, \mathcal{B}$ might. Prove the correctness of this:

$$(\exists x \cdot (\mathcal{N} \Rightarrow \mathcal{A}) \wedge (\neg\mathcal{N} \Rightarrow \mathcal{B})) \quad \equiv \quad (\mathcal{N} \Rightarrow (\exists x \cdot \mathcal{A})) \wedge (\neg\mathcal{N} \Rightarrow (\exists x \cdot \mathcal{B})) \quad .$$

Exercise E.8 (p. 288) Prove the correctness of this, for any formula $\mathcal{A}$ that might contain a and b:

$$(\exists a \cdot (\forall b \cdot \mathcal{A})) \quad \Rightarrow \quad (\forall b \cdot (\exists a \cdot \mathcal{A})) \,.$$

Is the converse $\Leftarrow$ true? $\boxed{\text{Ex. E.10}}$

Exercise E.9 (p. 288) Show that $(\exists x, y \cdot x \neq y) \Rightarrow (\forall x \cdot (\exists y \cdot x \neq y))$.

The converse $\Leftarrow$ is very straightforward. Together that gives equivalence.

Hint: First, change (temporarily) the consequent to $(\forall z \cdot (\exists w \cdot z \neq w))$, which keeps those variables from getting mixed up with the x, y in the antecedent; at the end, the z, w can be renamed back to x, y by alpha conversion. Then structure the argument as follows: since $x \neq y$, we can't have z equal to both of them: it must differ from one or the other. That is the w we seek. And to refer to the postulated x, y, do your reasoning inside the $\exists x, y$ that introduces them.

Exercise E.10 (p. 291) Try adapting your answer to Ex. E.8 so that you prove also the converse:

$$(\exists a \cdot (\forall b \cdot \mathcal{A})) \quad \Leftarrow \quad (\forall b \cdot (\exists a \cdot \mathcal{A})) \,.$$

What goes wrong?

Illustration of heap behaviour during garbage collection

F.1 Mark–and–sweep garbage collection

The illustrations in Fig. F.1(a)–(g) show a successful mark-and-sweep garbage collection as described in Sec. 17.4: it begins with the heap in a "random" state, where there are not only reachable nodes coloured white (which we want to change to black), but also unreachable nodes coloured black (which we want to change to white). The small numbers in the first illustration, Fig. F.1(a), show the reference counts as well, so that we can see the pair at bottom left would never be collected if we used reference-counting collection. (Pointers to null are omitted in the diagrams.)

Thus we use mark–sweep, where –without interference– the program would be paused, "reachability" propagated from the roots, and then the unreachable nodes collected. The program would then be resumed.

In (h) we show what can go wrong, however, when the "Mutator" program is *not* paused and therefore interferes with the scanning.

F.2 Woodger's scenario

"Woodger's scenario", mentioned in Sec. 17.11.1, is shown in Fig. F.2 adapted to our current black/white and black-counting scheme:

(a) Initially `Root1` points to `Null`, `Root2` points to `T` and `T` points to `Null`. A scan has completed; all nodes are black; and there is no garbage.

(b) The Mutator decides that it will swing `Root1` from `Null` to `T`, and as its first step (in incorrect order, i.e. before the actual swing) it has blackened `T` (which was however already black).

Its second step (f) will be to complete the swing of `Root1` from `N` to `T`; but before it can do that...

(c) ...the Mutator is suspended in State (b), and the Scanner–Collector makes a complete cycle: again all nodes are already black; there is no garbage; and there is therefore nothing for it to do.

It then begins a second cycle: its first step is to whiten all nodes (including `T`), and the state is now as at (c), where the dotted arrow reminds us that the Mutator will blacken `T` when it resumes. But not yet...

(d) ...because the Scanner goes on to blacken the roots `R1`, `R2` and `N`, its initial action before scanning begins. Node `T` however remains white, because it is not a root.

Figure F.1 Illustration of mark–sweep (App. F.1): continued below

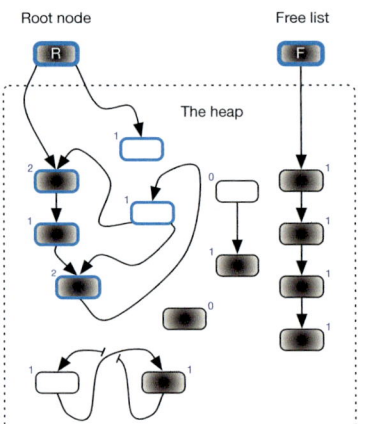

(a) Initially the colours are "randomly" assigned, and don't correspond properly to reachability (except for the two roots R and F).
(The node-pair at bottom left would never be collected using reference counting.)

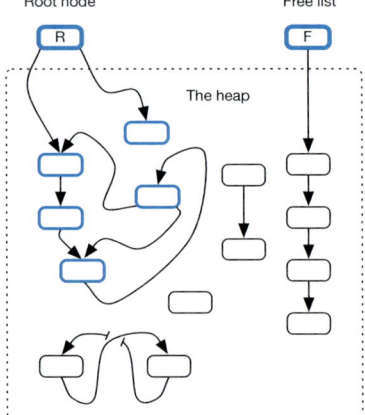

(b) The first step in mark–sweep is to whiten every node: all the blacks in (a) are now white.
(We have removed the reference counts.)

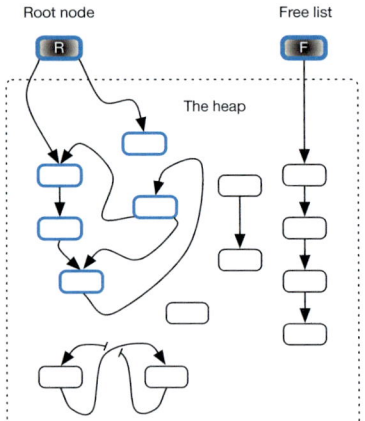

(c) First the roots are blackened. (Here there are only two.)
Then the nodes are examined in arbitrary order, in this example from top to bottom within right to left, in order 1–16 shown in (d).
(Those numbers are not reference counts.)

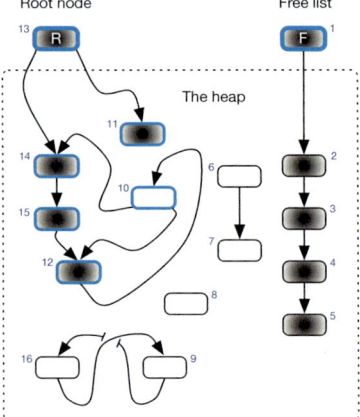

(d) Any black node propagates black to its "children". Here we have scanned all the nodes once; but node 10 will be blackened (from node 12) only on the *next* scan.
Then the third scan will blacken no more nodes, and the overall scanning loop will terminate.

Figure F.1 Illustration of mark–sweep in garbage collection (concluded)

(e) The (top to bottom within right to left here) scanning and propagation finishes when no more propagations occur.

(f) Once that is done, any nodes that are still white must be garbage. (They're coloured grey here, for illustration only.)

(g) The garbage nodes are added to the free list. (Here they have been added at the front.

(h) Here we illustrate possible interference from the Mutator in Step (d).

The collection of garbage has completed successfully in Step (g). But in (h)...

...we show what interference can do, that is if the user's program is *not* paused while the scan is going on. After the Scanner has examined node 11 in (d), but before it examines node 12, the Mutator uses node 12's pointer to find node 10, and changes node 11's null pointer to point there, i.e. to node 10 ✓. And then it sets node 12's pointer to null ✗. The Scanner resumes, and completes in (d) as before –no nodes blackened– but node 10 is reachable and white: instead of (e) we will end up with (h), after which the reachable node 10 will be collected as garbage.

(e) The Scanner now begins the scanning proper, but gets only as far as examining R1 before it is suspended, and the Mutator re-activated. Since R1 already points to black N, the black-count does not increase. But then...

(f) ...the re-activated Mutator finally (and disastrously) completes its swing of Root1 to T, not noticing that T has become white. That is, *it does not blacken* T — because it has done that already (b).

(g) The Mutator continues with a swing of Root2 from T to Null, first colouring N black (which colour it is already), and then...

(h) ...completes the swing of Root2 from T to Null.

(i) The Scanner completes, scanning the remaining nodes R2, N and T. But because R1 has already been scanned, its black is not propagated to T; and because of the Mutator's swing (h), the black at R2 is not propagated either.

The scan completes, because the number of blacks has not increased: it is still 3, and collection can begin.

(j) And so the Collector collects T, because it is white. But it is pointed to by R1, and so is not garbage.

Figure F.2 Woodger's scenario

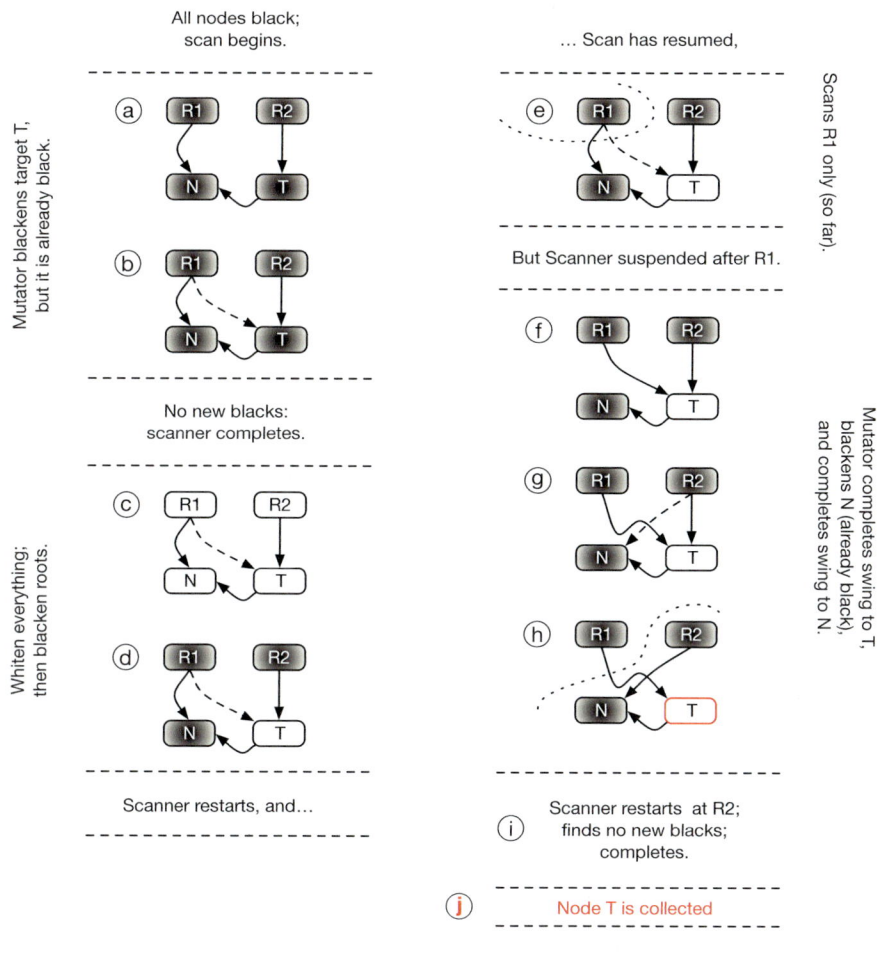

Python-**specific issues**

G.1 Multiple assignments

Multiple assignments in *C* are of the form a= b= c= 3 , for example, in which 3 is assigned to all three of a, b and c. (More precisely, it is read a= (b= (c= 3)) , where for example c= 3 is an expression whose value is 3 but as a "side effect" assigns that value to c.)

Multiple assignments (also perhaps called *parallel* assignments) in **Python** are instead of the form a,b,c= 1,2,3, and assign 1,2,3 to a,b,c respectively. For example, the assignment x,y= y,x swaps the values of x and y.

G.2 Block structure (and assertions)

In **Python**, control structures are as usual indicated explicitly by a keyword at their beginning (with if, while etc.) but the *body* of the structure does not have an explicit keyword to indicate its end: instead, indentation is used. A slight disadvantage of that convention is that postconditions, say *after* a loop rather than after the last statement of the loop body, are identified only because they are "outdented". Thus for example in (3.2), partly repeated here, we have

```
n,r= 0, FUN([])
while n!=N:
  ...
  n= n+1
  {r == FUN(A[:n])}
{n==N and r == FUN(A[:n])}    ;
```

the assertion r == FUN(A[:n]) is *within* the loop, at the end of the body (indicating in fact that the loop invariant is restored). But the assertion n==N and r == FUN(A[:n]) is *outside* the whole loop, is in fact the loop's postcondition: its invariant *and* the negation of its guard.

The only indication of the difference is that the second assertion is out-dented, left-aligned with the while above.

G.3 `for`-**loops vs.** `while`-**loops in** Python

In Python, a typical `for`-loop is written

```
for n in range(start,end,increment): body
```

and –like a `while`-loop– it executes the loop body for varying values of the variable n (in this case), usually the values

```
start
start+increment
start+2*increment
⋮
```

until (but not including) the first value that goes to `end` *or beyond.*

Indeed `for`-loops seem (and sometimes are) an attractive alternative to `while`-loops, because:

(a) You don't need to initialise n explicitly — the loop executes n= `start` automatically for you, before it begins.

(b) You don't need to increment n explicitly — the loop executes n= n+increment automatically for you, at the end of (almost) every iteration.

(c) You don't need to test n explicitly to exit the loop.

So, for example, instead of

```
n= 0
while n!=N:
   body
   n= n+1
```

you might instead write the more concise `for n in range(N): ` *body* .

But (!) you must be careful about the *last* value the variable n takes. And so we give below an example of what programmers should bear in mind when they use `for`-loops. Always consult the precise definition for the language you are using. In Python, the for-loop

```
for n in range(N):
   body
   {n == N-1}
```
(G.1)

establishes ` n == N-1 ` at loop end, provided N>=1. But the "corresponding" while-loop

```
n= 0
while n!=N:
   body
   {n==N}
```

instead establishes ` n==N ` at loop end, provided N>=0.

Thus although the two loops execute the loop bodies the same number of times, and with the same values of ` n `, the two loop forms are *not* equivalent.

The `while`-loop equivalent (in Python) of (G.1) is actually

```
if N>0:
   n= 0
   while True:
      body
      if n >= N-1: break
      n= n+1    .
```

Note that if N==0 in the fragment above, then n is not assigned-to at all (not even set to 0) and that, otherwise, on loop-end the variable n will be N-1, not N.

G.4 Object orientation in Python, and in general

In Python, encapsulated data-types are made using "classes" and "instances" of them; and the procedures and/or functions used to access them are called "methods". The variables within the class, or its instances, are called "attributes."

What we studied in Part II were the initial simple approaches (historically) to encapsulation alone –in particular, without multiple instantiations– so that we could see where the rules for checking encapsulation come from and why they are the way they are.[1]

In modern object-oriented languages, however, i.e. those with classes, instantiation and inheritance, the *maintenance* of coupling invariants, all of those ideas that were set out in Chapter 10, are sometimes quite difficult to enforce by compile-time checks: they are affected by each programming language's choice of "access modifiers" that control the degree to which the interior of a class or instance can be accessed from the outside.

Ex. G.1

To address the encapsulation issue in that broader context, at least partially, each object-oriented language has its own bespoke collection of "access modifiers" which control how the encapsulation "boundary" is allowed to be broken and by whom: the modifiers have names like "private", "protected", "public" and "package"; and each object-oriented language has its own rules for what they mean and what they guarantee.

G.5 Exercises

Exercise G.1 (p. 301) In (10.1) we saw an abstract class implementing a set of maximum size N, and in (10.3) we saw a concrete version of that class, using an array to store the set's values. Both makeEmpty and add were "public" procedures accessible from outside the class. (The procedure find was annotated "local", i.e. not accessible from outside the class.)

What problem might you encounter if one public procedure in a class called another public procedure in the same class, either directly or via other intermediate procedures possibly defined elsewhere?

Exercise G.2 Python has a continue statement that returns control immediately to the beginning of the enclosing while-loop. What is the connection between that practice and the potential problem mentioned in Ex. G.1?

Does a similar problem arise in the use of break?

---

[1] A very early approach to encapsulation was Niklaus Wirth's *Modula*, and its successors [54].

Answers to selected drills

Answer to Drill A.1 (p. 230)

(a) First (x+1)==0, then x==-1.

(b) First (x//2)==2, then x==4 or x==5 .

(c) First 2==2, then True. (You can omit the parentheses if it is clear you don't need them.)

(d) First 0==2, then False.

(e) First x-(x-y-1)>=3, then y>=2.

Answer to Drill A.3 (p. 231)

(a) Just hi-lo, with no +1 or −1 needed. That's why inclusive/exclusive is preferred.

(b) Just $\sum$A[lo:hi]. Here again inclusive/exclusive helps: there's no over- or underlap.

(c) $\sum$A[lo:mid+1].

(d) None, i.e. zero. It does not depend on n.

(e) Its value is 0.

Answer to Drill A.7 (p. 232)

In each of the following we include the "housekeeping" invariant 0<=n<=N implicitly.

(a) A good invariant would be s == $\sum$A[:n] (and the housekeeping 0<=n<=N). The program could then be

```
s,n= 0,0
while n!=N: s,n= s+A[n],n+1   .
```

(b) A good invariant would be s == MAX A[:n] if going from low to high. The program could then be

```
{PRE: N>0}
mx,n= A[0],1
while n!=N: mx,n= mx max A[n],n+1   .
```

(c) The postcondition for your program (a) should be {POST: s==$\sum$A}.

(d) There should be a precondition {PRE: N>=0} at the beginning of your program for item (a).

(e) A good invariant is b == "a is in A[:n]". The program could be

```
b,n= False,0
while n!=N: b,n= b or (A[n]==a), n+1   .
```

For efficiency, you might insert a break, however, to get instead

```
b,n= False,0
while n!=N:
  if A[n]==a: b= True; break
  n= n+1   .
```

(f) A good invariant would be "a is not in A[:n]." That invariant suggests that if a is not there at all then n==N should hold finally.

The program could be

```
n= 0
while n!=N and A[n]!=a: n= n+1   .
```

Answer to Drill A.9 (p. 233)

(a) The increasing variant could be n bounded above by the constant N, or it could be the decreasing N-n, bounded below by 0.

(b) The decreasing variant n could be bounded below by 0.

(c) As for (a). The program needs the precondition N>0 to ensure that the variant n is bounded above by N, which it wouldn't be if n were initialised to 1 when N==0.

(d) As for (c). Whether the *in*variant describes largest or smallest does not affect the loop's termination.

Answer to Drill A.12 (p. 234)
It's still true: if $A \cap B$ is empty then it's a subset of both A, B because the empty set is a subset of any set.

Answer to Drill A.14 (p. 234)

(a) "if A then B" is $A \Rightarrow B$.

(b) "A if B" is $A \Leftarrow B$.

(c) "A unless B" is $A \Leftrightarrow \text{not } B$.

(d) "A if and only if B" is $A \Leftrightarrow B$.

(e) "A just when B" is (also) $A \Leftrightarrow B$.

(f) "A only if B" is $A \Rightarrow B$.

(g) "A iff B" is (again) $A \Leftrightarrow B$.

Answer to Drill A.17 (p. 235)
Use the identity for natural (i.e. non-negative) numbers

$$(a-b)(c-d) + ad + bc = ac + bd \quad,$$

which even negative-number deniers will accept provided $a \geq b$ and $c \geq d$, because in that case no negative numbers are involved. Then postulate that the rule should apply to negative numbers too. Take as an example $a = c = 0$ and $b = d = 1$, in which case the above becomes

$$(0-1)(0-1) + 0 \cdot 1 + 1 \cdot 0 = 0 \cdot 0 + 1 \cdot 1 \quad,$$

i.e. that $-1 \times -1 = 1$.

The idea behind this question is that it illustrates the way we discover things like $\sum [] == 0$, because for non-empty sequences you have

$$\sum (as + bs) \quad == \quad \sum as + \sum bs \quad .^1$$

If you extend *that* rule (to the empty case) you get

$$\sum [] + \sum as \quad == \quad \sum([] + as) \quad == \quad \sum as \quad .$$

Similarly

$$\text{MAX}[] \text{ max MAX as} \quad == \quad \text{MAX}([] + as) \quad == \quad \text{MAX as} \quad ,$$

so that MAX [] must be $-\infty$.

Answer to Drill A.19 (p. 235)

(a) {x==0} x= x+1 {x==1}

(b) {x==8 or x==9} x= x//2 {x==4}

(c) {x==1} y= x*x-2*x+1 {y==0}

(d) {x==1 or x==2} y= x*x-3*x+1 {y==0}

(e) {False} y= x*x+1 {y==0}

Answer to Drill A.20 (p. 235)

(a) {x==X and y==Y}
   {y==Y and x==X}
   {y==Y and (x+y)-y == X}
   x= x+y
   {y==Y and x-y==X}
   {x == (x-y)+Y and x-y == X}
   {x == X+Y and (x-y)==X}
   y= x-y
   {x == X+Y and y==X}

   These three assertions are equivalent; but in general the upper must imply the lower.

(b) {x==X and y==Y}
   {x+Y == X+Y and y==Y}
   { (x+y)==X+Y and y==Y}
   x= x+y
   {x == X+Y and y==Y}
   {x == X+Y and (X+Y)-y == X}
   {x == X+Y and (x-y)==X}
   y= x-y
   {x == X+Y and y==X}
   {x-X == Y and y==X}
   { (x-y) == Y and y==X}
   x= x-y
   {x==Y and y==X}

---

^{1} Remember that (+) is sequence concatenation (on the left).

Answer to Drill A.22 (p. 236)

They are

(a) { *pre* } *init* { *inv* } — establish the invariant before the loop.

(b) { *inv* and *test* } *body* { *inv* } — maintain the invariant inside the loop.

(c) *inv* and not *test* $\Rightarrow$ *post* — establish the postcondition after the loop.

Answer to Drill A.24 (p. 237)

All of them.

Answer to Drill A.26 (p. 238)

The invariants are "ℓ is the length of a longest almost-consecutive x-run in `A[:n]`" and "e is the length of a longest almost-consecutive x-*suffix* of `A[:n]` ."

Answer to Drill A.28 (p. 238)

The key to this algorithm is clearly the inequality `bL<=r<=bH` that ensures (A.7); and – remembering that `b,c` are the numbers of remaining bears, children respectively– an invariant `bL<=⌊b/c⌋` and `⌈b/c⌉<=bH` would achieve it.

To avoid a multitude of special cases, we use these two general facts about floors and ceilings: for all integers i and reals r we have[2]

$$i \leq \lfloor r \rfloor \quad \equiv \quad i \leq r$$
$$\text{and} \quad \lceil r \rceil \leq i \quad \equiv \quad r \leq i \quad . \tag{H.1}$$

The inequality

$$\lfloor b/c \rfloor \quad \leq \quad \left\lfloor \frac{b - \lceil b/c \rceil}{c-1} \right\rfloor \tag{H.2}$$

describes the case where a child receives the maximum handout $\lceil b/c \rceil$ (the second term in the numerator on the right), and yet the lower bound calculated from the b, c remaining afterwards has not decreased as a result. Using (H.1) several times, we establish (H.2) as follows without –note!– needing to consider awkward special cases:

$$\lfloor b/c \rfloor \leq \left\lfloor \frac{b - \lceil b/c \rceil}{c-1} \right\rfloor$$

$\equiv \quad \lfloor b/c \rfloor \leq \frac{b - \lceil b/c \rceil}{c-1}$ "(H.1) upper statement"

$\equiv \quad (c-1)\lfloor b/c \rfloor \leq b - \lceil b/c \rceil$ "arithmetic"

$\equiv \quad \lceil b/c \rceil \leq b - (c-1)\lfloor b/c \rfloor$ "arithmetic"

$\equiv \quad b/c \leq b - (c-1)\lfloor b/c \rfloor$ "(H.1) lower statement"

$\equiv \quad b/c - b + c\lfloor b/c \rfloor \leq \lfloor b/c \rfloor$ "arithmetic"

$\equiv \quad b/c - b + c\lfloor b/c \rfloor \leq b/c$ "(H.1) upper statement"

$\equiv \quad \lfloor b/c \rfloor \leq b/c \quad ,$ "arithmetic"

which is trivially true, by definition of $\lfloor \cdot \rfloor$.

Although that might have seemed a lot of reasoning, each step is strongly suggested by the one before and (H.1) — thus it might take time, but not too much insight.

The upper bound is treated similarly.

---

[2] These two equivalences (H.1) express that the functions floor and ceiling together form a *Galois* connection between integers and reals, as noted for example by Roland Backhouse [5].

Now –finally– we turn to the actual program. We use (H.1) to modify the first part of our proposed invariant –again, to avoid having to worry about dividing by zero– so that it becomes

$$c*bL \ <= \ b \ <= \ c*bH \qquad . \tag{H.3}$$

And so we must consider the maintenance of the invariant (H.3) by the loop in (A.5), whose loop body is (H.4) below: that is what we must check. Read its comments from bottom to top, remembering that each assertion must be implied by the one before:

```
{PRE: c*bL <= b <= c*bH and c!=0} # Invariant, guard
# Proved above.
{(c-1)⌊b/c⌋ <= b-⌈b/c⌉   and   b-⌊b/c⌋ <= (c-1)⌈b/c⌉}
"Set r to some integer such that ⌊b/c⌋ <= r <= ⌈b/c⌉."
{(c-1)⌊b/c⌋ <= b-r <= (c-1)⌈b/c⌉} # From PRE above.
{(c-1)bL <= b-r <= (c-1)bH} # Substitution.
b,c= b-r,c-1 # Recall App. B.1.1.
{POST: c*bL <= b <= c*bH} # Invariant of loop.
```
(H.4)

And finally: when the program has terminated with c==0 we have 0<=b<=0, that is (A.6), from the invariant.

Answers to selected exercises

Answer to Exercise 1.2 (p. 18)

With the requirements removed, and all assertions written in the $\{\cdots\}$ form, the program becomes

```
# --- Find the maximum of all elements in A[0:N].
{ 0<=N }
m= -∞
for n in range(N): # INV: 0<=n<=N and m == MAX A[0:n]
  { 0<=n<N and 0<=n<=N and m;== MAX A[0:n] }
  { 0<=n+1<=N and (m max A[n]) == MAX A[0:n+1] }
  m= m max A[n]
  { 0<=n+1<=N and m == MAX A[0:(n+1)] }
  # There is a hidden n= n+1 below, implicit in the "for".
  # n= n+1
  { 0<=n<=N and m == MAX A[0:n] } # ...mostly.
# m == MAX A[0:N]    ,
```

where the extra `0<=n<N` comes from the range-expression `n in range(N)` of the `for`-loop. And then the check we have to do is

$$
\begin{aligned}
& \texttt{0<=n<N} \quad \text{and} \quad \texttt{m} \qquad\quad \texttt{== MAX A[0:n]} \\
\Rightarrow\ & \texttt{0<=n+1<=N and (m max A[n]) == MAX A[0:(n+1)]} \quad .
\end{aligned}
$$

The qualifier "mostly" reminds us that Python's `for`-loop does *not* increment `n` on the very last iteration: the last value that `n` takes in this loop is `N-1` — and so it's the *previous* assertion in the loop we must rely on for the program's overall postcondition. See App. G.3.

Answer to Exercise 1.3 (p. 19)

The exact text of the condition, after substitution, is

$$
\texttt{0<=(n+1)<=N and (s+A[n]) == } \sum \texttt{A[0:(n+1)]}
$$

except that parentheses have been added.

Adding parentheses is usually a good idea: you can always remove most of them; but it occasionally avoids later calculational mistakes that might arise for example from substituting `c+d` for `b` in `a*b`. (See "operator precedence" in App. D.9.)

Answer to Exercise 1.5 (p. 19)
This one you have to do yourself!

Answer to Exercise 1.7 (p. 20)

```
# --- Calculate the continued fraction
# --- corresponding to sequence A[0:N].
# PRE: N>0 and all elements of A[0:N] are integers.
n= N-1
f= A[n]
# INV: f is the continued fraction for A[n:N].
while n!=0:
  n= n-1
  f= A[n]+1/f
# POST: f is the continued fraction for A[0:N].
```


Answer to Exercise 1.8 (p. 21)
The program is

```
# --- If 1/1/1980 was Day 1,
# --- and today is Day d counting from there,
# --- determine the Year y of today.
# PRE: d>=1 and "Today is the dth day counting from 1/1/80."

y= 1980
# INV: d>=1 and "Today is the dth day counting from 1/1/y."
while d>DiY(y):
  d,y= d-DiY(y),y+1
# 1<=d<=DiY(y) and "Today is the dth day counting from 1/1/y."

# POST: y is today's year.
```

See Ex. 1.9 for checking that the program terminates.

Answer to Exercise 1.10 (p. 21)
The variant for (1.20) is just r, bounded below by 0.

Answer to Exercise 1.16 (p. 22)
No, there is no intermediate assertion that checks — there cannot be, because the program itself does not work, which can easily be shown by a counter-example.

The reason is that the substitution-generated assumption is the weakest one that can be placed before the second program component and still will achieve the overall postcondition: if *it* doesn't work, nothing else will.

Answer to Exercise 1.17 (p. 22)
See Fig. I.1.

Figure I.1 Flowchart for the answer to Ex. 1.17

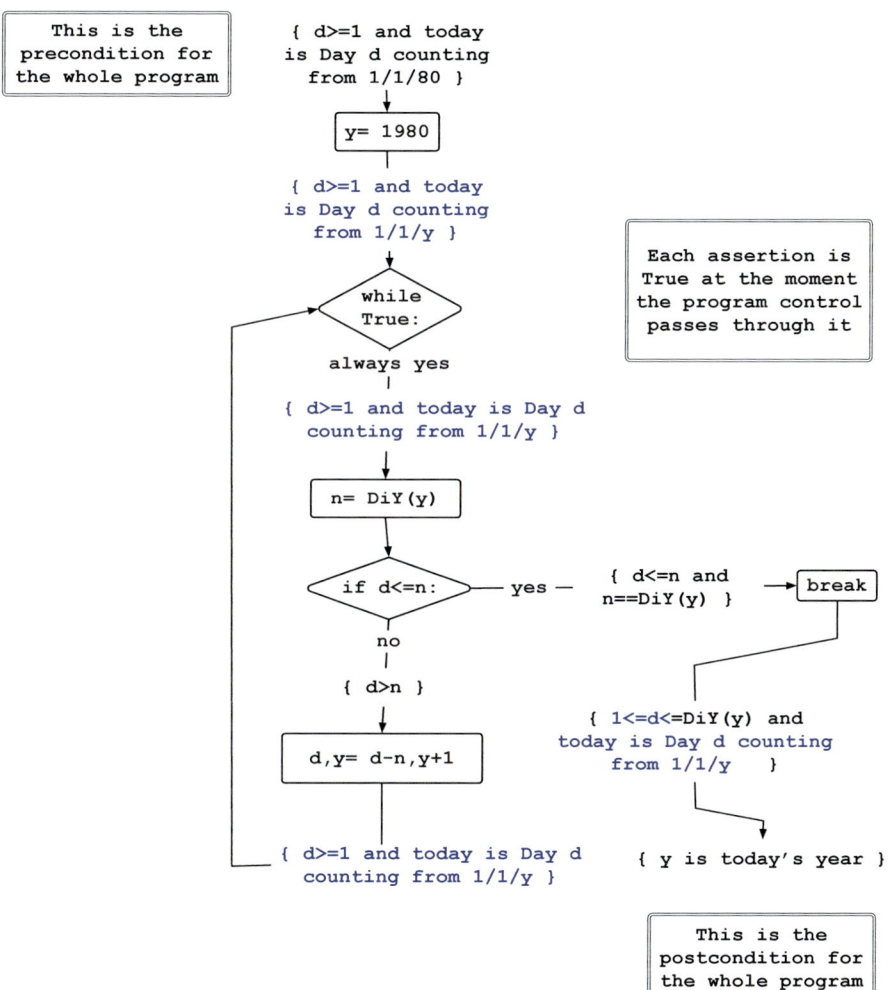

The assertion d>=1 and "today is Day d counting from 1/1/y" (as Day 1) appears three times on the left of the flowchart above, in different positions but the same at each occurrence: that is because it is the invariant. It is also carried through the break.

Answer to Exercise 1.19 (p. 22)

For a matrix of size n the determinant is a sum of $n!$, that is n factorial, products of n scalars. For the given three matrices, the sums are of

$$1! \quad \text{product of length 1} \quad a$$
$$2! \quad \text{products of length 2} \quad ad \quad -bc$$
$$3! \quad \text{products of length 3} \quad aei \quad -afh \quad bfg \quad -bdi \quad cdh \quad -ceg \quad .$$

When n is zero, that's a sum of 0! instances of the product of 0 numbers, that is 1 instance of 1. Thus the empty matrix has determinant 1.

Answer to Exercise 2.1 (p. 31)

Because of the conjunct `if n>=2:` , the call to `Bad` cannot index `A[-1]`. And the highest value `n` can take in the loop is `N-1`, in which case `Bad(n-2)` indexes `A[N-1-2]`, `A[N-1-1]`, `A[N-1]`, that is `A[N-3]`, `A[N-2]`, `A[N-1]`.

The for-loop version uses the same invariants; it is

```
# PRE: Bad(n) is well defined for 0<=n and n+3<=N.

# Inv1(n):  As in (2.5).
# Inv2(n):  As in (2.5).

good,low= 0,0
for n in range(N):     # Inv1(n) and Inv2(n) and 0<=n<=N
  if n>=2 and Bad(n-2): low= n-1
  good= good max (n+1-low)

# POST: Inv1(N).
```

No, it is not true. Although if `N` is at least 2 then indeed `good` must be at least 2; if `N` is 0 or 1 then `good` will be only `N`.

Answer to Exercise 2.3 (p. 31)

The caterpillar operates *conceptually* in two nested loops, although in the code given we have collapsed them to one: the outer loop is the hopping from one non-extendable *Good* subsegment to the next, as the remark suggests; and the inner loop is the step-by-step extension of the caterpillar's head, until it encounters the next *Bad* subsegment. The suggested invariant holds only for the outer loop; nevertheless, it is useful to be aware of it.

If we had written two nested loops then the invariant for the inner loop would be that the caterpillar's tail is resting on a *Bad* subsegment, and the head is not yet resting on the next *Bad* subsegment — i.e. that it can move another step forward.

Answer to Exercise 3.2 (p. 49)

(a) Replace (just) `A` in the postcondition by the more explicit `A[0:N]`.

(b) Introduce a new variable `n` and rewrite the postcondition to be

$$r == \text{FUN}(A[n:]) \text{ and } n==0 \quad .$$

(c) Split the conjunct (Sec. 3.2), and use the invariant

$$0<=n<=N \text{ and } r == \text{FUN}(A[n:]) \quad .$$

The program becomes

```
# PRE: A is a sequence of length N.
n,r= N, FUN([])
# INV: 0<=n<=N and r == FUN(A[n:])
while n!=0:
  { PRE: 0<n<=N and r == FUN(A[n:]) }
  n= n-1
  { POST: r == FUN(A[n+1:]) }
  ... # Examine A[n], update r.
  { POST: r == FUN(A[n:]) }
# POST: r == FUN(A)      .
```

Answer to Exercise 3.4 (p. 49)
The for-loop is

```
# PRE: 0<=N
r= 0
if N!=0:
  for n in range(1,N): r= r max abs(A[n]-A[n-1])
# POST: r == lad(A)      .
```

However –we now notice– when N==1, the iterator range(1,N) will be empty and the for-loop will exit immediately, leaving r set to 0. Since it does that anyway when N==0, we could even simplify the program one step further, to just

```
# PRE: 0<=N
r= 0
for n in range(1,N): r= r max abs(A[n]-A[n-1])
# POST: r == lad(A)      .
```

Would that be a good idea?

Answer to Exercise 3.8 (p. 50)
We used it in the checking of program fragments (3.6) and (3.7) of program (3.5). The precondition of the assignment m= p+1 is (only) that A[p]<x; but the postcondition (i.e. after the assignment) requires A[:p+1]<x, leaving A[m:p]<x still to be established — which follows from A[p]<x provided A is ascending.

For (3.7) the reasoning is similar.

Answer to Exercise 3.12 (p. 51)
Although the algorithm in Ex. 3.10 is correct –it *does* take the citizen to Rome from Paris by a shortest (i.e. green) route– it's the *checking* of the algorithm that concerns us.

Suppose for a contradiction that there were a shorter route P′, from Paris to c, than the P the citizen actually took by following the algorithm. Then the citizen could construct a shorter *overall* route from Paris to Rome by replacing P with P′ — contradicting that the algorithm is correct.

Answer to Exercise 3.15 (p. 52)

In (3.15)'s first case, r is assigned 1 when r==0; so that assignment can be replaced by r= r+1. In the third case, we have x==A[n], and so an added assignment x= A[n] has no effect. Once both of those replacements are done, the code in the first and third cases is the same.

Answer to Exercise 3.18 (p. 52)

The reason for visiting all the empty segments is that being able to leave them out in *this* program is due essentially to the coincidence that the function $(\sum)$ applied to an empty segment gives the identity of max *and* that the function does not depend on where the (empty) segments are, that is on their specific indices. If either of those facts were not true, we would be risking an error "downstream" if someone else borrowed our program structure and altered it in order to "max" something other than summation $\sum$. It's thus a *social* responsibility as well as a technical one.

So we retain the "visit everywhere" structure but avoid the indexing error by exiting early: ironically, the attempted access to A[N] is not used anyway, since the for-loop exits immediately after it. The program becomes

```
m= 0
for l in range(N+1):   # Inv1: m==muh(l,0)
  s,h= 0,l
  # Inv2: m==muh(l,h) and s==∑A[l:h]
  while True:
    m= max(m,s)
    if h==N: break
    s,h= s+A[h],h+1     ,
```

and is $O(N^2)$.

Answer to Exercise 3.19 (p. 52)

For the $O(N^2)$ version, we adjust the for-loop ranges so that only non-empty subsegments are summed:

```
m= -∞ # At this point, we are MAX'ing over no elements.
for l in range(N): # Inv1: m==muh(l,N)
  s= 0
  for h in range(l+1,N): # Inv2: m==muh(l,h) and s==∑A[l:h]
    m= m max s
    s= s+A[h]    .
```

The invariants look the same, but in fact the definition of muh has changed behind the scenes: "up to here" now includes only non-empty segments.

For the $O(N)$ version, we adjust the definitions of mss and mes as well. Only the update to e is affected:

```
# Pre: 0<=N
m,e= -∞,0
for n in range(N): # Inv: 0<=n<=N and m==mss(n) and e==mes(n)
  e= e+A[n] max A[n] # Establish e==mes(n+1) given e==mes(n).
  m= m max e # Establish m==mes(n+1) given m==mes(n) and e==mes(n+1).
# Post: m= mss A    .
```

Answer to Exercise 3.22 (p. 53)
In both cases the initial `m= -∞` can be replaced by `m= A[0]`, because we know the maximum segment sum must be at least the sum of the (length-1) segment `A[0:1]`.
   The new invariant is `m == A[0] max mss(n)`.

Answer to Exercise 4.1 (p. 60)
We actually have `{ b<=a and a!=b }`, where the second conjunct is from the `while`-condition.
   It's important because it is used to check that the invariant `a>0` is maintained, which –in turn– is necessary to check that the variant strictly decreases on every iteration (in this case, the very next one).

Answer to Exercise 4.2 (p. 60)
Working from postcondition to precondition gives

```
         ss == 20*(L+p) + (S+s)
↓ substitution from final assignment S= (S-s)%20
         ss == 20*(L+p) + (S-s)%20 + s
simplifies to
         ss == 20*L + 20*p + (S-s)%20 + s
↓ substitution from initial assignment L= L-p + (S-s)//20
         ss == 20*(L-p + (S-s)//20) + 20*p + (S-s)%20 + s
simplifies to
         ss == 20*L + 20*((S-s)//20) + (S-s)%20 + s
using (4.6) simplifies to
         ss == 20*L + (S-s) + s
simplifies to
         ss == 20*L + S    .
```

The significance of the reasoning is that it shows how the program correctly debits £p/s from the account £L/S. The value of `ss` is the number of shillings in the account, once the pounds have been converted.

Answer to Exercise 4.4 (p. 60)
Nothing bad: the program works regardless. See Ex. 4.2.

Answer to Exercise 4.6 (p. 60)
The connection is that, say, the ordering of pairs

```
(0,0),(0,1),...,(0,N),(1,1),(1,2)...
```

is indeed lexicographic (ascending), since `(0,N)` is followed by `(1,1)` in which the second element has potentially *decreased* from N to 1. But it is restricted to those pairs where the first element is no more than the second.

Answer to Exercise 4.7 (p. 61)
We don't need an upper bound for B: see Sec. 4.4.
   The pair `(a,b)` cannot lexicographically decrease forever: the `a` component must stop decreasing at some point, since it's bounded below: after that, all the `a` values are the same — and from then on only the `b` values change. But they too are bounded below, no matter how big `b` might be at the moment `a` stops decreasing.

Answer to Exercise 4.11 (p. 61)

A family with only one member has that member as a minimum, a descendant of all others because there *are* no others. Another example is just two parents and one child: the child is a minimum element.

Answer to Exercise 4.12 (p. 61)

Use the length of the list.

It's not a lexicographic variant. A lexicographic variant for strings depends on the actual value of the string: remember "banana" and "apple␣". This variant depends only on the string's length.

Answer to Exercise 4.19 (p. 62)

Choose any row or column with a strictly negative sum, and negate it. The (increasing) variant is the total of all numbers in the matrix, bounded above by the sum of their absolute values.

What's interesting is about this example is (1) that the variant has little or nothing to do with how many iterations you must make (or have made): it's not "counting" anything. And (2) the variant does not actually have to reach its bound for termination to have occurred.

Answer to Exercise 4.21 (p. 63)

Are you sure you don't want to try this yourself, before looking up the answer?

Answer to Exercise 4.22 (p. 64)

Termination is proved with a strictly increasing variant expression and its upper bound.

Let the circles be the integer number line, extending indefinitely from low to high in both directions; number the P people from $p=0$ sequentially to $p=P–1$ by tallying them from the lowest occupied circle to the highest, with multiple occupancies in a circle c being tallied within that circle. For example, initially person $p=0$ could be on circle $c=2$, people 1, 2 together on circle 3 and person 3 on circle 10 (far away). Circles 4–9 would be empty, and the overall length of the queue, from 2 to 10 including the empty circles in between, would be 9.

An increasing variant V is then the sum of the squares of the people's positions, in this initial state $2^2 + 3^2 + 3^2 + 10^2 = 122$, because a single separation –one moves lower and one moves higher– increases that variant by exactly 2, no matter where it occurs. Here the only possible move leads to $2, 2, 4, 10$ where $V=124$, and the next move would be to $1, 3, 4, 10$ giving $V=126$ (and termination).[1]

Now –to bound V above– we *confine* the queue, using as invariant that each person p can never be more than p higher than where she started. For p can move 1 step higher *only* when she is sharing a circle with $p–1$ who –by the invariant– is herself no more than $p–1$ higher than where *she* started. Thus also p is no more than (the same) $p–1$ from where *she* started, since p cannot have started lower than $p–1$ did.

And so, after her move, person p is no higher than $p–1$ plus that 1 step, that is no higher than the p from where she started. That shows the invariant to have been preserved.

Our invariant therefore confines the queue on the high side, with a symmetric argument sufficing for low. In the example above the queue is confined to positions $(2–3)\cdots(10+3)$ inclusive, which bounds its V by 4×13^2.

---

[1] The variant above was motivated by statistical variance.

Answer to Exercise 5.1 (p. 70)

The implication to be checked is $V==(N-n)>0 \Rightarrow V>(N-(n+1))>=0$. In general variants can either strictly decrease, or increase, provided they are bounded below or above respectively, because they can always be reduced to "strictly decrease while bounded below by 0" as we did here.

Answer to Exercise 5.6 (p. 71)

(a) `range(?1?)` should be `range(N,0,-1)`.

(b) `range(?2?)` should be `range(i-1)` and `?5?` should be `A[:i-1]<=A[i-1]`.

(c) The code of the inner-loop body should be

```
{PRE: A[:j]<=A[j] }
if A[j]>A[j+1]: A[j],A[j+1]= A[j+1],A[j]
{PRE: A[:j+1]<=A[j+1] }
```

(d) For the `else`-part, we see that `A[:j]<=A[j]` and `A[j]<=A[j+1]` together already imply `A[:j+1]<=A[j+1]`. For the `if`-part, we note that swapping them with the statement `A[j],A[j+1]= A[j+1],A[j]` reduces to the `else`-part.

Answer to Exercise 5.8 (p. 72)

The invariant is `noSwaps` $\Rightarrow$ `A[:n+1] is sorted`. The variant is the number of inversions in `A[0:N]`, which every swap strictly decreases. (An *inversion* in a sequence is a pair of elements that are out of order: count all pairs, adjacent or not.) The assertion `???` is `A[0:N] is sorted`, which follows from the invariant and the `if`-condition `noSwaps`.

Answer to Exercise 8.1 (p. 91)

```
# --- Determine whether the "set" qs contains element s.

b= False
for q in qs: # INV: b == "s is in qs so far examined."
  if q==s: {"s in qs"} b= True; break
{ If b then "s is in qs so far examined."
       else "s is not in qs at all."       }

# POST: b == "s is in qs."
```

Handling the **break** is interesting, and takes a bit of practice.

At the end of the **for**-loop, the invariant is still true; but we also have the assertion given there. If b is (still) false, then the loop exited normally and "qs so far examined" has become "all of qs". If b is True, however, the "so far examined" is possibly only "some of it". But if s is in some of qs, it is also in all of qs.

Another, more concise version of the program is

```
for q in qs:
  if q==s: {"s in qs"} b= True; break
  else b= False {"s not in qs"}     ,
```

which uses an **else** for the **for**-loop, executed only if the loop completes all iterations. (If this were in a function, it could be made even more concise, using explicit **return True** and **return False**.)

In both cases, however, it's better to develop the **while**-loop version first, using the normal invariant technique, and then adapt it to a more concise formulation (if there is one).

Answer to Exercise 8.4 (p. 91)

The simplification is a specific example of "Boolean arithmetic" (Appendix D), in this case the two facts

$$
\begin{array}{llll}
& \text{P and False} & \equiv & \text{False} \\
\text{and} & \text{False or Q} & \equiv & \text{Q} \quad,
\end{array}
$$

for any P and Q.

Answer to Exercise 8.6 (p. 91)

Here is how the two postconditions differ. With the missing 0<=n<=N included, they become

$$
\begin{array}{lll}
& \text{0<=n<=N and (A[n]==x if x}\in\text{A else n==N)} & (8.3) \\
\textit{and} & \text{0<=n<=N and (A[n]==x if n!=N else x}\notin\text{A)} & (8.6) \quad.
\end{array}
$$

The first case (8.3) is *not defined* when x∈A and n==N — it (tries to) evaluate A[N], which is an indexing error. The second case (8.6) cannot get an indexing error.

"But what does that matter?" you might say. "The program can never end up in the state x∈A and n==N anyway."

The point brought out here is that *you cannot expect someone to have to reason about what the program* does *in order to understand what its postcondition* means. (Think about it.) Precisely the reverse is true: it is the postcondition's job to tell you what the program establishes, not the program's job to make the postcondition well defined. (See also program (12.1).)

Here is the methodological reason we end up preferring the second version, i.e. (8.6). When originally we formulated the postcondition (8.3) we were (probably) thinking "operationally", i.e. "Look for x and, if you do (or do not) find it, set n appropriately." We were "executing the potential algorithm in our heads".

Guided by a more systematic approach, our postcondition delivered a means (i.e. testing n==N) of determining whether x∈A or not and –if so– where it is. That's precisely what any code following this program is likely to need.

And in case all this seems "overly subtle", bear in mind that it's *precisely* this kind of subtlety that is overlooked by human-led code reviews and occasionally unlocks a disaster. If programming weren't so full of subtle traps like these, we wouldn't have to be so careful when doing it.

Answer to Exercise 8.7 (p. 91)

Using the same case analysis gives

$$
\begin{array}{ll}
& \text{n==N and x}\notin\text{A[0:N] and True} \\
\text{or} & \text{n!=N and x}\notin\text{A[:n] and x==A[n]} \quad,
\end{array}
$$

which simplifies to

$$
\text{x}\notin\text{A if n==N else x==A[n] and x}\notin\text{A[:n]} \quad.
$$

This is stronger than the postcondition we gave for the original (8.3).

Answer to Exercise 8.8 (p. 92)
A reasonably concise formulation is

```
n is largest such that 0<=n<=N and x∉A[:n]     .
```

Answer to Exercise 8.10 (p. 92)
The invariant is

```
b == "s in the part of qs examined so far"     .
```

   The checking rule is that when one assertion is followed by another (on a new line), the first must imply the second. (See App. B.2.2.) That implication holds here because the coupling invariant holds at that point too, i.e. that s∈qs and s∈ss are equal: it's a precondition of this function, and the function body did not change it.

Answer to Exercise 8.11 (p. 92)
The simplified code is

```
class Set:  # This is the actual implementation.
   ⋮
   def isIn(s):
     for q in qs:
        if q==s: return True
     return False     ,
```

and it is all right to change it as long as the new code and the old code do exactly the same thing under all conditions that any preconditions guarantee. Again, we can carry out that reasoning entirely separately from all the other work we have done, with no risk of invalidating earlier checks.

Answer to Exercise 9.1 (p. 98)
The basic idea is that the actual parameters of the recursive call assume the role of the state over which the loop iterates: both the invariant and variant are defined over those, and then the same rules apply.

Answer to Exercise 9.4 (p. 99)

```
# --- Calculate the Nth Fibonacci number.
{PRE: N>=0}
f,g=1,0
{f == FIB(0) and g == FIB(-1)}
for n in range(N): # INV: f == FIB(n) and g == FIB(n-1)
  {f == FIB(n) and g == FIB(n-1)}
  {f+g == FIB(n+1) and g == FIB(n-1)}
  f= f+g
  {f == FIB(n+1) and g == FIB(n-1)}
  {f == FIB(n+1) and f-g == FIB(n)}
  g= f-g
  {f == FIB(n+1) and g == FIB(n)}
  # Implicit n= n+1 from for-loop.
  {f == FIB(n) and g == FIB(n-1)}
{POST: f == FIB(N)}
```

Answer to Exercise 10.1 (p. 113)
Without |ss|!=N, program (10.2) would have been just

```
{ PRE: |ss|<=N }
ss= ss ∪ {s}
{ POST: |ss|<=N }      ,
```

and its assignment statement does not check: using substitution (Sec. 5.2) would give the implication |ss|<=N ⇒ |ss ∪ {s}|<=N, which is not valid. The data-type invariant is not maintained.

Answer to Exercise 10.3 (p. 114)
Given that the data-type invariant |ss|<=N must hold at the beginning of add(s), we know from Ex. 10.2 that the assertion can be as weak as

$$|ss|<=N \Rightarrow (|ss|<=N \text{ and } (s \notin ss \Rightarrow |ss|!=N)) ,$$

which simplifies to $s \notin ss \Rightarrow |ss|!=N$.
See Appendix D for more on how to do such simplifications.

Answer to Exercise 10.5 (p. 114)
Each procedure is required to leave the coupling invariant true, and relies on its still being true when the next procedure is called. If the external program can change variables in the coupling invariant *without* calling a procedure in the class, it could falsify the coupling invariant "without the class's knowledge". (Recall Sec. 9.6.)

Answer to Exercise 10.6 (p. 114)
Using **return** i would be incorrect, as (in **Python**) the value of i at that point would be n-1, not n. And if n were 0, in fact i at that point would be undefined.

Answer to Exercise 10.7 (p. 114)
We answer the second question first: "What should the abstract specification of remove(s) do if s is not in ss?" The answer is *"whatever we like"*. When you are writing a specification, it's up to you how you specify the behaviour. If it's useful behaviour then your type will be popular. Otherwise, perhaps not so much. Once you have specified it, however, any implementations must respect your choice.
    If we decide to ignore the $s \notin ss$ case then the extra abstract procedure for (8.7) would be

```
def remove(s): ss= ss-{s}
```

and the corresponding implementation procedure could be

```
def remove(s):
  i= find(s)
  if i<n: ar[i],n= ar[n-1],n-1    .
```

If on the other hand we wanted to specify that you "can't" remove elements that are not there, or more accurately "that you shouldn't try to", then we'd have

```
def remove(s): assert s∈ss; ss= ss-{s}      ,
```

and now the corresponding implementation procedure could be the slightly simpler

```
def remove(s):
  i= find(s)
  ar[i],n= ar[n-1],n-1     ,
```

which would get an index-out-of-range error if called with s∉ss. This is *allowed*, but it might be better to have, "defensively",

```
def remove(s):
  i= find(s)
  assert i<n, "To-be-removed element is not present."
  ar[i],n= ar[n-1],n-1     .
```

But the (second) specification does not *require* that.

Answer to Exercise 10.9 (p. 114)

As we saw in Ex. 10.7, the new procedure remove(s) might simply ignore an attempt to remove an element that is not there. Or it might not. What it *should* do in that case is entirely up to you, since that procedure was not there before. That is why adding new procedures is always allowed.

Removing procedures might be allowed too, but for a different reason. If the procedure is not being used then nobody will notice. If it *is* being used then the program using the data-type will no longer compile. Thus in neither case will the running program become incorrect "in the field". But you would not be popular with your colleagues if suddenly the system were no longer compilable.

If procedures are loaded dynamically at runtime, however, then removing a procedure should not be done: already-installed systems might suddenly fail in the field because they can no longer load the (now missing) procedure.

In terms of engineering practice, removing a procedure "without asking" is probably a bad idea either way.

Answer to Exercise 10.12 (p. 114)

These two versions of Set would be exactly equal in terms of their *behaviour* if we had used the slightly weaker assertion s∉ss⇒|ss|!=N on the left. That would mean that no surrounding program could ever tell the difference: they are related by what they do, not by how they are written. In just the same way the Roman numerals IV are related to the addition 2+2 in Arabic notation: they both mean "four".

In fact the right-hand version of Fig. 10.4 is slightly better than the left because its behaviour is better (not because of the way it's written, or the fact that it uses "real" data-types rather than "pretend" ones). It is guaranteed to work properly even if you add an element when the set is "full", provided that element is already in the set. The left-hand version *might* work properly in that case — but that is not guaranteed.

Answer to Exercise 10.16 (p. 115)

With the explicit assertion, the procedure add(s) would become

```
  ⋮
def add(s):
  assert n==N ⇒ s∈ar
  i= find(s)
  if i==n: ar[n],n= s,n+1     .
  ⋮
```

It might be a good idea to put it in, because it is then easier to check the program that calls add(s) in this version of the class. Rather than having to figure out the assertion by examining the concrete code that follows it, instead the job can be split into two pieces: first check

$$\vdots$$

```
# PRE: n==N ⇒ s∈ar
i= find(s)
if i==n: ar[n],n= s,n+1
# POST: True
```

$$\vdots$$

to make sure that n==N $\Rightarrow$ s∈ar guarantees that add(s) will not crash; and then separately check that the surrounding code guarantees that n==N $\Rightarrow$ s∈ar holds at the point of call. It's another example of defensive programming.

Answer to Exercise 10.17 (p. 115)
It's possibly true.
  It could be argued that the person writing (and checking) the surrounding code will be looking only at the abstract version of the class. After all, as Sec. 10.4 explains, the whole point of the abstract/concrete approach is that you can understand what the concrete one is doing by pretending that it is the abstract one. And the abstract one is usually simpler.
  Yet, on the other hand, someone modifying the concrete version might appreciate seeing the precondition explicitly, rather than having to deduce it from the abstract version.

Answer to Exercise 11.1 (p. 120)
No, it isn't necessary. (It could be considered good documentation, though, an example of defensive programming.) The reason it's not necessary is that the *abstract* program (11.2) contains assert nb!=⟨⟩, and so any arbitrary behaviour that dividing by 0 might cause has been allowed by the specification.

Answer to Exercise 12.1 (p. 128)
Yes, that specification is allowed to change x if it crashes, even though x is not mentioned. A "crash" is allowed to do anything, at least in the model of programming we are using.

Answer to Exercise 12.3 (p. 128)
Although the condition s∉ar[:n] $\Rightarrow$ n!=N is precisely the condition for termination of the concrete code for add(s), that is not where it comes from.
  It is the concrete version of the explicit assumption s∉ss $\Rightarrow$ |ss|!=N of the *abstract* version of add. The fact that it is exactly (or implies, which would be enough) the termination condition of the concrete version of add is a result of the coupling-invariant process.
  If we had used the stronger (but simpler) assumption |ss|!=N for the abstract version of add, then we would have added just n!=N to the PRE for the check in Ex. 12.2. Since that is stronger than what we did use, the check would still succeed.

Answer to Exercise 12.4 (p. 129)
Remaining quite informal, we could write

```
A:[ sequence A is of length N,
    sequence A is sorted ]    ,
```

$$\vdots$$

with an important point however being that the PRE and POST are gone.
  The specification above does not tell the whole story, though: to be more precise we would need also that the elements of A before and after are the same (as a multiset), even if their order has changed. Just how much precision is needed in the specification is usually discovered later, when you need to use its postcondition. Then you can come back and increase the precision, step by step.

In this case the important property is probably that all equal values in A occur together (Inv2) — it does not actually matter that they are in order otherwise. That being so, a better replacement might be

```
A:[ sequence A is of length N,
    the values in A are as before, but now
    all equal values in A are grouped together ]    ,
 ⋮
```

which could later (perhaps by someone else) be *implemented* by a sorting program.

Answer to Exercise 12.5 (p. 129)
Notations (a)–(c) are all used for checking; none of them is part of the executable program. We have been using the #-form for conditions that we would like to retain finally as part of the program's documentation; the { ... }-form is for checks we might discard, used only to help us write the program. And the addition of an annotation PRE or similar is to remind us of what the condition is being used for: again, it does not affect the meaning.

Notations (d) and (e) however are program statements, i.e. not merely conditions used only for checking programs as they are being written. In particular, assert *cond* halts an executing program "abruptly" if the condition does not evaluate to True, useful for testing and defensive programming, whereas the { ... }-form of (b) suggests more that you should be concentrating on checking *beforehand* that the condition can never be false at that point.

And assume *cond* forces the programmer to write code that makes *cond* true at that point, because otherwise the program cannot be compiled to executable code.

Some might argue that there would be no point in performing a runtime test if the program had been checked beforehand. But you never know... and it is sometimes better to be defensive, i.e. extra cautious.

Answer to Exercise 12.6 (p. 129)
If the initial state satisfies *pre* then assert *pre* does nothing, leaving it up to assume x:*post* to change x (if necessary) in a way that makes *post* true, in the final state. If the initial state does not satisfy *pre*, then assert *pre* can do anything, including ignoring the following statement altogether. And that is exactly the description of x:[*pre*,*post*] .

Answer to Exercise 13.1 (p. 144)
Yes, assuming atomicity is reasonable: even if the actual code executed is

```
r0= x      ← Another thread reads x here,
r0= r0+1   ← or here.
x=  r0    ,
```

another thread's reading x in either of those two places would have the same overall effect as its having read x before the whole on-the-single-line x= x+1.

Answer to Exercise 13.2 (p. 144)
This time, we suppose that global x is initially 0, considering

```
{ x==0 }
r0= x      ← Another thread's x= 2 occurs here,
r0= r0+1   ← or here.
x=  r0    .
```

In both cases, the final value of x would then be 1, and the other thread's assignment x= 2 would effectively be "lost".

If we considered x= x+1 with global x to be atomic, however, there would be only the two cases

```
{ x==0 }   ← The other thread's x= 2 occurs here,
x= x+1    .  ← or here.
```

In the first case x is 3 finally, and in the other case x is 2: but in neither case could the final value of x be 1 as it was further above.

Thus here asserting the atomicity of x= x+1 is *not* reasonable: since x is global, the read access and the write access together count as two.

Answer to Exercise 13.5 (p. 144)
Usually the thread suspends itself (it "yields"), explicitly giving control to a scheduler that will then resume other threads (multiprogramming case) or sending the core into a special idle state where it remains until receiving an interrupt. The improved code, taking advantage of that, would be

> while $bb!=$*Th*:
>   "Suspend this thread."   ←*"yield" until resumed.*
>   "Compare $bb with ⊥ and   ← *CAS: Atomic in hardware.*
>   assign *Th* if they are equal."

Answer to Exercise 13.6 (p. 144)
The loop in (13.7) depends for its termination on activity in *other* threads. If its termination is to be guaranteed, a variant must be found whose strict decrease is guaranteed by progress made in those other processes, and which cannot become negative while $bb!=⊥, i.e. showing that execution in those other processes will eventually establish $bb==⊥.

But even that is not enough — it must also be shown that this process will *actually be scheduled* at some point when $bb==⊥. If the scheduler is not "fair", so that the thread cannot make progress because of that unfairness alone, the scheduler is said to be "unfair" and the thread to be "starved".

Answer to Exercise 14.1 (p. 150)
The assertion *assn* does have to be checked for local correctness, i.e. that it is established by *stmt1*, at least if it is needed for subsequent reasoning — for example, if the correct execution of *stmt2* depends on it.

It does not have to be checked for global correctness, however, because no statement in another thread can execute while control in this thread is between *stmt1* and *stmt2*, if we are following the convention that multiple statements on the same line are collectively atomic.

Global invariants do not have to be checked against *stmt1* on its own (or *stmt2* on its own); but they do have to be checked against *stmt1*; *stmt2* together.

Answer to Exercise 14.3 (p. 150)
At the beginning or end of the whole system, none of its statements can execute: either the system has not yet begun or it is already finished. So none of its fragments can interfere with anything.

Answer to Exercise 14.5 (p. 150)
The given reasoning is not circular: even if both "attempted" interferences were to occur, still one –say *stmt1*'s interfering with *pre2*– must have occurred before the other in the interleaving of the threads' executions.

At that point, however, the other assertion *pre1* is still true — because we have assumed that *stmt2* at (14.6) has not yet executed. And so from (14.7) we see that *stmt1*'s attempt to interfere with *pre2* does not succeed.

Figure I.2 Figure 15.2 with added assertions establishing deadlock freedom

$$\{\,\textsc{Pre: not } \texttt{c} \text{ and } \texttt{t}==\bot\,\} \qquad \leftarrow \textit{overall precondition}$$
$$\{\,\textsc{Inv: } \texttt{t}==\bot \Rightarrow \text{not } \texttt{c}\,\} \qquad \leftarrow \textit{global invariant}$$

`# `*`Th1`*` repeats this forever.`	`# `*`Th2`*` repeats this forever.`
"other business 1."	*"other business 2."*
`{ t!=1 }`	`{ t!=2 }`
`await not c: c,t= True,1`	`await not c: c,t= True,2`
`{ c and t==1 }`	`{ c and t==2 }`
"critical section 1."	*"critical section 2."*
`{ t==1 }`	`{ t==2 }`
`c,t= False,`$\bot$	`c,t= False,`$\bot$

The auxiliary variable `t` has been given a third possible value "$\bot$" and extra assertions have been added before the `await` statements.

Answer to Exercise 15.2 (p. 159)
Because the invariant is maintained by each of the two fragments individually, that is by `if c1<=bb: bb= bb-c1` and by `if c2<=bb: bb= bb-c2`, it will be maintained when they are interleaved atomically — equivalently, one `if`-body cannot execute between the `if`-condition and the `if`-body of the other.

Non-atomic interleaving is prevented in this case, guaranteed never to happen, by the inconsistent assertions `t==1` and `t==2` that the critical section imposes.

Answer to Exercise 15.7 (p. 159)
Extend the use of `t` as shown in Fig. I.2 with an extra possible value "$\bot$" and extra assignments and assertions. Note that `t` remains auxiliary.

Check the global invariant and the local correctness of the two new assertions; then check their global correctness as well.

Finally, note that if both `await` statements are "pending", i.e. both their preconditions are true, then `t` can be neither 1 nor 2 — and so it must be $\bot$. (That it is one of those three values is also a global invariant, but we have left it out because it is trivial.)

Thus `t` must be $\bot$, whence `not c` evaluates to `True`, from the global invariant — and so in fact either of the `await` statements may execute. Deadlock cannot occur.

The implementation is unsatisfactory because it doesn't enforce fairness: one thread can starve the other.

Answer to Exercise 16.1 (p. 161)
Finding an answer here is the principal topic of the whole of this Chapter 16. It's harder than it looks, however short the answer might turn out to be.
First try to find it by yourself.

You might start with this simpler version of (15.6):

```
{ not c } # Global initialisation.
```

```
# Th1 repeats this forever.
"other business 1."
await not c
c= True
   "critical section 1."
c= False


# Th2 repeats this forever.

"other business 2."
await not c
c= True
   "critical section 2."
c= False    .
```

But you will quickly see that the above is not safe. A second attempt (if you have forgotten our earlier Fig. 15.1) might be

```
"other business 1."
await not c: c= True
   "critical section 1."
c= False


"other business 2."
await not c: c= True
   "critical section 2."
c= False    ,
```

which *is* safe: but it uses **await** statements with bodies, which we have disallowed in this exercise. And even then it is not correct, because it allows overtaking, as we illustrated in Sec. 15.3 with (15.7): if say *Th2* is scheduled only while *Th1* is in its critical section then *Th2* will never get past its **await**, no matter how often it tries.

Solving those issues is where we are going.

Answer to Exercise 16.5 (p. 168)
Something like

```
with name:
   critical section    ,
```

which would place this (and all other) **with** *name* constructions in a critical section managed by a Boolean $name, as in Sec. 13.4, would do.
   The rule for checking it would simply be to exempt any statement within a "**with** *name*" from being considered for possible interference with an assertion within a "**with** *name*" (for the same *name*) in another thread

Answer to Exercise 16.11 (p. 169)
The implementation is correct because t==1 is *stable* at that point in *Th1* — it cannot be falsified by *Th2*.

Answer to Exercise 16.14 (p. 169)

We have been following the convention that statements written on a single line are atomic, because mostly that is true and it would be a nuisance to have to indicate atomicity explicitly. That means `t1,t= True,2` in (16.3) is atomic, and (by our convention) also `t1= True; t= 2` is atomic: they both would need a critical section for their execution, and –since Peterson's algorithm itself is designed to *implement* critical sections– it would make the exercise pointless. Thus the purpose of Sec. 16.3 was to show that the two statements could be executed one after the other without invalidating the algorithm.

We will in general try to avoid writing expressions that need locks for their evaluation, whether as conditions or as right-hand sides of assignments.

Answer to Exercise 17.3 (p. 191)

To check our program, we will have to check every step it might take: but if there is only one kind of step it can take, we have only one kind of thing to check. It does not matter how many times that operation is done: if it works any time, it works every time, no matter how many "every time" turns out to be.

Answer to Exercise 17.5 (p. 193)

Setting `c= W` initially makes the outer invariant true, simplifying the checking.

Answer to Exercise 17.7 (p. 193)

If the condition `if n.left.colour == W:` were not there then `c= W` would be executed every time a B node was encountered, meaning that the outer loop would not terminate unless all nodes were W already. So the assertion that should be there is something like

$$\{\,\texttt{n.left.colour == W} \text{ or "number of W's"} < W\,\} \qquad ,$$

where W is the value of the variant "number of W's" at the beginning of the outer-loop iteration. That *is* globally correct with respect to the mutator.

Answer to Exercise 17.9 (p. 193)

It *would* work if we used `nB= cB`; but then `cB` would no longer be auxiliary and so couldn't be removed. We would simply have regressed to evaluating `|blacks|` atomically so that we could assign it to `cB` in the statement just before.

It is only because `cB` is auxiliary that we don't have to have actual code at runtime that carries out the assignment `cB= |blacks|` .

Answer to Exercise 17.12 (p. 194)

See Fig. I.3. The "dot-dash" arrow indicates that the Mutator *will* blacken that target but has not yet done so. In Step 2 it's immaterial, because T is already black. But in Step 5, as before, Node T has become white: the Mutator "intends" to blacken it, but has not yet done so.

But in Step 6 the dangerously white T is blackened by the *Scanner*, because the swing has already occurred and the Scanner's visit to black R1 notices the white T, and blackens it. And so the number of blacks increases, from three to four. A further scan will occur (though it is not necessary).

Figure I.3 Woodger's scenario defeated (App. F.2 and Ex. 17.12)

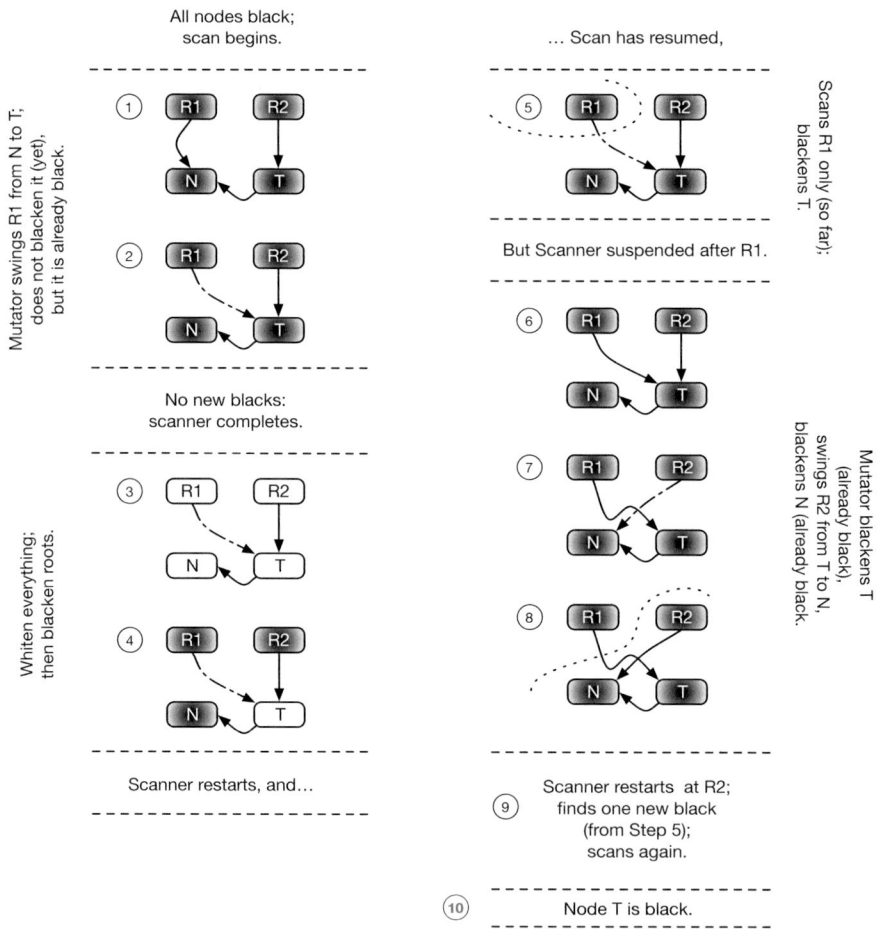

The "dot-dash" arrow indicates that its target *will be* blackened by the Mutator.

Answer to Exercise 17.13 (p. 194)

The process is not complete: all it takes is for the Mutator to wait until scanning is finished, and then –before the Collect phase– to swing a pointer away from a node that is not pointed to by anything else: it will become black garbage.

But black garbage can survive for at most more one cycle: it must remain garbage, since it's unreachable, and so it will be caught in the next sweep. The Mutator cannot swing away from it again: it can't even refer to it — precisely *because* it is garbage.

Answer to Exercise 17.14 (p. 194)

The first thing to note is that the Mutator cannot access n at all while the Collector is active, as at (17.20), because n is coloured W and therefore it is unreachable for the Mutator. That is precisely what the Scanner accomplished: the `n.colour == W` implies that n is unreachable by the Mutator.

Answer to Exercise 18.1 (p. 203)

Like `Python`, `Dafny` implements "extended" integers, i.e. integers that can be as large as will fit into the programs's available memory as a whole (rather than merely into a single computer word). If an upper bound, say `MaxInt`, were introduced, and appropriate assertions added then the error *would* be caught. Just what assertion to add, though, is not obvious: the obvious `assert low+high<=MaxInt` might not suffice. (Why not?) Perhaps `assert low<=MaxInt-high`?

Since the answer might depend on how the hardware/compiler implements comparisons, perhaps just going with `low:= low + (high-low)//2` is safest.

Answer to Exercise 19.2 (p. 213)

It could be seen as an *MUA*, in this case the assumption (unwarranted, but also unarticulated) that only printable characters –and not too many of them– would be typed in. But it could also seen as not using assertions: after an input, should there be a postcondition that the input was not too long, used as a precondition to justify say an array access just afterwards?

Can you think of other classifications for this kind of failure?

Another example (same company) is that of a programmer who was assured (but not in writing) that there would be no more than 20 items that the system had to handle at once. In spite of that, on his own initiative he allocated space for 50 *and* coded a runtime check that no more than 50 were supplied. The in-house trial run (with its ≤20 items) was a success. At the *actual* presentation, however, the client supplied 100.

The programmer's check caught that excess, and printed an error. Had it not, the extra items would have over-run onto other data, causing the whole system to crash, in front of the clients and –worse– to do so *without* any ready explanation (that being a "feature" of overruns).

Whose head would have rolled?

Answer to Exercise B.1 (p. 251)

App. B.2.2 allows the rule (B.1) in App. B.4.1 to be recovered by adding the *pre* before, and the *post* after, provided their implications check. They are the same implications set out at (B.1).

Answer to Exercise B.3 (p. 251)

There isn't any difference: in both cases considered, a {PRE: *pre*} ⋯ {POST: *post*} enclosing the statement checks just when *pre* and *cond* ⇒ *post*. The statement –in either form– cannot be executed unless *cond* is true.

There is a conceptual difference however in the way they are used. An `assume` *cond* forces an earlier `x= ?` to make its choice in a way that establishes *cond*, which is useful for data refinement. An `await` *cond* forces the thread to wait until some *other* thread makes *cond* true (rather than some earlier `x= ?` in this thread's *having made cond* true), which is useful for ensuring noninterference.

Answer to Exercise C.1 (p. 261)

The program would still be meaningful, but unimplementable: the `assume` cannot (now) be removed. The specification would essentially be saying "Any call of `add` must succeed, even if it would make the number of elements in the set greater than N."

Answer to Exercise C.2 (p. 261)

The general answer is this: that checking the (concrete) code for (C.3) is not done with respect to pre- and/or postconditions that (C.3) itself contains. Instead, we must check that it is an acceptable replacement (refinement) for the *original* abstract code from Fig. 10.4 that was "de-sugared" at (C.1) — and that is guaranteed *automatically* provided we follow the rules explained in Appendix C. That process is called "correctness by construction".

The specific answer is that because the original abstract code contained `assert |ss|<=N`, that specification was allowed explicitly to "misbehave" in the "too full" case, and so the concrete code is allowed to do the same. That is *precisely* the reason that the assertion was there.

Answer to Exercise C.3 (p. 261)

As usual, we work from the back towards the front. Start with the modified (11.6) here:

```
was {···} → assert s-n == ∑(nb-⌊n⌋) and c-1 == |nb-⌊n⌋|
            assert n∈nb
            nb= nb-⌊n⌋
            s,c= s-n,c-1
was {···} → assume s == ∑nb and c == |nb|          ← Start with the assume here.
```

Then move the `assume` one step forward, as here:

```
            assert s-n == ∑(nb-⌊n⌋) and c-1 == |nb-⌊n⌋|
            assert n∈nb
            nb= nb-⌊n⌋
            assume s-n == ∑nb and c-1 == |nb|
            s,c= s-n,c-1     .
```

And then finally move it once again so that we now have

```
            assert s == ∑nb and c == |nb|
            assert n∈nb
            assume s-n == ∑(nb-⌊n⌋) and c-1 == |nb-⌊n⌋|
            nb= nb-⌊n⌋
            s,c= s-n,c-1     ,
```

which means we can alter the code of (11.6) to become just

```
def del(n):
   nb= nb-⌊n⌋
   s,c= s-n,c-1     ,
```

because the two `assert` statements allow the `assume` to be removed. The implication from the two `assert` statements' conditions before (as antecedents) to the condition of the `assume`, that is

$$s==\sum nb \text{ and } c==|nb| \text{ and } n\in nb$$
$$\Rightarrow \quad s-n==\sum(nb-\{n\}) \text{ and } c-1==|nb-\{n\}| \quad ,$$

holds because it is a property of bags that

$$n\in nb \quad \Rightarrow \quad \sum(nb-\{n\}) \quad == \quad \sum nb - n$$
$$\text{and} \quad n\in nb \quad \Rightarrow \quad |nb-\{n\}| \quad == \quad |nb| - 1 \quad ,$$

and that means the `assume` can be removed altogether.

And then the `assert` statements and the abstract `nb` (now auxiliary) can be removed as well: an `assert` can always be removed, as can auxiliaries.

Answer to Exercise D.1 (p. 278)

The simple answer is "It depends." Some programming languages don't have `assert` statements; almost none have `assume` statements.

If the language *does* have `assert` statements then they can be evaluated at runtime. In that case, a statement `assert cond` will abort program execution immediately if the condition *cond* does not evaluate to `True` at that point. Sometimes that produces a useful message, but sometimes not: it depends on the programming language. Either way, such "executable" `assert`'s are helpful for debugging, but they certainly do not help the program give the answer you were expecting: it's too late for that. Rather they tell you (at runtime) that if the program were to proceed further, it would in fact be *unlikely* to give the right answer. Thus "It's better to stop now."

Some languages have both `assert` statements *and* `assume` statements. In `Dafny`, they are both evaluated at compile time, by `Dafny` itself, to help you reason about your program *before* you run it. An `assert cond` tells the programmer/`Dafny` to check at program-development time that *cond* will always be true at runtime — and so will never abort. But we all make mistakes; and that is why runtime `assert` statements are useful.

On the other hand, an `assume cond` statement left in an executing program would insist that its condition be True if execution is to proceed further; and so –if the condition is False– execution cannot proceed. Because compiled programs are not supposed to do that, an `assume` statement should be rejected at compile time if the "generate executable code" option is selected.[2]

Thus an `assume cond` statement is a reasoning tool, forcing the programmer to check that *cond* will always be true at that point, so that the program can be compiled to code. One way of doing that is to resolve an earlier demonic choice at compile time. (Recall App. B.6.2.)

Answer to Exercise D.3 (p. 278)

The connection between predicates and sets is that a predicate simply describes a set of program states, all –and only– those in which the predicate is True: they are "isomorphic" points of view, meaning that it doesn't really matter whether you think of them as one or the other — as long as you calculate correctly in either case.

---

[2] This is what happens in `Dafny` (Sec. 18.2).

Figure I.4 Answer to Ex. D.7(a)

$\mathcal{A}$	$\mathcal{B}$	$\mathcal{A}$	$\Rightarrow$	$(\mathcal{B}$	$\Rightarrow$	$\mathcal{A})$
True	True	True	True	True	True	True
True	False	True	True	False	True	True
False	True	False	True	True	False	False
False	False	False	True	False	True	False

$\uparrow$

The indicated column $\uparrow$ is all True.

Answer to Exercise D.4 (p. 278)
The corresponding set operators are as follows:

(a) For "$\Rightarrow$" between propositions, you take ($\subseteq$) between the corresponding sets. But note! Even when A, B are sets, it's not the case that $A \subseteq B$ is a set as well: instead, either it's true or it's false. That's in fact the essence of the difference between $\Rightarrow$ and $\Rightarrow$. (See (c) below.)

(b) For "$\neg$" on propositions, you complement (take the opposite of) the corresponding sets, provided there is an agreed-upon "universal" set that contains everything of relevance.

(c) For "$\Rightarrow$" between propositions, you take all elements that are either *not* in the first set (even if they are in the second set as well) –or– *are* in the second set (even if they are in the first set as well).

As for negation, you need a universal set.

As a logical equivalence, we're relying on $\mathcal{A} \Rightarrow \mathcal{B} \equiv \neg\mathcal{A} \vee \mathcal{B}$ (E.26). Note that what you make here *is* a set. (See (a) above.)

Answer to Exercise D.5 (p. 279)
Items (a), (c), (d), (e) are terms. And (b) is a term if you take the (usual) view that it's an abbreviation for (c). For Item (f), we could stretch a point, saying it abbreviates $2 \times x$. And Item (g) would be a term if we regarded $<$ as a Boolean-valued function of arity 2; but it would not be a term if $<$ were taken to be a predicate symbol (again of arity 2). In the latter case, it would be a formula.

Answer to Exercise D.7 (p. 279)
The truth table for the first formula $\mathcal{A} \Rightarrow (\mathcal{B} \Rightarrow \mathcal{A})$ is shown in Fig. I.4. The other formulae are arrived at similarly.

Answer to Exercise D.8 (p. 279)
Only (d) is a propositional formula.

Item (a) is a variable (with a four-letter name which would be written **true** in a **Python** program), not necessarily of Boolean type; or perhaps it's an English word in italics.

Item (b) is *also* an English word, but one we reserve for describing whether some formula holds in a state. If written **True**, it would be a Boolean term (a constant) in a **Python** program.

Item (c) is type-incorrect, because z is not a formula.

Answer to Exercise D.11 (p. 280)

In any state where $\mathcal{A}$ is True, we know from Fig. D.6 that the implication $\mathcal{B} \Rightarrow \mathcal{A}$ is also True.

On the other hand, $(\mathcal{A}{\Rightarrow}\mathcal{B}) \Rightarrow \mathcal{A}$ is not correct (valid) — any state in which $\mathcal{A}$ is False would make the antecedent $\mathcal{A}{\Rightarrow}\mathcal{B}$ of $\Rightarrow$ True but its consequent $\mathcal{A}$ False.

Answer to Exercise D.12 (p. 280)

since $\mathcal{A} \Rrightarrow \mathcal{A}'$ Making the antecedent of an implication "(possibly) more often True" makes the implication as a whole "less often True" — because there are now potentially situations in which the antecedent has become True but the consequent remains False. Thus in this situation $\mathcal{A}' \Rightarrow \mathcal{B}$ is less often true than $\mathcal{A} \Rightarrow \mathcal{B}$.

    But $\mathcal{A} \Rightarrow \mathcal{B}$ is itself the antecedent of $(\mathcal{A} \Rightarrow \mathcal{B}) \Rightarrow \mathcal{C}$ and, if it becomes $\mathcal{A}' \Rightarrow \mathcal{B}$, i.e. less often True as just above, then the whole of $(\mathcal{A}' \Rightarrow \mathcal{B}) \Rightarrow \mathcal{C}$ has become more often True, so justifying the $\Rrightarrow$.

since $\mathcal{B} \Lleftarrow \mathcal{B}'$ Similar reasoning applies here, but this time starting with the consequent $\mathcal{B}$. Try it!

What we are using –more precisely and in general– is

$$\text{if } \mathcal{X} \Rrightarrow \mathcal{X}' \text{ then } \mathcal{X}{\Rightarrow}\mathcal{Y} \Lleftarrow \mathcal{X}'{\Rightarrow}\mathcal{Y} \quad ,$$

and similar inferences. It's called "contravariance", in this case that an "arrow" applied within an antecedent has the reverse effect on the whole implication. If it's applied in the consequent, however, then it is *not* reversed: that is covariance.

Answer to Exercise D.13 (p. 280)

We assume $a{\neq}0$ and then reason

$$
\begin{aligned}
&& a + bc &\neq (a + b)(a + c) \\
&\equiv& a + bc &\neq a^2 + ac + ba + bc \\
&\equiv& a &\neq a^2 + ac + ba \\
&\equiv& &\text{``since } a \neq 0\text{''} \\
&& 1 &\neq a + c + b \quad ,
\end{aligned}
$$

whose final inequality we can make True by choosing any b, c with $b{+}c \neq 1{-}a$.

Answer to Exercise D.14 (p. 280)

    (a) $(\forall i{:}\mathbb{Z} \cdot \mathsf{even}\,i \vee \mathsf{odd}\,i)$

    (b) $(\forall m{:}\mathbb{N} \cdot \mathsf{odd}\,m \Rightarrow (\exists n{:}\mathbb{N} \cdot \mathsf{even}\,n \wedge m = n{+}1)\,)$

    (c) $(\exists i{:}\mathbb{Z} \cdot \mathsf{even}\,i \wedge \neg\,(\exists n{:}\mathbb{N} \cdot \mathsf{odd}\,n \wedge i = n{+}1)\,)$

Answer to Exercise D.16 (p. 280)

$(\exists y \cdot (\forall x \cdot \mathcal{A} \Rightarrow x = y))$.

Answer to Exercise E.1 (p. 290)

If $\mathcal{B} \Rightarrow \mathcal{A}$ means "In all states in which $\mathcal{B}$ is True, then $\mathcal{A}$ is also true", and if $\mathcal{B}$ is in fact true, then it is (trivially) True in all states: therefore so must $\mathcal{A}$ be. Choosing default false instead would be pointless, because then $\Rightarrow \mathcal{A}$ would be correct for all $\mathcal{A}$'s.

A more interesting reason is that true is the identity of conjunction, so you could imagine a comma-separated *list* of formulae on the left as being conjoined. The empty conjunction is True, after all.

Similar reasoning on the right suggests the default false. Taking true would be pointless, and false is the identity of disjunction. So a list of formulae on the right could be taken to be implicitly disjoined. That is, more generally, we'd have that

$$\mathcal{A}, \mathcal{B} \quad \Rightarrow \quad \mathcal{C}, \mathcal{D} \tag{I.1}$$

means "In any state in which both $\mathcal{A}$ and $\mathcal{B}$ are True, either $\mathcal{C}$ or $\mathcal{D}$ is True."

Answer to Exercise E.4 (p. 290)

Reason by cases: if no value for x makes $\mathcal{A}$ (in the antecedent, left of $\Rightarrow$) True in the current state, then there can be no x that makes $\mathcal{A}$ in the consequent (right of $\Rightarrow$) True in the current state either. And so, in that state and whatever x might be, the formula $\mathcal{A} \Rightarrow \mathcal{B}$ is True because its antecedent is False.

If on the other hand there *is* an x that makes $\mathcal{A}$ true, then (from the antecedent) there must be an x that makes $\mathcal{B}$ True, even if it is a different x. But that (different) x makes $\mathcal{A} \Rightarrow \mathcal{B}$ True, even if $\mathcal{A}$ is True and $\mathcal{B}$ is False for the original x.

Answer to Exercise E.7 (p. 291)

$$\quad (\exists x \cdot (\mathcal{N} \Rightarrow \mathcal{A}) \wedge (\neg \mathcal{N} \Rightarrow \mathcal{B}))$$
$$\equiv \quad \text{"Exercise E.6"}$$
$$\quad (\exists x \cdot \mathcal{N} \wedge \mathcal{A}) \vee (\exists x \cdot \neg \mathcal{N} \wedge \mathcal{B})$$
$$\equiv \quad \text{"(E.86)"}$$
$$\quad \mathcal{N} \wedge (\exists x \cdot \mathcal{A}) \vee \neg \mathcal{N} \wedge (\exists x \cdot \mathcal{B})$$
$$\equiv \quad \text{"(E.42)"}$$
$$\quad (\mathcal{N} \Rightarrow (\exists x \cdot \mathcal{A})) \wedge (\neg \mathcal{N} \Rightarrow (\exists x \cdot \mathcal{B})) \quad .$$

Bibliography

[1] Abrial, J.R.: The *B* Book: Assigning Programs to Meanings. Cambridge University Press (1996)

[2] Abrial, J.R., Schuman, S.A., Meyer, B.: A specification language. In: A.M. Macnaghten, R.M. McKeag (eds.) On the Construction of Programs. Cambridge University Press (1980)

[3] Back, R.J.: On the correctness of refinement steps in program development. Ph.D. thesis, Department of Computer Science, University of Helsinki (1978)

[4] Back, R.J., von Wright, J.: Refinement Calculus: A Systematic Introduction. Springer (1998)

[5] Backhouse, R.C.: Program Construction and Verification. Prentice-Hall (1996)

[6] Backhouse, R.C.: Program Construction: Calculating Implementations from Specifications. John Wiley (2003)

[7] Ben-Ari, M.: Algorithms for on-the-fly garbage collection. ACM ToPLaS **6**, 333–344 (1984)

[8] Bentley, J.: Programming Pearls. Addison-Wesley (1986)

[9] Broda, K., Eisenbach, S., Khoshnevisan, H., Vickers, S.: Reasoned Programming. Prentice-Hall, Inc., USA (1994)

[10] Cohen, E.: Programming in the 1990s: An Introduction to the Calculation of Programs. Springer (1991)

[11] Dijkstra, E.W.: A note on two problems connected with graphs. Numerische Mathematik **1**, 269–71 (1959)

[12] Dijkstra, E.W.: Over seinpalen (1964). EWD 74 at https://www.cs.utexas.edu/~EWD/indexBibTeX.html

[13] Dijkstra, E.W.: Guarded commands, nondeterminacy and formal derivation of programs. Communications of the ACM **18**(8), 454–457 (1975)

[14] Dijkstra, E.W.: A Discipline of Programming. Prentice-Hall (1976)

[15] Dijkstra, E.W.: A note on "tail invariants". Tech. Rep. EWD1195-0, University of Texas at Austin (1993)

[16] Dijkstra, E.W., Lamport, L., Martin, A., Scholten, C., Steffens, E.: On-the-fly garbage collection: An exercise in cooperation. Communications of the ACM **21**(11), 966–975 (1978)

[17] Enderton, H.B.: A Mathematical Introduction to Logic. Academic Press (1972)

[18] Feijen, W.H.J., van Gasteren, A.J.M.: On a Method of Multiprogramming. Prentice-Hall (1990)

[19] Floyd, R.W.: Assigning meanings to programs. In: J. Schwartz (ed.) Mathematical Aspects of Computer Science, no. 19 in Proc. Symp. Appl. Math., pp. 19–32. American Mathematical Society (1967)

[20] Gödel, K.: Über formal unentscheidbare Sätze der Principia mathematica und verwandter Systeme I. Monatshefte für Mathematik und Physik **38**(1), 173–198 (1931)

[21] Gries, D.: An exercise in proving parallel programs correct. Communications of the ACM **20**(12), 921–930 (1977)

[22] Gries, D.: The Science of Programming. Springer (1981)

[23] Hayes, I.J. (ed.): Specification Case Studies. Prentice-Hall (1987).
http://www.itee.uq.edu.au/~ianh/Papers/SCS2.pdf

[24] Hehner, E.C.R.: A Practical Theory of Programming. Springer (1993)

[25] Hoare, C.A.R.: An axiomatic basis for computer programming. Comm ACM **12**(10), 576–80, 583 (1969)

[26] Hoare, C.A.R.: Proof of correctness of data representations. Acta Informatica **1**, 271–281 (1972)

[27] Jackson, D.: Software Abstractions: Logic, Language and Analysis. MIT Press (2006)

[28] Jones, C.B.: Development methods for computer programs including a notion of interference. D.Phil. thesis, Oxford University (1981)

[29] Jones, C.B.: Systematic Software Development Using VDM. Prentice Hall International (1986)

[30] Kaldewaij, A.: Programming: The Derivation of Algorithms. Prentice-Hall (1990)

[31] Kingston, J.H.: Algorithms and Data Structures: Design, Correctness, Analysis. Addison Wesley (1990)

[32] Kline, M.: Mathematical Thought from Ancient to Modern Times. Oxford University Press (1972)

[33] Knuth, D.: The Art of Computer Programming, Vol. 3: Sorting and Searching. Addison-Wesley (1973)

[34] Lamport, L.: My writings. https://lamport.azurewebsites.net/pubs/pubs.pdf

[35] Lamport, L.: A new solution of Dijkstra's concurrent programming problem. Communications of the ACM **7**(8), 453–488 (1974)

[36] Leino, K.R.M.: Program Proofs. MIT Press (2023)

[37] Meltzer, B.: On Formally Undecidable Propositions of *Principia Mathematica* and Related Systems (translation of [20]). Dover (1992)

[38] Meyer, B.: Object-Oriented Software Construction. Prentice-Hall (1988)

[39] Meyer, B.: Applying "Design by Contract". Computer **25**(10), 40–51 (1992)

[40] Milner, R.: An algebraic definition of simulation between programs. In: D.C. Cooper (ed.) Proceedings of the 2nd International Joint Conference on Artificial Intelligence. London, UK, September 1–3, 1971, pp. 481–489. William Kaufmann (1971)

[41] Misra, J.: A Discipline of Multiprogramming. Springer New York (2001)

[42] Misra, J.: Effective Theories in Programming Practice, *ACM Books*, vol. 47. ACM (2023)

[43] Morgan, C.C.: Programming from Specifications, 2nd edn. Prentice-Hall (1994)

[44] Morgan, C.C.: (In-)formal methods: the lost art. In: Z. Liu, Z. Zhang (eds.) Engineering Trustworthy Software Systems – First International School, SETSS 2014, Chongqing, China, September 8–13, 2014. Tutorial Lectures, *LNCS*, vol. 9506, pp. 1–79. Springer (2016)

[45] Morgan, C.C., Sanders, J.W.: Laws of the logical calculi. Technical Monograph PRG-78, Oxford University Computing Laboratory, Programming Research Group (1989)

[46] Nipkow, T., Klein, G.: Concrete Semantics with Isabelle/HOL. Springer (2014)

[47] Owicki, S.S.: Axiomatic proof techniques for parallel programs. Ph.D. thesis, Cornell (1975)

[48] Owicki, S.S., Gries, D.: An axiomatic proof technique for parallel programs. Acta Informatica **6**, 319–340 (1976)

[49] Reynolds, J.C.: The Craft of Programming. Prentice-Hall (1981)

[50] van de Snepscheut, J.L.A.: "Algorithms for on-the-fly garbage collection" revisited. Information Processing Letters **24**, 211–216 (1987)

[51] Spivey, J.M.: Understanding Z: a Specification Language and its Formal Semantics. Cambridge University Press (1988)

[52] Wirth, N.: Program development by stepwise refinement. Comm ACM **14**(4), 221–7 (1971)

[53] Wirth, N.: Algorithms + Data Structures = Programs. Prentice Hall (1976)

[54] Wirth, N.: MODULA: a language for modular multiprogramming (1976). at `https://doi.org/10.3929/ethz-a-000199440`

[55] Woodcock, J.C.P., Davies, J.: Using Z – specification, refinement, and proof. Prentice Hall international series in computer science. Prentice Hall (1996)

Index of symbols and terms

"or" between Booleans in `Python`, **272**, **275**

⇔ means if-and-only-if (iff), corresponding to "==" in `Python` if between Booleans, **272**

¬ is negation, corresponding to "not" applied to a Boolean in `Python`, **272**

"iff" is short for "if and only if", **288**

∴ "therefore" is archaic; we use ⇒, **289**

∵ "because" is archaic; we use ⇐, **289**

⊨ is semantic entailment (but here we write it as ⇒), **289**

⊢ is logical entailment (but here we write it ⇒ as well), **289**

∀, for all, *see* quantification

∃, there exists, *see* quantification

Index of terms

`A[low:high]` is a subsegment, 31

  `A[:high]` is short for `A[0:high]`, 27∘, 38

  `A[low:]` is short for `A[low:len(A)]`, 38

  "··· < x" means "every element of the (sub)segment ··· is < x", **38**

  index-ranges are

    inclusive/exclusive, **5**, 31, 39, 49

  `A[0]` is the head of `A`, 162

  `A[1:]` is the tail of `A`, 162

  `A[n:n]` is the empty sequence, 52

J.-R. **Abrial**, [219↓], [222], [222, 223], [225]

absorption, 282

abstract data-type, 83, 86–87

  See also concrete data-type.

abstract/concrete hybrid, *qv*

access modifier, *see* object orientation

accreditation

  of engineers, 73

  of programmers, 73

`acquire()` in `Python`, 135↓

aeroplane, *see* building an aeroplane

algorisms of reasoning about programs, 230

  See also Al-Khwārizmī.

algorithm

  can be incorrectly coded, xii

    ... or can be wrong in principle, xii

  is the "essence" of a program, xi

  See also Al-Khwārizmī.

Al-Khwārizmī, 229↓

(for) all ∀, *see* quantification

"all the way down", *see* mathematics

alpha conversion, 242↓, **277**, 286, 288, 291

example, 277

sometimes necessary in substitutions, 242↓

analyst vs. customer, 118

"**and**" is Boolean conjunction, *qv*

animals, people behaving like, 288↓

antecedent

  contravariance

    of implication, 333

    of quantification, 287

  is false means the overall implication is true, 156

  left-hand side of implication, **9**, 272

  See also consequent, implication.

antisymmetric, **59**

anything, set x to, *qv*

arithmetic, of Booleans, *qv*

arity of operator, function or predicate, **270**

"arrays" in `Python`, 105

`assert` statement, 106, **125**, 129

  at runtime, 219

  encourages colleagues to respect your preconditions, 104, 106

  how to check, 104, **249**

  if it fails, allows

    unpredictable behaviour, 115

  in `Python`, 104↓

  used to validate data refinement, 253, 261, 331

  vertical stacking indicates *conjunction*, not implication, 198↓

  See also `Dafny`.

`assume` statement, *see* `Dafny`

assertions {···} or # ··· , **9**, 8–10, 16, **118**

  are often checked from the end (post-condition) towards the beginning (precondition) of a program fragment, 19, 67, 68, 70, 87, 201, 265

  braces vs. comment, 18, 129

  compile time vs. run time, 104↓, 198

  effective even if written informally as comments (e.g. in English), 21, 281

  horizontal vs. vertical format, 10, 12↓

  "housekeeping" assertions, 20, 303

  how to check, **250**

  intermediate, 19, 20, 22, 66, 201, 310

  pre-, postconditions and invariants are special cases of, 16

  several in a row vertically, 10, 12↓, 14, 34, 67, 68, 305

  trivial, 244

  used as "scaffolding", 30

Printed in the United Kingdom by TJ Clays Ltd.